The Video Collection

Collection

**ADOBE PREMIERE PRO CS6,
AFTER EFFECTS CS6, AUDITION CS6, ENCORE CS6**

The Video
Collection

ADOBE PREMIERE PRO CS6,
AFTER EFFECTS CS6, AUDITION CS6, ENCORE CS6

Debbie Keller

Revealed

DELMAR
CENGAGE Learning·

Australia · Brazil · Japan · Korea · Mexico · Singapore · Spain · United Kingdom · United States

DELMAR
CENGAGE Learning

The Video Collection CS6 Revealed
Debbie Keller

Vice President, Career and Professional Editorial:
 Dave Garza

Director of Learning Solutions: Sandy Clark

Senior Acquisitions Editor: Jim Gish

Managing Editor: Larry Main

Product Managers: Jane Hosie-Bounar, Nicole Calisi

Editorial Assistant: Sarah Timm

Vice President Marketing, Career and Professional:
 Jennifer Baker

Executive Marketing Manager: Deborah S. Yarnell

Associate Marketing Manager: Erin DeAngelo

Senior Production Director: Wendy Troeger

Production Manager: Andrew Crouth

Content Project Manager: Allyson Bozeth

Developmental Editor: Sasha Vodnik

Technical Editor: Sebastian Guerra

Director of Design: Bruce Bond

Cover Design: Riezebos Holzbaur/Tim Heraldo

Cover Photo: Riezebos Holzbaur/Andrei Pasternak

Text Designer: Liz Kingslein

Production House: Integra Software Services Pvt. Ltd.

Copy Editor/Proofreader: Kim Kostmatka

Indexer: Alexandra Nickerson

Technology Project Manager: Jim Gilbert

For product information and technology assistance, contact us at **Cengage Learning Customer & Sales Support, 1-800-354-9706**

For permission to use material from this text or product, submit all requests online at **www.cengage.com/permissions**

Further permissions questions can be emailed to **permissionrequest@cengage.com**

Adobe® Premiere Pro®, Adobe® Premiere Elements, Adobe® After Effects®, Adobe® Soundbooth®, Adobe® Bridge®, Adobe® Encore, Adobe® Photoshop®, Adobe® InDesign®, Adobe® Illustrator®, Adobe® Flash®, Adobe® Dreamweaver®, Adobe® Fireworks®, and Adobe® Creative Suite® are trademarks or registered trademarks of Adobe Systems, Inc. in the United States and/or other countries. Third party products, services, company names, logos, design, titles, words, or phrases within these materials may be trademarks of their respective owners.

Adobe product screenshot(s) reprinted with permission from Adobe Systems Incorporated. The Adobe Approved Certification Courseware logo is a proprietary trademark of Adobe. All rights reserved. Cengage Learning and *The Video Collection CS6—Revealed* are independent from ProCert Labs, LLC and Adobe Systems Incorporated, and are not affiliated with ProCert Labs and Adobe in any manner. This publication may assist students to prepare for an Adobe Certified Expert exam in Premiere Pro; however, neither ProCert Labs nor Adobe warrant that use of this material will ensure success in connection with any exam.

Library of Congress Control Number: 2011945474

Hardcover edition:
ISBN-13: 978-1-133-81500-6
ISBN-10: 1-133-81500-6

Delmar
5 Maxwell Drive
Clifton Park, NY 12065-2919
USA

Cengage Learning is a leading provider of customized learning solutions with office locations around the globe, including Singapore, the United Kingdom, Australia, Mexico, Brazil, and Japan. Locate your local office at: **international.cengage.com/region**

Cengage Learning products are represented in Canada by Nelson Education, Ltd.

To learn more about Delmar, visit **www.cengage.com/delmar**

Purchase any of our products at your local college store or at our preferred online store **www.cengagebrain.com**

Notice to the Reader
Publisher does not warrant or guarantee any of the products described herein or perform any independent analysis in connection with any of the product information contained herein. Publisher does not assume, and expressly disclaims, any obligation to obtain and include information other than that provided to it by the manufacturer. The reader is expressly warned to consider and adopt all safety precautions that might be indicated by the activities described herein and to avoid all potential hazards. By following the instructions contained herein, the reader willingly assumes all risks in connection with such instructions. The publisher makes no representations or warranties of any kind, including but not limited to, the warranties of fitness for particular purpose or merchantability, nor are any such representations implied with respect to the material set forth herein, and the publisher takes no responsibility with respect to such material. The publisher shall not be liable for any special, consequential, or exemplary damages resulting, in whole or part, from the readers' use of, or reliance upon, this material.

Printed in the United States of America
1 2 3 4 5 6 7 16 15 14 13 12

Revealed Series Vision

The Revealed Series is your guide to today's hottest multimedia applications. For years, the Revealed Series has kept pace with the dynamic demands of the multimedia community, and continues to do so with the publication of 13 new titles covering the latest Adobe Creative Suite products. Each comprehensive book teaches not only the technical skills required for success in today's competitive multimedia market, but the design skills as well. From animation, to web design, to digital image editing and interactive media skills, the Revealed Series has you covered. We recognize the unique learning environment of the multimedia classroom, and we deliver textbooks that include:

- Comprehensive step-by-step instructions
- In-depth explanations of the "Why" behind a skill
- Creative projects for additional practice
- Full-color visuals for a clear explanation of concepts
- Comprehensive online material offering additional instruction and skills practice
- Video tutorials for skills reinforcement as well as the presentation of additional features
- NEW icons to highlight features that are new since the previous release of the software. With the Revealed series, we've created books that speak directly to the multimedia and design community—one of the most rapidly growing computer fields today.

—The Revealed Series

About This Edition

This edition of *The Video Collection Revealed* is updated with an entire chapter of new information on Adobe Audition.

CourseMate

A CourseMate is available to accompany *The Video Collection Revealed*, which helps you make the grade! This CourseMate includes:

- An interactive eBook, with highlighting, note-taking, and search capabilities
- Interactive learning tools including:
  - Chapter quizzes
  - Flash cards
  - Instructional video lessons from Total Training, the leading provider of video instruction for Adobe software. These video lessons are tightly integrated with the book, chapter by chapter, and include assessment.
  - And more!

Go to login.cengagebrain.com to access these resources you have purchased.

AUTHOR'S VISION

It's amazing how much has happened since writing the first edition of *The Video Collection Revealed*. Since then I have written two more books for Cengage Learning, *Adobe Creative Suite 5 ACA Certification Preparation: Featuring Dreamweaver, Flash and Photoshop* and *Adobe® Creative Suite 5 Projects Binder BASICS*, which are also being revised for CS6. In addition, I have been recording four courses for Total Training that are aligned to the ACA certification exams. In fact, you will be able to see some of those videos on the CourseMate website for this book.

A big thank you goes out to my new developmental editor on this book, Sasha Vodnik, for taking on such a heavy load, which allowed me the time I needed to not only teach high school full time, but work on those training courses for Total Training.

And of course, thank you to my husband Glenn for his continued support and understanding as my free time becomes less. This summer I will be working on my fourth book, *Creating 2D Animation with Adobe CS6*. Fortunately, I may find some more free time while school is out for the summer.

—Debbie Keller

Introduction to The Video Collection Revealed

Welcome to *The Video Collection—Revealed*. This book offers creative projects, concise instructions, and complete coverage of basic to advanced video skills, helping you to create polished, professional-looking video. Use this book both in the classroom and as your own reference guide.

The text is written with an integrated approach to each of the four applications: Adobe Premiere Pro, After Effects, Audition, and Encore. A chapter is dedicated to each application to help you gain familiarity with the program, followed by three chapters that incorporate what you have learned and have you work with more than one application, or work dynamically with more than one application using Adobe Dynamic Link. (Note that this feature is only available if your software was installed as part of a suite and not as individual point products.)

What You'll Do

A What You'll Do figure begins every lesson. This figure gives you an at-a-glance look at what you'll do in the chapter, either by showing you a screen from the current project or a tool you'll be using.

Comprehensive Conceptual Lessons

Before jumping into instructions, in-depth conceptual information tells you "why" skills are applied. This book provides the "how" and "why" through the use of professional examples. Also included in the text are tips and sidebars to help you work more efficiently and creatively, or to teach you a bit about the history or design philosophy behind the skill you are using.

Step-by-Step Instructions

This book combines in-depth conceptual information with concise steps to help you learn about working with video in CS6. Each set of steps guides you through a lesson where you will create, modify, or enhance a file. Step references to large colorful images and quick step summaries round out the lessons. The Data Files for the steps are provided on the DVDs packaged with this book.

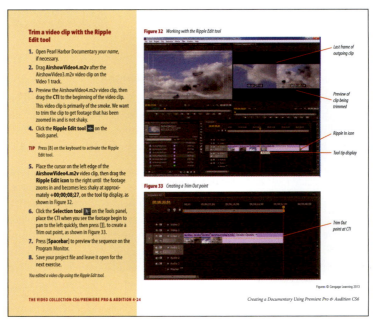

Trim a video clip with the Ripple Edit tool

1. Open Pearl Harbor Documentary *your name*, if necessary.

2. Drag **AirshowVideo4.m2v** after the AirshowVideo3.m2v video clip on the Video 1 track.

3. Preview the AirshowVideo4.m2v video clip, then drag the **CTI** to the beginning of the video clip.
   This video clip is primarily of the smoke. We want to trim the clip to get footage that has been zoomed in and is not shaky.

4. Click the **Ripple Edit tool** on the Tools panel.

   TIP Press [B] on the keyboard to activate the Ripple Edit tool.

5. Place the cursor on the left edge of the **AirshowVideo4.m2v** video clip, then drag the **Ripple Edit** icon to the right until the footage zooms in and becomes less shaky at approximately **+00;00;08;27**, on the tool tip display, as shown in Figure 32.

6. Click the **Selection tool** on the Tools panel, place the CTI when you see the footage begin to pan to the left quickly, then press [ ], to create a Trim out point, as shown in Figure 33.

7. Press [Spacebar] to preview the sequence on the Program Monitor.

8. Save your project file and leave it open for the next exercise.

You edited a video clip using the Ripple Edit tool.

Figure 32 *Working with the Ripple Edit tool*

Last frame of outgoing clip

Preview of clip being trimmed

Ripple In icon

Tool tip display

Figure 33 *Creating a Trim Out point*

Trim Out point at CTI

Figures © Cengage Learning 2013

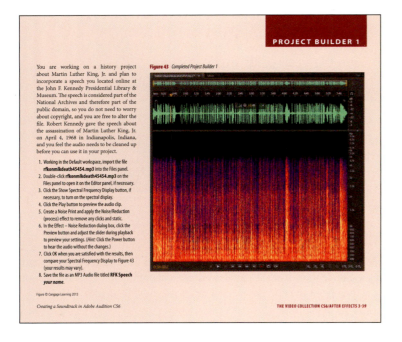

PROJECT BUILDER 1

You are working on a history project about Martin Luther King, Jr. and plan to incorporate a speech you located online at the John F. Kennedy Presidential Library & Museum. The speech is considered part of the National Archives and therefore part of the public domain, so you do not need to worry about copyright, and you are free to alter the file. Robert Kennedy gave the speech about the assassination of Martin Luther King, Jr. on April 4, 1968 in Indianapolis, Indiana, and you feel the audio needs to be cleaned up before you can use it in your project.

1. Working in the Default workspace, import the file **rfkonmlkdeath45454.mp3** into the Files panel.

2. Double-click **rfkonmlkdeath45454.mp3** on the Files panel to open it on the Editor panel, if necessary.

3. Click the Show Spectral Frequency Display button, if necessary, to turn on the spectral display.

4. Click the Play button to preview the audio clip.

5. Create a Noise Print and apply the Noise/Reduction (process) effect to remove any clicks and static.

6. In the Effect – Noise Reduction dialog box, click the Preview button and adjust the slider during playback to preview your settings. (*Hint:* Click the Power button to hear the audio without the changes.)

7. Click OK when you are satisfied with the results, then compare your Spectral Frequency Display to Figure 43 (your results may vary).

8. Save the file as an MP3 Audio file titled **RFK Speech** *your name*.

Figure © Cengage Learning 2013

Creating a Soundtrack in Adobe Audition CS6

Figure 43 *Completed Project Builder 1*

Creating a Documentary Using Premiere Pro & Audition CS6

Projects

This book contains a variety of end-of-chapter materials for additional practice and reinforcement. The Skills Review contains hands-on practice exercises that mirror the progressive nature of the lesson material. The chapter concludes with three projects: two Project Builders, and one Portfolio Project. The Project Builders require you to apply the skills you've learned in the chapter. The Portfolio Project encourages you to address and solve challenges based on the content explored in the chapter, and to develop your own portfolio of work.

What Instructor Resources Are Available with This Book?

The Instructor Resources are Delmar's way of putting the resources and information needed to teach and learn effectively into your hands. All the resources are available for both Macintosh and Windows operating systems. These resources can be found online at: **http://login.cengage.com**. Once you login or create an account, search for the title under 'My Dashboard' using the ISBN. Then select the instructor companion site resources and click 'Add to my Bookshelf.'

Instructor's Manual

The Instructor's Manual includes chapter overviews and detailed lecture topics for each chapter, with teaching tips.

Sample Syllabus

The Sample Syllabus includes a suggested syllabus for any course that uses this book.

PowerPoint Presentations

Each chapter has a corresponding PowerPoint presentation that you can use in lectures, distribute to your students, or customize to suit your course.

Data Files for Students

To complete most of the chapters in this book, your students will need Data Files, which are available on the DVDs packaged with the book. Instruct students to use the Data Files List at the end of this book. This list gives instructions on organizing files.

Solutions to Exercises

Solution Files are Data Files completed with comprehensive sample answers. Use these files to evaluate your students' work. Or distribute them electronically so students can verify their work. Sample solutions to lessons and end-of-chapter material are provided with the exception of some Portfolio Projects.

Additional Resources and Certification

To access additional materials for this book, including information about ACE certification, take the following steps:

1. Open your browser and go to http://www.cengagebrain.com.
2. Type the author, title, or ISBN of this book in the Search window. (The ISBN is listed on the back cover.)
3. Click the book title in the list of search results.
4. When the book's main page is displayed, click the Access button under Free Study Tools.
5. Click ACE Information or, to access additional materials, click the Additional Materials tab under Book Resources to download the files.

Test Bank and Test Engine

ExamView is a powerful testing software package that allows instructors to create and administer printed and computer (LAN-based) exams. ExamView includes hundreds of questions that correspond to the topics covered in this text, enabling students to generate detailed study guides that include page references for further review. The computer-based and LAN-based/online testing component allows students to take exams using the EV Player, and also saves the instructor time by grading each exam automatically.

BRIEF CONTENTS

CONTENTS

 CHAPTER 1: CREATING A VIDEO MONTAGE IN ADOBE PREMIERE PRO CS6

CHAPTER 2: WORKING IN ADOBE AFTER EFFECTS CS6

CHAPTER 3: CREATING A SOUNDTRACK IN ADOBE AUDITION CS6

CHAPTER 5: DEVELOPING A PSA & COMMERCIAL USING PREMIERE PRO & AFTER EFFECTS CS6

CHAPTER 6: WORKING WITH SPECIAL EFFECTS TO ENHANCE VIRAL VIDEOS - ADOBE PREMIERE PRO & ADOBE AFTER EFFECTS CS6

Supported Features

The Adobe Dynamic Link feature is only available if your software was installed as part of a suite and not as individual point products. In addition, please note that if you installed a trial version of the Suite, Encore and other features will be disabled.

Intended Audience

This book is designed for the beginner or intermediate user who wants to learn applications from the Production Premium Suite. The book is written in a project-based format to provide basic and in-depth material that not only educates, but also encourages you to explore the nuances of each of the applications discussed in this book.

Approach

The text is designed so you can work at your own pace through step-by-step tutorials. A concept is presented and the process explained, followed by the actual steps. To take advantage of what this text has to offer, you should work as follows:

- Read the introduction for each chapter to understand the overall concept that is being used to teach the tools and techniques the applications have to offer.

- The introduction for each lesson provides greater explanation than the actual steps. Refer to the introduction while working on the steps.
- As you work on the steps, pay attention to what you are doing and why; do not just go through the motions of following directions.
- After completing a set of steps, ask yourself if you could use these skills without referring to the steps. If you feel you could not, review the steps.

Icons, Buttons, and Pointers

Symbols for icons, buttons, and pointers are shown each time they are used in the steps. Try to become familiar with their names and their location.

Data Files

To complete the lessons in this book, you need the Data Files located on the DVDs provided with this book. Your instructor will tell you where to store the files as you work, such as to your hard drive or network server. The instructions will refer to the drive and folder where these Data Files are stored.

The software in this text creates reference files to assets or footage being used in the individual applications. As a result, there may

be instances when your files are missing. The application may alert you to this when it is opening a project, or it may show a missing link in the Project panel. In either case, it will be necessary to locate the missing files in order for the project to work properly. Once the files have been re-linked and the project file saved, it will not be necessary to locate these files again. Therefore, it is extremely important not to move or delete any files that are being used.

Building an Electronic Portfolio

The final chapter in this book addresses Encore, which will be used to create an electronic portfolio of the portfolio projects from each chapter in this book. It is suggested you work on the chapters in the book in consecutive order so that as your skills are developed you are able to utilize them in later chapters.

Windows and Macintosh

The Production Premium Suite works virtually the same on both the Windows and Macintosh operating systems. In those cases where there is a difference, the abbreviations (Win) and (Mac) are used.

System Requirements for Adobe Creative Suite 6 Production Premium

Windows

- 64-bit support required: Intel® Pentium® 4 or AMD Athlon® 64 processor (Intel Core™ 2 Duo or AMD Phenom® II recommended); Intel Core 2 Duo or AMD Phenom II required for Adobe Premiere® Pro
- 64-bit operating system required: Microsoft® Windows Vista® Home Premium, Business, Ultimate, or Enterprise with Service Pack 1 (Service Pack 2 recommended) or Windows 7
- 2 GB of RAM (4 GB or more recommended)
- 16.3 GB of available hard-disk space for installation; additional free space required during installation (cannot install on removable flash-based storage devices)
- 1280x900 display (1280x1024 recommended) with qualified hardware-accelerated OpenGL graphics card, 16-bit color, and 256 MB of VRAM
- Adobe-certified GPU card for GPU-accelerated performance in Adobe Premiere Pro
- Some features in Adobe Bridge rely on a DirectX 9–capable graphics card with at least 64 MB of VRAM
- 7200 RPM hard drive for editing compressed video formats; RAID 0 for uncompressed
- Adobe-certified card for capture and export to tape for SD/HD workflows
- OHCI-compatible IEEE 1394 port for DV and HDV capture, export to tape, and transmit to DV device
- Sound card compatible with ASIO protocol or Microsoft Windows Driver Model
- DVD-ROM drive compatible with dual-layer DVDs (DVD+-R burner for burning DVDs; Blu-ray burner for creating Blu-ray Disc media)
- Java™ Runtime Environment 1.5 (32 bit) or 1.6
- QuickTime 7.6.2 software required for QuickTime features
- Adobe Flash® Player 10 software required to play back DVD projects exported as SWF files
- Broadband Internet connection required for online services

Macintosh System Requirements

- Multicore Intel processor with 64-bit support
- Mac OS X v10.5.7 or v10.6.3; Mac OS X v10.6.3 required for GPU-accelerated performance in Adobe Premiere Pro
- 2 GB of RAM (4 GB or more recommended)
- 20.6 GB of available hard-disk space for installation; additional free space required during installation (cannot install on a volume that uses a case-sensitive file system or on removable flash-based storage devices)
- 1280x900 display (1280x1024 recommended) with qualified hardware-accelerated OpenGL graphics card, 16-bit color, and 256 MB of VRAM
- Adobe-certified GPU card for GPU-accelerated performance in Adobe Premiere Pro
- 7200 RPM hard drive for editing compressed video formats; RAID 0 for uncompressed
- Core Audio–compatible sound card
- DVD-ROM drive compatible with dual-layer DVDs (SuperDrive for burning DVDs; external Blu-ray burner for creating Blu-ray Disc media)
- Java Runtime Environment 1.5 or 1.6
- QuickTime 7.6.2 software required for QuickTime features
- Adobe Flash Player 10 software required to play back DVD projects exported as SWF files
- Broadband Internet connection required for online services

Certification

You can find information about obtaining ACE certification for Premiere Pro CS6 on Cengage Brain. To access the online certification materials, follow the instructions on page ix, under "Additional Resources and Certification."

CHAPTER 1

CREATING A VIDEO MONTAGE
IN ADOBE PREMIERE
PRO CS6

1. Create a new project and explore the workspace
2. Import assets
3. Work with the Timeline panel and sequences
4. Apply video transitions
5. Work with motion effects
6. Design and insert titles
7. Export a movie

CHAPTER

1

CREATING A VIDEO MONTAGE
IN ADOBE PREMIERE PRO CS6

Adobe Premiere Pro CS6 is a professional digital video editing application that allows you to capture, edit, and publish video. It can be purchased as a stand-alone application or as part of either the Creative Suite 6 Production Premium or the Creative Suite 6 Master Collection.

You have probably heard of Adobe Systems and have already used some of their applications such as Photoshop or Illustrator. Premiere Pro should therefore have some familiarity to you as you begin to work with it because of the similarity in workspace design with other Adobe products.

When working with Premiere Pro you bring together video clips, digital images, audio, and vector graphics to create a **project file**, which contains the movie you are creating. A project file is saved with the .prproj file extension.

In this chapter, you will create a video montage. A **video montage** is a video created with digital images, words, transitions, and music.

TOOLS YOU'LL USE

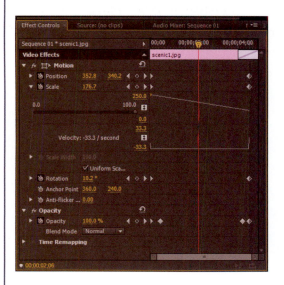

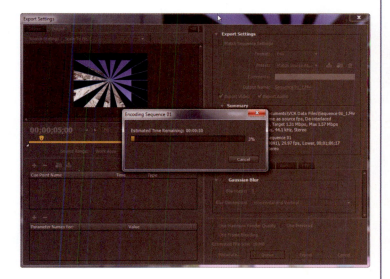

Figures © Cengage Learning 2013

Create a New Project
AND EXPLORE THE WORKSPACE

What You'll Do

Figure © Cengage Learning 2013

 In this lesson, you will start Premiere Pro, create a new project, and explore the workspace.

Exploring the Premiere Pro Workspace

When you start Premiere Pro, you will be prompted to create a new project or open an existing project. Once you have done that, you will see the **application window**, which is the main window comprised of various panels. The arrangement of panels in the application window is known as the **workspace**. Premiere Pro offers several preformatted workspaces which are designed for specific tasks. Figure 1 shows the default workspace which is called **Editing**. The Editing workspace, as its name implies, is designed to facilitate video editing. The

Figure 1 *Editing workspace*

Menu bar

Source Monitor

Effect Controls panel

Project panel

Media Browser panel

Sequence

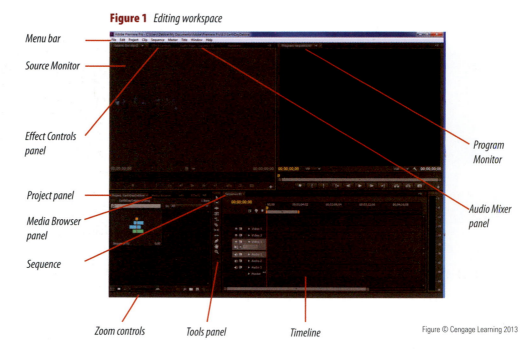

Program Monitor

Audio Mixer panel

Zoom controls

Tools panel

Timeline

Figure © Cengage Learning 2013

panels that are necessary to perform editing functions are the active panels.

QUICK TIP

The editing workspace has been updated for CS6. If you prefer the CS5 or CS5.5 workspace choose Editing (CS5.5) from the Workspace command on the Window menu.

The workspace can be changed by selecting a preformatted workspace or by rearranging the panels to your individual preference. You can switch between preformatted workspaces using the Workspace command on the Window menu.

QUICK TIP

The workspace drop down menu has been removed from the Tools panel. To view the workspace drop down menu, also known as the **Workspace Switcher**, open the Options panel from the Window menu.

Panels can be moved by clicking and dragging the **panel tabs**. As you drag a panel, an area becomes highlighted; this is called the **drop zone**, as shown in Figure 2, and provides a visual reference to where the panel can be placed.

If you wish to save a custom workspace, you may do so by selecting the New Workspace command on the Workspace menu. A **custom**

workspace is one that has been created by the user and saved with a unique name.

The panels used most often in Premiere Pro are:

Project panel: The Project panel organizes all the assets for your project. **Digital assets** can include video clips, digital images, and audio clips.

Timeline panel: The Timeline panel is where you assemble assets and edit them. It is here that you can also add special effects, transitions, and titles. The Timeline plays the items from left to right creating a movie.

Figure 2 *Moving panels in the workspace*

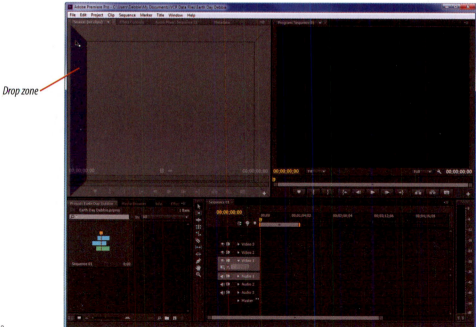

Drop zone

Figure © Cengage Learning 2013

Source and Program Monitor panels: The Source Monitor is used to preview assets from the Project panel or the Media Browser before you place them in a sequence, and the Program Monitor displays the contents of the Timeline—your project in progress.

Capturing Video from an External Device

Adobe Premiere Pro supports the control of devices such as camcorders and VCRs for capturing video via the Control Settings dialog box. DV and HDV devices are controlled with IEEE 1394 (FireWire, i.Link) connections. On the Windows platform, Adobe Premiere Pro can also control serial devices by way of RS-232 or RS-422 controllers if they are installed on the computer.

The Control Settings dialog box can be activated via the Device Control panel in the Preferences dialog box or from the Settings pane of the Capture panel. This controls how Premiere Pro transfers video and audio from a VCR or a camera. The options may differ depending on installed software or capture cards. In the Capture panel, if you are connecting a DV or HDV Device, select the device you want to control from the Device pop-up menu. You will then have the option to select the model, or one from the same family. If these are not available options, choose Standard. If you are connecting a serial device, make your selections from the Protocol, Port, Time Source, and Time Base menus. Check either or both check box selections available for the protocol you choose.

The Capture panel, activated from the File menu, provides controls similar to those in the Source and Program Monitor panels to operate the device during playback and capture. These are called transport controls and include a Record button. The Record button is used for a manual capture.

In the Logging pane, you can create metadata for your imported footage and set up the capture to import the entire footage as one clip or based on scene detection. You can also set extra frames, or **handles**, to the clip to provide additional frames at each end to assist in editing. Additionally, you can log clips and identify In/Out points without capturing so that you can utilize batch capturing. Batch capturing allows you to capture logged clips automatically and then leave them unattended, allowing you to minimize Premiere Pro and switch to another application without stopping capture. (*Note*: This option is selected from the File menu.)

Premiere Pro supports editing footage from a multi-camera shoot of up to four cameras. Make sure each camera has a sync point, such as a clapper slate, to easily synchronize the footage. Capture your footage as you normally would, stack the synchronized footage on separate video tracks, and create a nested sequence. You can then open the Multi-Camera Monitor panel and target the nested sequence. You will then be able to see the footage from each of the cameras and edit from this panel. You will have the ability to switch between camera footage and assemble an edited sequence from the footage from each of the cameras while viewing all of them at one time. The Capture panel is shown in Figure 3 and the DV/HDV Device Control Settings dialog box is shown in Figure 4.

Figure 3 *Using the Capture panel*

Capture panel

Status area

Preview

Transport controls

Figure 4 *DV/HDV Device Control Settings*

Device Control Options button

Understanding the New Project Dialog Box

When you create a new project, the New Project dialog box opens. The New Project dialog box is where you specify the settings for your Premiere Pro project. It has two tabs: General and Scratch Disks. The General tab is where you adjust settings regarding safe margins and video/audio formats. It is recommended that these settings be left to their defaults. You will be using the DV Capture setting. If you capture or have access to your own high definition footage, you will need to change this setting to HDV. The General tab is also where you name your project file and set the location where you will be saving it.

The Scratch Disks tab, as shown in Figure 5, provides settings for a variety of files associated with the video editing process including where they are stored. Premiere Pro sets the default for each of these files as the Same as Project. Using the Same as Project setting is an excellent way to keep your project organized and to be able to clean up project files as they become memory intensive. You will be using the default settings as you work through the projects in this book.

Figure 5 *Scratch Disks tab in the New Project dialog box*

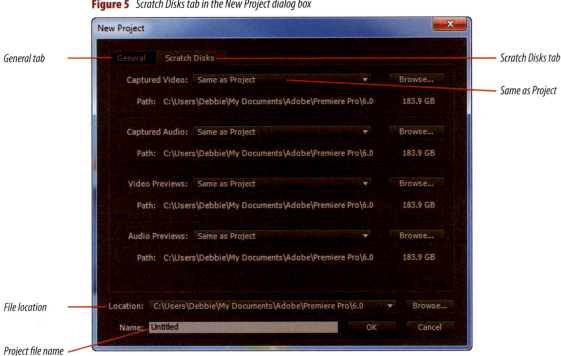

General tab

Scratch Disks tab

Same as Project

File location

Project file name

Figure © Cengage Learning 2013

Understanding the New Sequence Dialog Box

The New Sequence dialog box appears after you click OK in the New Project dialog box. A *sequence* is where the digital assets are placed and edited. At least one sequence is required in a Premiere Pro project, which is why you are prompted to create one when beginning a project. The New Sequence dialog box has three tabs: Sequence Presets, Settings, and Tracks.

You will be working with the default settings, as shown in Figure 6, unless otherwise noted.

The Sequence Presets tab has a number of categories of sequence settings for commonly used capture devices. It is recommended that you choose the preset that matches the settings for your device if it is available.

The Settings tab is available to customize settings if there is not a preset available for your device. It is recommended that you use the preset that is the closest match to your device and continue with any necessary customizations on the Settings tab. You can then save this custom preset.

The Tracks tab allows you to indicate how many video and audio tracks will be added when the sequence is created; by default, three video tracks and three stereo audio tracks are created. Tracks can be added or deleted later.

Figure 6 *New Sequence dialog box*

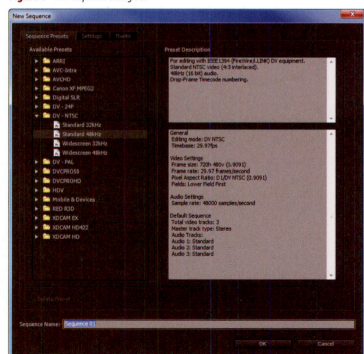

Create a new project and explore the workspace

1. Click **Start** on the taskbar, point to **All Programs**, then click **Adobe Premiere Pro CS6** (Win) or open the **Finder** from the dock and click **Applications** from the sidebar, select the **Adobe applications folder** then click **Adobe Premiere Pro CS6** (Mac).

   You may need to look in a subfolder if you have installed the Creative Suite.

   TIP Pressing and holding [Ctrl][Alt][Shift] (Win) or ⌘ [Shift][option] (Mac) while starting Premiere Pro restores default preference settings.

2. Click **New Project** in the Welcome to Adobe Premiere Pro window as shown in Figure 7.

   The New Project dialog box opens.

3. Click the **Browse button** and navigate to the drive and folder where your Data Files are located.

4. Click **OK** to close the Browse for Folder window but keep the New Project dialog box open.

   The Browse button allows you to choose a destination to save the project in. As shown in Figure 8, the path where the project will be saved appears in the Location field.

   (continued)

Figure 7 *Welcome to Adobe Premiere Pro window*

New Project

Figure 8 *New Project dialog box*

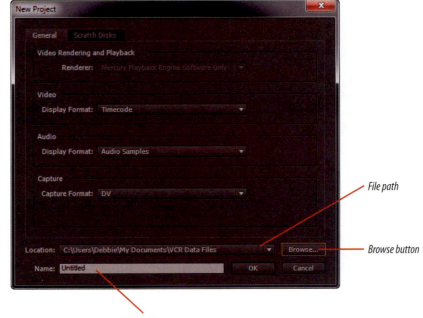

File path

Browse button

Project / file name

Figures © Cengage Learning 2013

Creating a Video Montage in Adobe Premiere Pro CS6

Figure 9 *Effects workspace*

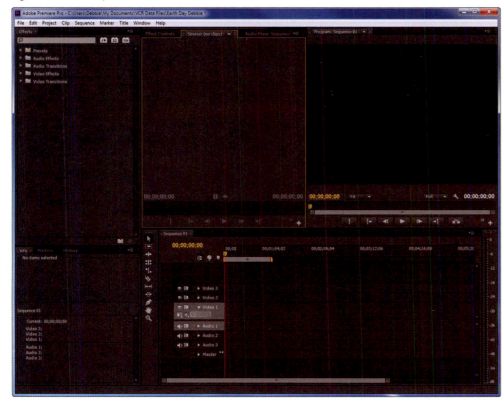

Figure © Cengage Learning 2013

5. In the Name text box of the New Project dialog box, replace the existing text with **Earth Day** followed by your name.

6. Click **OK** to close the New Project dialog box.

   The New Sequence dialog box appears.

7. Click **OK** to accept the default settings.

   The Premiere Pro CS6 workspace appears.

8. Locate the Project panel, Source Monitor, Program Monitor, and Timeline.

9. Click **Window** on the Menu bar, point to **Workspace**, then click **Effects**.

   The Effects workspace is used for working with video and audio effects. As shown in Figure 9, the Source window was resized to make room for the Effects panel and the Info panel replaced the Project panel.

10. Click **Window** on the Menu bar, point to **Workspace**, then click **Editing** to return to the default workspace.

You started Adobe Premiere Pro CS6, created a new project named Earth Day, and explored the workspace.

LESSON 2

Import ASSETS

What You'll Do

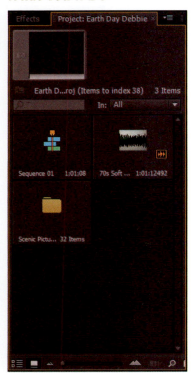

Figure © Cengage Learning 2013

 In this lesson, you will continue to work with the project you began in Lesson 1 and familiarize yourself with the Project panel and the Media Browser.

Importing Assets

A Premiere Pro CS6 project is a single file that stores all references to digital assets used in the project. Digital assets may include video, audio, still images, and Photoshop and Illustrator files. A project file also contains sequences (or timelines); these are where the digital assets are placed and edited. Only one project may be open at a time. When you save a project, the name will appear in the title bar along with the path to where it is being saved.

The assets you use for your project are imported into the Project panel. You will have the option when importing to select single or multiple clips, folders and their content, and numbered stills. Video projects characteristically take up a lot of memory so to help keep the file size down, Premiere Pro creates **reference files** that point to the original files being imported.

> **QUICK TIP**
> To ensure that Premiere Pro can find digital assets that you've imported, don't move or delete reference files.

Organizing the Project Panel

The Project panel is your "file cabinet" of assets. You can create **bins** to help organize your Project panel, as shown in Figure 10. Bins work the same way as folders in Windows Explorer

Figure 10 *Project panel with bins and assets*

Project panel

Asset preview

Bin

Assets

New Bin button

Figure © Cengage Learning 2013

Creating a Video Montage in Adobe Premiere Pro CS6

or the Mac OS Finder. Bins may contain assets, sequences, or other bins. You may want to use them to organize your source files by category, such as text or images, or if you are creating multiple sequences, to organize sequences with their own source files.

Working with the Media Browser

The Media Browser provides a convenient way to locate, sort, preview, and import assets that you plan to use in your Premiere Pro project, as shown in Figure 11. It also provides access to the assets that you are using while you edit. Because the Media Browser is a panel it can be treated like any other panel—docked, left open, or floating.

Organizing a Storyboard

In addition, the Project panel can be used for storyboarding when in Icon view.

Storyboarding is a way to plan your video by placing **clips** or digital assets in the order you plan to have them play. **Icon view** shows **thumbnails**, which are smaller versions of the digital assets you imported, as shown in Figure 12.

Figures © Cengage Learning 2013

Figure 11 *Media Browser*

Media Browser

Computer directory

Folders and files

To arrange the thumbnails, click and drag any square. As you drag, a vertical bar indicates where the item is going; when you release the mouse button the thumbnail drops into place.

Figure 12 *Organizing a storyboard in Icon view*

Return to Parent bin

List View button

Icon View button   *Zoom controls*

Import assets using the Media Browser

1. Open your Earth Day *your name*.prproj file, if necessary.

2. Click the **Media Browser panel tab**, if it is not already active.

   The Media Browser displays the hard drive(s) on your computer.

3. On the Media Browser, navigate to the drive and folder where the Chapter 1 Data Files are located as shown in Figure 13.

4. Select **70s Soft Rock - 60.mp3** in the Chapter 1 folder.

5. Click **File** on the Menu bar, then click **Import from Media Browser**.

TIP You can also right-click a file on the Media Browser and select Import or drag the file from the Media Browser into the Project panel.

   The reference to the 70s Soft Rock - 60.mp3 file from the Chapter 1 folder can now be found in the Project panel.

6. Save your project file and leave it open for the next exercise.

You used the Media Browser to import an audio file for your Earth Day project.

Figure 13 *The Media Browser panel*

Media Browser
Recent directories
Chapter 1 Data Files folder
File types displayed
Directory viewers
Chapter 1 Data Files contents in thumbnail view
Thumbnail View icon

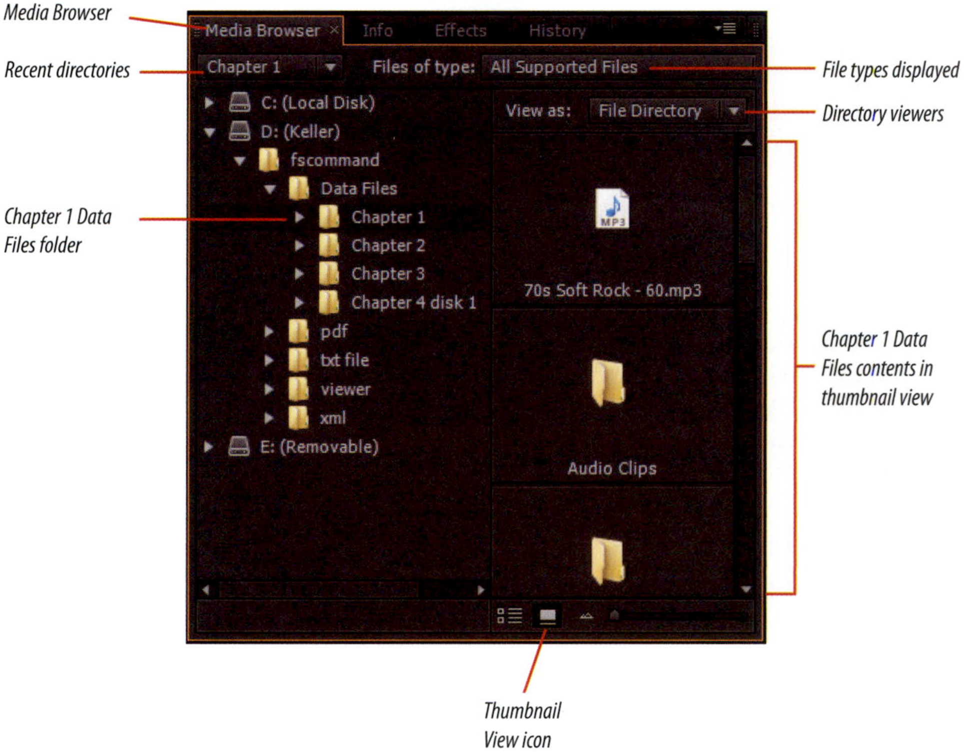

Viewing Files in the Media Browser

To view only files of certain types in the Media Browser, click the Files of type list arrow in the Import dialog box, and select a file type. To select an additional type, open the menu again and make another selection. Repeat until all desired types are selected. Select one or more files from the list of files. To select more than one noncontiguous file, [Ctrl]-click (Win) or ⌘-click (Mac) the filenames. To select more than one contiguous file, [Shift]-click the filenames.

Figure © Cengage Learning 2013

Creating a Video Montage in Adobe Premiere Pro CS6

Figure 14 *Creating a new bin*

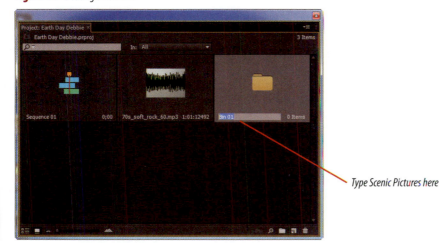

Type Scenic Pictures here

Figure 15 *Scenic Pictures bin opened as a dockable panel*

Bin name

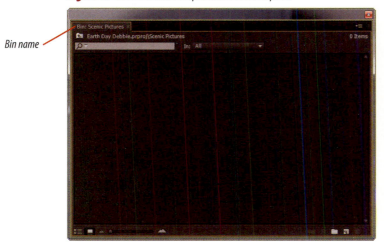

Work with bins

1. Open your Earth Day *your name*.prproj file, if it is not already open.

2. Click the **New Bin button** 📁 on the Project panel to create a new bin.

   You may need to open the Project panel by clicking on its tab to the left of the Media Browser tab.

3. Type **Scenic Pictures**, as shown in Figure 14, to rename the bin.

4. Double-click the **Scenic Pictures bin** to open the bin as a dockable panel.

   Opening a bin as a dockable panel, as shown in Figure 15, allows you to resize the window to get a better view.

   TIP To open a bin on the Project panel, [Ctrl]-double-click (Win) or ⌘-double-click (Mac) the bin. Click the Parent bin button 📁 to close the bin if you opened the bin on the Project panel.

5. Click the **Close box** ❎ to close the Scenic Pictures dockable panel.

6. Save your project file and leave it open for the next exercise.

You created a new bin titled Scenic Pictures, opened it as a dockable panel, and then closed it.

Import assets with the Import command

1. Open your Earth Day *your name*.prproj file, if necessary.

2. [Ctrl]-double-click (Win) or ⌘-double-click (Mac) the **Scenic Pictures bin** to open it within the Project panel.

3. Click **File** on the Menu bar, click **Import**, as shown in Figure 16, then navigate to the drive and folder where your Data Files are located.

   TIP Alternatively, you can right-click a bin, then click Import.

4. Select the range of files **scenic1** through **scenic32** located in the Earth Day Pictures folder, then click **Open**.

   TIP To select more than one contiguous file, click the first file, press and hold [Shift], then click the last file in the sequence.

(continued)

Figure 16 *Import command on the File menu*

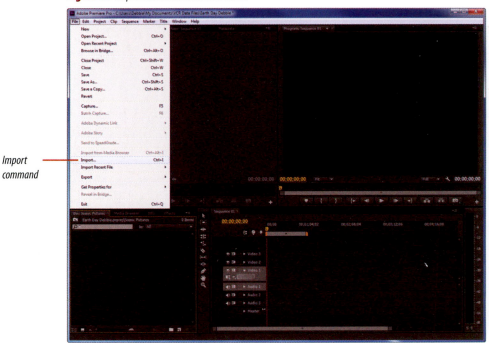

Import command

Creating a Video Montage in Adobe Premiere Pro CS6

Figure 17 *Scenic Pictures bin with imported images*

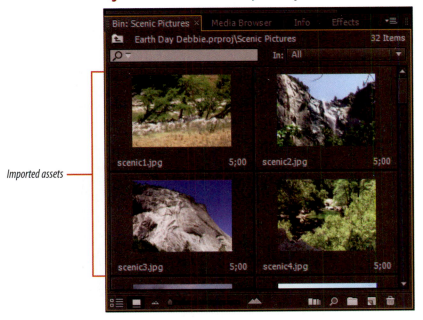

Imported assets

The Scenic Pictures bin now contains the references to the files from the Data Files folder, as shown in Figure 17.

5. Click the **Parent bin button** 🔲 to close the Scenic Pictures bin.

6. Save your project file and leave it open for the next exercise.

You imported images into the Scenic Pictures bin using the Import command.

Create a storyboard

1. Open your Earth Day *your name*.prproj file, if necessary.

2. Double-click the **Scenic Pictures bin** to open it as a dockable panel.

3. Click the **Icon View button** 🔲 on the Scenic Pictures bin.

(continued)

Configure Premiere Pro Preferences for a Project

Premiere Pro can be customized using the Preferences panel. Options range from setting the brightness of the interface under the Appearance category, to changing the default length of transitions under the General category. Some preferences remain for all projects, while others such as setting a location for scratch disks, under the Media category, are specific to a project file.

Figure © Cengage Learning 2013

4. Click the **scenic3.jpg image**, drag the image after **scenic1.jpg**, then release the mouse button.

As you drag, a vertical line appears to show you where the item will be placed, as shown in Figure 18.

(continued)

Figure 18 *Dragging an image in the Scenic Pictures bin*

Vertical line

Preparing Still Images for Import

To reduce rendering time and improve quality, images should be prepared prior to importing into your Adobe Premiere Pro project. The pixel dimensions should be set to the resolution you will use in Adobe Premiere Pro. If you plan to scale the image, set the image dimensions to the largest size the image will be in the project. Scaling an image larger than its original size can cause loss of sharpness. Crop the parts of the image that you don't want to be visible in Adobe Premiere Pro.

Figure © Cengage Learning 2013

Creating a Video Montage in Adobe Premiere Pro CS6

Figure 19 *Images rearranged in the Scenic Pictures bin*

Odd numbered images

Even numbered images

Icon View button

5. Reorder all of the images so that the odd numbered images are first (scenic1.jpg, scenic3.jpg, scenic5.jpg, and so on).

TIP You may need to resize the Scenic Pictures bin to drag all of the images.

Your bin should resemble Figure 19.

6. Close the Scenic Pictures bin.

7. Save your project file and leave it open for the next exercise.

You created a storyboard by rearranging the images in the Scenic Pictures bin.

Work with the Timeline Panel
AND SEQUENCES

What You'll Do

Figure © Cengage Learning 2013

In this lesson, you will work with a sequence in the Timeline panel by placing clips on the sequence.

Understanding the Timeline Panel

A **sequence** is located in the Timeline panel, shown in Figure 20, and is where most editing takes place. Adobe Premiere Pro can have multiple sequences and you can place sequences inside other sequences to break your project up into manageable pieces. Sequences are comprised of video and audio tracks. **Tracks** are where the clips are assembled, edited, and enhanced with effects and transitions. A sequence can consist of multiple audio and video tracks, but must contain at least one of each. Multiple tracks are used to blend clips together.

Exploring the Timeline Panel Controls

The Timeline panel includes the following features:

Time ruler: The Time ruler measures the time in the sequence horizontally. Icons for markers and In and Out points are also displayed here.

Current-time display: The Current-time display shows the timecode for the current frame. **Timecodes** mark specific frames with unique addresses and is recorded onto

videotape during the recording process. To change the timecode, click the timecode display and enter a new timecode, or place the pointer over the display and drag left or right. Changing the Current-time display is a way to adjust the location of the Current-time Indicator.

Play head and Current-time Indicator (CTI): The Current-time Indicator (CTI) indicates the current frame displayed in the Program Monitor. The CTI is a light gold triangle in the Time ruler with a vertical red line extending through the video and audio tracks. The CTI can be moved by clicking and dragging on the gold triangle. This can also be used as a preview method, referred to as **scrubbing**.

Work area bar: The Work area bar indicates the area of the sequence that you want to preview or export. The brackets on either end, located just below the Time ruler, are adjustable so you can export portions of a large project for preview.

Horizontal Zoom bar: The Horizontal Zoom bar is the area that corresponds with the visible portion of the Timeline panel and allows you to quickly move to different parts of the sequence. The ends of the Horizontal Zoom bar can be used to increase or decrease the number of visible frames in the viewing area. It is located just above the Time ruler.

The Horizontal Zoom bar also allows you to adjust the range of time being viewed in the Timeline panel.

QUICK **TIP**

Click and drag on the square at either end of the Horizontal Zoom bar to increase or decrease the number of visible frames within the current viewing area.

Adding Clips to a Sequence

There are many options for adding clips to a sequence on the Timeline panel. The most obvious is to simply drag the clip from the Project panel to the sequence. If it is an audio clip it needs to be placed on an audio track; all other clips are placed on video tracks.

Any edits or effects that are done to the clip do not alter the clip on the Project panel, so you are able to use clips multiple times in the same project and apply different effects to the same clip.

You are also able to add clips to a sequence while previewing them on the Source Monitor. You can either drag an image from the Source

Monitor to a track, or use the Insert button or the Overwrite button on the Source Monitor to place the clip on the sequence.

Using the Insert button places the clip at the location of the CTI and shifts any clips at that location to the right to make room for the clip. The Overwrite button replaces the clip, as shown in Figure 21.

QUICK **TIP**

If you are placing items on a video track and have already placed audio on an audio track, you need to lock the audio track to keep it from shifting. To lock a track, you click the Toggle Track Lock box to the left of the track name. A padlock icon appears, indicating that the track is locked.

Figure 20 *Timeline panel*

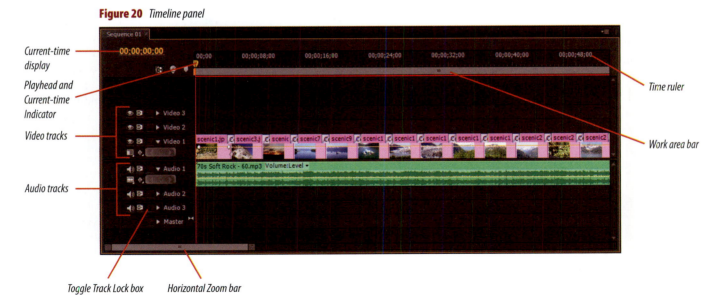

Figure © Cengage Learning 2013

Using the Automate to Sequence Command

In a previous lesson, you learned how to organize digital images in a storyboard. Premiere Pro has a command that lets you place the images from a storyboard on a sequence in the order that they were organized. This feature is called Automate to Sequence.

The clips you would like to be included in the Automate to Sequence process must be selected. The Automate to Sequence command is located on the Project panel menu, which you open by clicking the Project panel options button. You can also use the Automate to Sequence button on the Project panel.

If you do not want to organize your clips using a storyboard, you may select the clips in the order that you would like them placed in the sequence while pressing and holding [Ctrl] (Win) or ⌘ (Mac) and then choosing Selection Order from the Ordering list in the Automate To Sequence dialog box, as shown in Figure 22.

Figure 22 *Automate To Sequence dialog box*

Ordering

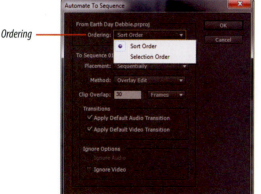

Figure 21 *Example of Insert and Overwrite insertions*

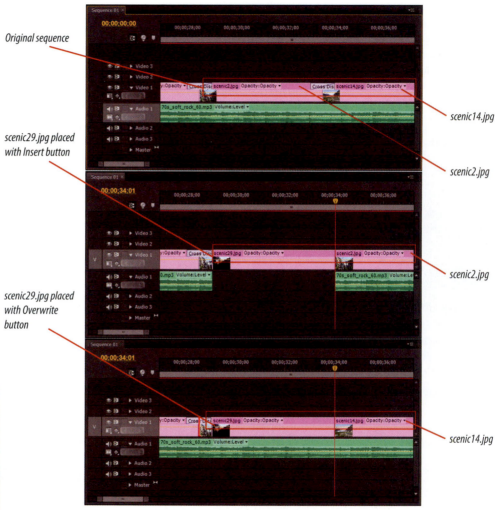

Original sequence

scenic29.jpg placed with Insert button

scenic29.jpg placed with Overwrite button

scenic14.jpg

scenic2.jpg

scenic2.jpg

scenic14.jpg

Figures © Cengage Learning 2013

Creating a Video Montage in Adobe Premiere Pro CS6

Deleting Clips from a Sequence

If during the editing process you decide you want to remove a clip from a sequence, it is not removed from the Project panel. If you remove a clip from the Project panel, and it is still in a sequence, it is removed from the sequence. In this case, Premiere Pro gives you a warning before it deletes the clip from the Project panel.

The Selection tool is the main tool used in Premiere Pro. It is used to select menu items and objects in the Premiere Pro workspace, and it is used for selecting clips in a sequence and in the Project panel.

The Track Select tool selects everything to the right of where you click in the sequence. See Figure 23. To select the clip and everything to the right on all tracks, [Shift]-click the clip.

The **Ripple Delete** command removes a clip from the sequence without leaving any gaps if the clip being removed is located between two other clips. Be cautious when working with this command if you have assets on other tracks; it shifts the clips on those tracks as well. In order to keep clips from shifting on other tracks they need to be locked before using the Ripple Delete command.

Previewing Your Project in the Program Monitor

The Program Monitor plays back the clips you are assembling in the active sequence on the Timeline panel for you to preview. The Play-Stop Toggle button plays and stops the sequence from the location of the CTI. The Shuttle button moves either forward or backward, fast or slow, depending on how you adjust the slider. The more you move the slider to the right the faster the video will play forward, the more you move the slider to the left the faster the video will rewind.

Figure 23 *Selecting clips with the Track Select tool*

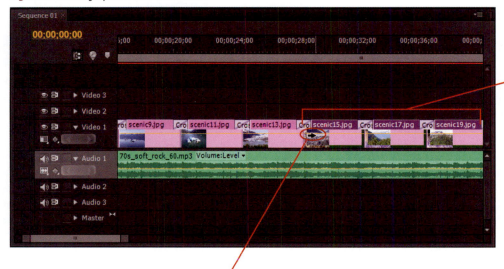

All tracks to the right are selected, including scenic15.jpg

Track Select tool

Figure © Cengage Learning 2013

Add clips to a sequence by dragging

1. Open your Earth Day *your name*.prproj file, if necessary.

2. Verify that the Current-time Indicator (CTI) is at the beginning of the sequence, as shown in Figure 24, by clicking the CTI 🔧 and dragging it to the left until the Current time display shows all zeroes.

TIP Another method for placing the CTI at the beginning of the sequence is to click the Timeline panel tab and then press [Home]. The [Home] key equivalent is [fn]+left arrow (Mac).

3. Click the **Project panel tab** to activate the Project panel.

4. Double-click the **Scenic Pictures bin**.

5. Click **scenic5.jpg**, then drag the clip to the beginning of the Video 1 track on the Timeline panel.

    When you drag a clip to add it to a sequence, you target the track by dropping the clip into the track.

TIP To make clip edges align when you drag them, make sure that the Snap button 🔲 is active on the Timeline panel.

(continued)

Figure 24 *CTI with timecode displaying all zeroes*

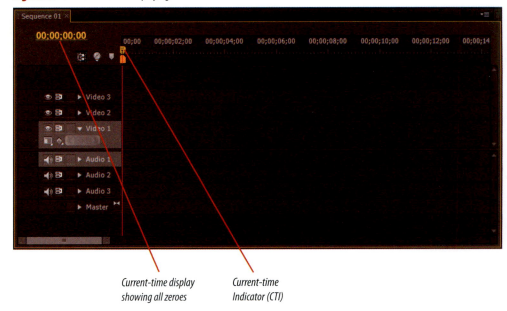

Current-time display showing all zeroes

Current-time Indicator (CTI)

A Note About Rendering

Rendering is the process of compiling the information in your projects sequence into its final format as a video. Rendering is part of the exporting process and it is what determines the quality of the playback of the final product. Video in a rendered project plays more smoothly and much closer to real time. You may have noticed a red or green line below the Work area bar in the Timeline panel. This line indicates whether your project has been rendered. A red line indicates that Premiere Pro is not able to play back your project in real time in the Project Monitor. A green line indicates that the project has been rendered. Adjusting the length of the Viewing area bar allows you to control portions of the video you wish to preview in rendered mode. **Note:** Each time you render your project, a unique preview file is created; this can become memory intensive. Premiere Pro creates a folder titled *Adobe Premiere Pro Preview Files* where these files are saved. This folder can be deleted to conserve hard drive space without harming your project file.

Figure 25 *The scenic5.jpg clip on the Video 1 track*

Snap
button

Video
track 1

Horizontal Zoom bar

scenic5.jpg

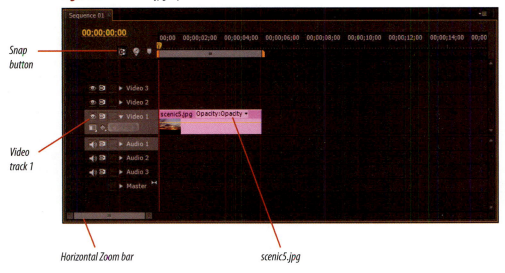

Figure 26 *The Video 1 track with five clips*

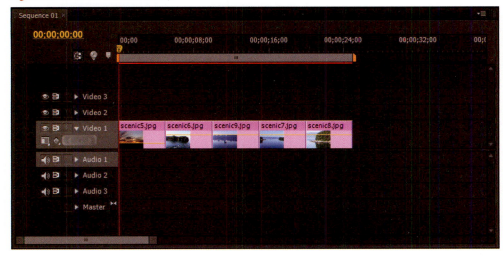

Lesson 3   Work with the Timeline Panel and Sequences

6. Click the **Horizontal Zoom bar** on the Timeline panel as needed to enlarge the thumbnail of the image on the Video 1 track until you can view the image better, as shown in Figure 25.

7. Drag the clips **scenic6.jpg**, **scenic7.jpg**, and **scenic8.jpg** to the sequence one after the other.

8. Drag the clip **scenic9.jpg** directly on top of **scenic6.jpg**.

    The scenic9.jpg file replaces scenic6.jpg in the sequence.

9. Drag **scenic6.jpg** directly on top of **scenic9. jpg** and press and hold [**Ctrl**] (Win) or ⌘ (Mac) before releasing the mouse button.

    The scenic6.jpg is added to the sequence and scenic9.jpg is shifted to the right.

10. Compare your sequence to Figure 26, make adjustments with the Horizontal Zoom bar as necessary, then save your project file and leave it open for the next exercise.

You added five clips to the sequence by dragging them from the Project panel.

Use the Automate to Sequence command

1. Open your Earth Day *your name*.prproj file, if necessary.

2. Be sure the Current-time Indicator (CTI) is at the end of the sequence by dragging it to the right until the Current-time display shows **00;00;25;00**.

TIP Another method for placing the CTI at the end of the sequence is to click the Timeline panel tab and press [End]. The [End] key equivalent is [fn]+right arrow (Mac).

3. Click the **Project panel tab** to activate the Project panel.

4. Open the Scenic Pictures bin as a dockable panel, if necessary.

   The bin should still be in Icon view and sorted with odd numbers first.

5. Select all of the images in the bin.

TIP You can select all images by pressing [Ctrl][A] (Win) or ⌘ [A] (Mac).

6. Click the **Scenic Pictures panel options button** , then click **Automate to Sequence**, as shown in Figure 27.

   The Automate To Sequence dialog box opens.

TIP You can also use the Automate to Sequence button on the Project panel to access the Automate To Sequence dialog box.

(continued)

Figure 27 *Using the Automate to Sequence command*

Scenic Pictures panel options button

Automate to Sequence command

All images selected

Creating a Video Montage in Adobe Premiere Pro CS6

Figure 28 *Automate To Sequence dialog box*

Sort Order

Figure 29 *Source Monitor*

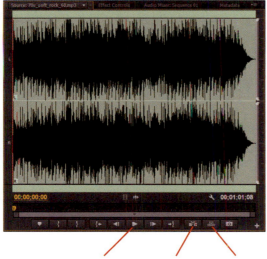

Play-Stop Toggle button   Insert button   Overwrite button

7. In the Automate To Sequence dialog box, click the **Ordering list arrow**, click **Sort Order**, as shown in Figure 28, then click **OK**.

   The clips are added to the sequence in sort order beginning at timecode 00;00;25;00, after the previous five clips that were already on the sequence.

8. Close the Scenic Pictures bin.

9. Save your project file and leave it open for the next exercise.

You added clips to the sequence using the Automate To Sequence dialog box.

Place clips in a sequence using the Source Monitor

1. Open your Earth Day *your name*.prproj file, if necessary.

2. Move the CTI 🔧 to the beginning of the sequence.

3. Double-click the **70s Soft Rock-60.mp3** audio file on the Project panel to preview the clip in the Source Monitor.

   The Source Monitor, as shown in Figure 29, allows you to preview any asset from either the Project panel or the Media Browser.

4. Click the **Play-Stop Toggle button** ▶ on the Source Monitor to preview the audio file.

   (continued)

5. Click in the **header area** of the Video 1 track, as shown in Figure 30, to turn off the target on the Video 1 track.

The highlight needs to be removed to indicate that when the audio file is placed from the Source Monitor, it should affect only the Audio 1 track.

6. Verify that the Audio 1 source track indicator and header area are both highlighted and click the **Collapse-Expand Track arrow** ▶ on the Audio 1 layer to expand the audio track, as shown in Figure 31.

Each area highlights independently; both areas need to be highlighted for the next steps to work properly. The **source track indicator** represents that an audio clip is open on the Source Monitor.

7. Click the **Insert button** 🔲 on the Source Monitor to place the audio file on the sequence in the Audio 1 track.

To accommodate inserting the audio track, all of the digital images shift to the right, as shown in Figure 32. You want the music to play with the images, so you need to undo your last action.

8. Click **Edit** on the Menu bar, then click **Undo**.

TIP You can also undo your last step by pressing [Ctrl] [Z] (Win) or [⌘] [Z] (Mac).

(continued)

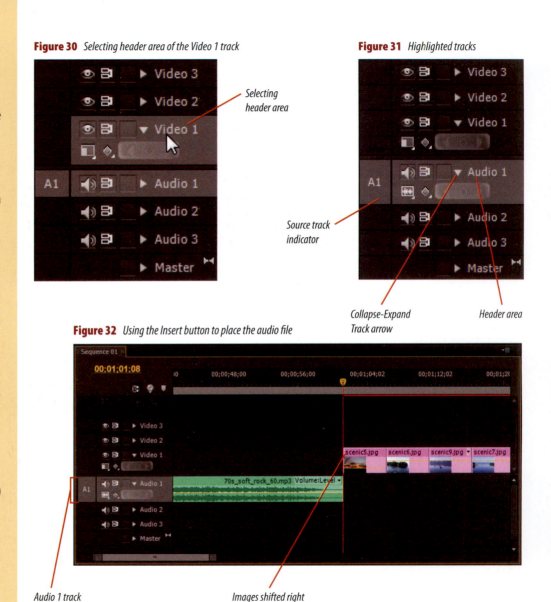

Figure 30 *Selecting header area of the Video 1 track*

Selecting header area

Figure 31 *Highlighted tracks*

Source track indicator

Collapse-Expand Track arrow

Header area

Figure 32 *Using the Insert button to place the audio file*

Audio 1 track is selected

Images shifted right

Figures © Cengage Learning 2013

Creating a Video Montage in Adobe Premiere Pro CS6

Figure 33 *The audio file placed with the Overwrite button*

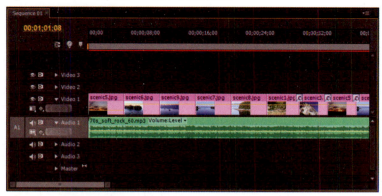

Figure 34 *Closing the file on the Source Monitor*

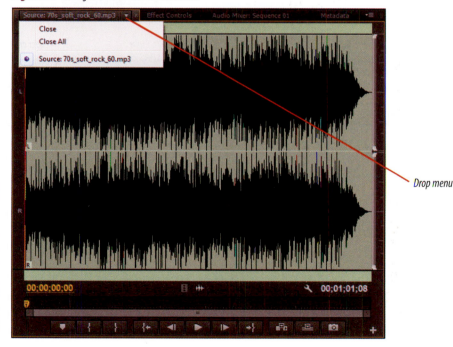

Drop menu

9. Click the **Overwrite button** on the Source Monitor to place the audio file on the sequence.

   Notice this time the audio track is lined up directly below the images on the video track, as shown in Figure 33.

10. Click the **drop-down menu button** next to **70s Soft Rock-60.mp3** on the Source Monitor, as shown in Figure 34, then click **Close** to close the audio clip.

11. Save your project file and leave it open for the next exercise.

You added an audio clip to the Audio 1 track using the Insert and Overwrite buttons on the Source Monitor.

Delete clips from a sequence

1. Open your Earth Day *your name*.prproj file, if necessary.

2. Verify that the Editing workspace is chosen.

3. Select the first five clips in the sequence: **scenic5.jpg**, **scenic6.jpg**, **scenic9.jpg**, **scenic7.jpg**, and **scenic8.jpg**.

4. Zoom in on the sequence if necessary to read the clip names.

TIP To select more than one clip, [Shift]-click the clips or drag a selection marquee over them.

(continued)

5. Press **Delete** on the keyboard.

   Notice that the clips are removed, but a gap is left as shown in Figure 35.

6. Click **Edit** on the Menu bar, then click **Undo**.

   You will use the Ripple Delete command to remove the clips without leaving a gap in the sequence.

7. Click **Edit** on the Menu bar, then click **Ripple Delete**.

   The Ripple Delete command closes the gap and removes the clips from the sequence.

TIP Alternatively, you can press [Shift] + [Delete] (Win) or [fn] + [shift] + [delete] (Mac) on the keyboard to apply the Ripple Delete command.

8. Click the **Track Select tool** on the Tools panel, click **scenic2.jpg**, then adjust your view of the timeline if necessary.

   The Track Select tool is used to quickly select a range of items. The range of images beginning with scenic2.jpg to the end of the sequence is selected.

9. Press **Delete**.

   Since these images are at the end of the sequence, you do not need to use the Ripple Delete command.

10. Click the **Selection tool** on the Tools panel before continuing.

11. Save your project file.

You deleted clips from a sequence using the Ripple Delete command.

Figure 35 *Removing clips with the Delete key*

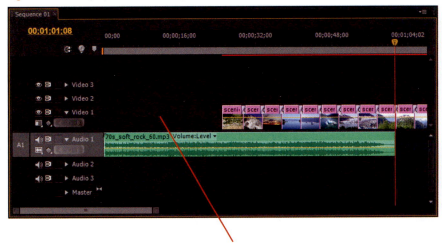

Gap left after clips deleted

Archive your Premiere Pro Project with the Project Manager

The Project Manager can be used to archive a project by consolidating all of the project's source media files, or to create a variation of the project called a trimmed project. There are options to consider in the Project Manager dialog box to conserve disk space. If the Include Preview Files and Include Audio Conform Files options are selected, the rendered effects remain rendered and the conformed audio remains conformed in the project, thus taking up more disk space. You can remove the check marks to conserve disk space. (Note: These options are available only if the Collect Files And Copy to New Location option is selected.) When the project is opened again, the audio is conformed and the file can be rendered.

The Rename Media File To Match Clip Names option provides the opportunity to organize footage files based on the names given to the footage in the Project panel.

The Include Handles option specifies the number of frames that are preserved before and after the In and Out points of each trimmed clip; the default value is 30 frames. This provides extra frames in the new project if minor adjustments need to be made.

Figure © Cengage Learning 2013

Creating a Video Montage in Adobe Premiere Pro CS6

Figure 36 *Edited Timeline panel*

Preview contents of the Timeline on the Program Monitor

1. Open your Earth Day *your name*.prproj file, if necessary.

2. Be sure the CTI is at the beginning of the sequence.

3. Press the **Play-Stop Toggle button** ▶ on the Program Monitor to view the contents of the Timeline.

   The project transitions from one image clip to another as the CTI moves from left to right in the sequence. Premiere Pro applies the default transition, called Cross Dissolve, to all clips.

   TIP Pressing [Spacebar] also previews the sequence. Pressing [Enter] (Win) or [return] (Mac) previews the sequence and begins the rendering process.

4. Drag the **CTI** 🛡 on the Timeline panel left and right to preview the sequence on the Program Monitor.

   TIP Viewing the clip in this manner is referred to as scrubbing (so named because of the back-and-forth motion).

5. Compare your Timeline panel to Figure 36.

6. Save your project file and leave it open for the next exercise.

You previewed the sequence in the Program Monitor.

Apply Video
TRANSITIONS

What You'll Do

Figure © Cengage Learning 2013

 In this lesson, you will apply video transitions to images.

Applying Video Transitions

A **transition** is used to move from one clip to the next in your sequence. Transitions can add additional interest to your video and can be as simple as phasing out one image and phasing in another. Adobe Premiere Pro CS6 has a large library of video transitions to choose from, with categories that include Dissolve, Page Peel, Slide, and Zoom. Video transitions are stored on the Effects panel. Cross Dissolve is set as the default transition and has already been placed between each of your clips in the Timeline panel.

Applying a Transition Between Clips

After you find the transition you want to apply on the Effects panel, simply drag the transition to the vertical line between two clips, known as the **cut line**, and release the mouse button when you see the cut icon for the alignment option you want to apply. As shown in Figure 37, you can place or align the transition in one of three ways: Center at Cut, End at Cut, or Start at Cut. By default, the transition is placed centered on the **cut**, which is the space between two clips. The other options either start or end the

Figure 37 *Three alignment options for placing a transition*

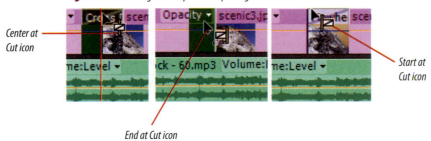

Center at
Cut icon

End at Cut icon

Start at
Cut icon

Figure © Cengage Learning 2013

transition at the cut. These options can also be chosen on the Effect Controls panel using the Alignment drop-down menu.

Customizing Transitions on the Effect Controls Panel

When working with transitions, it is a good idea to change to the Effects workspace. In this workspace, you can use the Effect Controls panel, shown in Figure 38, to customize transitions. Different options are available on the Effect Controls panel for each transition.

Some transitions have **edge selectors**, which are arrows that change the orientation or direction of a transition. To change either of these aspects, you click an edge selector arrow on the transition's thumbnail. For example, the Slide transition can be oriented vertically, horizontally, or diagonally.

Start and **End sliders** can be changed with the three alignment settings as previously mentioned. You can also create a custom setting by pressing and holding [Shift] to move the start and end sliders together or by dragging one slider to change the position of one end.

The **Show Actual Sources** setting displays the starting and ending frames of the clips.

The **Border Width** setting adjusts the width of the optional border on the transition. The default border width setting is 0.0. Some transitions do not have borders.

The **Border Color** setting specifies the color of the transition's border. For the border color to show, the border width setting must be a value higher than 0.0.

The **Reverse** setting plays the transition backward.

Figure 38 *Additional transition options on the Effect Controls panel*

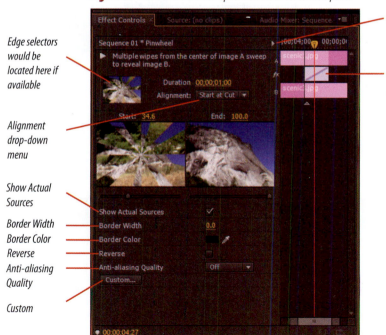

Edge selectors would be located here if available

Alignment drop-down menu

Show Actual Sources

Border Width
Border Color
Reverse
Anti-aliasing Quality

Custom

Show/Hide Timeline View button

Click and drag to adjust the position of the transition

Figure © Cengage Learning 2013

The **Anti-aliasing Quality** setting adjusts the smoothness of the transition's edges.

The **Custom** setting changes settings specific to the transition. Most transitions do not have custom settings.

Figure 39 *Effects panel for Windows and Mac*

Windows

Mac

Contains box

Effects bins

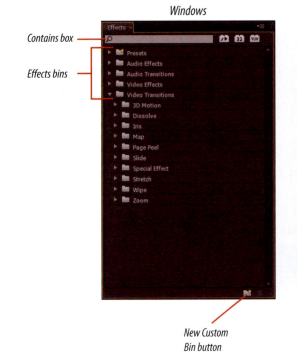

New Custom
Bin button

Searching for Video Transitions

The Effects panel contains an extensive library of transitions filed in several folders and subfolders as shown in Figure 39. If you know the name of the transition you are looking for, or even if you have an idea of what it might be called, you can search for it by typing its name in the Contains box on the Effects panel to find it more quickly.

Figure © Cengage Learning 2013

Figure 40 *Viewing the default transition between clips*

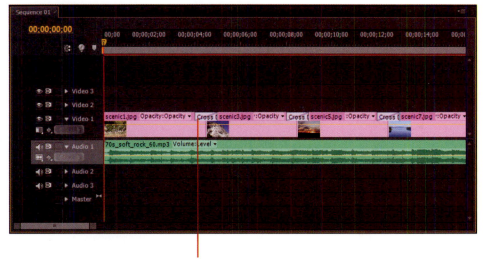

Cross Dissolve transition

Figure 41 *Center at Cut placement of Pinwheel transition*

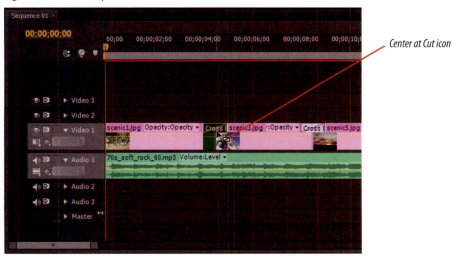

Center at Cut icon

Figures © Cengage Learning 2013

Apply a transition between two clips

1. Open your Earth Day *your name*.prproj file, if necessary.

2. Click **Window** on the Menu bar, point to **Workspace**, then click **Effects** to change the workspace to the Effects workspace.

   You will be working with the Effects panel and the Effect Controls panel during this lesson.

3. If necessary, move the CTI to the beginning of the sequence, then zoom in on the Timeline panel, if necessary, so you can easily see the transitions between the clips, as shown in Figure 40.

   The Cross Dissolve transition has already been applied between the clips placed on the Timeline.

4. Target the **Video 1 track** by clicking in the **Video 1 header**.

5. Click the **triangle** to the left of the Video Transitions bin on the Effects panel to expand it.

6. Inside the Video Transitions bin, expand the Wipe bin.

7. Click and drag the **Pinwheel transition** to the Cross Dissolve transition between **scenic1.jpg** and **scenic3.jpg**, then release the mouse button when you see the **Center at Cut icon** 🔁 as shown in Figure 41.

8. Click the **Pinwheel transition** on the sequence between **scenic1.jpg** and **scenic3.jpg** to select it.

   The Effect Controls panel displays the settings for the Pinwheel transition because it is selected on the Timeline. The settings can be changed to customize the transition.

   (continued)

9. Click the **Show/Hide Timeline View button** ▶ on the Effect Controls panel to show the timeline section of the Effect Controls panel, if necessary.

10. Click and drag the **CTI** 🛡 over the transition to preview it on the Program Monitor.

11. Save your project file and leave it open for the next exercise.

You applied a video transition between two clips in a sequence.

Customize a transition

1. Open your Earth Day *your name*.prproj file, if necessary.

2. Verify that the Effects workspace is chosen.

3. Click the **Pinwheel transition** between the **scenic1.jpg** and the **scenic3.jpg** clips to preview the transition on the Effect Controls panel.

4. On the Effect Controls panel, click the **Show Actual Sources check box** to select it, as shown in Figure 42.

    The scenic1.jpg and scenic3.jpg images replace the A-roll/B-roll format. A preview window appears above the two thumbnails and is useful for previewing the transition as it will look applied to the clips.

5. Click the **Alignment list arrow**, then click **Start at Cut**.

    The transition moves to the right in the timeline section on the Effect Controls panel so that it is placed at the beginning of the second clip.

    (continued)

Figure 42 *Effect Controls panel*

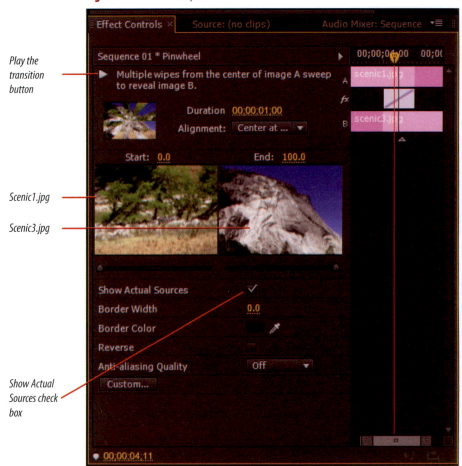

Play the transition button

Scenic1.jpg

Scenic3.jpg

Show Actual Sources check box

Creating a Video Montage in Adobe Premiere Pro CS6

Figure 43 *Customizing the pinwheel transition*

12 wedges

Start at Cut

2.0 Border width

Light blue border color

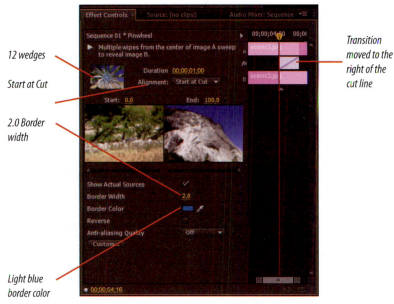

Transition moved to the right of the cut line

Figure 44 *Play the transition button on the Effect Controls panel*

Play the transition button

Figure 45 *Custom Pinwheel transition*

6. Click the **Custom button** on the Effect Controls panel to open the Pinwheel Settings dialog box.

7. Type **12** in the Number of wedges text box to add extra wedges to the wheel, then click **OK**.

TIP You may need to scroll down in the Effect Controls panel to see additional options if they are available.

8. Click the **Border Width value**, then type **2.0** to change the width of the border.

9. Click the **color box** next to Border Color to open the Color Picker dialog box, pick a **light blue color**, then click **OK**.

   Your Effect Controls panel should resemble Figure 43.

10. Click the **Play the transition button** ▶ on the Effect Controls panel, as shown in Figure 44, to preview any changes you make, then. Click the button again to stop the preview.

11. Click the **Play-Stop Toggle button** ▶ on the Program Monitor to preview the changes made to the transition, as shown in Figure 45, then click the button again to stop the preview.

TIP If the transition is not smooth on the Program Monitor you will need to render the sequence. Press [Enter] (Win) or [return] (Mac) to do so.

12. Save your project file and leave it open for the next exercise.

You customized the Pinwheel transition using settings on the Effect Controls panel.

Search for video transitions

1. Open your Earth Day *your name*.prproj file, if necessary.

2. On the Effects panel, type **SW** in the Contains box 🔍, as shown in Figure 46.

   As you type, the Effects panel filters out any effects not containing the characters you have typed.

   TIP Click the Close button on the right side of the Contains box to clear what has been typed.

3. Drag the **Swirl transition** between **scenic3.jpg** and **scenic5.jpg** on the Timeline panel and place it as a Center at Cut transition ⊹.

4. Save your project file and leave it open for the next exercise.

You searched for a video transition on the Effects panel.

Copy video transitions

1. Open your Earth Day *your name*.prproj file, if necessary.

2. Click the **Pinwheel transition** between **scenic1.jpg** and **scenic3.jpg**.

3. Click **Edit** on the Menu bar, then click **Copy**.

4. On the Timeline panel, drag the **CTI** 🔖 to the cut line between scenic3.jpg and scenic5.jpg.

5. Click **Edit** on the Menu bar, then click **Paste**, as shown in Figure 47.

   TIP Press [Shift] + [End] (Win) or [shift] + [down arrow] (Mac) to jump quickly to the next cut line from the location of the CTI.

(continued)

Figure 46 *Searching for a transition*

Search term

Swirl transition

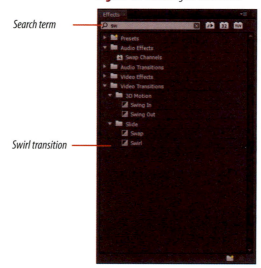

Figure 47 *Pasting transitions*

Paste command

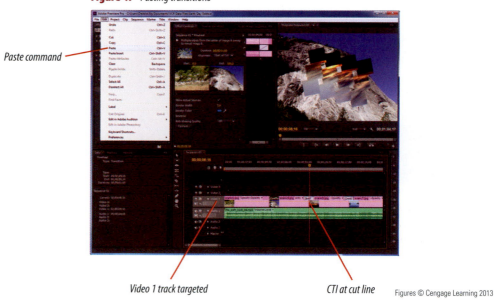

Video 1 track targeted   CTI at cut line

Figures © Cengage Learning 2013

Figure 48 *Sequence after pasting Pinwheel transition*

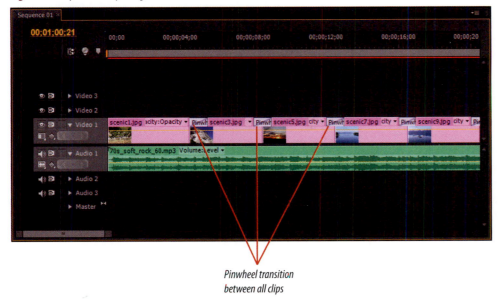

Pinwheel transition
between all clips

6. Repeat Steps 4 and 5 to continue pasting the copied transition over the remaining cut lines in the sequence, then compare your Timeline panel to Figure 48.

7. Preview the changes in the Program Monitor.

8. Save your project file and leave it open for the next exercise.

You copied and pasted video transitions between the remaining clips in the sequence.

Specifying a Default Transition

If you prefer to use another video transition instead of Cross Dissolve, you can change the default. Changing the default transition does not affect transitions already applied to a sequence; it only affects future projects.

To change the default, first expand the Video Transitions bin on the Effects panel. Select the transition that you want to set as the default. Click the Effects panel options button, then click Set Selected As Default Transition.

Figure © Cengage Learning 2013

In this lesson, you will add motion effects and video transition images.

Work with
MOTION EFFECTS

Working with Motion Effects

Motion effects are commonly used on still images in documentaries to make the footage more visually interesting when video isn't available. This effect of panning and zooming has been commonly termed the "Ken Burns Effect." The director Ken Burns popularized the use of the effect in his widely seen Civil War documentary on PBS in the fall of 1990. A motion effect can be created by scaling or changing the position or the rotation of an image. These effects are created using keyframes. A **keyframe** is a snapshot of how you want a clip to look at a specified time, and is defined on the Effect Controls timeline, as shown in Figure 49. Premiere Pro recognizes each keyframe you create and fills in the gaps to create a smooth movement between keyframes. For motion effects to work properly, at least two keyframes need to be created.

Understanding Keyframes in More Detail

When working with keyframes you always need to define at least two keyframes: a start point and an end point. It is a good idea to

create two keyframes before making any changes. In Figure 50, start and end keyframes have been created for the Position, Scale, and Rotation properties.

By clicking the Toggle animation button, the first keyframe is inserted for you at the location of the CTI. To insert or remove additional keyframes, the Add/Remove Keyframe button needs to be clicked. Remember to move the CTI to the location where you would like the keyframe to be placed. Keyframes can always be adjusted later if you don't get the location quite right the first time.

You'll work with the Position property in greater detail first. The CTI needs to be positioned on a keyframe before you can change the property values to the keyframe. To return to the start keyframe, click the Go to Previous Keyframe button.

When creating the Pan effect (scrolling across the image) you need to look at the image and decide what you want the final view of the image to be. For instance, if the goal is to have the image in its original state in the final frame, the start keyframe needs to be adjusted.

In Figure 49, the position coordinates 360.0, 240.0 represent the center of the screen—the upper-left corner is 0, 0 and the lower-right corner is 720.0, 480.0 because 720 × 480 is the standard NTSCDV screen size and is the sequence preset. These coordinates can get quite confusing; therefore, one of the simpler ways to adjust the coordinates is by using the mouse pointer. Hover the mouse pointer over one of the coordinates and it becomes a pointing finger cursor with a double-sided arrow.

Adjusting the coordinates is a matter of dragging left or right. As you drag the first coordinate (360.0) to the left, the image moves left; move it to the right and the image moves right. Likewise, dragging the second coordinate (240.0) to the left moves the image up, and dragging it to the right moves the

Figure 49 *Working with keyframes on the Effect Controls panel*

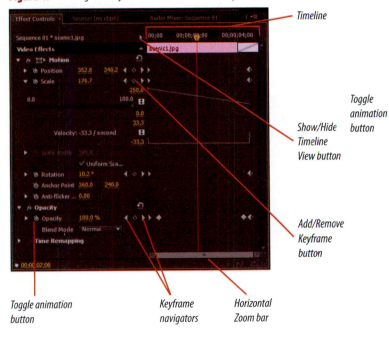

Toggle animation button

Keyframe navigators

Horizontal Zoom bar

Timeline

Show/Hide Timeline View button

Add/Remove Keyframe button

Figure 50 *Working with keyframes in greater detail*

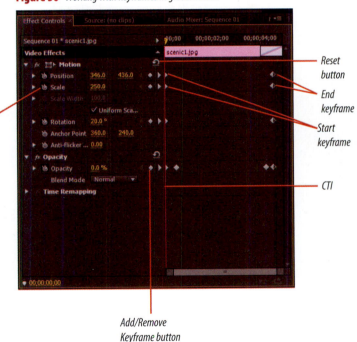

Toggle animation button

Add/Remove Keyframe button

Reset button

End keyframe

Start keyframe

CTI

Figures © Cengage Learning 2013

image down. As you adjust the coordinates on the Effect Controls panel, you see the image change location on the Program Monitor, as shown in Figure 51.

Zoom is the second part of the Pan and Zoom effect, and Scale is the Motion Effects property that is used to create this effect. Adjusting the Scale property works in much the same way as adjusting the Position property. It can be done by either typing the percentage or using the pointing finger cursor. If you deselect the Uniform Scale

check box, you have the option to scale the image's height and width. On the Program Monitor, the image scale changes to assist you visually, as shown in Figure 52.

While these figures illustrate a very basic example, the Pan and Zoom effect can be as creative as you want to make it. The Reset button is available on the Effect Controls panel to reset the motion effects back to their default settings without removing the keyframes. If you want to delete keyframes and start over, just click the Toggle animation

button. A Warning dialog box appears asking you if you want to remove all of your keyframes from that effect. When you click OK, all the keyframes are removed.

Fading an Image

A basic effect that provides a lot of impact is to fade an image in and out. **Fading** is created by applying the Opacity effect. **Opacity** adjusts the level of transparency on a scale of 0% to 100%. If you set the Opacity at 0% your clip is completely transparent; at 100% it has no

Figure 51 *Adjusting the Position property*

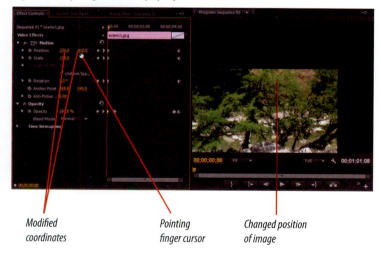

Modified coordinates

Pointing finger cursor

Changed position of image

Figure 52 *Adjusting the Scale property*

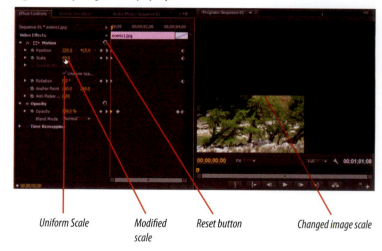

Uniform Scale

Modified scale

Reset button

Changed image scale

transparency. Figure 53 shows two clips set at 100% Opacity and another clip with the same images overlapping with the top clip set with a 50% Opacity. Notice how the two images become blended together.

When creating a fade-in/fade-out effect you need to create four keyframes. The start and end keyframes are set to 0% Opacity, and the second and third keyframes remain at 100% Opacity. Click the triangle to the left the Opacity property to display a graphical representation of the keyframes actions, as shown in Figure 54. Preview the effect on the Program Monitor. If the fade in is too fast, click and drag the second keyframe to the right to slow the effect down. To reset the Opacity settings, select the start keyframe, click the Reset button, select the end keyframe, and click the Reset button.

Using the Program Monitor to Apply Motion Effects

The Program Monitor provides another option to work with applying motion effects. The Motion properties—Position, Scale, and Rotate—are spatial in nature and therefore easier to manipulate on the Program Monitor where you have the ability to adjust clips with handles. The handles allow you to move, size, and rotate a clip visually.

Figure 53 *Examples of Opacity*

100% opacity

Images layered, with picture from upper-right set at 50% opacity

100% opacity

Figure 54 *Adjusting the Opacity property*

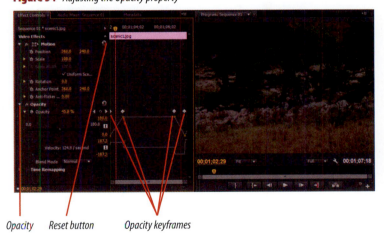

Opacity   *Reset button*   *Opacity keyframes*

Figures © Cengage Learning 2013

To activate the Motion Effects controls, click the Transform button, found to the left of Motion on the Effect Controls panel. You may need to adjust the Zoom Level on the Program Monitor to see the transform handles, as shown in Figure 55.

When working with Motion Effects controls, you need to create only one keyframe. Additional keyframes are created automatically at the location of the CTI.

Simply adjust the CTI to the location where you would like the change to occur and then make your adjustments in the Program Monitor. Using the mouse pointer, click the handles to resize, scale, and rotate the image, then notice the changes in the property values on the Effect Controls panel as you adjust the image on the Program Monitor, as shown in Figure 56.

QUICK TIP

The Rotation effect is applied in the same manner as the Position and Scale effects. It can be manipulated either on the Effect Controls panel or on the Program Monitor.

QUICK TIP

The Transform button to the left of a video effect name indicates that the effect's properties can be manipulated on the Program Monitor. Lightning, Twirl, Transform, Lens Flare, and Checkerboard are examples.

Figure 55 *Applying motion effects on the Program Monitor*

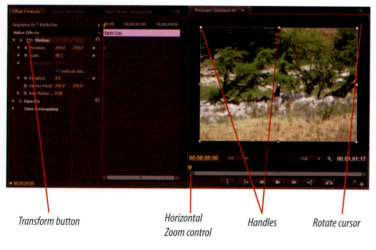

Transform button

Horizontal Zoom control

Handles

Rotate cursor

Figure 56 *Adjusting motion effects on the Program Monitor*

Property values adjusted based on location in Program Monitor

Resize cursor

Figures © Cengage Learning 2013

Figure 57 *Viewing scenic1.jpg in the Timeline section of the Effect Controls panel*

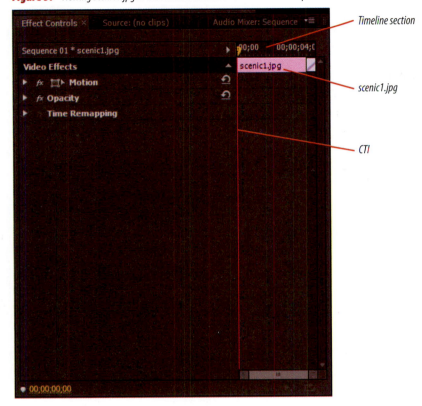

Timeline section

scenic1.jpg

CTI

Fade an image in and out

1. Open your Earth Day *your name*.prproj file, if necessary.

2. Set the workspace to the Effects workspace, if necessary.

3. Be sure the CTI 🔲 is at the beginning of the sequence, then click **scenic1.jpg**.

4. If necessary, click the **Show/Hide Timeline View button** ▶ on the Effect Controls panel to show the Timeline section, as shown in Figure 57.

5. Click the **triangle** to the left of **Opacity** on the Effect Controls panel to expand the Opacity properties.

6. Click the **Toggle animation button** ⏱ to the left of Opacity on the Effect Controls panel.

   A keyframe is added where the CTI is located on the Effect Controls panel. Keyframes do not become available until you activate them with the Toggle animation button, and the first keyframe is added automatically when the Toggle animation button is clicked.

7. Press the → **key** 10 times to move the CTI 1/10 of a second to the right.

8. Click the **Add/Remove Keyframe button** ◆ to add another keyframe.

9. Press [**Shift**] + [**End**] (Win) or [**shift**] + [**fn**] + [**right arrow**] (Mac) to move the CTI 🔲 to the end of the clip, then add a third keyframe.

10. Press the ← **key** 10 times to move the CTI 1/10 of a second to the left, then add a fourth keyframe.

(continued)

You should now have four keyframes on the Timeline section of the Effect Controls panel, as shown in Figure 58.

11. Click the **Go to Previous Keyframe button** 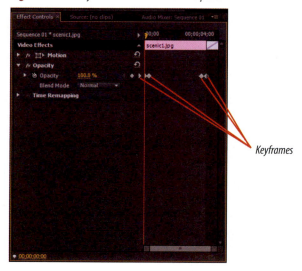 repeatedly until you return to the first keyframe.

12. Click the **Opacity value**, **100.0%**, then type **0**.

The first keyframe now has 0% opacity. This means the image is invisible and fades into the next keyframe, as shown in Figure 59.

(continued)

Figure 58 *Four keyframes on the Effect Controls panel*

Keyframes

Figure 59 *First keyframe set to 0% Opacity*

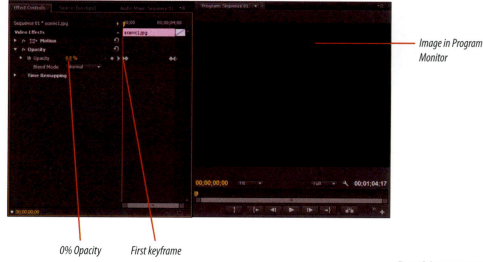

Image in Program Monitor

0% Opacity   First keyframe

Figure 60 *Opacity effect shown as a graph*

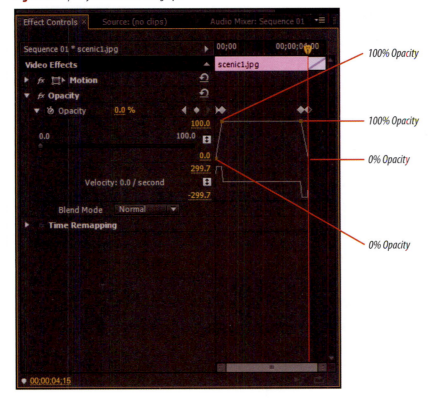

100% Opacity

100% Opacity

0% Opacity

0% Opacity

Figure © Cengage Learning 2013

13. Click the **Go to Next Keyframe button** ▶ repeatedly until you return to the last keyframe, then change its Opacity to **0%**, as shown in Figure 60.

14. Click the **expand arrow** in front of the Opacity Toggle animation button.

    A line graph in the Timeline section of the Effect Controls panel is revealed, which provides a visual representation of opacity.

15. Return the CTI 🛡 to the beginning of the Timeline and preview the transition on the Program Monitor.

TIP Keyframes can be adjusted by clicking and dragging them to adjust the speed at which the effect takes place.

16. Drag the **second keyframe** to the right to fade the image in more slowly.

17. Preview the clip again to see how the effect has changed.

18. Save your project file and leave it open for the next exercise.

You faded an image in and out using the Opacity property.

Add a Pan and Zoom effect

1. Open your Earth Day *your name*.prproj file, if necessary.

2. Be sure the CTI 🔖 is at the beginning of the sequence.

   Remember, the Opacity for this clip is set to 0% so you will not be able to preview the image in the Program Monitor.

3. Click the **triangle** to the left of Motion on the Effect Controls panel to expand the Motion properties.

4. Click the **Toggle Animation button** ⏱ to the left of Position and Scale to activate keyframes, as shown in Figure 61.

   This adds keyframes at the beginning of the clip for both Position and Scale.

5. Move to the end of the clip and add another keyframe ◆ for both Position and Scale.

TIP Another way to move to the end of the clip is to click the Go to Next Keyframe button ▶ in the Opacity effect.

6. Go back to the first keyframe, change the Scale setting to **250.0**, then change the Position settings to: **346.0**, **436.0**, as shown in Figure 62.

7. Return the CTI 🔖 to the beginning of the Timeline and preview it? on the Program Monitor.

8. Save your project file and leave it open for the next exercise.

You added a pan and zoom effect.

Figure 61 *Adding a keyframe to the Position and Scale effect*

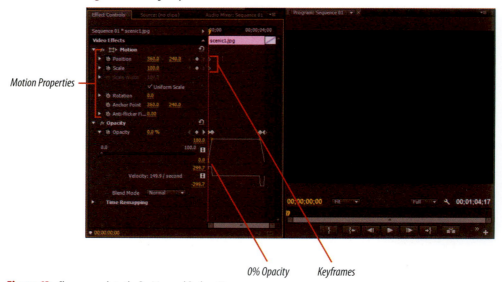

Motion Properties

0% Opacity   Keyframes

Figure 62 *Changes made to the Position and Scale settings*

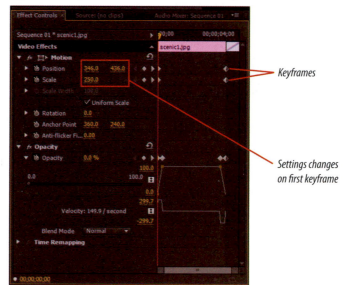

Keyframes

Settings changes on first keyframe

Figures © Cengage Learning 2013

Figure 63 *Changing the Rotation setting*

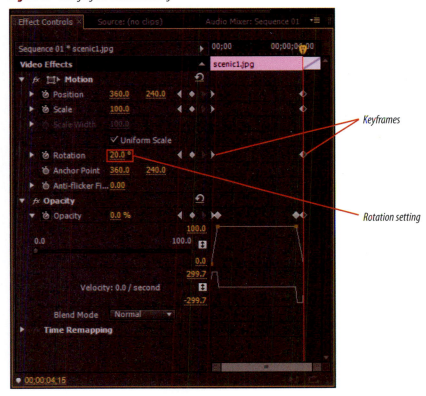

Keyframes

Rotation setting

Add a Rotation effect to a clip

1. Open your Earth Day *your name*.prproj file, if necessary.

2. Be sure the CTI 🎸 is at the beginning of the sequence and the Motion properties are visible in the Effect Controls panel.

3. Click the **Toggle Animation button** 🕰 to the left of Rotation to activate keyframes and to add the first keyframe at the beginning of the clip.

4. Move to the end of the clip, then add another keyframe to Rotation.

5. Go to the first keyframe, then change the Rotation setting to **20.0°**, as shown in Figure 63.

6. Return the CTI 🎸 to the beginning of the Timeline and preview on the Program Monitor.

7. Save your project file and leave it open for the next exercise.

You applied a rotation effect to a clip.

Pan, zoom, and rotate in the Program Monitor

1. Open your Earth Day *your name*.prproj file, if necessary.
2. Move the CTI 🛠 to the beginning of the second clip and verify that the Motion properties are visible in the Effect Controls panel.
3. Activate keyframes for Position, Scale, and Rotation.
4. Add keyframes at the end of the clip for Position, Scale, and Rotation, and return the CTI to the first keyframe on the clip.

TIP Press the Down Arrow to jump to the end of the clip.

5. Click the **Transform button** 🔳▸ to the left of Motion on the Effect Controls panel.

    A transform box appears around the clip on the Program Monitor.

6. Click the **Select Zoom Level arrow** on the Program Monitor, then click **50%**, as shown in Figure 64.

    Using your cursor, you can now position, scale, and rotate the clip.

7. Position your cursor over the upper-right handle on the transform box until you see the rotate cursor ↻, click, then drag until you see **26.0** ° in the Rotation setting, as shown in Figure 65.

TIP Accuracy can be a challenge when dragging with the cursor; try and get as close as you can.

(continued)

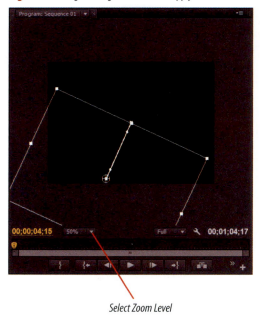

Figure 64 *Using the Program Monitor to apply effects*

Select Zoom Level

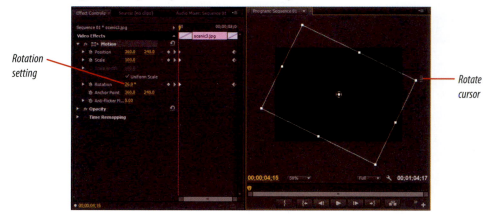

Figure 65 *Using the Program Monitor to rotate the image*

Rotation setting

Rotate cursor

Figures © Cengage Learning 2013

Creating a Video Montage in Adobe Premiere Pro CS6

Figure 66 *Using the Program Monitor to resize the image*

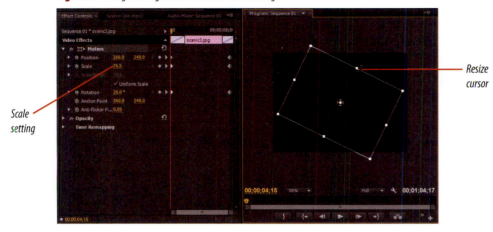

Scale setting

Resize cursor

Figure 67 *Using the Program Monitor to move the image*

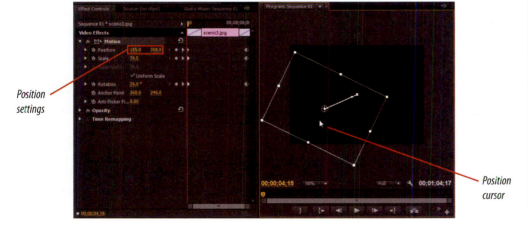

Position settings

Position cursor

8. Position your cursor over the top-middle handle until you see the Resize cursor ⤢, then drag down until the Scale setting becomes **76.5%**, as shown in Figure 66.

9. Position your cursor near the center of the image until you see the Position cursor ▶, then drag your image to the bottom-left corner until your Position settings become **185.0** and **308.0,** as shown in Figure 67.

10. Return the CTI ⬇ to the beginning of the Timeline and preview on the Program Monitor.

11. Save your project file and leave it open for the next exercise.

You rotated, resized, and moved the image in the Program Monitor.

Design and
INSERT TITLES

What You'll Do

Figure © Cengage Learning 2013

In this lesson, you will add text to your project using the Titler.

Adding Text to a Video Montage

Titling is an important way to enhance your message and to provide credit by adding text to the video montage. In the video montage you have been working on, you have been using photographs of images from various regions of the United States, but that only conveys a portion of your message. Titling allows you to bring a stronger message or meaning to your video montage through the addition of quotes.

As you continue to work in Premiere Pro, you will find other uses for titling. For example, you can superimpose a person's name on the screen while they are speaking as a way to introduce them, or later in an interview to re-introduce them to the viewer. Using titles, you can establish your video with an opening title sequence and provide closing credits at the end for the digital assets that you may have borrowed.

Working with the Titler

In Premiere Pro, you create titles in a mini application called the Titler. The **Titler** is

a free-floating window that is made up of a group of panels that are all related to creating titles. The panels in the Titler can be rearranged and docked to your liking. The following panels are included in the Titler, and shown in Figure 68:

- **Title panel** – The Title panel is where you design and preview your text and graphics. It is the central panel in the Titler window.
- **Title Properties panel** – The Title Properties panel is where you choose a font and change the font size, kerning, leading, or font characteristics, such as bold or italics.
- **Title Tools panel** – The Title Tools panel is where the tools are located to draw basic shapes, create text paths, and create vertical or horizontal text.
- **Title Actions panel** – The Title Actions panel is where you align, center, or distribute objects and text vertically and horizontally.
- **Title Styles panel** – The Title Styles panel is where you can apply preset styles to titles. You can also create and save your own titles to maintain consistency throughout a project.

Creating a New Title

Premiere Pro offers the option to create a title from either the File menu or the Title menu. If you choose to create a title from the Title menu you can choose among three types of titles: Default Still, Default Roll, or Default Crawl. You can base a new title on a template or the current title. Creating a title from the File menu creates a Default Still title.

A title that has fixed text is called **still**. Titles in which text moves vertically over the footage are called **rolls**. If the text moves horizontally, it is referred to as a **crawl**. On the Premiere Pro New Title submenu, they are referred to as Default Still, Default Roll, and Default Crawl.

Creating a title based on the current title does just what it sounds like: it duplicates the current title, allowing you to replace the text while maintaining the current formatting. The Based on a Template option opens up a library of templates in a preview window for you to select from, as shown in Figure 69. Once you select a template, it opens and you are able to replace the placeholder text with your own.

Figure 68 *Titler window*

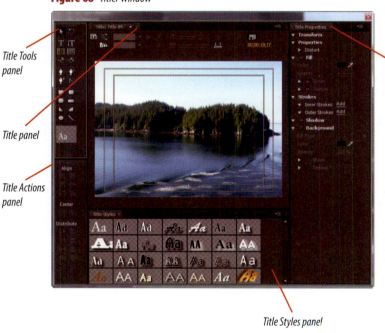

Title Tools panel

Title panel

Title Actions panel

Title Properties panel

Title Styles panel

Figure 69 *Templates dialog box*

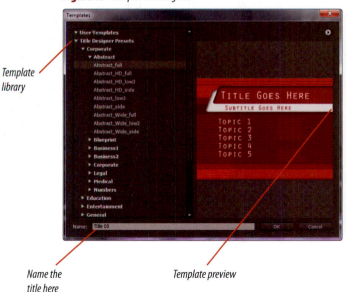

Template library

Name the title here

Template preview

After titles are created, they can be changed into one of the three available types: still, roll, or crawl. To modify a title, click the Roll/Crawl Options button on the Title panel; the Roll/Crawl Options dialog box appears, as shown in Figure 70. You can also choose to apply a template after you create a title, by clicking the Templates button on the Title panel.

Once created, titles are saved on the Project panel and can be edited by simply double-clicking the title clip from either the bin or the sequence. While designing your title, you have the ability to view the footage from the sequence to help with the placement and design of the title. This is done by

putting the CTI in the sequence where you plan to place the title, and activating the Show Background Video button on the Title panel. The CTI can be moved while in the Titler by changing the Background Video Timecode on the Title panel, as shown in Figure 71.

QUICK TIP

The length of a title clip in a sequence determines the speed of the text moving in the title. The longer you make the length of the title clip in the sequence, the slower the text will roll or crawl.

Figure 71 *Previewing a clip behind a title*

Show background video

Background Video Timecode

Figure 70 *Roll/Crawl Options dialog box*

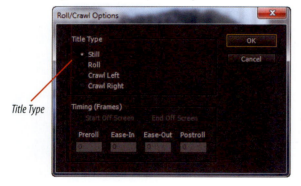

Title Type

Figures © Cengage Learning 2013

The Title panel is where you can make basic formatting decisions such as Font family, Font style, Font size, and Alignment options, as shown in Figure 72. You can also find many of these same options on the Title menu on the Menu bar. More advanced options can be found on the Title Properties panel, as shown in Figure 73. The Title Properties panel provides the opportunity to get very creative with your titles and their appearance using fills, strokes, and shadows.

Working with Title Styles

While working with the Title Properties panel, if you create a format you really like you can save it as a style and add it to the

Figure 73 *Title Properties panel*

Figure 72 *Title panel*

Title Styles panel. The style you create then becomes part of the Style library in Premiere Pro and is available to you in all projects that you create.

Styles are a great way to keep a consistent look and feel when working in a project without having to remember all the settings you chose to make the style.

Premiere Pro also has many preset styles available for you to use, as shown in Figure 74. Styles can be used as they are or as a great springboard for designing your own text and creating your own original styles.

QUICK TIP

You can base a new title on an existing title by clicking the New Title Based on Current Title button ⬚ on the Title panel. Enter a name for the new title in the New Title dialog box, click OK, then format the title to your liking.

Figure 74 *Title Styles panel*

Styles

New Style command

Figure 75 *New Title dialog box*

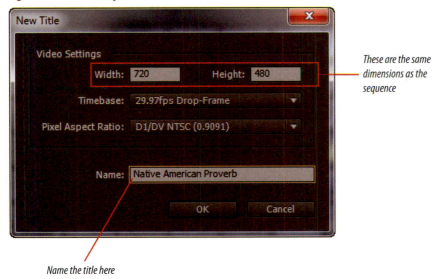

These are the same dimensions as the sequence

Name the title here

Create a new title

1. Open your Earth Day *your name*.prproj file, if necessary.

2. Set the workspace to the **Editing (CS5.5)** workspace.

3. Create a new bin on the Project panel and name it **Titles**.

4. [Alt]-double-click (Win) or [option]-double-click (Mac) the **Titles bin** to open it in place.

TIP Opening the Titles bin causes the titles you create to be automatically saved into the bin as you create them.

5. On the Media Browser, navigate to the drive and folder where the Chapter 1 Data Files are located.

6. Click the **Files of type list arrow** and select **All Files**.

   "All Files" is different than "All Supported Files." Be sure to select "All Files" so you will see the Notepad file.

7. Select **Earth Day Text.txt** in the Chapter 1 Data Files folder.

8. Click **File** on the Menu bar, then click **Import from Media Browser**.

   This is a text file that you will use to copy and paste text to and from the Title panel.

9. Double-click the **Earth Day Text file**, copy the first quote (**Native American Proverb**), then close the Earth Day Text file.

10. Drag the **CTI** 🎸 to **00;00;03;20**.

    The new title will start at the 3:20 mark on the sequence.

    (continued)

TIP Another way to move the CTI to a specific location is to click the Current time display on the Timeline, type the new timecode, and then press [Enter] (Win) or [return] (Mac). You do not have to type the semicolons (;).

11. Click **File** on the Menu bar, point to **New**, then click **Title**.

    The New Title dialog box opens. You can name the title and choose size options for it in the dialog box.

TIP You can also click the New Item button [icon] on the Project panel, and choose Title.

12. Type **Native American Proverb** in the Name text box of the New Title dialog box, as shown in Figure 75, then click **OK**.

13. Click the **Show Background Video button** [icon], if necessary, and notice that the Background Video Timecode matches the setting of **00;00;03;20** on the Timeline.

    Your Titler window should look like Figure 76.

14. Click the **Type tool** [icon] on the Title Tools panel.

15. Click in the Title panel, click **Edit** on the Menu bar, then click **Paste** to paste the quote.

    The text is much too big, so you need to make some adjustments on the Title Properties panel. You will start by reducing the font size.

16. Click the **Selection tool** [icon] on the Tools panel, then click the text.

    The text must be selected in order to modify it.

17. On the Title Properties panel, position the mouse pointer over the Font Size property and when you see the cursor change to a scrolling finger [icon], drag the mouse pointer left until the size changes to **62.0**, as shown in Figure 77.

    (continued)

Figure 76 *Creating a new title*

Background Video Timecode setting

Your clip should match this

Figure 77 *Changing the font size*

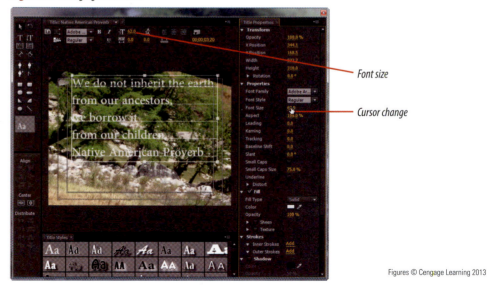

Font size

Cursor change

Figures © Cengage Learning 2013

Creating a Video Montage in Adobe Premiere Pro CS6

Figure 78 *Making adjustments on the Title Properties panel*

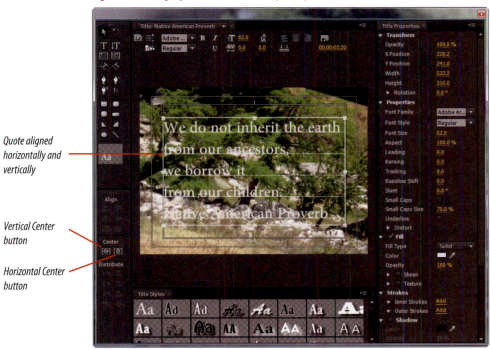

Quote aligned
horizontally and
vertically

Vertical Center
button

Horizontal Center
button

18. With the text still selected, click **Title** on
the Menu bar, point to **Position**, then click
Vertical Center to adjust the placement of the
text vertically.

19. Click **Title** on the Menu bar, point to **Position**,
then click **Horizontal Center** to adjust the
placement of the text horizontally, so that your
title is in the approximate location shown in
Figure 78.

TIP You can also align the title by clicking on the Vertical
Center and Horizontal Center buttons in the Title
Actions panel under Center.

20. Close the Native American Proverb title.

Titles save automatically when you close them.

21. Save your project file and leave it open for the
next exercise.

In this lesson, you created a new title.

Work with the Title Styles panel

1. Open your Earth Day *your name*.prproj file, if it is not already open.

2. [Alt]- (Win) or [option]- (Mac) double-click the **Titles bin** to open it in place.

3. Double-click the **Native American Proverb title**.

4. Verify that the Show Background Video button is selected and set the Background Video Timecode to **00;00;03;20**, if necessary.

5. Resize the Title Styles panel, as your screen permits, so you can see the available styles.

   TIP You can also scroll in the Title Styles panel to see all of the available styles.

6. Click the **Selection tool** on the Tools panel, select the **quote**, and choose the style **TektonPro Narrow Yellow 100** as shown in Figure 79.

   When hovering over a style, the name of the style appears as a tooltip.

   TIP If you click the Title Styles panel options button you can change the view to Text Only and find the style more quickly.

   (continued)

Figure 79 *Applying a title style*

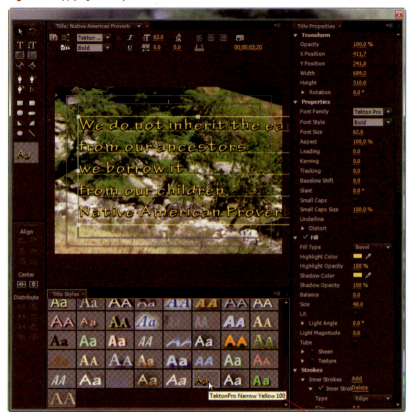

Style name

Creating a Video Montage in Adobe Premiere Pro CS6

Figure 80 *Making changes to the style*

Preview of new style

Height

Aspect

Fill Type

Color picker

Figure 81 *Placing the title in the sequence*

Timecode at 00;00;03;20

Snap button

Video 2 track

Overlay cursor

Lesson 6   Design and Insert Titles

7. With the quote still selected, make the following changes on the Title Properties panel: Height: **300.0**, Fill Type: **Solid**, Color: **White (FFFFFF)**, Aspect: **79.5%**, and then compare your title to Figure 80.

8. With the quote still selected, click the **Title Styles panel options button** , then click **New Style**.

    You will save this style so that you can use it again on other quotes.

9. Type **Quote Style** in the Name box of the New Style dialog box, then click **OK**.

    The new style appears at the bottom of the Title Styles panel.

10. Close the American Indian Proverb title.

11. Drag the **American Indian Proverb clip** to the Video 2 Sequence so it snaps to the right of the CTI (which should still be at the **00;00;03;20 Timecode**), as shown in Figure 81.

12. Preview the project on the Program Monitor.

TIP If the text looks blurry, render the sequence and preview again.

13. Save your project file and leave it open for the next exercise.

In this lesson, you created a new style and saved it on the Title Styles panel.

Create a rolling title

1. Open your Earth Day *your name*.prproj file, if necessary.

2. If necessary, [Alt]- (Win) or [option]- (Mac) double-click the **Titles bin** to open it in place.

3. Double-click the **Earth Day Text file** to open it in Notepad.

4. Copy the **credit information** for the song Subtle Storm, and for the photography, then close the file.

5. Place the CTI 🔻 at **00;00;56;15**.

6. Click **Title** on the Menu bar, point to **New Title**, then click **Default Roll**.

7. Name the new title **Credits** in the Name text box.

8. Click the **Type tool** T on the Title Tools panel then paste the credits into the Title panel.

9. Apply the **Quote Style** from the Title Styles panel.

10. Change the Font Size to **37.0**.

11. On the Title Properties panel, adjust the Leading to **52.0** to create more spacing between the lines of text.

12. Click the **Selection tool** and adjust the placement of the text as shown in Figure 82.

13. Click the **Roll/Crawl Options button** on the Title panel.

(continued)

Figure 82 *Rolling title preview*

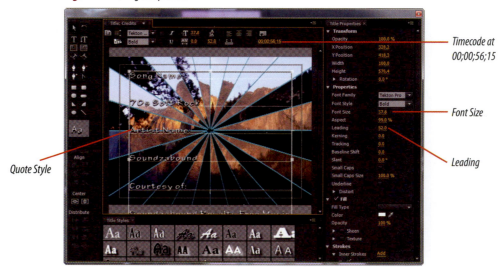

Timecode at 00;00;56;15

Font Size

Leading

Quote Style

Figure 83 *Settings for Roll/Crawl Options*

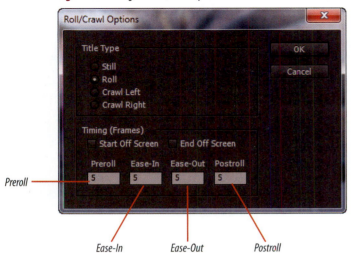

Preroll —

Ease-In   *Ease-Out*   *Postroll*

Figure 84 *Credits clip placed on sequence*

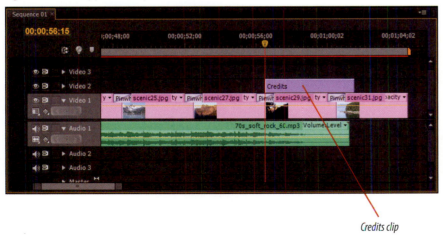

Credits clip

14. Specify the following options in the Roll/Crawl Options dialog box: Preroll: **5**, Ease-In: **5**, Ease-Out: **5**, Postroll: **5**, as shown in Figure 83, then click **OK**.

    The Preroll/Postroll values specify the number of frames to play before and after the roll begins. The Ease-In/Ease-Out values specify the number of frames the roll will ease in or out before playing at regular speed.

15. Close the Credits title.

16. Drag the **Credits clip** to the Video 2 Sequence so it snaps to the right of the CTI (which should still be at the 00;00;56;15 timecode), as shown in Figure 84.

17. Press **[Enter]**, to render, and preview the project on the Program Monitor panel.

18. Save your project file and leave it open for the next exercise.

In this lesson, you created a rolling title.

Create a title from a template

1. Open your Earth Day *your name*.prproj file, if necessary.

2. If necessary, [Alt]- (Win) or [option]- (Mac) double-click the **Titles bin** to open it in place.

3. Place the CTI 🛡 at **00;00;00;00**.

4. Click **Title** on the Menu bar, point to **New Title**, and then click **Based on Template**.

5. Click the **expand triangle** next to Title Designer Presets, if necessary, to open the Template library.

6. Scroll down in the Templates dialog box, expand the General category, then expand Inspire.

7. Select **Inspire_low3**, as shown in Figure 85, name the title **Earth Day**, then click **OK**.

   The Titler window appears ready for you to edit the placeholder text. This title will be used to introduce the project.

8. Click the **Type tool** 🅣 on the Title panel, highlight all of the NAME GOES HERE text and replace it with EVERY DAY IS EARTH DAY ~ ANONYMOUS.

9. Replace TITLE GOES HERE with **your name**, reconfigure both lines of text using fonts and sizes of your choice, then compare your title to Figure 86.

TIP You may need to reduce the font size of the first line of text before you can select the TITLE GOES HERE text.

(continued)

Figure 85 *Templates dialog box*

Inspire_low3

Preview of template

Name of title

Figure 86 *Earth Day title clip*

Sample layout of text

Figures © Cengage Learning 2013

Figure 87 *Locking the tracks*

Locked track

Click here to
lock the track

Figure 88 *Using the Insert command to place a clip*

Shifted clip

Inserted clip

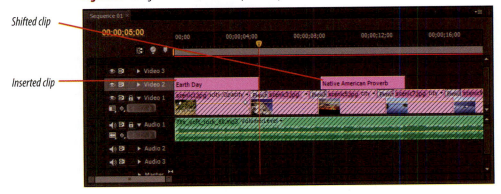

10. Close the Earth Day title clip.

11. Lock the Video 1 and Audio 1 tracks by clicking the **Toggle Track Lock box** on both tracks, as shown in Figure 87.

12. Target the **Video 2 track**.

13. Click the **Earth Day title clip** in the Titles bin on the Project panel, click **Clip** on the Menu bar, then click **Insert**.

    The clip is placed on the Video 2 track while shifting the Native American Proverb to the right, as shown in Figure 88.

14. Preview the project on the Program Monitor.

TIP If the text looks blurry, render the sequence and preview again.

15. Save your project file and leave it open for the next exercise.

In this lesson, you created a title based on a template, locked two tracks, and inserted the new title on the Video 2 track.

LESSON 7

Export a **MOVIE**

What You'll Do

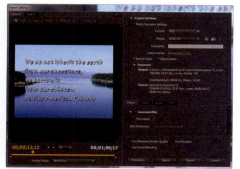

Figure © Cengage Learning 2013

In this lesson, you will export your project.

Exporting the Movie

Now it is time to export, or **encode**, your movie so that other people with be able to view it. Premiere Pro has a variety of options from which to choose. You can export to videotape, create a file for viewing on a computer or the Internet, or put your project on a DVD or Blu-ray disc with or without menus and other features. You will explore the DVD option in detail in Chapter 7 when you create an Electronic Portfolio using Adobe Encore CS6. Throughout the projects in this book, you will mainly focus on creating files for viewing projects on computers and the Internet.

You need to consider a few options when you export a movie for others to view on another computer or the Internet. Reducing file size is important for storage, transmission, and effective playback. Adobe Premiere Pro Help has an extensive chapter on exporting and options to consider when compressing video for playback on the Web and mobile devices. Adobe Premiere Pro Help is a Web-based feature and is updated frequently to support new mobile devices as they become available.

Exporting for the Web

When exporting video for the Web, your target audience becomes much larger and their software, hardware, and Internet access methods are too numerous to determine. Fortunately, there are a number of **codecs** (compressor/decompressors, also known as encoder/decoders) considered for this purpose to make video Web-friendly. According to Adobe, 98 percent of the world's computers that are connected to the Internet have a Flash Player installed, and of those Flash Players at least 90 percent are capable of playing the latest H.264 codec. Therefore, you will export using H.264 encoded video for Flash when saving video for the Web.

Many codecs use two types of technologies that should be considered when viewing videos on the Web: streaming video and progressive downloadable video. A **streaming video** is also referred to as **live streaming video**. Streaming video occurs when a video is played much like a traditional live broadcast on television, except that it is affected by the bandwidth that is available. **Buffering** (delay before the video begins to play) may occur when the bandwidth does not meet the required need of the video that is playing; that is, the video pauses until the bandwidth becomes sufficient again. **Progressive downloadable video** plays the movie without interruption. The movie player software determines how long it will take to download an entire movie for viewing and begins playing the movie when enough of the movie has been downloaded so it will playback uninterrupted. The H.264 codec with Flash takes advantage of progressive video technology.

The settings you will be using include the following: Format: F4V; Preset: Match Source Attribute (Medium Quality), as shown in Figure 89. When setting the Output Name, the Save As dialog box opens, prompting you to name the file and choose a location to save your project in its exported state.

You have two options for exporting a file from the Export Settings dialog box: you can choose either the Queue button or the Export button.

Figure 89 *Export Settings dialog box*

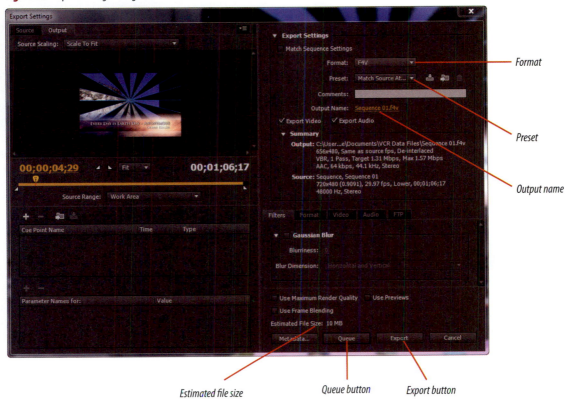

Estimated file size   Queue button   Export button

The Queue button launches the Adobe Media Encoder application using the designated export settings; this application then renders and saves the file. This is an excellent option when exporting to multiple file formats. The Adobe Media Encoder creates a rendering queue and processes the files in the order in which they were received, as shown in Figure 90.

If you wish to bypass the Adobe Media Encoder you can simply click the Export button instead. The Export button again uses the export settings designated in the Export

Figure 90 *Adobe Media Encoder dialog window*

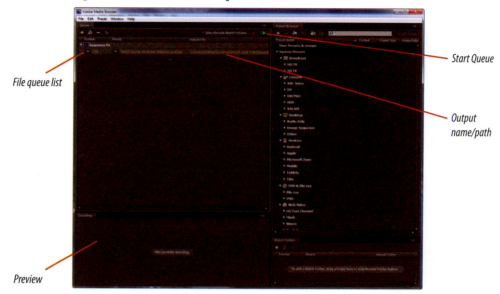

File queue list

Start Queue

Output name/path

Preview

Tips to Consider before Compressing

- Edit out any unnecessary content from your video to make it shorter.
- Work with raw footage whenever possible.
- Limit special effects and any unnecessary camera work with shaky movements and zooming.
- Consider your audience:
  - Work with appropriate frame dimensions based on your audience: for example, consider the type of Internet connection that most have.
  - Choose an appropriate frame rate based on the processing speed of your audience's computers.
- Preview the file on a system comparable to that of your intended audience, whenever possible.

Creating a Video Montage in Adobe Premiere Pro CS6

Settings dialog box. An Encoding dialog box launches showing the approximate time it will take to export the file, as shown in Figure 91.

QUICK **TIP**

The MPEG-2 file format is the compression standard for DVD video. When the Adobe Dynamic Link command is used to export directly to Adobe Encore, the MPEG-2 file format is the one utilized; therefore, you will be exporting all of your projects using the MPEG-2 file format to facilitate the creation of the Electronic Portfolio later in Chapter 7.

Figure 91 *Viewing the Encoding Sequence dialog box*

Status of job

Encoding dialog box

Working with Adobe Media Encoder

Adobe Media Encoder is a stand-alone encoding application used by Premiere Pro to export your movie to a format appropriate for movies. To start Adobe Media Encoder, you may need to look in a subfolder if you have installed the Creative Suite. Click File on the Menu bar, then click Add Premiere Pro Sequence. Navigate to the project file you wish to encode. Default presets are available, or click the Preset link to access the Export dialog box. Once a sequence is exported and in the queue, you can minimize the Adobe Media Encoder and continue to work in Adobe Premiere Pro while the Media Encoder continues to render in the background.

Figure © Cengage Learning 2013

Export a movie for the Web

1. Open your Earth Day *your name*.prproj file, if necessary.

2. Click **Sequence 01** on the Project panel to select it.

   A sequence needs to be selected before you export the movie.

3. Click **File** on the Menu bar, point to **Export**, then click **Media**.

4. In the Export Settings dialog box make the following selections on the right side: Format: **F4V**; Preset: **Match Source Attribute (Medium Quality)**; Output Name: **Earth Day *Your Name***.

   When you click Output Name to name your file, the Save As dialog box opens prompting you to name your file and browse to a new location.

   Note that an estimate is given for the file size at the bottom of the Export Settings dialog box, as shown in Figure 92.

5. Click **Export**.

   The Encoding dialog box launches to let you see the status of the file being saved.

6. Save your project file and leave it open for the next exercise.

You exported the Earth Day project in F4V format for viewing on the Web.

Figure 92 *Export Settings for the Web*

Format

Preset

Output Name

Estimated File Size

Creating a Video Montage in Adobe Premiere Pro CS6

Figure 93 *Export settings for the computer and to be put on a DVD*

Format

Preset

Output Name

Estimated
File Size

Figure 94 *Adobe Media Encoder dialog box*

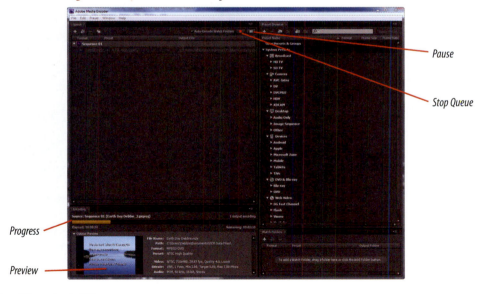

Pause

Stop Queue

Progress

Preview

Lesson 7   Export a Movie

Export a movie for playback on a computer

1. Open your Earth Day *your name*.prproj file, if necessary.

2. Select **File** on the Menu bar, point to **Export**, then click **Media**.

3. In the Export Settings dialog box, make the following selections: Format: **MPEG2-DVD**; Preset: **NTSC High Quality**; Output Name: **Earth Day *Your Name***, as shown in Figure 93.

4. Click **Queue**.

   The Adobe Media Encoder is launched with the settings you designated in the Export Settings dialog box.

5. Click **Start Queue**.

   The project is saved with the settings you designated as shown in Figure 94.

6. Close the project file and Adobe Media Encoder.

You exported your project to be viewed on a computer and later to be put on a DVD in your Electronic Portfolio in Chapter 7.

Create a new project and explore the workspace.

1. Start Premiere Pro. Create a new project titled **America the Beautiful *your name***, with a sequence and save it to your Data Files folder.
2. Change the workspace to Effects.
3. Change the workspace to Audio.
4. Change the workspace to Editing.
5. Save your project file.

Import assets.

1. Using the Media Browser, navigate to the drive and folder where your Data Files are located.
2. Import Subtle Storm - 60.mp3 into the Project panel.
3. Create a new bin and title it **U.S. Pictures**.
4. Open the U.S. Pictures bin as a dockable panel.
5. Import scenic16.jpg through scenic.32.jpg into the U.S. Pictures bin from the Earth Day Pictures folder in your Data Files folder.
6. Click the Icon View button on the U.S. Pictures bin and rearrange the images as you would like them to be placed on the sequence.
7. Close the U.S. Pictures bin.
8. Save your project file.

Work with the Timeline panel and sequences.

1. Be sure the Current-time Indicator (CTI) is at the beginning of the Timeline.
2. Open the U.S. Pictures bin as a dockable panel.
3. Select all the images in the bin.
4. Click the U.S. Pictures panel options button, then click Automate to Sequence.

5. In the Automate To Sequence dialog box, click the Ordering list arrow, click Sort Order, then click OK.
6. Close the Scenic Pictures bin.
7. Be sure the CTI is at the beginning of the sequence.
8. Zoom in on the Timeline to see the clips easily.
9. Open the Subtle Storm - 60.mp3 file in the Source Monitor.
10. Target the audio track by clicking in the header area and the source track. (*Hint*: Be sure the video track is no longer targeted.)
11. Click the Overwrite button on the Source Monitor to place the audio file on the sequence.
12. Select the first two clips in the sequence.
13. Click Edit on the Menu bar, then click Ripple Delete.
14. Click the Play-Stop Toggle button on the Program Monitor to view the contents of the Timeline.
15. Drag the CTI on the Timeline panel left and right to preview the sequence on the Program Monitor.
16. Save your project file.

Apply video transitions and work with motion effects.

1. Change the workspace to the Effects workspace.
2. Be sure the CTI is at the beginning of the sequence; zoom in on the Timeline panel so you can easily see the transitions between the clips.
3. Expand the Video Transitions bin on the Effects panel.
4. On the Effects panel, type **page** in the Contains box.
5. Drag Page Peel to the cut line between the first and second clip on the sequence, then place as a Center at Cut.

6. Click the Page Peel transition on the sequence where you just placed it.
7. Click and drag the CTI over the transition to preview it on the Program Monitor.
8. On the Effect Controls panel, click the Show Actual Sources check box to select it.
9. Move the mouse pointer over each of the edge selectors to view their names, then click the Northeast to Southwest edge selector and preview again.
10. Click the Page Peel transition between the first and second clip on your sequence.
11. Click Edit on the Menu bar, then click Copy.
12. On the Timeline panel, move the CTI to the cut line between the third and fourth clip.
13. Target the Video 1 track.
14. Click Edit on the Menu bar, then click Paste.
15. Continue pasting the copied transition over the remaining cut lines in the sequence.
16. Preview the changes on the Program Monitor.
17. Be sure the CTI is at the beginning of the sequence.
18. Select the first clip in your sequence.
19. Expand the Opacity properties on the Effect Controls panel.
20. Click the Toggle animation button to add a keyframe.
21. Highlight the Current time display, type **010**, then press [Enter] (Win) or [return] (Mac).
22. Click the Add/Remove Keyframe button to add another keyframe.
23. Press [Page Down] (Win) or [fn] + [down arrow] (Mac) to move the CTI to the end of the clip, then add a third keyframe.
24. Highlight the Current time display, type **320**, then press [Enter] (Win) or [return] (Mac).

25. Click the Add/Remove Keyframe button to add another keyframe.
26. Click the Go to Previous Keyframe button repeatedly until you return to the first keyframe.
27. Click the Opacity value, 100.0%, then type **0**.
28. Click the Go to Next Keyframe button repeatedly until you return to the last keyframe, then change its Opacity to **0%**.
29. Return the CTI to the beginning of the Timeline and preview the transition on the Program Monitor, as shown in Figure 95.
30. Drag the second keyframe to the right and drag the third keyframe to the left to fade the image more slowly.
31. Preview the clip again to see how the effect is changed.
32. Return the CTI to the beginning of the sequence.
33. Expand the Motion properties on the Effect Controls panel.
34. Click the Toggle Animation button to the left of Position and Scale to activate keyframes.
35. Move to the end of the clip and add another keyframe for both Position and Scale.
36. Return to the first keyframe, and change the Scale setting to 300%, and the Position settings to: 346.0, 436.0.
37. Preview on the Program Monitor.
38. Return the CTI to the beginning of the sequence.
39. Click the Toggle Animation button to the left of Rotation to activate keyframes.
40. Move to the end of the clip, then add another keyframe to Rotation.
41. Go to the first keyframe, then change the Rotation setting to -15 degrees.
42. Preview on the Program Monitor.

43. Move the CTI to the beginning of the second clip.
44. Activate keyframes for Position, Scale, and Rotation.
45. Add keyframes at the end of the clip for Position, Scale, and Rotation, and return the CTI to the first keyframe on the clip.
46. Click the Transform button on the Effect Controls Panel. (*Hint*: Adjust the Select Zoom Level on the Program Monitor if you cannot see the transform box.)
47. On the Program Monitor position, scale and rotate the clip using your own settings.
48. Apply various motion effects (fade, zoom, pan, rotate) to each of the clips on the Video track. You do not need to apply each effect to every image. Be creative.
49. Preview your project on the Program Monitor and render as needed.
50. Save your project file.

Design and insert titles.

1. Set the workspace to the **Editing (CS5.5)** workspace.
2. Create a new bin on the Project panel, name it **Titles for Project**, then open it in the Project panel.
3. On the Media Browser, navigate to the drive and folder where the Chapter 1 Data Files are located.
4. Click the Files of type list arrow and select All Files.
5. Select America Text.txt in the Chapter 1 Data Files folder.
6. Click File on the Menu bar, then click Import from Media Browser.
7. Open the America Text.txt file in Notepad.
8. Click File on the Menu bar, point to New, and then click Title.

9. Type **Nelson** in the Name text box of the New Title dialog box, then click OK.
10. Verify that the Show Background Video button is selected and set the Background Video Timecode to 00;00;09;25 on the Timeline.
11. Copy the Gaylord Nelson quote from the America Text file in Notepad and paste the text into the Title panel using the Type tool.
12. Select the text with the Selection tool, apply the Tekton White 45 title style, then resize the text to fit in the window.
13. Close the Nelson title.
14. Drag the title to the sequence so it is placed to the right of the CTI on the Video 2 track.
15. Place the CTI at 00;00;56;00.
16. Click Title on the Menu bar, point to New Title, then click Default Roll.
17. Type **Credits** in the Name text box of the New Title dialog box, then click OK.
18. Copy the Song and Photography credits from the America Text file in Notepad, and paste it into the Title panel using the Type tool.
19. Select the text with the Selection tool and apply the Minion Pro Black 89 title style.
20. Change the font size to 32.0.
21. On the Title Properties panel, adjust the Leading to 50.0 to create more spacing between the lines of text.
22. Click the Roll/Crawl Options button on the Title panel.
23. Specify the following options in the Roll/Crawl Options dialog box: Preroll: **5**; Ease-In: **5**; Ease-Out: **5**; Postroll: **5**.

24. Move the text box approximately one inch below the inner rectangle, then close the Credits title.

25. Drag the title to the sequence so it is placed to the right of the CTI on the Video 2 track.

26. Move the CTI to the beginning of the sequence.

27. Click Title on the Menu bar, point to New Title, then click Based on Template.

28. Expand the General category, then expand Woodland.

29. Select Woodland upper3rd, name it **Title**, then click OK.

30. Using the Type tool, replace OUTDOORS TITLE with: **America the Beautiful** and replace WOODLAND SUBTITLE with **Your Name**. (*Hint*: You will need to resize America the Beautiful to fit.)

31. Close the title you are working on.

32. Drag the Title clip to the Video 2 sequence above scenic1.jpg.

33. Preview the project on the Program Monitor.

34. Save your project file.

Export a movie.

1. Select the sequence on the Project panel.

2. Click File on the Menu bar, point to Export, then click Media.

3. In the Export Settings dialog box, make the following selections: Format: **FLV**; Preset: **Match Source Attribute (Medium Quality)**; Output Name: **America the Beautiful** *Your Name*.

4. Click Queue.

5. Return to Premiere Pro.

6. Select File on the Menu bar, point to Export, then click Media.

7. In the Export Settings dialog box, make the following selections: Format: **MPEG2-DVD**; Preset: **NTSC High Quality**; Output Name: **America the Beautiful** *Your Name*.

8. Click Queue.

9. Return to the Adobe Media Encoder.

10. Click Start Queue.

11. Close the project file.

Figure 95 *Completed Skills Review*

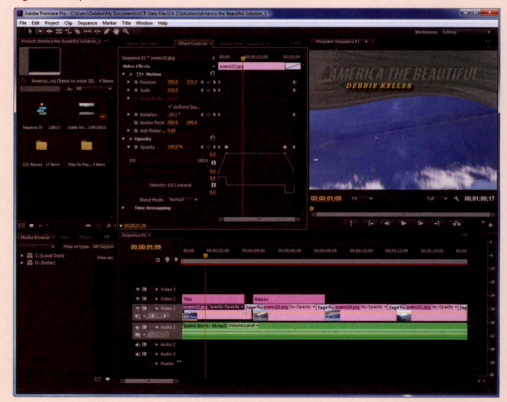

Figure © Cengage Learning 2013

A local travel agency has contacted your advertising firm to create an ad to help advertise a new trip they are promoting called the Tour of Italy! They have a very low budget and can afford to use only still images and music but have heard that you specialize in video montages. They would like you to create an eye-catching video montage highlighting this new vacation destination.

The agency has provided the beginning Premiere Pro project file, which includes bins that have already been created and an audio file already imported. The Pictures bin has 15 images of Italy already imported and ready to use. There is a Titles bin with titles available to be used in the project, including the credits, the travel agency information, and the tour announcement. They plan to run this ad on television and on the Internet, and therefore need you to supply the final version in F4V and MPEG2-DVD formats.

1. Open Italy.prproj from your Data Files folder, then save it as **Italy *your name***.
2. Open the Pictures bin and organize the images using a storyboard. Once you have the images in the order you like, automate them to the sequence on the Video 1 track. (*Hint*: Remove the check mark in the Apply Default Audio Transition check box, and leave the check mark in the Apply Default Video Transition check box.)

3. Place the audio track below the images on the Audio 1 track so that the audio aligns with the images. (*Hint*: Be careful that your clips on the Video track do not shift to the right when you place your audio track.)
4. Place the titles on the Video 2 track. Place the Intro title over your first clip. Place the other three titles where you think appropriate.

5. Preview your project on the Program Monitor, then compare the first frame of your project to the example shown in Figure 96 as a possible solution.
6. Export your movie to the F4V and the MPEG2-DVD formats.

Figure 96 *Program Monitor showing first frame*

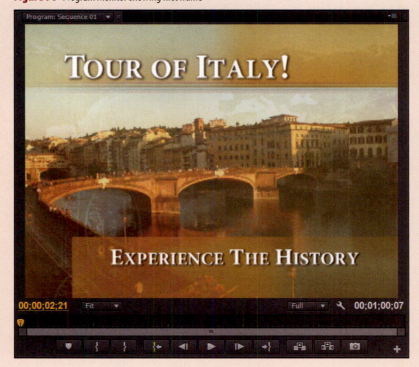

Creating a Video Montage in Adobe Premiere Pro CS6

You have been asked to complete the work on a video montage for the San Antonio Visitors Center, who would like to feature the San Antonio Missions, one of the city's historical attractions, on their Web site. You will apply the Ken Burns Effect (Pan and Zoom) to the images on the Video 1 track in the sequence.

1. Open SA Missions.prproj, from your Data Files folder, then save it as **SA Missions** *your name*.
2. Preview the movie on the Program Monitor to familiarize yourself with the project's current assets. Currently, there are no motion effects. Notice that the images have been placed without transitions to allow you more room on the Timeline to add your own effects.
3. Reset the workspace to the Effects workspace.
4. Create at least two keyframes for each clip. You will be adjusting the Position and Scale properties to create the Pan and Zoom Motion effects.
5. Compare your keyframes and Program Monitor to the example shown in Figure 97.
6. Preview your project on the Program Monitor. When you are pleased with your results, save your project.
7. Export your movie to the F4V format.

Figure 97 *Effect Controls panel and Program Monitor showing sample motion effects*

Figure © Cengage Learning 2013

Your history teacher has heard about the work you are doing in your multimedia class and wants you to incorporate your knowledge of Adobe Premiere Pro into a project for his class. You are currently studying the history of the United States space program. He would like you to gather images from the NASA images Web site (www.nasaimages.org) and make a two-minute video montage. Be sure to read the "Terms" at the bottom of the Web site and cite your sources correctly. After placing images on your sequence, resize them if necessary using the Scale property. You may also want to use the Pan and Zoom effect on some images to emphasize certain areas of a photograph or just to add motion to an image.

Descriptions are included with the pictures on the NASA Web site; use this information to create titles for your pictures to describe the images. (*Hint*: While you are downloading the images, you may want to create a text file that you can later reference when creating the titles.)

Your teacher would also like you to include background music while the images are playing. Since there will be descriptions on the images that will need to be read while the video is being viewed, he would prefer the music be instrumental. Audio clips are available in the Audio Clips folder on the resource disc that

came with this book, if you cannot find your own audio file from the Internet.

Note: If given an option to download either a low- or a high-resolution image, choose to download the low-resolution version. Create a folder to save your images in your Data Files folder.

1. Create a new Premiere Pro Project and sequence and save it as **Space Program** *your name*.
2. On the Project panel, create bins to organize the images you downloaded and to save your titles in.
3. Import your assets into the appropriate areas of the Project panel; compare your Project panel to the example shown in Figure 98.
4. Arrange your assets and place them on the sequence. (*Hint*: Consider whether you want a default transition between the clips if you are going to be working with the Pan and Zoom effect extensively.)
5. Apply the Pan and Zoom effect as you feel appropriate.
6. Create title descriptions for your images that you will place on the Video 2 track. (*Hint*: You may want to create your Intro title and Credit title as clips on the Video 1 track because you are placing descriptions on each picture. You will need to use the Insert command to shift the images to the right to place the Intro title at the beginning of the sequence. Remember to lock your Audio 1 track if you have already placed your music clip.)
7. Render and preview your project on the Program Monitor and make any changes before you export your project.

8. When you are finally satisfied with your work, export your video to the MPEG2-DVD format, so that it can be viewed on a computer and later be added to your electronic portfolio.

Figure 98 *Sample Project panel showing assets*

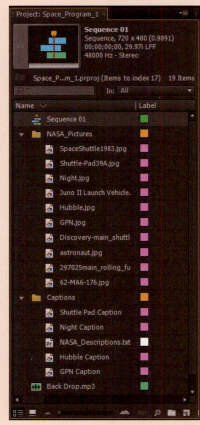

Figure © Cengage Learning 2013

CHAPTER 2

WORKING IN ADOBE
AFTER EFFECTS CS6

1. Explore the After Effects workspace
2. Create an on-screen graphic
3. Create a production logo
4. Create a title sequence

WORKING IN ADOBE
AFTER EFFECTS CS6

Adobe After Effects CS6 is a development tool for adding animated text, digital motion graphics, and realistic visual effects to video. After Effects is a nonlinear editing system that works with layers much like those you may have used in other Adobe programs such as Premiere Pro, Photoshop, and Illustrator. **Nonlinear editing** is the ability to access any frame in a video in order to make changes to it. Changes can include removing sections of the video, creating fades, or adding transitions. It is analogous to cutting, pasting, and formatting text in a word processor.

Adobe Dynamic Link provides integration between After Effects and Premiere Pro and Encore as long as you have installed these applications as part of the Creative Suite 6 Production Premium or the Creative Suite 6 Master Collection. **Dynamic Link** is a command on the File menu that allows you to import Premiere Pro sequences into the Project panel in After Effects and use them as layers. Any changes made to the sequence in Premiere Pro are automatically updated in the composition in After Effects without the need to render. A **composition** is the container that holds all the references for the movie. You can also dynamically link After Effects compositions to Premiere Pro as clips, or to Encore as projects.

In this chapter, you will be creating a digital on-screen graphic, a production logo, and a title sequence using After Effects CS6. Each of these projects is essentially working with motion graphics, for which After Effects is the ideal editing program.

A **digital on-screen graphic** is a logo overlaid on a portion of the television viewing area to identify the channel, much like a watermark. The use of this graphic also helps minimize copyright infringement. The digital on-screen graphic has expanded to included clocks, temperatures, and the score bug during athletic events. In the United Kingdom and New Zealand, it is known by the acronym **DOG**; in the United States and Canada, it is referred to as a **bug**.

Movie and television production companies use a **production logo** at the beginning of a theatrical movie or at the end of a television program or movie to brand what they produce. It is referred to as either an opening or closing logo. Production logos can even be found in many video games.

A **title sequence** is shown at the beginning of a movie or television program to provide the title and credit the actors.

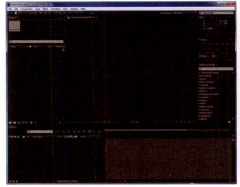

LESSON 1

Explore the After Effects
WORKSPACE

What You'll Do

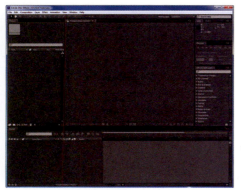

Figure © Cengage Learning 2013

In this lesson, you will start After Effects, examine the panels that make up the After Effects workspace, and learn how to change and customize the workspace.

Exploring the After Effects Workspace

After Effects has a customizable workspace with several default workspaces available, similar to Premiere Pro. The main window, comprising the various panels, is called the application window. The workspace is the arrangement of the panels. Figure 1 shows the default workspace, which is called **Standard**.

The workspace can be changed by selecting a preformatted workspace or by rearranging the panels to your individual preference, creating a **customized workspace**. You can switch between preformatted workspaces using the Workspace command on the Window menu or by making a selection from the drop-down menu on the **Tools panel**.

Each panel has a tab with the panel name. Panels can be moved by clicking and dragging panel tabs. As you drag a panel, an area becomes highlighted; this is called the drop zone, and provides a visual reference to where the panel can be placed.

If you wish to save a customized workspace, you may do so by selecting New Workspace on the Workspace menu or from the drop-down menu on the Tools panel.

A basic workflow for creating a project in After Effects follows six steps:

1. Import and organize footage.
2. Create compositions and arrange footage into layers.
3. Add various effects to layers.
4. Animate elements on layers.
5. Preview work on the Composition panel.
6. Export the final composition.

The panels you will use most often are:

Project panel: The Project panel organizes the references to all of the assets for the project. Assets can include video clips, digital images, and audio clips. In After Effects, assets are referred to as **footage**. The Project panel also lists compositions, which explain how you want to use the footage.

Timeline panel: The Timeline panel is where footage may be added to a composition in components called **layers** and is represented as a bar graph.

Figure 1 *Standard workspace*

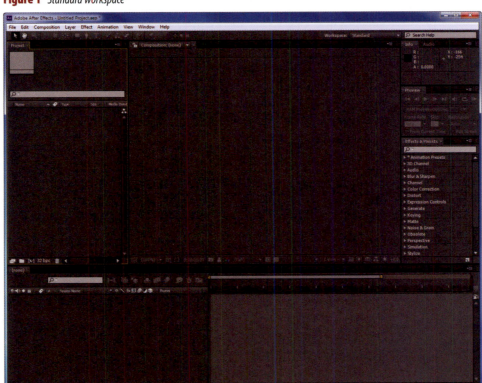

Figure © Cengage Learning 2013

Composition panel: The Composition panel represents layers spatially. The Composition panel displays compositions at the location of the Current-time Indicator (CTI) on the Timeline panel.

Showing Rulers and Grids

After Effects provides the option to display grids, rulers, guides, and safe margins. These options can be found on the View menu or by clicking the Choose grid and guide options

button on the Composition panel. Using these options can be very beneficial when working with the drawing tools to determine the size of the shapes you are creating. It is important to understand that the grid, guides, and margins do not render for previews or for final output.

The various default settings for the grid, rulers, guides, and safe margins can be modified in the Grids & Guides section of the Preferences dialog box, as shown in Figure 2. Various

colors and line styles can be selected based on personal preference to make the grid and guides easier to see. Spacing options on the grid can also be changed to provide greater detail to assist in the drawing and placement of objects. The unit of measurement is the **pixel**, which is $1/72^{nd}$ of an inch.

The grid and guide features work in much the same way as in other Adobe applications. To create a guide you drag from the ruler, and to reposition the guide you drag it with the

Figure 2 *Grids & Guides section of the Preferences dialog box*

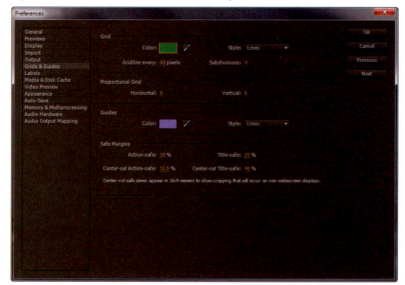

Selection tool. Locking guides prevents them from being moved. Guides can be cleared or hidden from view when you no longer need them.

Viewing area **safe zones**, or margins, are designed to ensure that certain content is not missed when being played on television screens. Programs like After Effects and Premiere Pro provide the option of turning on safe margin guides during editing. The safe zone is broken down into two areas: **title safe zone** and **action safe zone**.

As shown in Figure 3, the inner margin is the title safe zone and the outer margin is the action safe zone. Television stations that use a digital on-screen graphic place it just inside the title safe zone to ensure that it is visible on all television displays.

Figure 3 *Safe margin guides*

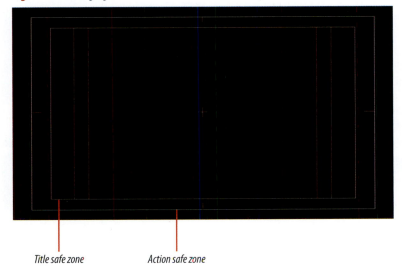

Title safe zone   Action safe zone

Figure © Cengage Learning 2013

Start Adobe After Effects and explore the workspace

1. Click **Start** 🏁 on the Menu bar, point to **All Programs**, then click **Adobe After Effects CS6** (Win) or open the Finder from the dock and click **Applications** from the sidebar, click the **Adobe applications folder**, then click **Adobe After Effects CS6** (Mac).

   You may need to look in a subfolder if you have installed the Production Premium or Master Collection Suite. The Welcome to Adobe After Effects window appears as shown in Figure 4. This window allows you to open an existing project, create a new composition, see recent projects, and view the Tip of the Day.

   TIP Pressing and holding [Ctrl][Alt][Shift] (Win) or ⌘ [option][Shift] (Mac) while starting After Effects restores default preference settings.

2. Click the **Close button** [Close] on the Welcome to Adobe After Effects window.

   An untitled project appears in the Standard workspace as shown in Figure 5.

3. Click **Window** on the Menu bar, then point to **Workspace**.

   You will see a variety of preformatted workspaces that are available. Note the check mark next to Standard; the check mark indicates the workspace you are currently viewing.

   (continued)

Figure 4 *Welcome to Adobe After Effects window*

Figure 5 *New untitled project*

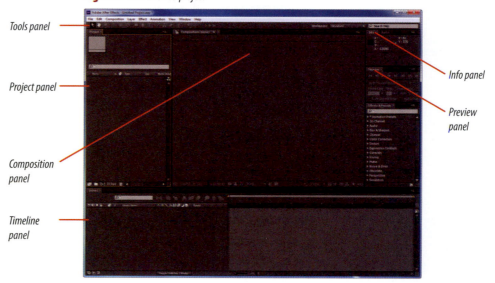

Tools panel

Info panel

Project panel

Preview panel

Composition panel

Timeline panel

Figures © Cengage Learning 2013

Figure 6 *Displaying the grid*

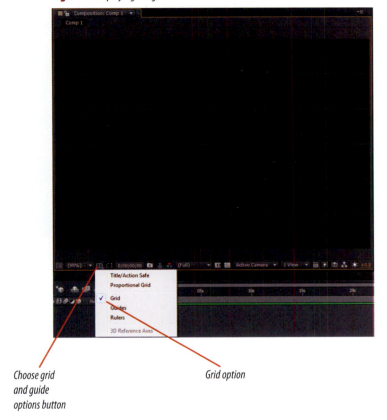

Choose grid
and guide
options button

Grid option

4. Click **Animation**.

   The Smoother, Wiggler, and Motion Sketch panels are added to the workspace on the right. These three panels are important when working with animation.

5. Continue to click through the various workspaces and notice how the window changes each time.

6. When you have finished looking at the various workspaces, switch back to the **Standard** workspace.

TIP After selecting Standard, you may want to click Reset "Standard" on the Workspace menu to ensure that the workspace has been reset properly.

7. Leave Adobe After Effects open for the next exercise.

You started Adobe After Effects CS6 and explored the workspace.

Work with the grid and guides

1. Open **GridPractice.aep** from your Chapter 2 Data Files folder.

2. Click the **Choose grid and guide options button** on the bottom of the Composition panel, then click **Grid** as shown in Figure 6.

3. Click **Edit** on the Menu bar (Win) or **After Effects** (Mac), point to **Preferences**, then click **Grids & Guides**.

(continued)

Figure © Cengage Learning 2013

Lesson 1 Explore the After Effects Workspace

4. Click the **Color box** to open the Grid Color dialog box, click on the yellow area of the spectrum, then click in the large color space to change the color to a bright yellow as shown in Figure 7.

5. Click **OK** in the Grid Color dialog box, then click **OK** in the Preferences dialog box.

   The gridline colors on the Composition panel have changed to bright yellow and are easier to see.

6. Click **View** on the Menu bar, then click **Show Rulers**.

   Rulers measuring in pixels are shown at the top and to the left of the Composition panel.

   (continued)

Figure 7 *Customizing the color of the grid*

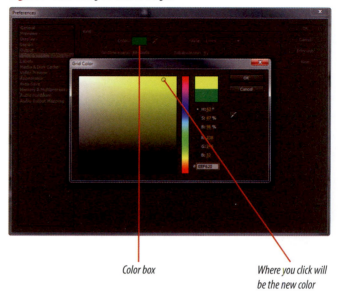

Color box

Where you click will be the new color

Figure © Cengage Learning 2013

Working in Adobe After Effects CS6

Figure 8 *Creating a ruler guide*

Left ruler —

Top ruler

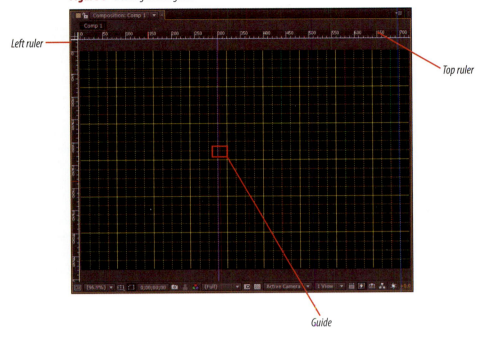

Guide

Lesson 1   Explore the After Effects Workspace

7. Position the mouse pointer over the **left ruler**, click and drag to the grid to create a vertical guide, then release the mouse pointer when it is approximately at the 300 px mark, as shown in Figure 8.

   Once the mouse pointer is over a ruler, it changes into a double-headed arrow.

   TIP The Info panel shows the location of the guide as you drag it.

8. Repeat this process from the top ruler to create a horizontal guide anywhere on the Composition panel.

   Guides can be moved by clicking and dragging them. To remove a guide, drag it back onto the ruler.

9. Click **View** on the Menu bar, then click **Lock Guides** to keep guides from being moved or selected accidentally.

10. Save your project file and close After Effects.

In this lesson, you showed the grid and rulers and customized the color of the grid. You also placed two guides on the Composition panel and locked them.

LESSON 2

Create an
ON-SCREEN GRAPHIC

What You'll Do

Figure © Cengage Learning 2013

 In this lesson, you will create a digital on-screen graphic, also known as a bug.

Creating a Composition

A **project** in After Effects is a single file that stores compositions and references to footage used in the project. Footage—what you referred to as digital assets in Premiere Pro—may include video, audio, animation, still images, text, Photoshop and Illustrator files, and even Premiere Pro project files.

The project file must contain at least one composition, which is the container that holds all the references for the movie. A composition may also be referred to as a **comp** within After Effects. It has its own timeline and layers, as shown in Figure 9.

Each layer can have only one footage item, which then can be manipulated in space and time. A composition is similar to a sequence in Premiere Pro or a movie clip in Flash Professional.

Composition settings are independent of the project settings and if you create multiple compositions, you can create different settings for each composition. For most composition settings, the presets should be acceptable. For your purposes, while working on projects in this book, you will use the NTSC DV and the NTSC DV Widescreen presets. It is always a good idea to make the composition settings

Figure 9 *Composition layers and timeline*

Composition ——

Layers ——

Timeline

Figure © Cengage Learning 2013

match the footage. Fortunately, if you do not know the information for your footage you can simply drag the footage to the Create a new Composition button on the Project panel or drag it to the Timeline panel and After Effects will create the composition for you with the appropriate settings. Figure 10 shows video footage about air pollution in Beijing that was imported into the Project panel, then dragged to the Timeline panel where a composition was automatically created with the default name of the footage and in this case, the preset NTSC DV and a duration of 8.03 seconds.

The Composition panel, as shown in Figure 11, displays the layers of footage at the Current-time Indicator (CTI) on the Timeline panel. You can use the Composition panel as a visual preview of the footage on the Timeline, similar to the Program Monitor in Premiere Pro.

Figure 10 *Composition settings created based on footage*

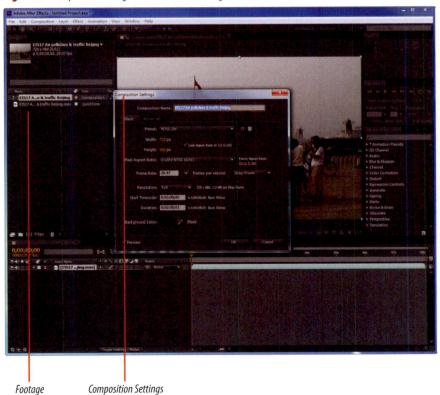

Footage   Composition Settings

Figure 11 *Composition panel sample preview of Timeline*

Composition panel   Current time

Figures © Cengage Learning 2013

Working with Footage

The Project panel is where the compositions and footage items are listed, as shown in Figure 12. After Effects supports practically every format for common file types of video, audio, and still images. A complete list can be found in After Effects Help. Files are not directly imported into the Project panel; instead a reference link to each source file is created. Therefore, if you delete, move, or change the name of a file you are referencing, the link will become broken. If a link becomes broken, the name of the source file will appear in italics on the Project panel, and the File Path column will identify the path as missing, as shown in Figure 13. If the source file is still available, double-click the reference on the Project panel and restore the link by selecting the file again.

You can create folders on the Project panel to store and organize footage. You can also embed folders within folders. If you have a folder selected when you choose the Import command, the footage will be placed in that folder. To reveal a folder's contents you simply click the expand arrow to the left of the folder icon. In Windows, can also choose the Import Folder option on the Import File dialog box, as shown in Figure 14. The imported folder will become a folder on the Project panel. (*Note*: The Import Folder button is not available on a Mac; however, clicking the Open button when a folder is selected is equivalent to clicking the Import Folder button on Windows.)

Color labels are assigned to footage items by default to represent different types of media;

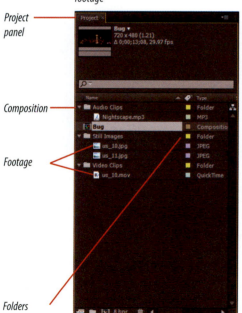

Figure 12 *Project panel showing sample footage*

Project panel

Composition

Footage

Folders

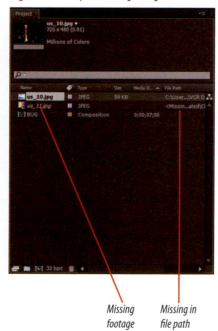

Figure 13 *Example of missing footage*

Missing footage

Missing in file path

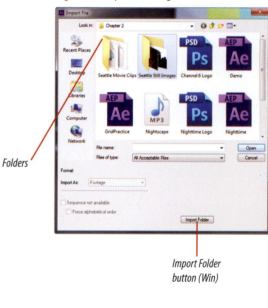

Figure 14 *Import File dialog box*

Folders

Import Folder button (Win)

for example, video clips are assigned the color Aqua. Color labels are also assigned to compositions and layers. You can change the default colors in the Labels section of the Preferences dialog box, as shown in Figure 15. The labels allow you to sort by color on the Project panel, or to select all layers with the same label color on either the Project panel or the Timeline panel, as shown in Figure 16.

After Effects projects can become quite large, and the Timeline can become quite long. If you are unable to locate a piece of footage on the Timeline, right-click (Win) or [Control]-click (Mac) the footage on the Project panel, click Reveal in Composition, then select the instance you are looking for. You can also use the Search box on the Project panel and on the Timeline panel to search for footage. As you begin to type in the Search box, the filter process begins and items that do not meet the criteria become hidden. After you find the item you are looking for, click the X on the Search box to clear it.

Creating a Layer

Layers are similar to tracks in Premiere Pro. Without layers, a composition would be empty. When you use the term layers in After Effects, you are referring to the layers on the Timeline panel, not on the Layer panel. The Layer panel in After Effects is similar to the Source Monitor in Premiere Pro; it is the panel where you can view source footage. One very important thing to remember is

that a layer in After Effects can have only one footage item (movie, still image, audio, text) as its source and every layer has properties that are unique to that particular layer.

There are several types of layers in After Effects. There are layers that are created to hold items created within After Effects such as text layers and shape layers. There are audio

Figure 15 *Labels section of the Preferences dialog box*

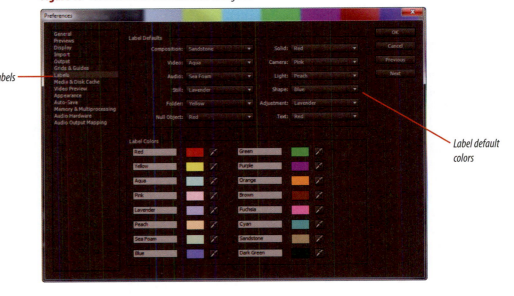

Labels

Label default colors

Figure 16 *Selecting layers based on label color*

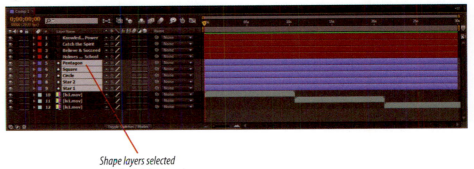

Shape layers selected based on label color

and video layers based on the type of footage that has been placed on them. Finally, there are special function layers that are also created within After Effects for cameras, lights, null objects, guide layers, and adjustment layers. Layers that are created without using source footage are called **synthetic layers**.

There are three panels that allow you to work with layers—the Timeline panel, the Composition panel, and the Layer panel. (You will use the Layer panel in later chapters as you continue to explore After Effects.)

The Timeline panel is where you can change layer properties by using keyframes, in a manner very similar to how you used them in Premiere Pro. Every layer by default begins with the Transform group of properties, as shown in Figure 17. All layer properties are **temporal**, meaning they can change the layer over time. Some layer properties are also **spatial**, meaning they have the ability to move, or to add motion across composition space.

Opacity is an example of a temporal property. It is temporal because the layer does not move; the property causes the layer to fade in or fade out, which is an effect that occurs over a period of time. Position is a property that shows movement of a layer—the layer is moved at different keyframes to indicate motion over a period of time. Therefore, position is an example of a property that is both temporal and spatial. (*Note*: Because all properties are temporal, if a property is spatial it is also temporal.)

On the Timeline panel, you can change a layer's starting time, length of time, and its stacking order. After Effects automatically numbers each layer based on its position in the stacking order, as shown in Figure 18. If the stacking order changes, the numbers assigned to each layer are updated to keep the numbering in numerical order. All layers are placed at the top of the stacking order by default when created.

However, a footage item can be dragged to the Timeline panel in the position of the stack where you want it to be placed.

The Composition panel is where you preview the changes you have made to a layer, and view the layer in context with other layers in the composition. This is also where you can manually modify layers.

Figure 17 *Transform group properties*

Transform group

Default settings

Figure 18 *Layers on the Timeline panel*

Timeline panel

Search box

Label colors

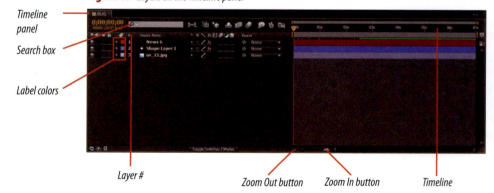

Layer #

Zoom Out button

Zoom In button

Timeline

Figures © Cengage Learning 2013

Adding Layer Effects

Effects can be found on the Effects & Presets panel or on the Effect menu. To apply an effect to a selected layer, double-click the effect you wish to apply. The Effect Controls panel opens and the effect you applied and its properties become active, as shown in Figure 19.

As a layer is modified and animated, properties are added, and the properties are organized into property groups. The Effects property group is added to the Layer properties on the Timeline panel, as shown in Figure 20. You can edit these properties either on the Timeline panel or on the Effect Controls panel.

Working with Animation Presets

An **animation preset** is a collection of animation settings that includes keyframes and effects that you have applied to a layer. Creating an animation preset allows you to apply the same settings to another layer in the composition or even in another After Effects project.

After Effects also includes a large library of animation presets. You can browse the available animation presets in the Effects & Presets panel or in Adobe Bridge. To preview the animation presets in Adobe Bridge, click Animation on the Menu bar then select Browse Presets.

Making a Movie

The term **movie** describes a file that is created by rendering a composition. Rendering is the process of compiling a composition into its

Figure 19 *Effect Controls panel*

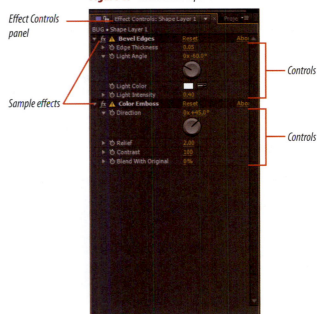

Effect Controls panel

Sample effects

Controls

Controls

Figure 20 *Viewing the Effects property group*

Timeline panel

Effects property group

Sample effects

Controls

Controls

Figures © Cengage Learning 2013

final output from all of its layers and settings. The preferred way to render and export movies from After Effects is by using the Render Queue panel.

The Render Queue panel is used to render compositions, adjust render settings, apply output module settings, name the file, adjust the file location if necessary, and monitor the rendering process, as shown in Figure 21. When a composition is added to the Render Queue it becomes a **render item**, and its status is listed as Queued. Clicking the Render button in the upper-right corner of the Render Queue panel begins the rendering process for all the items listed in the queue with the status Queued in the order they are listed. The status changes to Done when the process is complete. A render item remains in the Render Queue where it can be duplicated and added back to the queue with the same settings or different settings.

Just as you did with Premiere Pro, you will be saving to the MPEG-2 file format and the FLV format.

Figure 21 *Render Queue panel*

Render Queue panel

Output Module

Render button

Status   Output To

A Note About Special Function Layers

A **null object** is an invisible layer that can have all the properties of a visible layer; you can then apply those properties to other layers. Null object layers are often used as control layers when working with animations because they are often easier to select and see than when working with a camera or light layer. You will work with this type of layer in later chapters.

The **guide layer** can help you position and edit elements by providing a visual reference in the Composition panel; guide layers are created from existing layers. By default, guide layers do not become part of the final output.

An **adjustment layer** affects all layers that fall below it in the stacking order; therefore, adjustment layers are useful if you want to apply the same effects to many layers at the same time.

Figure 22 *Composition Settings dialog box*

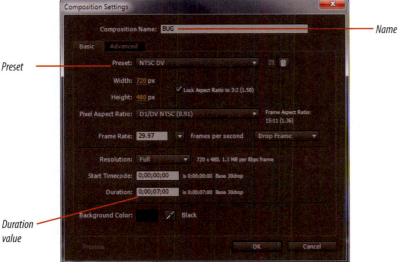

Name

Preset

Duration
value

Figure © Cengage Learning 2013

Create a composition

1. Press and hold [**Ctrl**][**Alt**][**Shift**] (Win) or ⌘ [**option**][**Shift**] (Mac), then start Adobe After Effects CS6 to reset the default preference settings.

2. Click **OK** in the warning dialog box in response to: "Are you sure you want to delete your preferences file?"

   After Effects deletes the old preferences file and creates a new one using default settings. Resetting the default preference settings will remove the bright yellow grid setting you applied in the last lesson.

3. Click the **Close button** ⓧ on the Welcome to Adobe After Effects window, if necessary.

4. Click **File** on the Menu bar, point to **Save As**, then click **Save As**, type **BUG** *your name* in the File name text box, navigate to the drive and folder where your Data Files are located, then click **Save**.

5. Click **Composition** on the Menu bar, then click **New Composition**.

   The Composition Settings dialog box opens.

TIP You can also press [Ctrl][N] (Win) or ⌘ [N] (Mac) to create a new composition.

6. Type **BUG** in the Composition Name text box.

7. Click the **Preset list arrow**, then click **NTSC DV**.

8. Change the Duration value to **0;00;07;00** by selecting the contents of the Duration box and typing **700** (7 seconds), press [**Tab**], compare your dialog box to Figure 22, then press [**Enter**] (Win) or [**return**] (Mac).

(continued)

Pressing [Enter] (Win) or [return] (Mac) after typing 700 will close the Composition Settings dialog box. If you need to edit the composition settings further, click Composition on the Menu bar then select Composition Settings.

A new composition named BUG appears on the Project panel, Composition panel, and Timeline panel, as shown in Figure 23.

9. Save your project and leave it open for the next exercise.

You started a new After Effects project and created a new composition.

Import footage

1. Open the BUG *your name* project file, if necessary.

2. Click **File** on the Menu bar, point to **Import**, then click **File**.

3. Navigate to the drive and folder where your Data Files are stored, click **us_11.jpg**, be sure the JPEG Sequence check box is not checked, then click **Open**.

The file appears on the Project panel, as shown in Figure 24.

TIP Be sure the JPEG Sequence check box is not checked to keep files in a possible sequence from being imported by mistake.

4. Save your project and leave it open for the next exercise.

You imported footage into the Project panel.

Figure 23 *New composition*

Project panel

Timeline panel

Composition panel

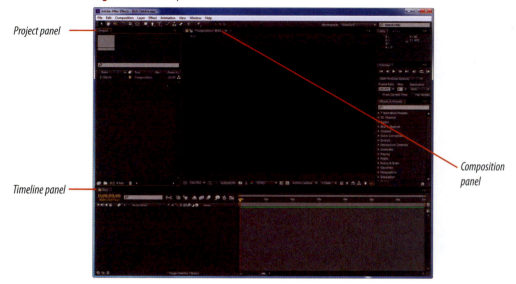

Figure 24 *Project panel showing imported footage*

Selected footage preview

Imported footage file

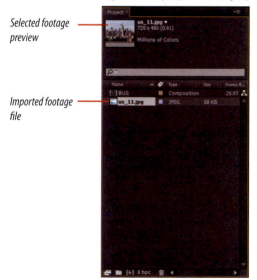

Figures © Cengage Learning 2013

Figure 25 *Shape Layer 1 added to Timeline panel*

Shape Layer 1

Figure 26 *Drawing a rectangle*

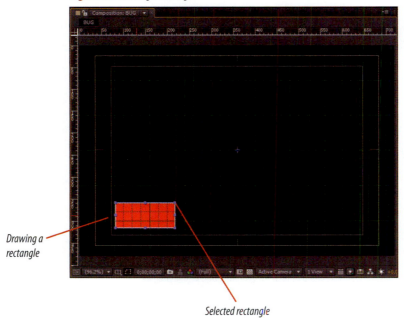

Drawing a rectangle

Selected rectangle

Figures © Cengage Learning 2013

Lesson 2   Create an On-Screen Graphic

Create a shape layer

1. Open the BUG *your name* project file, if necessary.

2. Click the **Choose grid and guide options button** on the Composition panel, then click **Title/Action Safe**.

3. Repeat Step 2 to select **Grid**, then **Rulers**.

4. Click the **Timeline panel** to select it.

5. Click **Layer** on the Menu bar, point to **New**, then click **Shape Layer**.

   A new layer named Shape Layer 1 is added to the BUG composition on the Timeline panel, as shown in Figure 25.

   TIP You can also right-click the Timeline panel, point to New, then click Shape Layer to create a new shape layer.

6. Click the **Rectangle tool** on the Tools panel, then draw a rectangle near the bottom-left corner of the title safe area of the Composition panel, as shown in Figure 26.

   Your rectangle size and location may differ slightly from the figure.

7. With the rectangle still selected, click the **Fill color box** on the Tools panel, replace the text in the # text box with **113355**, then click **OK**.

   The # text box in the Text Color dialog box refers to the hex color code which represents color in the RRGGBB form. RR represents the intensity of the color red, GG the intensity of the color green, and BB the intensity of the color blue. Color intensity is represented by a hexadecimal number from 00 to FF.

8. Click the **Stroke Width value** on the Tools panel, then drag the pointer to **0 px**.

(continued)

9. Click **Effect** on the Menu bar, point to **Perspective**, then click **Bevel Edges**.

The Effect Controls panel becomes active to show the Bevel Edges effect.

10. On the Effect Controls panel, change the Edge Thickness value to **0.05**.

11. Click **Effect** on the Menu bar, point to **Stylize**, then click **Color Emboss**.

The Color Emboss effect is added to the Effect Controls panel.

12. On the Effect Controls panel, change the Relief value to **2.00**, as shown in Figure 27.

13. Deselect the rectangle by clicking away from it on the Composition panel, then click the **Selection tool** ▶ on the Tools panel.

TIP You can also press [V] on the keyboard to select the Selection tool.

14. Save your project and leave it open for the next exercise, then compare your Composition panel to Figure 28.

You displayed the grid, rulers, and Title/Action Safe margins. Next, you created a new shape layer on the Timeline panel, drew a rectangle, and applied effects to it.

Create a text layer

1. Open the BUG *your name* project file, if necessary.

2. Click **Window** on the Menu bar, point to **Workspace**, then click **Text**.

The workspace changes to the Text workspace. The Character and Paragraph panels are included in the Text workspace, as shown in Figure 29.

(continued)

Figure 27 *Effects added to Effect Controls panel*

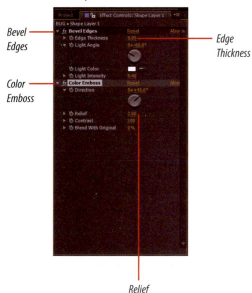

Bevel Edges

Color Emboss

Edge Thickness

Relief

Figure 28 *Rectangle with Bevel Edges and Stylize Color Emboss effects*

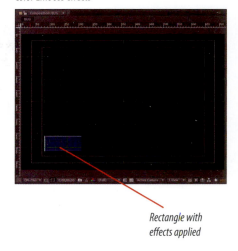

Rectangle with effects applied

Figure 29 *Text workspace*

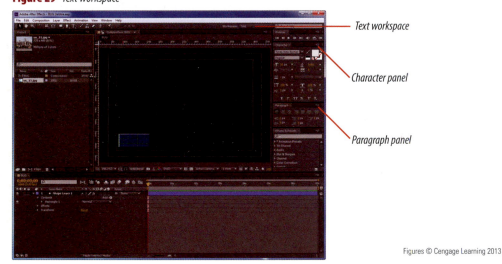

Text workspace

Character panel

Paragraph panel

Figures © Cengage Learning 2013

Figure 30 *Entering text on the Composition panel*

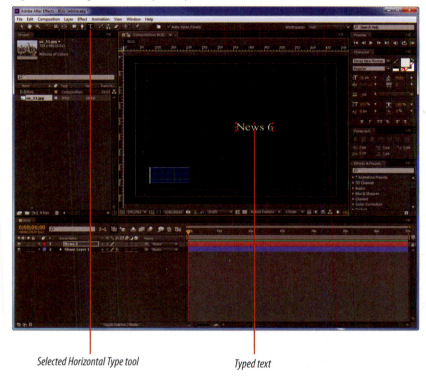

Selected Horizontal Type tool   Typed text

Figure 31 *New name of the text layer*

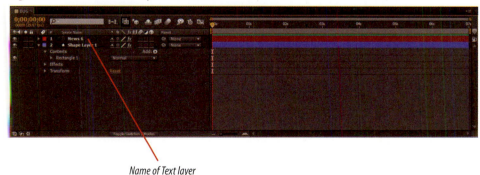

Name of Text layer

Figures © Cengage Learning 2013

3. Right-click the **Timeline panel**, point to **New**, then click **Text**.

   A Text layer named Text 1 is added to the Timeline panel. The Horizontal Type tool becomes selected on the Tools panel. A red cursor appears in the center of the Composition panel.

4. Type **News 6**, then press [**Ctrl**][**Enter**] (Win) or ⌘ [**return**](Mac) on the main section of the keyboard to exit text-editing mode.

   Selection handles appear around the text so that it may now be formatted, as shown in Figure 30. The Horizontal Type tool remains selected on the Tools panel. The name of the Text layer has changed to News 6 to reflect the text that has been typed on the layer, as shown in Figure 31.

TIP Pressing [Enter] on the numeric keyboard will also exit text-editing mode.

5. On the Character panel make the following selections: Font: **Verdana**; Font style: **Bold**; Fill color: **White (#FFFFFF)**; Font size: **30 px**.

TIP If the text is no longer selected, click the Selection tool ▶ on the Tools panel, then click News 6 on the Composition panel to select it.

6. Save your project and leave it open for the next exercise.

You changed the workspace to the Text workspace and created a text layer. You then typed text on the Composition panel and used the Character panel to format the text.

Add a layer effect to text

1. Open the BUG *your name* project file, if necessary.

2. Set the workspace to the **Text** workspace, if necessary.

3. On the Effects & Presets panel, type **drop shadow** in the Search box, then press [**Enter**].

4. Press [**V**] to access the Selection tool ![cursor icon], then click **News 6**.

5. Double-click **Drop Shadow** on the Effects & Presets panel.

   The Drop Shadow effect is applied to the News 6 text. The Effect Controls panel becomes active and displays the properties for the Drop Shadow effect.

6. Drag the **News 6** text over the rectangle, as shown in Figure 32.

   The News 6 text is above the rectangle because the News 6 text layer is above the Shape Layer 1 layer on the Timeline panel. The text layer was created after the shape layer so it is one level higher in the stacking order.

7. Save your project and leave it open for the next exercise.

You applied the Drop Shadow effect to the News 6 text then moved the text over the rectangle.

Place footage in a composition

1. Open the BUG *your name* project file, if necessary.

2. Click the **Project panel tab**, then drag **us_11. jpg** from the Project panel to the center of the Composition panel, as shown in Figure 33.

(continued)

Figure 32 *Placing the text over the rectangle*

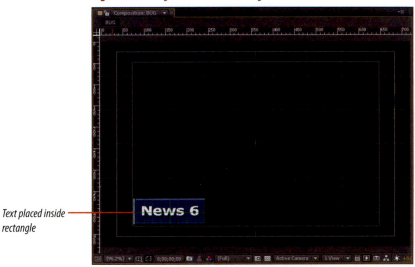

Text placed inside rectangle

Figure 33 *Placing footage on the Composition panel*

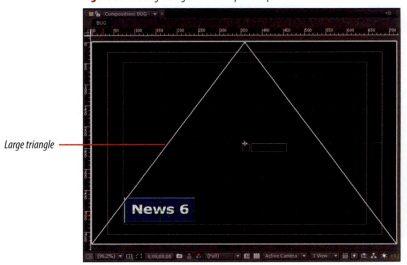

Large triangle

Figure 34 *us_11.jpg moved to #2 in stacking order*

Stacking order

Figure 35 *Changing the stacking order of layers on the Timeline panel*

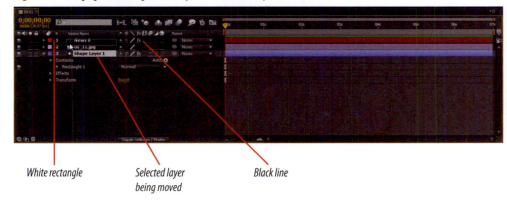

White rectangle

Selected layer
being moved

Black line

As you drag the footage, you will see a large triangle, which represents the item being dragged. When you drag an item from the Project panel to the Composition panel, a new layer is automatically created at the top of the stacking order. The us_11.jpg layer is above the other layers on the Timeline panel. You need to correct the stacking order.

3. Click **Layer** on the Menu bar, point to **Arrange**, then click **Send Layer Backward**.

   You should now be able to see "News 6". The us_11.jpg layer should now be #2 in the stacking order, as shown in Figure 34.

4. On the Timeline panel, click the **Shape Layer 1 layer**, then drag it above the us_11.jpg layer, as shown in Figure 35.

   You will see a white rectangle, which represents the layer being dragged, and a black line indicating where the layer will be relocated to when you release the mouse pointer.

5. Click the **Choose grid and guide options button** ⊞ on the Composition panel, then turn off the Title/Action Safe, Grid, and Rulers options.

   (continued)

Lesson 2   Create an On-Screen Graphic

6. Compare your screen to Figure 36.

7. Save your project and leave it open for the next exercise.

You placed footage in the composition, then rearranged the stacking order of layers on the Timeline panel.

Apply an animation preset

1. Open the BUG *your name* project file, if necessary.

2. Verify that the Current-time Indicator (CTI) is placed at **0;00;00;00** on the Timeline.

TIP With the Timeline panel selected, press [Home] to return the (CTI) to 0;00;00;00 and [End] to jump to the end of the duration of the composition. The [Home] key equivalent is [FN]+left arrow and the [End] key equivalent is [FN]+right arrow (Mac).

3. Click the **Selection tool** ▶ on the Tools panel, then click the **News 6 text**.

TIP If you have trouble selecting the text, click the Text layer on the Timeline panel.

4. Click **Animation** on the Menu bar, then click **Browse Presets**.

   Adobe Bridge opens, as shown in Figure 37.

5. Adjust the size of the thumbnails, if necessary, by dragging the slider at the bottom of the window.

6. Double-click the **Text folder**.

7. Double-click the **Animate In folder**.

8. Click **Center Spiral** to preview it on the Preview panel.

(continued)

Figure 36 *Completed BUG*

Title/Action Safe, Grid, and Rulers turned off

Stacking order

Figure 37 *Adobe Bridge Presets window*

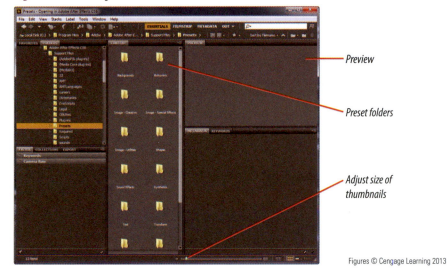

Preview

Preset folders

Adjust size of thumbnails

Figures © Cengage Learning 2013

Figure 38 *Animate In presets*

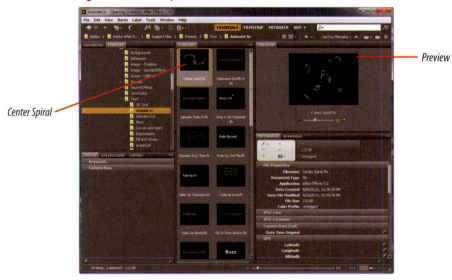

Center Spiral

Preview

Figure 39 *Placing a preset in After Effects*

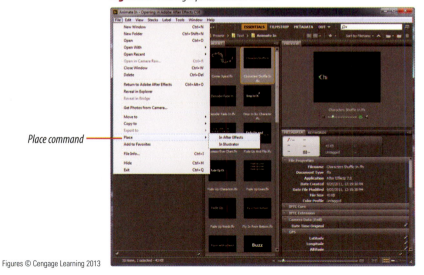

Place command

Figures © Cengage Learning 2013

9. Preview some other "Animate In" effects, as shown in Figure 38.

10. Click **Characters Shuffle In**, click **File** on the Menu bar, point to **Place**, then click **In After Effects**, as shown in Figure 39.

    This will apply the Character Shuffle In preset to the selected News 6 text.

11. Click the **Play/Pause button** ▶ on the Preview panel to preview the effect on the Composition panel.

    The preview will play slowly the first time because it is rendering the file.

12. Click the **Play/Pause button** ▶ to stop the animation.

13. Save your project and leave it open for the next exercise.

You added a preset animation to the News 6 text, then played the animation on the Preview panel.

Make a movie

1. Open the BUG *your name* project file, if necessary.

2. Click the **Composition panel** to select the BUG composition.

   The composition needs to be selected before you will be able to add it to the Render Queue.

3. Click **Composition** on the Menu bar, then click **Add to Render Queue**.

   The Render Queue panel appears at the bottom of the workspace, as shown in Figure 40.

4. Click **Lossless** next to Output Module on the Render Queue panel.

   The Output Module Settings dialog box opens, as shown in Figure 41.

5. Click the **Format list arrow**, click **MPEG2**, then click **OK**.

   Leave the Include Project Link check box checked. This will assist with compatibility when you import your MPEG2 files into Encore in a later chapter.

6. Click the text to the right of the **Output To** heading on the Render Queue panel.

   The Output Movie To dialog box opens, allowing you to name the movie and choose a location to save it in.

7. Name the movie **BUG Final *your name***, navigate to your Data Files folder, then click **Save**.

(continued)

Figure 40 *Render Queue panel*

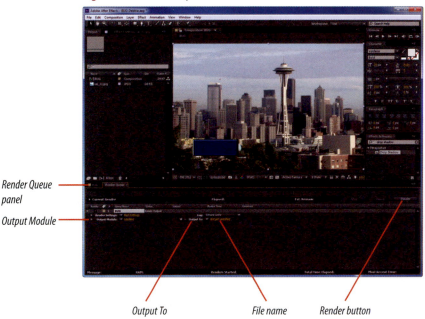

Render Queue panel

Output Module

Output To   File name   Render button

Figure 41 *Output Module Settings dialog box*

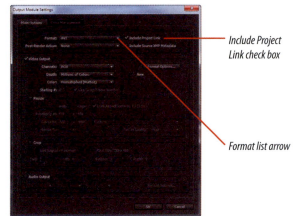

Include Project Link check box

Format list arrow

Figures © Cengage Learning 2013

Figure 42 *Watching BUG Final in Windows Media Player*

Text is in motion —

Lesson 2   Create an On-Screen Graphic

8. Click the **Render button** on the Render Queue panel.

   The rendering process begins. A status bar displays the approximate time remaining. Depending on the size, quality, complexity, and output method this could take seconds or hours. You will not be able to continue to work in After Effects until the process has completed. An audio alert indicates when the rendering process is complete.

9. Locate **BUG Final *your name*.m2v** where you save your work, then double-click to open your project in a digital media player, such as Windows Media Player, to see your movie.

   Your screen should resemble Figure 42.

10. Close the project.

You exported the movie to MPEG2 format and then watched it in a digital media player.

LESSON 3

Create a
PRODUCTION LOGO

What You'll Do

Figure © Cengage Learning 2013

 In this lesson, you will create a production logo.

Importing Photoshop Text

If you are already familiar with working with Photoshop features, such as formatting text and layer styles, it may be easier for you to prepare your text in Photoshop rather than create it in After Effects. After Effects includes the Photoshop rendering engine; it will import all the attributes of a Photoshop file, as shown in Figure 43. The text and the attributes will be editable in After Effects. This is also

Figure 43 *Photoshop file imported with attributes*

Layer styles

Figure © Cengage Learning 2013

true of working with still images created in Photoshop. For this reason, it is important to organize and name your layers in Photoshop. After Effects recognizes the names of the layers and imports them inside a folder by default, as shown in Figure 44, making it easier for you to work with the layers once they are imported. If you make any edits to the original Photoshop file, the Reload Footage command in After Effects will refresh the layers to reference the current Photoshop file. If you delete a layer, you will see the footage marked as missing from the Project panel, as shown in Figure 45. You can then make any edits to the layer styles in After Effects.

Figure 44 *Photoshop file imported into the Project panel as a composition*

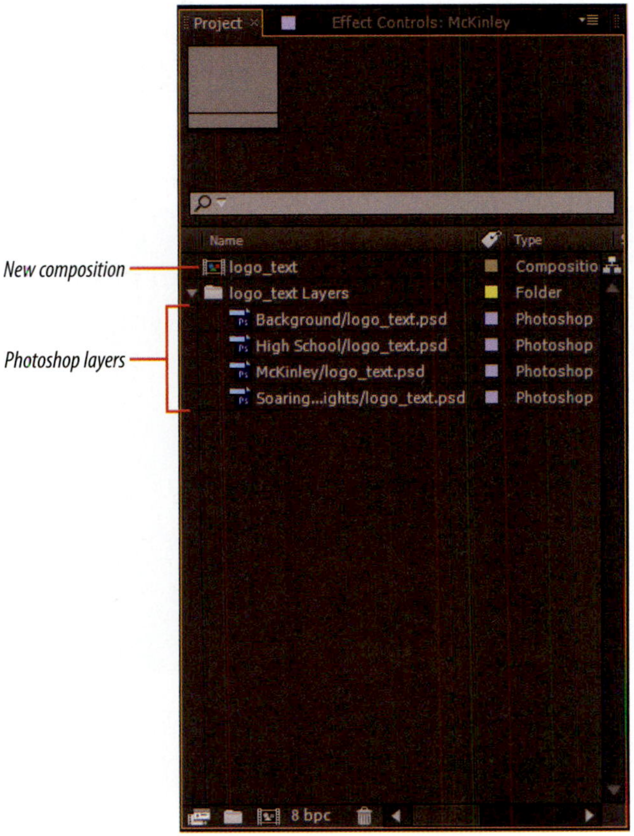

New composition

Photoshop layers

Figure 45 *Photoshop layer deleted*

Missing Photoshop layer

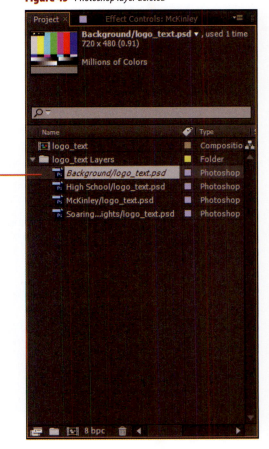

You can also convert a Photoshop layer to an After Effects Text layer, as shown in Figure 46. The layer will retain all the attributes it had when it was imported; however, it will no longer reference the Photoshop file and you will no longer be able to return to Photoshop to make edits to those layers that have been converted. The text, however, will be editable on the Composition panel in After Effects.

Formatting Text

When formatting text, it is a good idea to change your workspace to the Text workspace. The Text workspace activates the Character and Paragraph panels on the right side of the application window.

Changes you make on the Character panel affect only the text you have selected. If you select text with the Selection tool while making changes on the Character panel, all the text on that layer will change. If you highlight text with the Text tool, only the highlighted text will change, as shown in Figure 47. If you want to select all of the text on a layer and activate the Text tool, double-click the text layer on the Timeline panel with the Selection tool. With the Text tool selected, double-click a word to select it, triple-click to select a line of text, or quadruple-click to select a paragraph.

Nesting a Composition

Nesting a composition is the process of placing it inside another composition. The nested composition, sometimes referred to as a **precomposition**, appears as a single layer in the composition in which it is placed, also known as the **master composition**. You can apply effects to the nested composition like any other layer, and you can open the nested composition and make changes there as

Figure 46 *Photoshop file imported in After Effects*

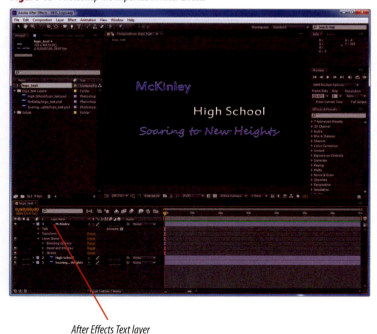

After Effects Text layer

Figure 47 *Highlighting text*

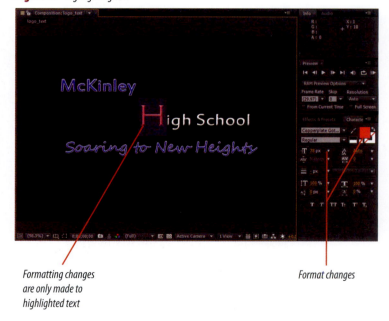

Formatting changes are only made to highlighted text

Format changes

Figures © Cengage Learning 2013

well. Importing Photoshop files encourages you to work with nested compositions. When importing a Photoshop file, selecting the composition option provides greater flexibility in working with Photoshop in After Effects. For instance, layers are preserved and text layers can be converted to editable text. If you choose the footage option, the Photoshop file is imported as a single layer. In addition, nesting is great for repetitive elements such as animated logos so that you can reuse them. You can also think of nesting as a way to organize layers into groups to break a composition into manageable parts.

The easiest way to navigate between nested compositions in After Effects is to use the Composition Navigator, as shown in Figure 48. Click the composition name to activate the composition. The directional arrow between the names of the compositions indicates the downstream composition to the left and the upstream composition to the right. **Upstream** is another term sometimes used for a nested composition. The composition most upstream is the master composition. **Downstream** is another term for the composition that contains a nested composition. There can be multiple nestings in a composition; the most downstream composition is referred to as the **root composition**.

Animating Text

There is an entire animation preset library dedicated specifically to text, as shown in Figure 49. The text animation presets

Figure 48 *Composition Navigator*

Root composition

Nested composition

Figure 49 *Library of text animation presets*

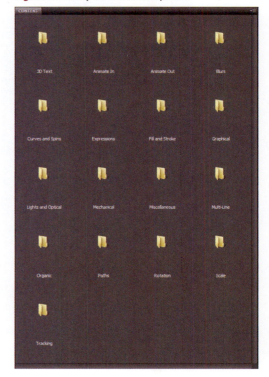

were created in an NTSC DV 720x480 composition using a text layer with the Myriad Pro, size 72-point font. If you use a text animation preset, you may need to adjust the size of the text. Additionally, when using presets from the Fill and Stroke category, the preset may change the colors of your text, and some presets require a stroke or fill in order for the animation to work. Adjustments can be made to the preset using the property settings on the Timeline, as shown in Figure 50.

Figure 50 *Adjusting a text animation preset*

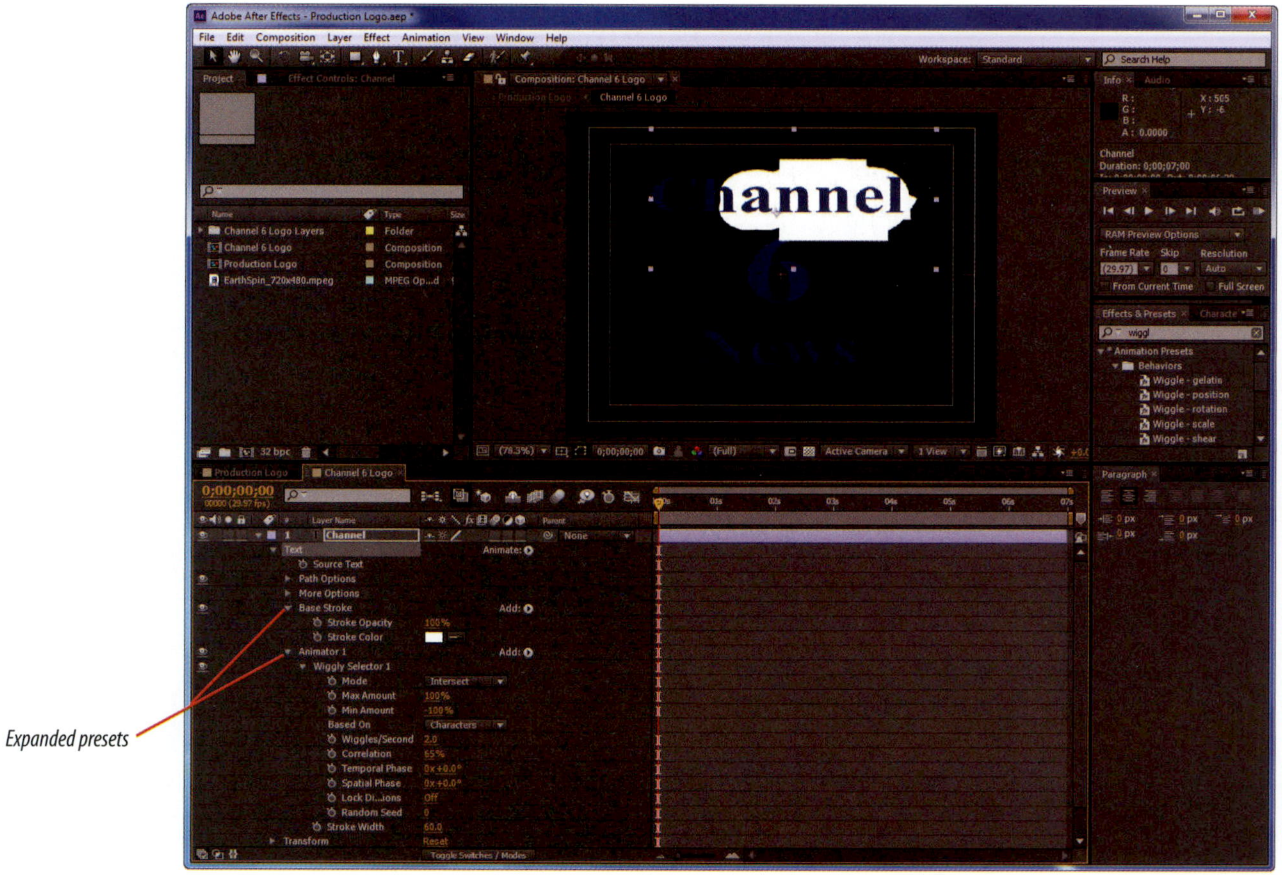

Expanded presets

Figure 51 *Settings for exporting for the Web*

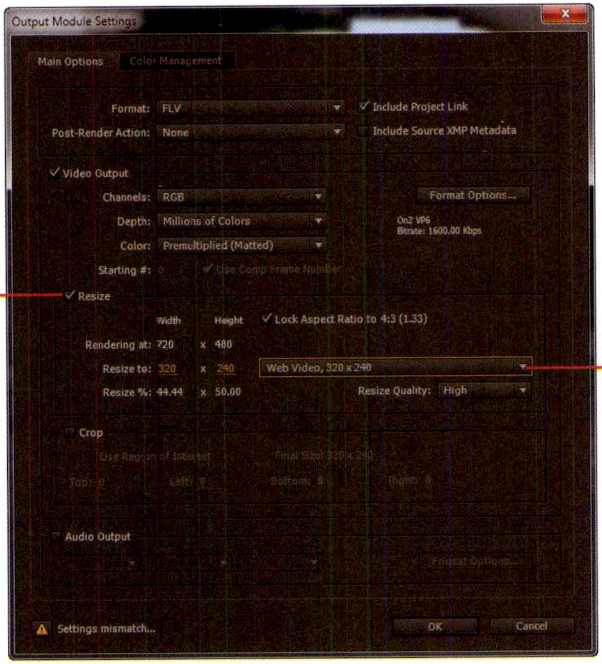

Resize check box ———

Custom menu ———

(screenshot: Output Module Settings dialog box)

Exporting a Production Logo for the Web

The method for exporting a movie is the same for all After Effects projects. However, when saving a file for the Web, the file extension that needs to be chosen is FLV.

In the Output Module Settings dialog box, the Resize option needs to be selected to reduce the size of the video from 720 x 480 px to a more manageable screen size, as shown in Figure 51. The Custom menu provides the Web Video 320 x 240 option, which you will use for the exercises in this book.

Import Photoshop text and convert it to editable text

1. Open Production Logo.aep, then save it as **Logo your name**.

2. Click **File** on the Menu bar, point to **Import** then click **File**.

3. Navigate to the drive and folder where the Chapter 2 Data Files are located, then click **Channel 6 Logo.psd**.

4. Leave the default settings in the Import File dialog box so that your Import File dialog box matches Figure 52, then click **Open**.

   Another dialog box appears, as shown in Figure 53.

5. If necessary, click the **Import Kind list arrow**, click **Composition**, then click **OK**.

   This option will allow you to edit the text that was created in Photoshop. Notice that there is now another composition on the Project panel titled Channel 6 Logo, as shown in Figure 54, and a folder with the various Photoshop layers.

   (continued)

Figure 52 *Import settings for importing Photoshop file*

Figure 54 *New composition based on Photoshop footage*

Figure 53 *Choosing Composition from the Import Kind menu*

Figures © Cengage Learning 2013

Figure 55 *Channel 6 Logo composition*

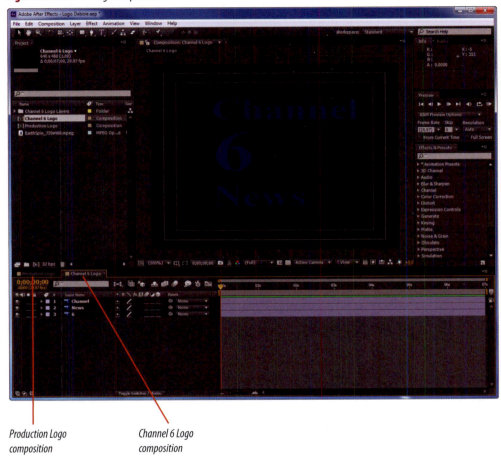

Production Logo
composition

Channel 6 Logo
composition

6. Double-click **Channel 6 Logo** on the Project panel to make it active on the Timeline panel and on the Composition panel, then compare your screen to Figure 55.

The Channel 6 Logo composition has three layers that were preserved from Photoshop during the import process when the composition option was selected. Each individual layer appears on the Timeline panel.

(continued)

Figure © Cengage Learning 2013

Lesson 3   Create a Production Logo

7. Click the **Channel layer** on the Timeline panel, click **Layer** on the Menu bar, then click **Convert to Editable Text**.

   The layer is converted to an editable After Effects text layer, as shown in Figure 56, and is no longer a Photoshop file.

8. Right-click the **News layer**, then click **Convert to Editable Text**.

9. Convert Layer 3 to editable text.

   All three layers on the Channel 6 Logo composition are text layers, as shown in Figure 57.

10. Close the Channel 6 Logo composition.

11. Save your project and leave it open for the next exercise.

You imported a Photoshop file as a composition, then converted the Photoshop layers to After Effects text layers so the text would be editable.

Figure 56 *Photoshop layer converted to editable text*

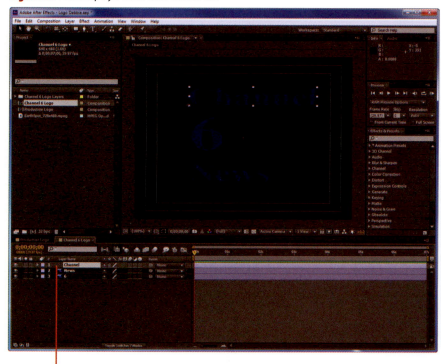

Editable text

Figure 57 *Converted text layers on the Channel 6 Logo composition*

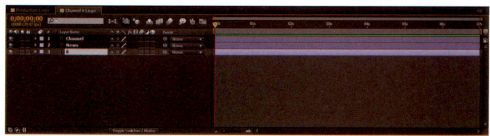

Figures © Cengage Learning 2013

Figure 58 *Channel 6 Logo composition nested in Production Logo composition*

Channel 6 Logo composition

Channel 6 Logo composition

Channel 6 Logo composition

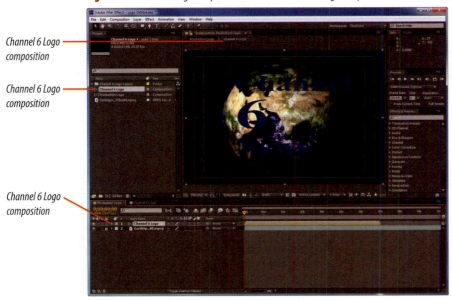

Figure 59 *Composition Navigator*

Composition Navigator

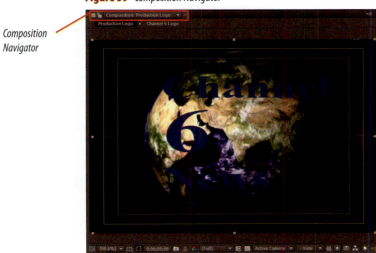

Nest a composition

1. Open the Logo *your name* project file, if necessary.

2. Click the **Production Logo composition** to activate it on the Timeline panel.

3. Drag the **Channel 6 Logo** composition from the Project panel to the **Production Logo composition** so that it is in the Layer 1 position, as shown in Figure 58.

   You are nesting one composition inside the other. This will allow you to switch between the two compositions, and to continue to format the text so that you will be able to preview your formatting changes while you work. The Composition Navigator bar appears on the Composition panel when there is more than one composition, as shown in Figure 59.

   (continued)

4. Click the **Composition Navigator list arrow**, then click **Channel 6 Logo** to switch to the Channel 6 Logo composition.

The Channel 6 Logo composition appears on the Composition panel, as shown in Figure 60.

5. Save your project and leave it open for the next lesson.

You nested a composition and navigated between compositions using the Composition Navigator on the Composition panel.

Format text

1. Open the Logo *your name* project file, if necessary.

2. Verify that the Channel 6 Logo composition is active on the Composition panel, and that the Text workspace is active.

3. Click the **Selection tool** on the Tools panel, then click **Channel** on the Composition panel, as shown in Figure 61.

(continued)

Figure 60 *Channel 6 Logo composition*

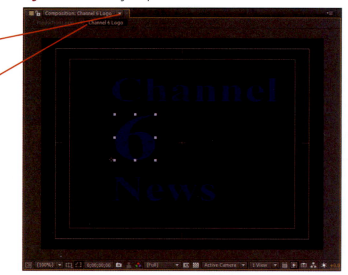

Composition
Navigator
list arrow

Channel 6 Logo

Figure 61 *Channel selected with Selection tool*

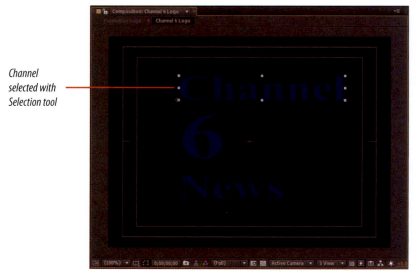

Channel
selected with
Selection tool

Figures © Cengage Learning 2013

Figure 62 *Activating the Stroke Color button*

Stroke Color button

Figure 63 *Formatting the stroke using the Character panel*

Stroke width

4. On the Character panel, click the **Stroke Color button**, as shown in Figure 62, to bring it in front of the Fill Color button.

5. Click the **Stroke Color button** again.

   The Text Color dialog box opens. Because the Stroke Color button is in front of the Fill Color button on the Character panel, the color you choose will be applied to the stroke—or border—of the text characters.

6. Click **White (#FFFFFF)**, then click **OK**.

7. Change the Stroke width to **0.5 px** as shown in Figure 63.

8. Click the **Composition Navigator list arrow**, then click **Production Logo** to preview the changes to "Channel" in front of the video footage, as shown in Figure 64.

9. Return to the Channel 6 Logo composition on the Composition panel.

(continued)

Figure 64 *Previewing the changes to the Production Logo composition*

Production Logo composition

Stroke color added to Channel

Lesson 3   Create a Production Logo

10. Make the same color and stroke width changes to the stroke for the "6" and the "News" text, then compare your Composition panel to Figure 65.

TIP You can format both items at the same time by pressing and holding [Shift] as you select them, then making your formatting selections on the Character panel.

11. Click the **Selection tool** on the Tools panel, press and hold [**Shift**], click **Channel**, click **6**, click **News**, click the **Character panel options button** , then click **Small Caps**.

12. With the text layers still selected on the Composition panel, click **Window** on the Menu bar, then click **Align**.

    The Align panel opens.

13. Click the **Align Layers to list arrow**, click **Composition**, then click the **horizontal center alignment button** , as shown in Figure 66.

(continued)

Figure 65 *Strokes applied to all three text layers*

Channel 6 Logo

Figure 66 *Align panel*

Align Layers to menu

Horizontal center alignment

Figure 67 *Edited text layers*

Figure 68 *Preview of Production Logo with animated text*

Lesson 3 Create a Production Logo

14. Preview your changes on the Production Logo composition panel, as shown in Figure 67.

15. Save your project and leave it open for the next exercise.

Using the Character panel, you edited text by adding a stroke and changing the font style to small caps. You also worked with the Align panel to align the text so that it is horizontally centered.

Animate text

1. Open the Logo *your name* project file, if necessary.

2. Activate the **Channel 6 Logo** composition on the Composition panel, then change the workspace to **Effects**.

3. Click the **Selection tool** on the Tools panel, select all three text layers then place the CTI at **0;00;00;00**.

4. Click the **Effects & Presets panel options button**, then click **Browse Presets**.

   Adobe Bridge launches the Presets preview.

5. Double-click the **Text folder**, then double-click **Lights and Optical**.

6. Right-click **Bubble Pulse**, point to **Place**, then click **In After Effects**.

   The Bubble Pulse animated preset is applied to all three text layers.

7. Select the **Production Logo composition** on the Composition panel, click the **Play/Pause button** on the Preview panel to play the composition, then compare your preview to Figure 68.

TIP Select Composition Preview RAM Preview if the preview is running too slow.

(continued)

8. Save your project and leave it open for the next exercise.

You added an animated preset to the three text layers and then previewed the composition.

Export a production logo for the Web

1. Open your Logo *your name* project file, if necessary.

2. Use the Composition Navigator to select the **Production Logo composition**.

You need to select the Production Logo composition because it is the root composition; the root composition is the one that is exported.

3. Click **Composition** on the Menu bar, then click **Add to Render Queue**.

4. Click **Lossless** next to Output Module on the Render Queue panel.

5. In the Output Module Settings dialog box, make the following selections: Format: **FLV**; check the **Resize check box**; Custom: **Web Video, 320 x 240**, as shown in Figure 69, then click **OK**.

You selected the FLV (Flash Video) file format because you are planning on using this for the Web.

6. Click the text to the right of the Output To heading on the Render Queue panel.

(continued)

Figure 69 *Output settings for Web*

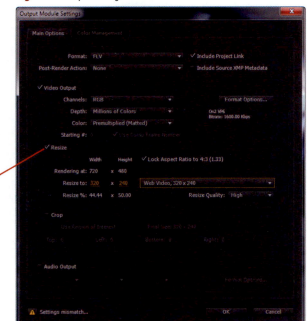

Check Resize

Figure © Cengage Learning 2013

Working in Adobe After Effects CS6

Figure 70 *Logo Final file*

7. Name your movie **Logo Final** *your name*, select your Data Files folder, then click **Save**.

8. Click the **Render button** on the Render Queue panel.

9. Locate Logo Final *your name*.flv where you save your work, then double-click the filename to see your movie, as shown in Figure 70.

10. Save and close the project.

You exported your movie for the Web using the FLV file format.

Create a
TITLE SEQUENCE

What You'll Do

Figure © Cengage Learning 2013

 In this lesson, you will create a title sequence.

Working with Keyframes

You worked with keyframes in Premiere Pro when you customized motion effects on the Effect Controls panel. Keyframes work much the same way in After Effects.

You can work with keyframes in either layer bar mode or Graph Editor mode. Layer bar mode is the default displayed on the Timeline panel. The duration of a layer is shown as a bar with its keyframes aligned vertically with their properties, as shown in Figure 71. Graph Editor mode shows keyframes in value and speed graphs, as shown in Figure 72. You will be using layer bar mode. A keyframe marks the point in time when you specify a change in value to a layer property such as position, scale, or opacity. Refer to Table 2-1 for more transform property shortcut keys. If you do not specify at least two keyframes when you change the value of a property, that value remains for the duration of the layer.

To activate keyframes on a specific property, the stopwatch icon on the Timeline needs

Figure 71 *Layer bar mode*

Figure © Cengage Learning 2013

to be selected, as shown in Figure 73. Once the keyframes are activated, the keyframe navigator is displayed. The keyframe navigator includes the Go to next and Go to previous keyframe buttons and the Add or remove keyframe at current time button. The yellow diamond on the Timeline represents the selected keyframe. If you click the Add or remove keyframe button, a keyframe is either added or removed at the location of the CTI. You can then quickly jump between keyframes with the Go to next and previous keyframe buttons. The keyframe navigator is specific to each layer property.

Keyframes can be deleted by selecting them and pressing [Delete], or to remove all the keyframes for a layer property, click the stopwatch button for that property. When you click the stopwatch, the value of the property defaults to the value at the location of the CTI.

In the previous lesson, keyframes were created when you used animation presets. Keyframes will be created automatically when you create motion paths in this lesson.

Working with Motion Paths

When you animate properties that can be changed over space as well as time, the movement is shown as a motion path. A **motion path** is a series of dots; each dot indicates the position of the layer at each frame. The number of dots indicates the relative speed of the layer: the closer the dots, the slower the speed; the farther apart, the faster the speed.

Figure 72   *Graph Editor mode*

Figure 73   *Working with keyframes*

Add or remove keyframe at current time button

Go to previous keyframe button

Go to next keyframe button

Inactive stopwatch

Active stopwatch

Selected keyframe

A path consists of two parts, segments and vertices (plural for vertex), as shown in Figure 74. A **vertex** is a point at which the direction of a path changes. A **segment** is the line or curve that connects two vertices. Motion paths can be modified using the Selection tool, the Add Vertex tool, or the Delete Vertex tool. The Selection tool allows you to move an existing vertex point, or to activate the direction handles and reshape the path, as shown in Figure 75. The Add and Delete Vertex tools allow you to add or delete vertex points to make adjustments that are more detailed to your motion path as needed.

After Effects includes the Motion Sketch panel, as shown in Figure 76, which records a motion path for you. You start by clicking the Start Capture button on the Motion Sketch panel. Recording begins when you click the relevant layer on the Composition panel; recording ends when you release the mouse button or the composition duration ends. The Motion Sketch panel records the position of the layer and the speed at which you draw, and generates a Position keyframe at each frame.

When working with the Motion Sketch panel, it is important to note that you are not able to adjust the start time of the recording. Keyframes are generated at the beginning of the Timeline. If you have set keyframes for other properties, those generated by the Motion Sketch panel are not affected.

A few options can be adjusted on the Motion Sketch panel, including the following:

Capture speed at: If the capture speed is set to 100%, the playback speed matches what was recorded. If the capture speed is greater than 100%, the recording plays back more slowly than what was recorded.

Figure 74 *Motion path*

Vertex point   Segment

Figure 75 *Adjusting a direction handle on a motion path*

Vertex point   Direction handle

Figure 76 *Motion Sketch panel*

Figures © Cengage Learning 2013

Smoothing: Smoothing eliminates unnecessary keyframes from a motion path; a higher value creates a smoother curve, but a value that is too high causes you to lose the shape of the curve.

Show: The Wireframe view displays a wireframe view of your layer while you are sketching, and the Background view displays a static view of the contents of the frame when you begin sketching.

Trimming Layers

There may be times when you do not want to use all of the frames in a movie clip. In addition, quite often you do not want a text or shape layer's duration to be the same length as the composition. Trimming a layer is a way to change its duration.

On the Timeline panel, each layer is represented by a duration bar. The **In point** marks the beginning of the layer, and the **Out point** marks the end. The span between the In point and the Out point is called the **duration**. The **layer duration bar** is the bar that extends between the In point and the Out point, as shown in Figure 77. Changing the In and Out points on the Layer panel or the Timeline panel is called **trimming**. Trimming a layer

does not affect the source footage or the original source file.

Trimming or extending a layer on the Timeline panel with keyboard shortcuts is probably the quickest and easiest way to adjust its duration. Place the CTI where you want to set the In or Out point. To set the In point at the current time, press [Alt][[] (Win) or [option][[] (Mac). To set the Out point at the current time, press [Alt][]] (Win) or [option][]] (Mac).

Once you have adjusted the duration of the various layers, After Effects has an automated

Figure 77 *Examples of In and Out points*

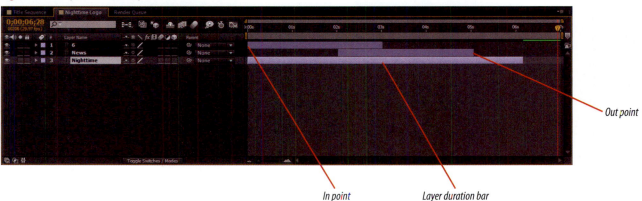

Out point

In point   Layer duration bar

process for arranging them that may prove beneficial. The Sequence Layers keyframe assistant automatically arranges layers based on the order that you select, as shown in Figure 78.

The Sequence Layers command is just one of the several Keyframe Assistant options designed to work with keyframes. Another example is Easy Ease, which creates smooth transitions in and out of a keyframe by adjusting the influence of the keyframe. **Influence** regulates speed of change as motion advances toward and retreats from a keyframe. Variations of Easy Ease are Easy Ease In and Easy Ease Out, which automatically adjust the influence in and out of a keyframe, respectively. The Keyframe Assistant command is found on the Animation menu.

Figure 78 *Example of sequencing layers*

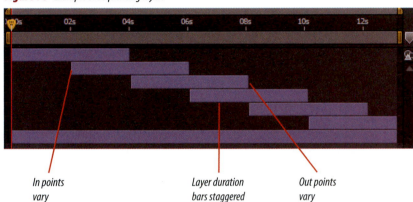

In points
vary

Layer duration
bars staggered

Out points
vary

Figure © Cengage Learning 2013

Figure 79 *Selecting multiple text layers*

Current time
display at 4
seconds

Layers #1—#6
selected

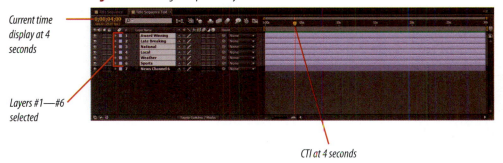

CTI *at 4 seconds*

Figure 80 *Trimmed text layers*

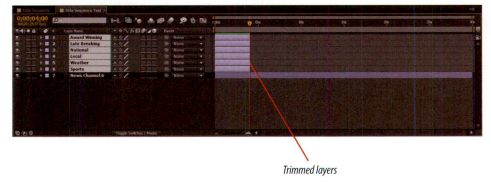

Trimmed layers

Lesson 4   Create a Title Sequence

Trim layers

1. Open Title Sequence.aep, then save it as **Title Sequence *your name***.

   Notice that there are two compositions already created, Title Sequence and Title Sequence Text.

2. Use the Composition Navigator to select the **Title Sequence Text composition**.

   You will be working with the text layers in the Title Sequence Text composition.

3. Click the **Current time display** on the Timeline panel, type **400**, then press [**Enter**] (Win) or [**return**] (Mac).

   The CTI 🛡 moves to the 4-second mark on the time ruler.

4. On the Timeline panel, use the **Selection tool** ▶ to select **Text Layer #1**, then [Shift]-click **Text Layer #6**, as shown in Figure 79.

5. Press [**Alt**][**[**] (Win) or [**option**][**[**] (Mac) to trim the layers to the CTI at 4 seconds, as shown in Figure 80.

   Notice that Layer 7 did not change because it was not selected.

6. Save your project and leave it open for the next exercise.

You trimmed text layers 1 through 6 on the Title Sequence Text composition.

Create a motion path

1. Open the Title Sequence *your name* project file, if necessary.

2. Select the **Title Sequence Text composition** on the Composition panel, then verify that the CTI  is at 0;00;00;00.

3. Change the workspace to **Minimal**.

4. Click **Window** on the Menu bar, then click **Motion Sketch**.

5. Click **Window** on the Menu bar, click **Preview**, then drag the **Preview panel** so it is below the Motion Sketch panel, as shown in Figure 81.

6. Turn on the Title/Action Safe margins.

7. Click the **Selection tool** on the Tools panel, click in the gray area of the Composition panel, then click **Award Winning** on the Composition panel.

8. On the Motion Sketch panel choose the following settings: Capture speed at: **50%**; Smoothing: **20**; Wireframe check box: **Check**, as shown in Figure 82.

(continued)

Figure 81 *Minimal workspace with Motion Sketch & Preview panels*

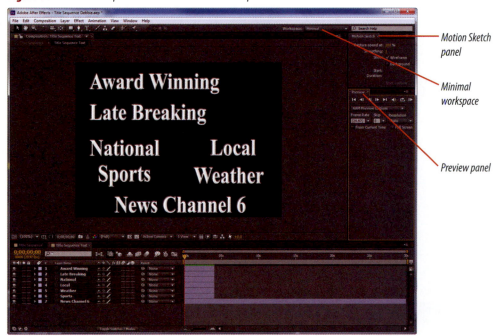

Motion Sketch panel

Minimal workspace

Preview panel

Figure 82 *Motion Sketch panel*

Smoothing

Capture speed

Wireframe

Figures © Cengage Learning 2013

Figure 83 *Drawing a path with the Motion Sketch panel*

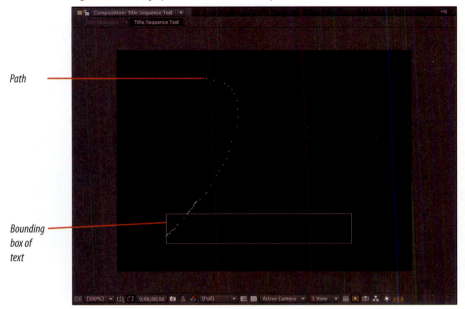

Path

Bounding
box of
text

9. Click the **Start Capture button**
   Start Capture   on the Motion Sketch
   panel, drag **Award Winning** on the Composition
   panel around the panel in an arc until you reach
   the bottom-left corner, just inside the Title Safe
   margin, as shown in Figure 83.

   The text layer and the bounding box disappear
   during the recording process. You will see a
   bounding box representing the size of your
   text layer and a path while you are dragging.
   Recording will stop when you release the
   mouse button.

10. Repeat Steps 7 - 9 for Layers 2 through 6 using
    the same settings on the Motion Sketch panel
    and creating different arcs.

    Placing the CTI 🛡 at 4 seconds will allow you
    to see the ending positions for the text layers as
    you work, as shown in the example in Figure 84.
    This will help you with the placement of the
    text so there is no overlap.

    (continued)

11. Return the CTI  to **0;00;00;00**, then select the **Title Sequence composition**.

12. Preview the Title Sequence composition by clicking the **Play/Pause button** ▶ on the Preview panel.

    You should see the preview of the animated text with the Seattle skyline.

13. Save your project and leave it open for the next exercise.

In this lesson, you placed the text on a motion path.

Modify the Scale property

1. Open the Title Sequence *your name* project file, if necessary.

2. Select the **Title Sequence Text composition**, then verify that the CTI 😊 is at **0;00;00;00**.

3. Reset the workspace to the **Effects** workspace.

TIP You may need to select Reset "Effects" on the Workspace menu if the workspace is already set to Effects.

4. Select **Text layers #1** through **#7**, then press [**S**].

    Pressing [S] filters the Scale property on all of the selected layers. See Table 2-1 for more Transform shortcuts.

    (continued)

Figure 84 *Previewing the end position of text*

CTI

Figure © Cengage Learning 2013

TABLE 2-1: TRANSFORM SHORTCUTS	
Shortcut	**Description**
[**P**]	Position
[**S**]	Scale
[**R**]	Rotation
[**T**]	Opacity
[**U**]	Properties with keyframes or expressions
[**UU**]	Properties that have been modified
[**Shift**]	Hold while pressing the above shortcuts, to reveal more than one property at the same time

© Cengage Learning 2013

Figure 85 *Working with the Scale property*

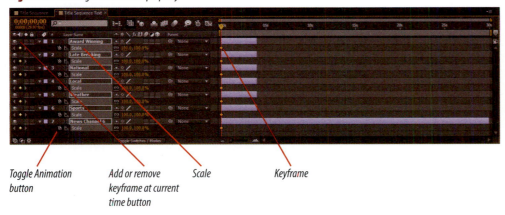

Toggle Animation
button

Add or remove
keyframe at current
time button

Scale

Keyframe

Figure 86 *Setting a beginning and ending keyframe*

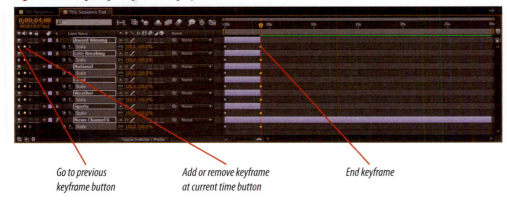

Go to previous
keyframe button

Add or remove keyframe
at current time button

End keyframe

Figures © Cengage Learning 2013

Lesson 4   Create a Title Sequence

5. Click the **Toggle Animation button** on the Timeline to activate keyframes for Scale, as shown in Figure 85.

6. Drag the **CTI** to 4 seconds, then create a keyframe for each Text layer by clicking the **Add or remove keyframe at current time button**, as shown in Figure 86.

7. Click the **Go to previous keyframe button**, while leaving all the layers still selected.

(continued)

8. To the right of Scale on the Timeline panel, change 100.0% to **50.0%**, then compare your window to Figure 87.

   The proportions are linked so you only need to change one of them. All the text layers change size.

9. With all the text layers still selected, press [**S**] to close the Scale property.

10. Return the CTI  to **0;00;00;00**, then select the **Title Sequence composition**.

11. Preview the Title Sequence composition by clicking the **Play/Pause button** ▶ on the Preview panel.

12. Save your project and leave it open for the next lesson.

You changed the Scale property for all of the text layers.

Arrange layers over time

1. Open the Title Sequence *your name* project file, if necessary.

2. Select the **Title Sequence Text composition**, if necessary, then verify that the CTI  is at **0;00;00;00**.

3. Click the **Selection tool** ▸ on the Tools panel, press and hold [**Shift**], then click **Text layer #1** through **Text layer #6** on the Timeline panel.

4. Click **Animation** on the Menu bar, point to **Keyframe Assistant**, then click **Sequence Layers**.

(continued)

Figure 87 *Preview after changing scale*

Scale

Figure 88 *Sequence Layers dialog box*

Overlap —————
Duration —————
Transition —————

Figure 89 *Layers arranged across time*

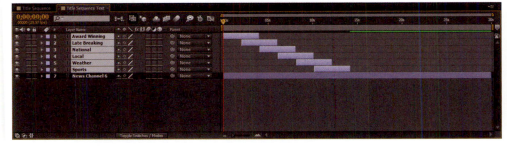

The Sequence Layers dialog box opens, giving you the option to overlap the layers, choose a transition type, and set the length of a transition. If you choose not to overlap the layers, the other selections become inactive and your layers are arranged one right after the other with no overlap.

TIP To leave a gap between your layers, click the Overlap check box and enter a negative number in the Duration field.

5. Make the following settings in the Sequence Layers dialog box: Overlap: **check mark**; Duration: **0;00;02;00**; Transition: **Cross Dissolve Front and Back Layers**, then compare your dialog box to Figure 88.

6. Click **OK**.

   The Layers are arranged across time based on their selection order, as shown in Figure 89. Each of the motion paths you created with the individual layers in the last exercise moves with its Text layer to its new position in time.

7. Click **Composition** on the Menu bar, then click **Composition Settings**.

   The Composition Settings dialog box opens. The duration is currently 0;00;30;00. You need to adjust the duration of the composition to match that of the Title Sequence composition.

8. Change the Duration setting to **0;00;13;05** and click **OK**.

   The Title Sequence Text composition now matches the duration of the Title Sequence composition.

(continued)

9. Compare your Timeline panel to Figure 90.

10. Return the CTI 🛡 to **0;00;00;00**, then select the **Title Sequence composition**.

11. Preview the Title Sequence composition by clicking the **Play/Pause button** ▶ on the Preview panel.

12. Save your project and leave it open for the next exercise.

You arranged Text layers 1 through 6 over time, and modified the duration of the Title Sequence Text composition. You then previewed your changes on the Title Sequence composition panel.

Modify a motion track

1. Open your Title Sequence *your name* project file, if necessary.

2. Select the **Title Sequence Text composition**, then verify that the CTI 🛡 is at **0;00;00;00**.

3. Verify that the workspace is set to Minimal, with the Motion Sketch and Preview panels displayed.

4. Move the CTI 🛡 to **0;00;03;00** so that you can see the motion path that was previously created.

5. Click the **Selection tool** 🔧 on the Tools panel, click in the gray area of the Composition panel, then click **Late Breaking** on the Composition panel then compare your screen to Figure 91, keeping in mind that your path will vary.

(continued)

Figure 90 *Title Sequence Text composition*

Composition duration shortened

Figure 91 *Motion path for Text layer 2*

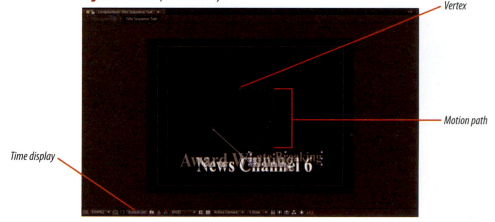

Vertex

Motion path

Time display

Figure 92 *Adjusting a motion path*

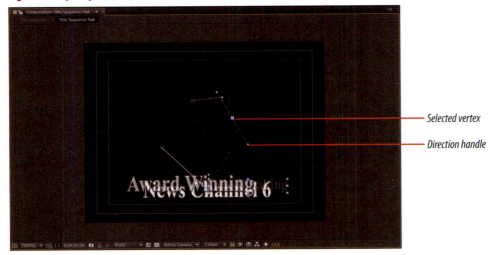

Selected vertex

Direction handle

Figure 93 *Adding more vertices*

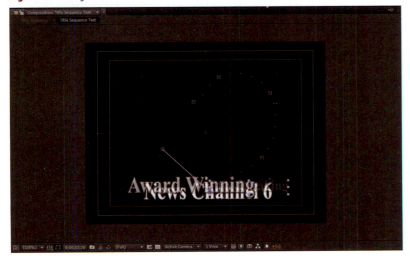

Figures © Cengage Learning 2013

6. Click a **vertex**, indicated by a square on the motion path, as shown in Figure 92.

   Direction handles appear so that you can adjust the curvature of the arc.

7. Click and hold the **Pen tool** on the Tools panel until the menu is displayed, then click the **Add Vertex tool**.

   The Add Vertex tool allows you to add additional points on the path that you have already drawn to create more detail, as shown in Figure 93.

8. Return the CTI to **0;00;00;00**, then select the **Title Sequence composition**.

9. Preview the Title Sequence composition by clicking the **Play/Pause button** on the Preview panel.

10. Save your project as an MPEG2 file, named **Title Sequence Final** *your name*.

In this lesson, you worked with motion paths and saved your project as an MPEG 2 movie file.

Explore the After Effects workspace.

1. Click Start on the Menu bar, point to All Programs, then click Adobe After Effects CS6 (Win) or open the Finder from the dock and click Applications from the sidebar, click the Adobe applications folder, then click Adobe After Effects CS6 (Mac).
2. Click the Close button in the Welcome dialog box.
3. Click Window on the Menu bar, point to Workspace, then click Effects.
4. Click Window on the Menu bar, point to Workspace, then click Minimal.
5. Click Window on the Menu bar, point to Workspace, then click Standard to change the workspace back to Standard.

Create a composition & import footage.

1. Click Composition on the Menu bar, then click New Composition.
2. Click the Preset list arrow, then click NTSC DV.
3. Change the Duration value to 0;00;07;00 by entering 700. (*Hint*: Pressing [Enter] (Win) or [return] (Mac) after entering 700 will close the Composition Settings dialog box.)
4. Click File on the Menu bar, point to Import, then click File.
5. Import us_10.jpg from your Data Files folder. (*Hint*: Be sure that the JPEG Sequence check box is not checked.)
6. Drag us_10.jpg to the Composition panel to add the footage to the Timeline panel.
7. Click File on the Menu bar, point to Save As, click Save As, type **Digital Graphic** *your name*, click Save then leave the file open.

Create layers and add effects and presets.

1. Click the Choose grid and guide options button on the Composition panel, then click Title/Action Safe.
2. Repeat Step 2 to select Grid, then Rulers.
3. Select the Timeline panel.
4. Click Layer on the Menu bar, point to New, then click Shape Layer.
5. Press and hold the Rectangle tool on the Tools panel until the menu is displayed, click the Rounded Rectangle tool, then draw a rounded rectangle with a fill color of #FA8E1C, and a stroke color of #953C01, and a width of 2 px, in the bottom-left corner of the title safe area on the Composition panel. (*Note*: Draw the rectangle approximately 5 grid squares wide and 3 grid squares tall.)
6. With the rounded rectangle still selected, click Effect on the Menu bar, point to Perspective, then click Bevel Edges.
7. On the Effect Controls panel, modify the Edge Thickness to .05.
8. With the rounded rectangle still selected, click Effect on the Menu bar, point to Stylize, then click Color Emboss.
9. Click the Choose grid and guide options button, then click Grid to remove the check mark.
10. Click Window on the Menu bar, point to Workspace, then click Text.
11. Right-click the Timeline panel, point to New, then click Text.
12. On the Composition panel, type **News 6**, press [Enter] (Win) or [return] (Mac), then type **Nighttime**.

13. Click the Selection tool on the Tools panel, then select the text on the Composition panel.
14. On the Character panel make the following selections: Font: Verdana; Font style: Bold; Fill color: White; Font size; 12 px; Stroke color: Black; Stroke width: 1 px.
15. Click the All Caps button on the Character panel, then click the Center text button on the Paragraph panel. Change the workspace to Effects.
16. Move the News 6 Nighttime text above the rounded rectangle.
17. On the Effects & Presets panel search for the "drop shadow" effect.
18. With the Text layer still selected, double-click the drop shadow effect to apply the effect. (*Hint*: Remove the search from the search box by clicking the X.)
19. Click Animation on the Menu bar, then click Browse Presets.
20. Open the Curves and Spins folder inside the Text folder and select Newton.ffx.
21. Click the Play/Pause button on the Preview panel to preview the effect in the Composition panel.
22. Right-click on Netwon.ffx, point to Place, then click In After Effects.
23. Save your project and leave it open.

Make a movie.

1. Select the digital graphic composition, click Composition on the Menu bar, then click Add to Render Queue.
2. Click Lossless next to Output Module on the Render Queue panel.

3. Click the Format list arrow, click MPEG2, then click OK.

4. Click the text to the right of the Output To heading on the Render Queue panel, name your movie **Digital Graphic Final** *your name*, then save it in your Chapter 2 Data Files folder.

5. Click the Render button on the Render Queue panel to render the movie.

6. Open Digital Graphic Final *your name*.mpeg, to see your movie, as shown in Figure 94.

7. Close your project.

Figure 94 *Completed Skills Review Part 1*

Figure © Cengage Learning 2013

Import Photoshop text.

1. Open Nighttime.aep, then save it as **Nighttime your name** in your Chapter 2 Data Files folder.
2. Change the workspace to Text.
3. Import the Nighttime Logo.psd footage to the Project panel. (*Hint*: Leave the default settings on the Import File dialog box, Import As: Footage; and leave the Photoshop Sequence check box deselected.)
4. In the Nighttime Logo.psd dialog box, make the following selection: Import Kind: Composition.
5. Double-click Nighttime Logo on the Project panel to open the composition in its own Timeline and Composition panels.
6. Shift-click to select all the Photoshop layers, right-click, then select Convert to Editable Text.
7. Save your project and leave it open for the next step.

Format text.

1. With the Selection tool, deselect any selected layers, then select Nighttime on the Composition panel.
2. On the Character panel, double-click the Stroke button to bring it forward and activate it.
3. Click White (#FFFFFF) in the Text Color dialog box, then click OK.
4. Change the Stroke width to 0.5 px.
5. Make the same changes to the stroke on "6" and on "News".

6. Select Nighttime, 6, and News by using the [Shift]-click method, click the Character panel options button, then click Small Caps.
7. With all the text layers still selected, change the Font size to 13 px.
8. Save your project and leave it open for the next step.

Trim layers.

1. With the Nighttime Logo composition still active, Shift-click to select all the text layers.
2. Click the Current time display, type **300**, then press [Enter] (Win) or [return] (Mac).
3. Click the Selection tool, click Text Layer #1 on the Timeline panel, press and hold [Shift], then click Text Layer #3.
4. Press [Alt][[]] (Win) or [option][[]] (Mac) to trim the layers to the location of the CTI at 3 seconds.
5. Save your project and leave it open for the next step.

Create a motion path.

1. Verify that the Nighttime Logo composition is still active, and that the CTI is at 0;00;00;00.
2. Drag Skyline.jpg to the Timeline panel so it is layer #4. (*Note*: You will be using this footage while you draw your motion path to help you with placement; you will delete it from the Nighttime Logo composition when you are finished.)

3. Change the workspace to Minimal, then add the Motion Sketch panel and Preview panel, if necessary.
4. Turn on Title/Action Safe margins.
5. Click Nighttime on the Composition panel.
6. On the Motion Sketch panel, enter the following: Capture speed at: 50%; Smoothing: 20; Wireframe check box: Check.
7. On the Motion Sketch panel, click the Start Capture button, click Nighttime on the Composition panel, then drag the text around the panel in an arc from the bottom-left corner around to the right so the text settles in the upper-left corner just inside the Title Safe margin. (*Hint*: Create the appearance of the text rising from behind the buildings.)
8. Repeat this procedure, keeping the same settings on the Motion Sketch panel for Layers 2 and 3.
9. Preview the Nighttime Logo composition by clicking the Play/Pause button on the Preview panel.
10. Save your project and leave it open for the next step.

Modify a motion track.

1. Verify that the Nighttime Logo composition is still active.
2. Move your CTI to 3 seconds so you can see the motion path that was created in the last step, and the text layers.

3. Click Nighttime on the Composition panel with the Selection tool.
4. Click a vertex, then make adjustments to the curves as you think appropriate.
5. If needed, use the Add/Delete Vertex tool to make additional adjustments to the Nighttime layer.
6. Repeat this process to Layer 2 and 3 as needed.
7. Select Layer 4 then press [Delete].
8. Preview the Nighttime Logo composition by clicking the Play/Pause button on the Preview panel.

Animate text.

1. Verify that the Nighttime Logo composition is still active, then change the workspace to Effects.
2. Select all three text layers and be sure the CTI is at 0;00;00;00.
3. Click the Effects & Presets options button, then click Browse Presets.
4. Double-click the Text folder, double-click the Organic folder, right-click Insects.ffx, point to Place, then click In After Effects.
5. Click the Play/Pause button on the Preview panel to play the composition, return the CTI to 0;00;00;00 when you have finished previewing.
6. Save your project and leave it open for the next step.

Arrange layers over time.

1. Select Nighttime Logo from the Composition Navigator, if necessary, then verify that the CTI is at 0;00;00;00.
2. On the Timeline panel, click Text layer #1, press and hold [Shift], then click Text layer #3.
3. Click Animation on the Menu bar, point to Keyframe Assistant, then click Sequence Layers.
4. Choose the following settings: Overlap: check mark; Duration: 0;00;01;00; Transition: Off.
5. Click OK.
6. Click Composition on the Menu bar, then click Composition Settings.
7. Change the Duration to 0;00;09;00.
8. Select Title Sequence on the Composition Navigator.
9. Drag the Nighttime Logo composition to the Timeline panel to the #1 position in the stacking order.
10. Drag the Nighttime composition to the Timeline panel again, to the #2 position in the stacking order.
11. [Shift]-click Layer #1, then click Layer #2.
12. Click Animation on the Menu bar, point to Keyframe Assistant, then click Sequence Layers.
13. Click OK in the Sequence Layers dialog box , then uncheck Overlap, if necessary.

(*Note*: You do not want the layers to overlap so you are not making any selections.)
14. Save your project and leave it open for the next step.

Export production logo for the Web.

1. Select Title Sequence on the Composition Navigator.
2. Click Composition on the Menu bar, then click Add to Render Queue.
3. Click on Lossless next to Output Module on the Render Queue panel.
4. In the Output Module Settings dialog box make the following selections: Format: FLV; Resize: check mark; Custom: Web Video, 320 x 240; Audio Output: check mark.
5. Click the text to the right of the Output To heading on the Render Queue panel.
6. Name the movie **Nighttime Final *your name***, save it in your Chapter 2 Data Files folder, then click Save.
7. Click the Render button on the Render Queue panel.
8. Open Nighttime Final *your name*.flv to see your movie, as shown in Figure 95.
9. Close your project.

Figure 95 *Completed Skills Review Part 2*

Working in Adobe After Effects CS6

You and a coworker just completed training in After Effects. Your boss has asked that you collaborate on a small demo movie showing off some of the text animation presets that are available. So far your movie has a composition and text layers named after an animation preset. You are expected to complete the project for the next staff meeting.

1. Open Demo.aep, then save it as **Animation Preset Demo** *your name*.
2. Format the text on each text layer using the Character panel and layer styles.
3. Browse the animation presets to find the animation preset named for each text layer.
4. Apply the appropriate animation preset to the appropriate text layer. (*Hint*: Be sure the CTI is at 0;00;00;00 when you apply the preset.)
5. Trim the duration of the layers based on the length of the effect. (*Hint*: Press UU to see keyframes and help you decide where to place the Out point.)
6. Adjust the sequence of the layers so that the text does not all play at the same time, as shown in Figure 96. (*Hint*: Use the Sequence Layers command that can be found under Keyframe Assistant.)
7. Add the demo composition to the Render Queue and export the movie as an MPEG2 named **Animation Preset Demo Final** *your name*.

Figure 96 *Completed Project Builder 1*

Figure © Cengage Learning 2013

The elementary school principal in your district has heard about your video production class. The principal is planning a video to be presented at the school's annual awards ceremony in the spring and would like you to design a creative opening title sequence for the video that would be appropriate for elementary age students. She thinks that using many colorful shapes with vibrant music would be fantastic. She would like the video to last 25 seconds and include the name of the school and some slogans.

1. Create an After Effects project titled **Elementary Title Sequence**, with a composition with the default preset NTSC DV, and duration of 30 seconds. (*Note*: Select a background color of your choice.)
2. Create a minimum of five shape layers with your choice of shapes and colors and apply layer styles.
3. Create a text layer for the name of the school with your choice of formatting and layer styles. The name of the school is **Holmes Elementary School**.
4. Create a text layer for each of the following slogans with your choice of formatting and layer styles, as shown in Figure 97:
   - Believe & Succeed
   - Catch the Spirit
   - Knowledge is Power

5. Apply animation effects with motion paths and animation presets.
6. Adjust the duration of the various layers and sequence the layers to vary the timing of the layers.
7. Export the movie to the MPEG2 video format with the name **Elementary Title Sequence Final** *your name*.

Figure 97 *Completed Project Builder 2*

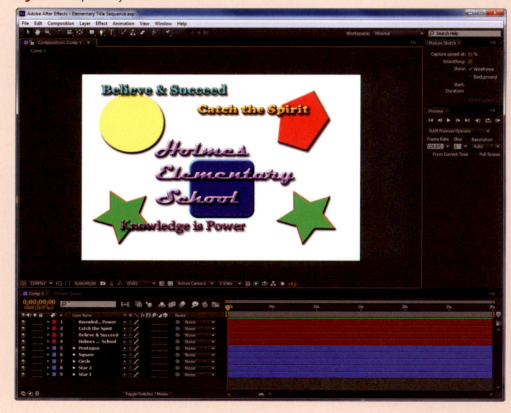

Figure © Cengage Learning 2013

Your video production teacher has asked you to create an animated production logo for your own video production company. He would like you to place this logo at the end of all the video projects you create while working through this book.

1. Come up with a creative title for your production company.
2. Create a composition with the NTSC DV Preset and Duration of 15 seconds, and the background color of your choice.
3. Obtain at least one good quality still image or video that works well with the theme of your production company.
4. Include a background audio clip. You may download one from the Internet, or look in the Audio folder that can be found with the resource files provided with this book. (*Note:* Be sure to check the terms of use regarding any media you may download to use with your project.)
5. Import your footage and create layers with the footage.
6. Create a text layer with the name of your production company, as shown in Figure 98.
7. Format your text, apply layer styles, and animate your text.
8. Add a shape layer to place behind the text, and add effects to the shape of your choice to enhance its look.
9. Your animated production logo should be exported so it is available for both MPEG2 and FLV formats; name your file after the name of your production company.

Figure 98 *Portfolio Project*

Figure © Cengage Learning 2013

Working in Adobe After Effects CS6

CHAPTER 3

CREATING A SOUNDTRACK IN
ADOBE AUDITION CS6

1. Explore Audition

2. Work with multitrack sessions

3. Clean Up Audio Files

CHAPTER 3
CREATING A SOUNDTRACK IN
ADOBE AUDITION CS6

Adobe Audition CS6 is a professional audio editing application designed to be easy to learn for those who are not sound professionals. Audition is compatible with most standalone audio files such as MP3, WAV, and WMA, as well as with files that combine video and audio, such as AVI, MPEG2, and FLV.

An Audition document is called a **session** and allows you to edit audio, create voiceovers, and produce your own musical scores. In addition, Audition supports round-trip editing with Premiere Pro. **Round-trip editing**

means you can edit an audio clip that has been imported into Premiere Pro in Audition and the updated audio clip then can be returned back to Premiere Pro, keeping you from having to import and export files.

In this chapter, you will explore the Audition workspace, import and play audio files, work with scores, and save your sessions to the Audition SESX format. The SESX file format provides maximum flexibility in editing and sharing files with Premiere Pro and After Effects.

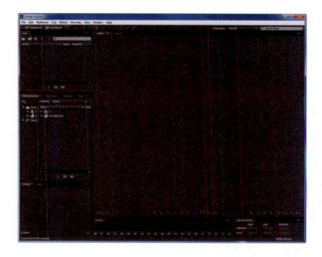

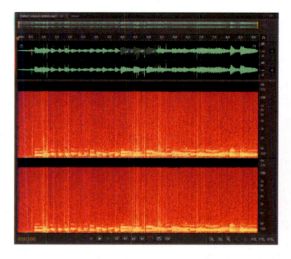

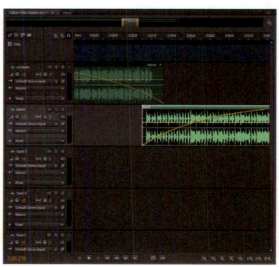

Figures © Cengage Learning 2013

Explore
AUDITION

What You'll Do

Figure © Cengage Learning 2013

 In this lesson, you will explore Audition and clean up an audio file.

Exploring the Audition Workspace

Adobe Audition, like Premiere Pro and After Effects, includes a number of preformatted, customizable workspaces that optimize the arrangement of panels for particular tasks. When you select one of the preformatted workspaces, the current workspace is adjusted accordingly. Figure 1 shows the default

Figure 1 *Default workspace*

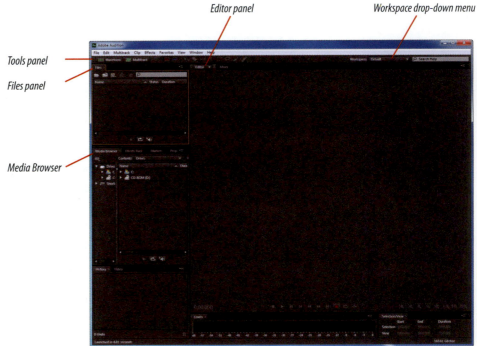

Figure © Cengage Learning 2013

workspace for Audition, which is called Default. The Default workspace is designed to optimize audio editing by providing a large view of the Editor panel.

The workspace can be changed by selecting a default workspace or by rearranging the panels to your individual preference. Default workspaces can be changed using the Workspace command on the Window menu or by making a selection from the drop-down menu on the Tools panel.

Panels can be moved by clicking and dragging panel tabs. As you drag the panel, an area becomes highlighted; this is called the drop zone, and provides a visual reference to where the panel can be placed.

If you wish to save a customized workspace, you may do so by selecting New Workspace on the Workspace menu or on the drop-down menu on the Tools panel.

Understanding Sound

Audition is designed for the non-musical professional to edit and create musical scores. However, an understanding of some fundamental digital audio concepts will help you as you work with Audition.

Sound is created by a vibration in the air created by an object that causes the air pressure to change. This vibration eventually reaches the eardrum causing it to vibrate, which is then interpreted as sound. The object creating the vibration could be vocal

cords, guitar strings, drums—anything that we interpret as making sound.

Sound is represented in a waveform, which is a line that visually depicts the variations in the waves being created by the air pressure, much like the way wind creates waves in water. Figure 2 shows a sample waveform. The line

at its high point, caused by higher pressure, is called its crest. Lower pressure is represented at the line's lowest point and is called its trough. When there is no air pressure, the sound wave is at zero, which is indicated by the red zero line in Figure 2. In Audition, you'll work with several properties that describe

Figure 2 *A sample waveform on the Editor panel*

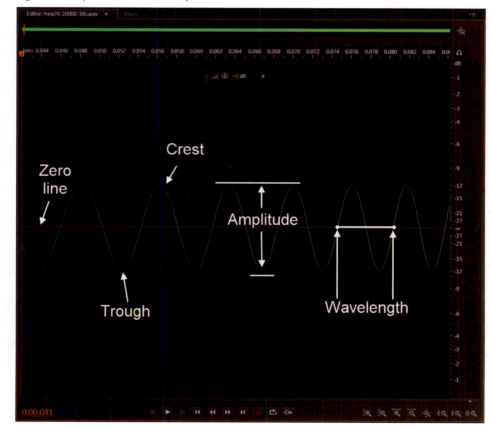

sound waveforms. Refer to Figure 2 as you read the definitions that follow. Amplitude is the change in pressure from crest to trough; high-amplitude waveforms are loud and low-amplitude waveforms are quiet. The number of cycles per second, measured in hertz, is called frequency. A wavelength is the distance in inches or centimeters measured between any two points, at the same height on the waveform. Waveforms and their properties can be viewed and edited in the waveform display on the Editor panel in Audition. The waveform is displayed on the Editor panel when you open an audio file in Audition or when you double-click an audio clip on the Files panel.

The waveform is displayed with either one or two channels. If you see two channels displayed one above the other, the audio file was recorded in stereo to give the sense of spatial placement of sound from two sound sources. If you only see one channel, the audio file is called a monophonic signal, or mono, and contains only one sound source.

Working with Audio Files

You can use Audition to import audio files or to record audio. A variety of audio and video file formats are supported, including mp3, WAV, AVI, and MPEG. Visit Audition Help to view the complete list. In this chapter, you will be working with audio files that have already been created. An audio file can be imported through the File menu, the Files panel, or the Media Browser. The Media Browser allows you to preview a file before you import it into your session. Audio can also be extracted from a CD with the Extract Audio From CD command. The Files panel organizes the references to all of the files used in a session and also lists the multitrack sessions, as shown in Figure 3. A multitrack allows you to combine more than one track of music to create a musical composition.

Figure 3 *Files panel displaying references*

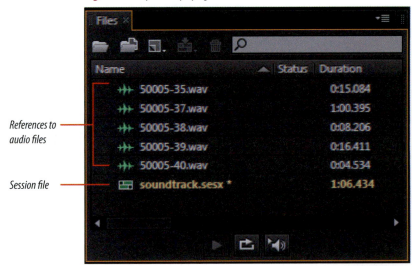

References to audio files

Session file

Working with External Devices

You can use a wide range of audio input devices, such as microphones and tape decks, and output devices, such as headphones and speakers. If you are having trouble with any device, check in the Audio Hardware section of the Preferences dialog box and refer to Adobe Help for more information for your particular device.

Figure © Cengage Learning 2013

Editor Views

Audition has two different editors that can be used when working with audio files. The Waveform Editor is used to edit individual files, as shown in Figure 4. The Multitrack Editor is used to mix multiple audio files and can be used to integrate them with video, as shown in Figure 5. To change the editor view, click the View button located on the toolbar at the top of the Audition workspace for the editor you would like to work in.

It is important to understand that the editors use different editing methods. The Waveform Editor uses a destructive method of editing. Destructive editing means that any changes that are made are permanent and cannot be undone. A destructive edit is not applied until you save the file. The Multitrack Editor uses a nondestructive method. Nondestructive editing means that the audio file is not changed permanently and can be undone. Nondestructive editing requires more processing power but provides greater flexibility. In this lesson, you will be working in the Waveform Editor.

Figure 4 *Waveform Editor*

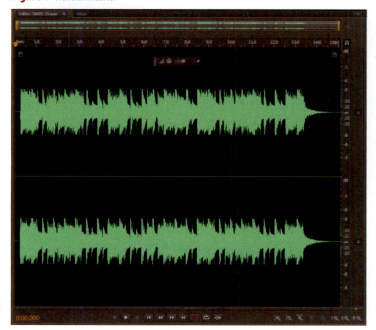

Figure 5 *Multitrack Editor*

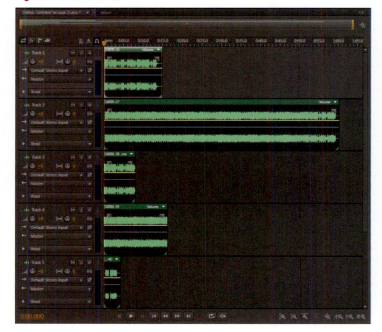

Figures © Cengage Learning 2013

Start Adobe Audition CS6 and explore the workspace

1. Click **Start** 🔵 on the Menu bar, point to **All Programs**, then click **Adobe Audition CS6** (Win) or open the Finder from the dock, click **Applications** from the sidebar, click the **Adobe applications folder**, then click **Adobe Audition CS6** (Mac).

   You may need to look in a subfolder if you have installed the Video Collection or Master Collection.

   TIP Pressing and holding [Shift] while starting Audition restores default preference settings.

2. Click **Window** on the Menu bar, point to **Workspace**, then click **Edit Audio to Video**.

   The Edit Audio to Video workspace is shown in Figure 6. The panels on the left are adjusted to make room for the Video panel at the top of the workspace.

3. Continue to click through the various workspaces and notice how the window changes for each one.

4. Return the workspace to the Default workspace.

   TIP After selecting Default, you may want to click Reset "Default" on the Workspace menu to ensure that the workspace has been reset properly.

5. Leave Adobe Audition open for the next exercise.

You started Audition CS6 and explored the workspace.

Figure 6 *Edit Audio to Video workspace*

Edit Audio to Video workspace

Video panel

Editor panel

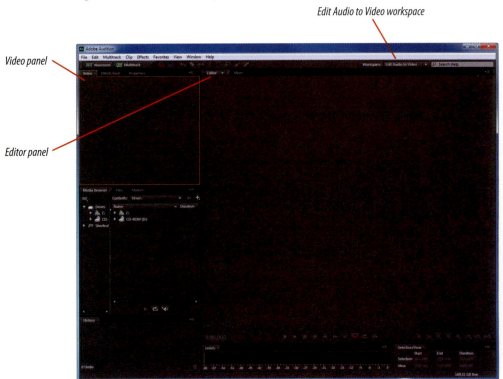

Figure © Cengage Learning 2013

Creating a Soundtrack in Adobe Audition CS6

Figure 7 *The Media Browser panel*

Media Browser panel

Click to view locations

Chapter 3 folder

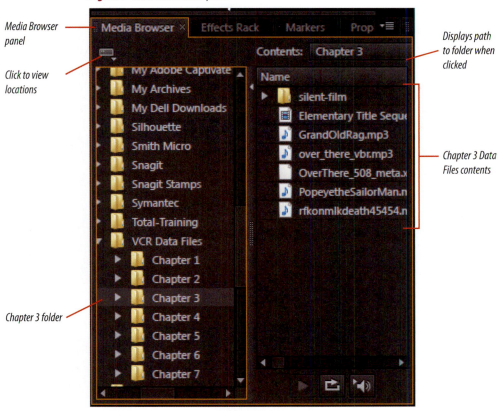

Displays path to folder when clicked

Chapter 3 Data Files contents

Work with Audio Files

1. Open Audition, if necessary, then reset the workspace to Default.

2. Click the **Media Browser panel tab** if it is not already active.

   The Media Browser displays the hard drive(s) on your computer.

3. On the Media Browser, navigate to the drive and folder where the Chapter 3 Data Files are located as shown in Figure 7.

   (continued)

4. Double-click **PopeyetheSailorMan.mp3** in the Chapter 3 Data Files Folder.

   The audio file is imported into the Files panel and displayed in the Waveform Editor, as shown in Figure 8.

5. Leave Adobe Audition open for the next exercise.

You imported an audio file into Audition.

Switch Between the Editor Views

1. Open Audition, if necessary, then reset the workspace to Default.

2. Import the PopeyetheSailorMan.mp3 file into the Files panel, if necessary.

3. Click the **View Multitrack Editor button**
   ![Multitrack].

   The New Multitrack Session dialog box opens, as shown in Figure 9. A multitrack session needs to be created before you can view the Multitrack Editor.

4. Type **Popeye** followed by *your name* in the Session Name text box of the New Multitrack Session dialog box.

(continued)

Figure 8 *Waveform Editor view*

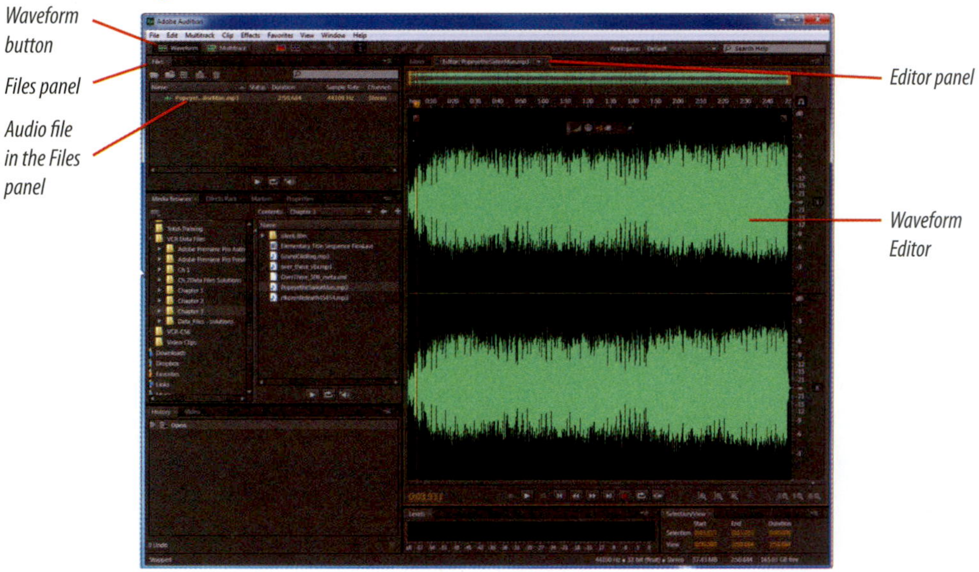

Waveform button
Files panel
Audio file in the Files panel

Editor panel

Waveform Editor

Figure 9 *New Multitrack Session dialog box*

Session Name text box

New Multitrack Session

Session Name: Untitled Session 1
Folder Location: C:\Users\Debbie\Documents\Adobe\Audi... ▼ Browse...
Template: None ▼
Sample Rate: 44100 ▼ Hz
Bit Depth: 32 (float) ▼ bits
Master: Stereo ▼

OK   Cancel

Creating a Soundtrack in Adobe Audition CS6

Figure 10 *Multitrack Editor view*

Multitrack button

Multitrack session

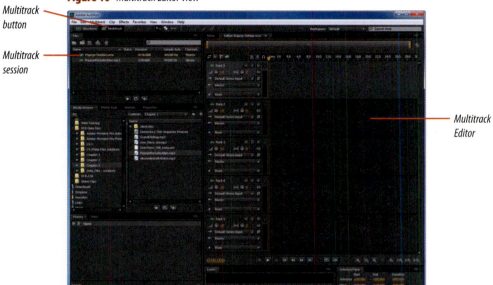

Multitrack Editor

5. Click **OK** to close the New Multitrack Session dialog box.

   The new session is added to the Files panel and the editor is changed to the Multitrack Editor view, as shown in Figure 10.

6. Click the **View Waveform Editor button** [Waveform].

   The view is changed back to the Waveform Editor.

7. Click **File** on the Menu bar, click **Close All**.

You created a multitrack session and switched between editors.

LESSON 2

Work with
MULTITRACK SESSIONS

What You'll Do

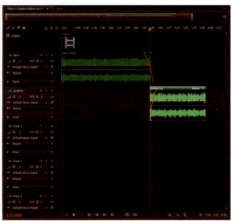

Figure © Cengage Learning 2013

 In this lesson, you will learn to work with multitrack sessions.

Working with Multitrack Sessions

Audition allows you to combine audio files and mix settings to create soundtracks for videos that you can then import into Premiere Pro or After Effects. A multitrack session is a file that contains references to source files and mix settings of multiple tracks, keeping the file relatively small. The extension for an Audition document is .sesx. Because a multitrack session file does not embed any of the source files or settings, it is recommended that you create a folder with a unique name for each session file to help you keep organized.

Multitrack sessions support importing video files to use as references while mixing a soundtrack, allowing you to synchronize your music. (*Note:* A session can include only one video.) The Video panel becomes active when you create a video track for previewing a video clip with the audio as you work. You can also choose the Edit Audio to Video workspace, as shown Figure 11. You can create a track by dragging a video clip to an audio track from the Files panel, or by clicking the Tracks list arrow on the Editor panel and selecting Add Video Track.

A multitrack session can be created before or after you import your movie file. The New command found under File on the Menu bar allows you to create either a multitrack session or an audio file. To create a multitrack session after importing a video file, select the file in the Files panel, click the New File button, then select New Multitrack Session from the menu.

Multitracks appear on the Multitrack Editor panel, and you can quickly switch between audio files by selecting the drop-down menu on the Editor panel, as shown in Figure 12. By default, tracks are named Track 1, Track 2, Track 3, etc. Tracks can be renamed by clicking the current name and typing a new name. If you have several audio tracks, it is helpful to assign them descriptive names so that you can easily keep track of where each sound effect or audio clip is located.

Audio files on the Files panel can be placed on an audio track by dragging them to the Multitrack Editor panel. An audio file that has been placed on a track is known as a clip. If you drag an audio file to the empty area below an existing track, a new track will be created. To insert a clip at a specific time,

Creating a Soundtrack in Adobe Audition CS6

Figure 11 *Previewing a video on the Video panel*

Edit Audio to Video workspace

Video Reference

Insert into Multitrack button

Multitrack Editor

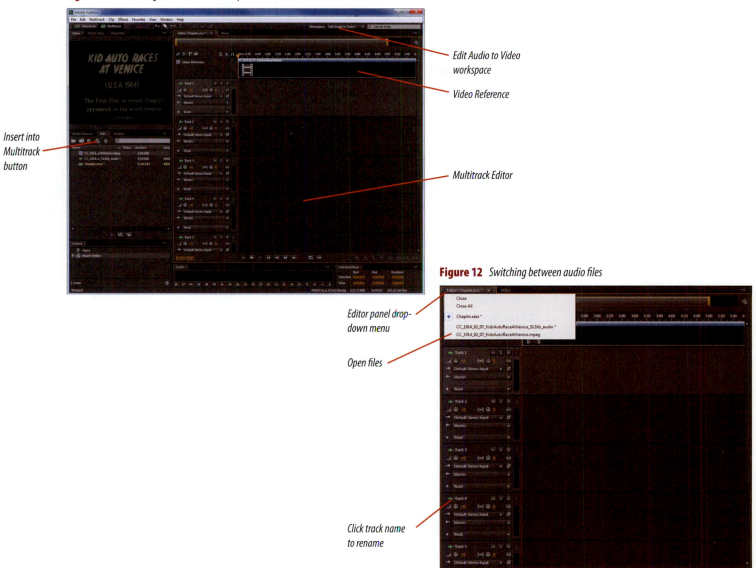

Figure 12 *Switching between audio files*

Editor panel drop-down menu

Open files

Click track name to rename

place the CTI where you would like the audio clip to be inserted, select the appropriate track, then with the audio file selected, click the Insert into Multitrack button on the Files panel. The clip will be placed at the location of the CTI.

Adjusting the length or duration of an audio clip is as simple as clicking and dragging, as shown in Figure 13. When you place the pointer at the edge of a clip, the cursor changes into a red E; if you are on the right side of the clip, the E is backwards. You click and drag the E icon to adjust the length of the clip.

Figure 13 *Trimming a clip*

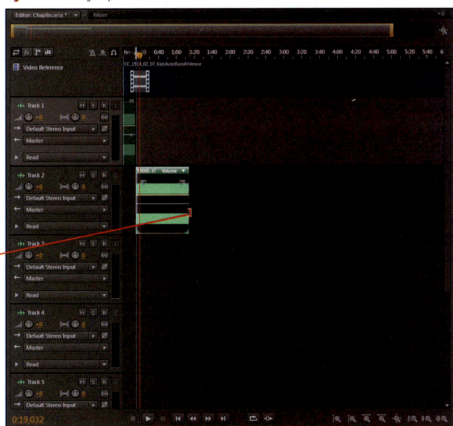

Cursor at the end of clip

The placement of a clip on a track can also be adjusted by clicking and dragging the clip with the Move tool. It is a good idea to place clips on separate tracks so that you can overlap them to eliminate the cut from one audio clip to the next. You can also add keyframes, as you used in Premiere Pro and After Effects, for the volume level, allowing you to create a fade from one audio clip to the next, as shown in Figure 14.

You can also create a fade in or a fade out effect between audio clips by right-clicking

Figure 14 *Creating a fade on an audio clip*

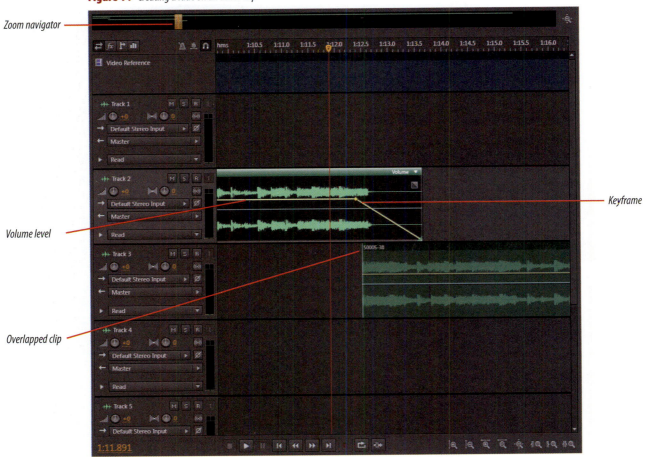

Zoom navigator

Volume level

Overlapped clip

Keyframe

Figure © Cengage Learning 2013

the fade icon, which is located at the top corner of each audio clip. You will see several options from the context menu, as shown in Figure 15. You can then adjust the length of the fade by dragging the fade icon. You can also adjust the amount of fade by dragging up or down to create a curve.

QUICK TIP

Click the zoom navigator located at the top of the Multitrack Editor panel to navigate to a different position in the session.

Figure 15 *Using the fade in effect*

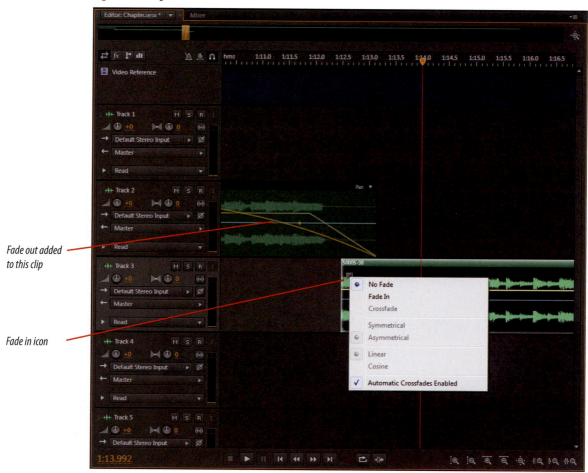

Fade out added to this clip

Fade in icon

Applying Effects in the Multitrack Editor

When working in the Multitrack Editor, each clip and track has its own Effects Rack panel, as shown in Figure 16. Effects are nondestructive in the Multitrack Editor and can be changed at any time. The Effects Rack panel allows you to apply up to 16 different effects to each track or clip. When working in Multitrack Editor mode, effects can be edited in the Editor panel, the Mixer panel, or the Effects Racks panel. The stacking order of effects can be modified by simply clicking and dragging an effect to a new location in the stack. You can also temporarily disable an effect by clicking the Power button for that effect. This allows you to compare what the clip sounds like with and without the effect.

Audition includes numerous effects in many categories, including Reverb Effects, Special Effects, and Modulation Effects. Choose Adobe Audition Help by selecting Help on the Menu bar for more information.

Saving a Multitrack File

While you are performing edits on a soundtrack and syncing it to video, you should keep it in the Audition SESX file format. The SESX format allows you to add effects and to adjust fades. You can also import a file in the SESX format directly into Premiere Pro and

Figure 16 *Effects Rack panel in Multitrack Editor View*

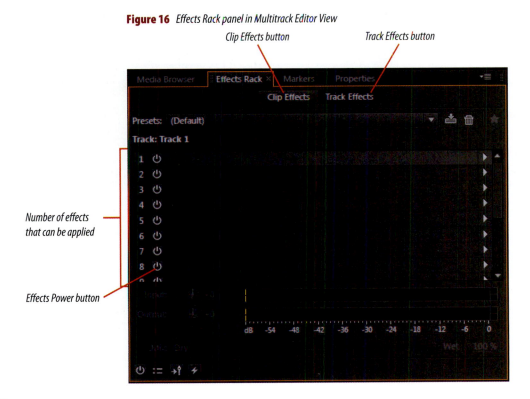

Clip Effects button

Track Effects button

Number of effects that can be applied

Effects Power button

After Effects and access the file from those applications for editing. The Save As dialog box allows you to rename a multitrack session and change the location where it is saved, as shown in Figure 17. By default, Adobe creates a folder titled Adobe for you and places a folder named Audition within it. By default, all Adobe session files are save to this location. (*Note:* Be sure the multitrack session is selected in the Editor window before choosing Save As.)

When you are done editing your file and ready to save it for playback or for use on other devices, you need to do what is called a mix down, which is a process that combines all of your audio tracks and outputs them together. This is accomplished using the Export Multitrack Mixdown command. As part of this process, you need to choose an audio file format to save in.

The MP3 file format is one of the most widely used file formats for portable media players and Web-based audio. MP3 has a highly compressed file size to make downloads faster, but also results in poorer quality. Use the MP3 file format when saving for the Web or for portable media players.

Windows Waveform, or WAV, is the standard, uncompressed audio format for the Windows operating system. Audio Interchange File Format, or AIF, is the standard, uncompressed audio file format for Mac OS. You should use these file formats when you plan to share your files with other applications or burn them to discs.

You have the option to save the entire file or a selected range. You also have the option to add the saved file to the Files panel. The WAV file format provides additional options regarding compression that the AIF file format does not.

Figure 17 *Save As dialog box*

Click the Browse button to change where the file is saved

Figure © Cengage Learning 2013

Creating a Soundtrack in Adobe Audition CS6

Figure 18 *Files added to Files panel*

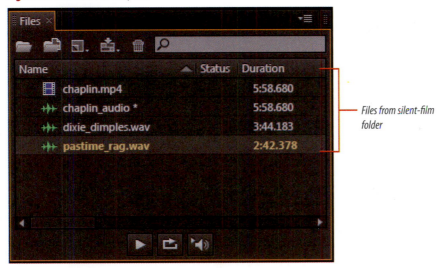

Files from silent-film folder

Create a multitrack file

1. Open Audition, then if necessary reset the workspace to Default.

2. Click **File** on the Menu bar, point to **Import**, then click **File**.

3. In the Import File dialog box, navigate to the drive and folder where you store your Data Files, open the folder titled **silent-film**, select the contents of the folder, then click **Open**.

   Movie and audio files are added to the Files panel, as shown in Figure 18. This will allow you to view the movie clip at the same time you create a soundtrack for the silent movie.

4. In the Files panel, select **chaplin.mp4**.

5. In the Files panel, click the Insert into **Multitrack button**, then click **New Multitrack Session**.

   The New Multitrack Session dialog box opens.

6. In the **Session Name field**, enter **Chaplin *your name*** as shown in Figure 19, click the **Browse button**, select the destination folder for your project, then click **OK**.

   (continued)

Figure 19 *Creating a Multitrack Session*

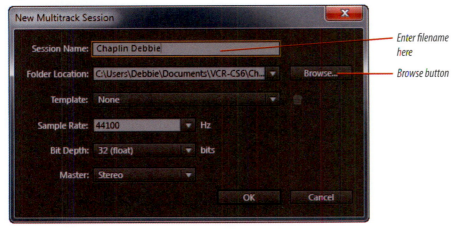

Enter filename here

Browse button

The file is saved as an Audition Multitrack Session file and a Video Reference is created for you at the top of the multitrack editor window, as shown in Figure 20.

7. Leave Audition open for the next exercise.

You imported files, created a multitrack file, and saved an Audition SESX document.

Place Audio on Tracks

1. Open Chaplin *your name*, if necessary.

2. Change the workspace to **Edit Audio to Video**.

   The Chaplin *your name* multitrack file should be open on the Editor panel.

3. Click and drag **dixie_dimples.wav** from the Files panel to the Audio 1 track on the Editor panel, as shown in Figure 21, then in the dialog box indicating sample rate of the file needs to be changed, click **OK**.

   The Audio 1 track moves below the video reference track.

4. Adjust the audio clip as needed so that it starts at **00:00:00.000**.

(continued)

Figure 20 *A New Multitrack Session with a Video track*

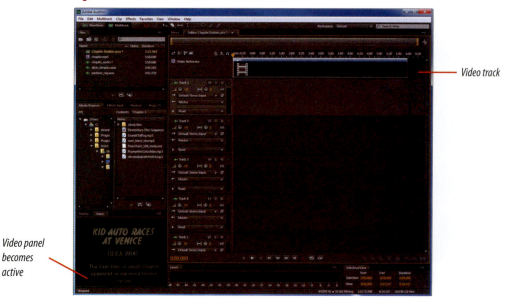

Video track

Video panel becomes active

Figure 21 *Adding an audio file to Track 1*

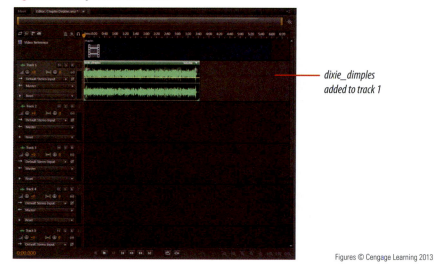

dixie_dimples added to track 1

Figures © Cengage Learning 2013

Creating a Soundtrack in Adobe Audition CS6

Figure 22 *Rename a track in the multitrack editor view*

Track renamed chaplin

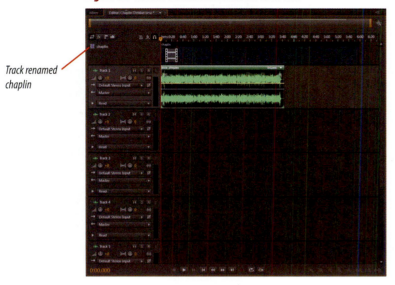

Figure 23 *Adding another audio file*

Toggle Snapping button

pastime_rag audio clip

Figures © Cengage Learning 2013

5. Click **Video Reference** in the Editor panel, then type **chaplin**, as shown in Figure 22.

    Renaming a track allows you to identify its content more easily.

6. Rename Track 1 **dixie**.

7. Click the **Play button** [icon] on the Editor panel to preview the audio clip with the movie clip, then click the **Pause button** [icon] to stop the preview.

TIP Press [Home] (Win) or [fn] + [left arrow] (Mac) to return the CTI to 00:00:00.000.

8. Select **File** on the Menu bar, then click **Save** to save the Chaplin *your name* multitrack file.

9. Leave Audition open for the next exercise.

You created a new video track, placed an audio file on an audio track, then renamed tracks. Finally, you previewed the Audition document.

Adjust the length of an audio clip

1. Open Chaplin *your name*, if necessary, then verify that the workspace is set to Edit Audio to Video.

    The Chaplin *your name* multitrack file should be open on the Editor panel, and the CTI should be at 00:00:00.000.

2. In the Editor panel, click **Track 2**.

3. In the Files panel, select **pastime_rag**, click the **Insert into Multitrack button** [icon], select **Chaplin your name**, then in the dialog box indicating sample rate of the file needs to be changed, click **OK**.

    The audio clip is added to the selected track.

4. Adjust the placement of the audio clip so that it begins to play after the dixie_dimples clip ends, as shown in Figure 23.

(continued)

TIP Be sure the Toggle Snapping button  is selected so the audio clip will snap at the end of the previous clip.

5. Rename the Track 2 layer **pastime**.

   The pastime audio track is much too long; you will need to trim its length to match that of the video clip track.

6. Hover the mouse pointer over the right edge of the audio clip ↔ on the pastime audio track, then drag the clip to the left until the right edge lines up with the video clip on the video track, as shown in Figure 24.

   The mouse pointer should resemble a backwards red E as you drag.

7. Adjust the **CTI** to **3:30.00**, then click the **Play button** ▶ on the Editor panel to preview the two audio clips, then click the **Pause button** ❚❚ to stop the preview.

   Notice there is a gap in the music, which you will adjust in the next exercise.

8. Save your file and leave Audition open for the next exercise.

You added an additional audio track and trimmed the length of the audio clip.

Figure 24 *Trimming an audio clip*

Adjusted length of the audio clip

Creating a Soundtrack in Adobe Audition CS6

Figure 25 *Adding a Fade Out effect to a clip*

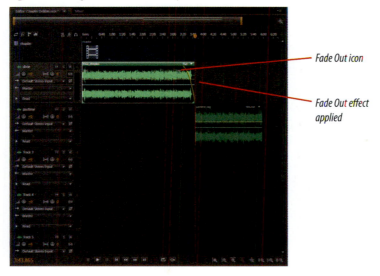

Fade Out icon

Fade Out effect applied

Lesson 2   Work with Multitrack Sessions

Add Fade In and Fade Out Effects

1. Open Chaplin *your name*, if necessary, then verify that the Edit Audio to Video workspace is active.

2. Select the **dixie clip** in the Editor panel, right-click on the **Fade Out icon** then click **Fade Out**, as shown in Figure 25.

   The Fade Out icon is located at the end of the clip in the upper-right corner.

3. Select the **pastime clip**, in the Editor panel, right-click on the **Fade In icon** then click **Fade In**.

   The Fade In icon is located at the beginning of the clip in the upper- left corner.

   (continued)

4. Adjust the placement of the **pastime_rag audio clip** so that it begins at **3:35.000**, as shown in Figure 26.

5. Adjust the **CTI** to **3:30.00**, then click the **Play button** 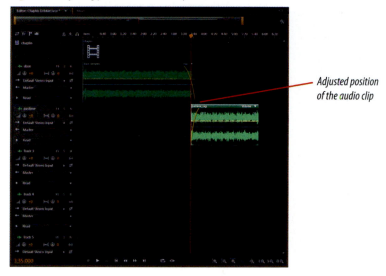 on the Editor panel to preview the two audio clips, then click the **Pause button** to stop the preview.

   The gap in the music has been removed.

6. Adjust the length of the pastime track to match the end of the movie, then add a Fade Out effect to the track.

7. Leave Audition open for the next exercise.

You added fade in and fade out effects.

Figure 26 *Adjusting position of an audio clip*

Adjusted position
of the audio clip

Figure © Cengage Learning 2013

Creating a Soundtrack in Adobe Audition CS6

Figure 27 *Resetting the workspace*

Default workspace

Effects Rack panel made active

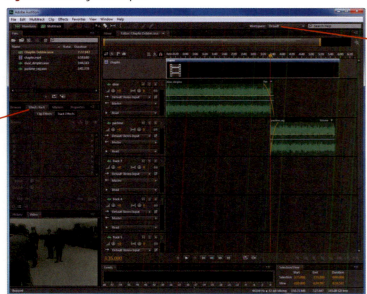

Apply effects in the Multitrack Editor

1. Open Chaplin *your name*, if necessary.
2. Reset the workspace to Default and make the Effects Rack panel active, as shown in Figure 27.
3. Select the **dixie track**.

(continued)

Figure © Cengage Learning 2013

Lesson 2   Work with Multitrack Sessions

4. In the Effects Rack panel, click the **Track Effects button** Track Effects , select the **Presets menu**, then click **AM Radio**, as shown in Figure 28.

   The AM Radio effect you applied will tone down the music to fit the mood of the era better.

5. Repeat Step 4 for the **pastime track**.

6. Click the **Play button** ▶ on the Editor panel to preview the audio clips.

   The AM Radio effect you applied will tone down the music to fit the mood of the era better.

7. Leave Audition open for the next exercise.

You applied effects in the Multitrack Editor.

Figure 28 *Applying a Track Effect to a Track*

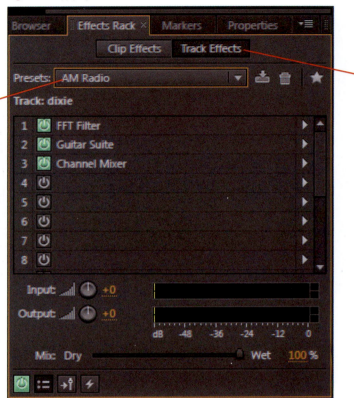

Presets menu with AM Radio selected

Track Effects button

Creating a Soundtrack in Adobe Audition CS6

Figure 29 *Export Multitrack Mixdown dialog box*

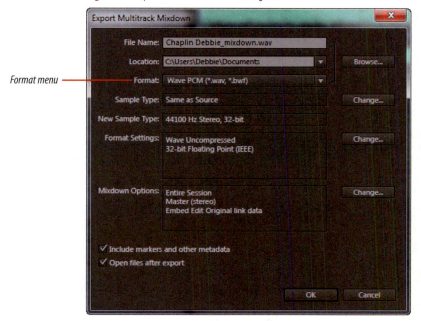

Format menu

Figure 30 *MP3 file in the Files panel*

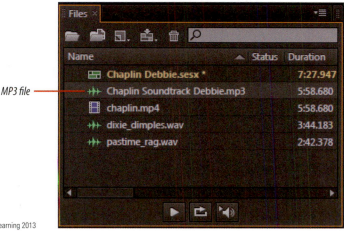

MP3 file

Export an MP3 file

1. Open Chaplin *your name* if necessary, then verify that the workspace is set to Default.

   The Chaplin *your name* multitrack file should be open on the Editor panel, and the CTI should be at 00:00:00.000.

2. Click **File** on the Menu bar, point to **Export**, point to **Multitrack Mixdown**, then click **Entire Session**.

   The Export Multitrack Mixdown dialog box opens, as shown in Figure 29.

3. Navigate to the drive and folder where you store your Data Files, then name the file **Chaplin-Soundtrack** *your name*.

4. Click the **Format arrow**, click **MP3 Audio (*.mp3)**, then click **OK**.

   A progress dialog box appears while the file is saving; the newly generated MP3 file is listed on the File panel, as shown in Figure 30.

5. Click **File** on the Menu bar, then click **Save All** to save all the files that are open on the Files and Editor panels.

6. Click **File** on the Menu bar, then click **Close All** to close all the files that are open on the Files and Editor panels.

7. Leave Audition open for the next exercise.

You saved the Chaplin-Soundtrack your name file as an MP3 file.

Clean Up
AUDIO FILES

What You'll Do

Figure © Cengage Learning 2013

In this lesson, you will clean up vintage audio files.

Cleaning Up Audio

Audition can be used to clean up and restore audio files. For example, crackling noises from old vinyl records or microphone recordings can be removed with the Automatic Click Remover effect, and background noise such as wind or humming can be removed with the Adaptive Noise effect. These effects can be used in either the Waveform Editor or the Multitrack Editor.

If you want to correct multiple problems or identify the noise you want removed, the Noise Reduction effect can be used. Using the Noise Reduction effect can significantly reduce any unwanted noise that is constant throughout the waveform. The Noise Reduction effect is only available in the Waveform Editor and is therefore a destructive edit.

By default, the Waveform Editor displays an audio file as a waveform showing amplitude changes. The Waveform Editor can also display an audio file as a Spectral Frequency display, or spectral display, as shown in Figure 31. In this display, the x-axis measures time and the y-axis measures frequency. The display can be activated by clicking the Show Spectral Frequency Display button on the Tools panel; the display appears below the waveform display on the Editor panel. (*Note:* This display is not available in the Multitrack Editor.) The colors in the spectral display represent amplitude and range from bright yellow to dark blue. Bright yellow represents high amplitude and is located near the bottom of the display; dark blue represents low amplitude and is located near the top of the display. The spectral display is used for removing unwanted noise such as clicks, hums, coughs, and other artifacts. Removing noise with the spectral display is known as frequency-space editing.

You can use the spectral display to identify and select noise. Bright vertical bars that extend from the top to the bottom are usually clicks and crackles. Light red clouds that extend across the top of the display are usually hissing noises. By studying the spectral display you can begin to identify problem areas by looking at the colors, as shown in Figure 32.

Figure 31 *Spectral Frequency display*

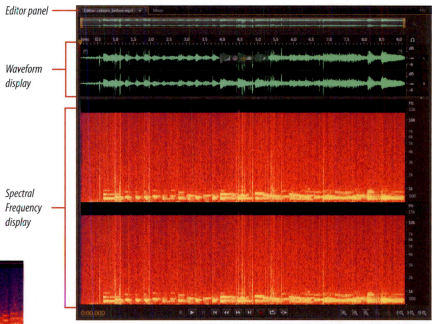

Editor panel

Waveform display

Spectral Frequency display

Figure 32 *Identifying noises in the Spectral Frequency display*

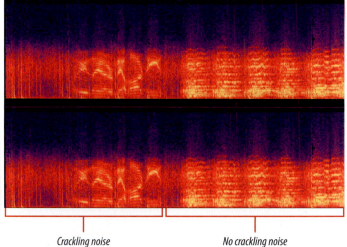

Crackling noise   No crackling noise

The Noise Reduction command can be used to remove noises like hisses and hums that remain constant in the background. Figure 33 displays the same audio file from the previous figure with the crackling noise removed.

Before you can apply the Noise Reduction command, you need to identify the noise. A noise can be selected with the Rectangular Marquee tool in the spectral display to generate a sample of the noise you wish to remove, as shown in Figure 34. If you are working on an audio file that was recorded in stereo, the second channel is automatically selected for you. The Capture Noise Print command creates a noise print, which is a sample of the artifact you want to remove from the audio file. This command is found on the Effects menu under the submenu Noise Reduction/Restoration. After you create a noise print, you can clean up the audio by selecting Noise Reduction (process) which is found on

Figure 33 *Spectral Frequency display of repaired audio file*

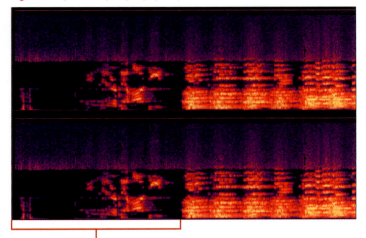

Removed crackling noise

Figure 34 *Creating a noise print*

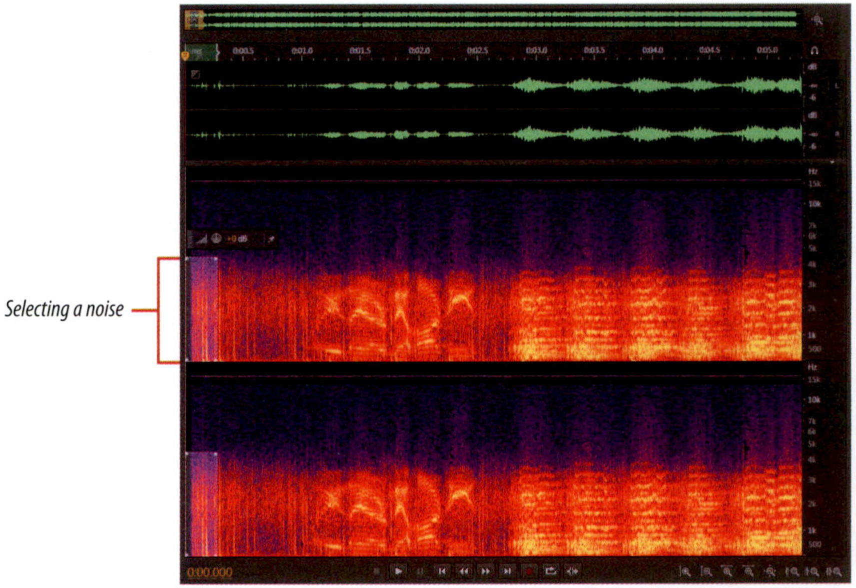

Selecting a noise

Creating a Soundtrack in Adobe Audition CS6

the Effects menu under the Noise Reduction/ Restoration submenu. This opens the Effect – Noise Reduction dialog box, as shown in Figure 35. The Noise Reduction setting in the Effect – Noise Reduction dialog box sets the amplitude of the noise floor. The noise floor is the level of amplitude representing the near-constant background noise that you have identified and are trying to remove, as

Figure 35 *Effect – Noise Reduction dialog box*

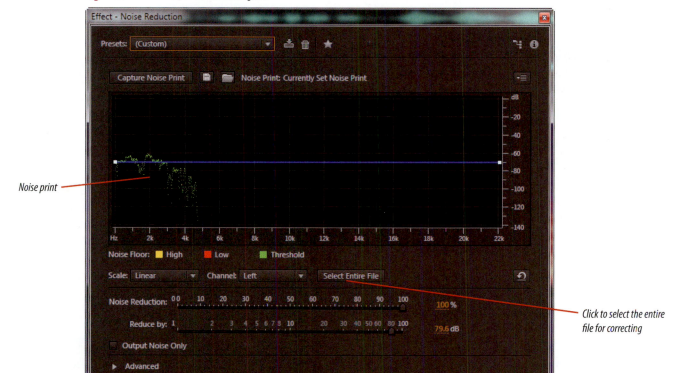

shown in Figure 36. The control curve sets the amount of noise reduction based on frequency and can be adjusted. By default, it is set based on the noise print. Audio that falls below the noise floor is dropped, or not heard. This can be adjusted with the Reduce By setting. You can preview your chosen settings in the Effect – Noise Reduction dialog box before processing the file.

Figure 36 *Analyzing a noise print*

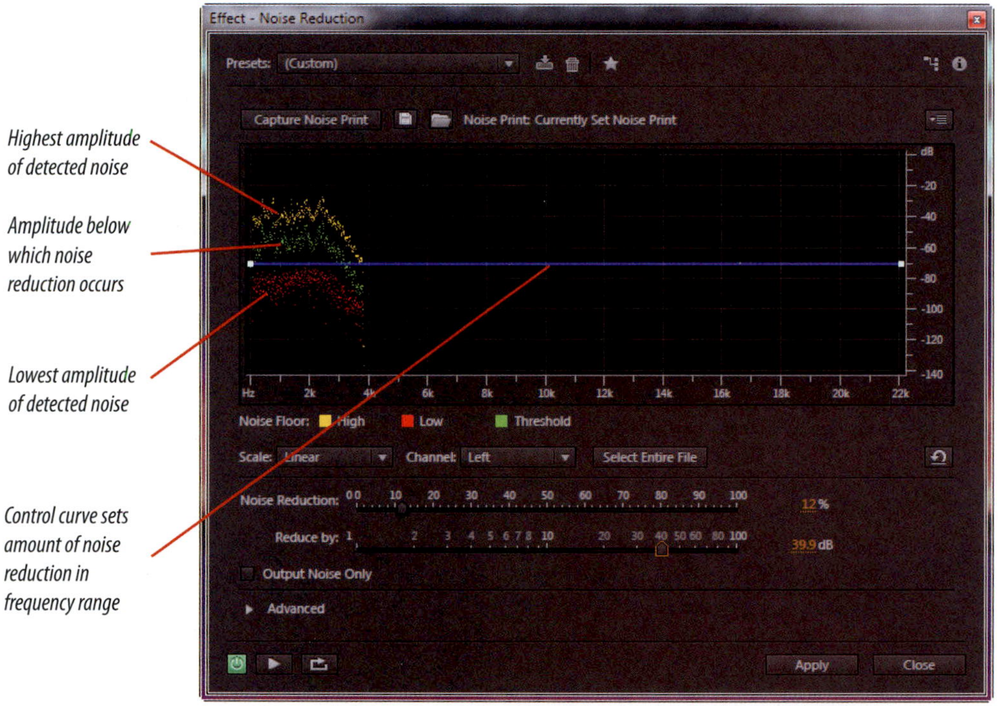

Highest amplitude of detected noise

Amplitude below which noise reduction occurs

Lowest amplitude of detected noise

Control curve sets amount of noise reduction in frequency range

Using Automatic Noise Removal Techniques

Audition provides two methods to automatically remove unwanted noise or artifacts from vintage recordings. The first method is the Automatic Click Remover effect, which is used to remove crackle and static from vinyl recordings. This method can be used to make corrections in large areas of a recording or to remove single instances of clicks or crackles. The second method is the Automatic Phase Correction effect, which is used to remove audio mistakes that were created during the recording process from improper microphone placement or misaligned tape heads.

Figure © Cengage Learning 2013

Creating a Soundtrack in Adobe Audition CS6

Figure 37 *Imported audio file on Files panel*

Files panel →

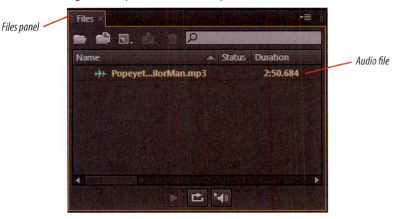

← Audio file

Figure 38 *Spectral frequency display*

Waveform display →

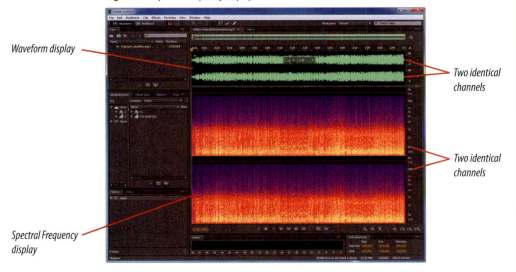

→ Two identical channels

→ Two identical channels

Spectral Frequency display →

Remove background noise

1. Open Audition, if necessary, then verify that the workspace is set to Default.

2. Click **File** on the Menu bar, point to **Import**, then click **File**.

   The Import Files dialog box opens.

3. Navigate to the drive and folder where you store your Data Files, click **PopeyetheSailorMan**, then click **Open**.

   The PopeyetheSailorMan audio file is imported into the Files panel, as shown in Figure 37.

4. Click the **Spectral Frequency Display button** on the Tools panel to activate the spectral display on the Editor panel, as shown in Figure 38.

5. Click the **Play button** on the Editor panel to hear the audio file, then click the **Pause button** to stop the preview.

   The audio file starts with a crackling noise at the beginning; you will select that portion of the audio and use the Capture Noise Print and Noise processes to remove the artifact. As the music is playing, observe the colors in the Spectral Frequency Display to help you identify problem areas.

   (continued)

6. Click the **Marquee Selection Tool** 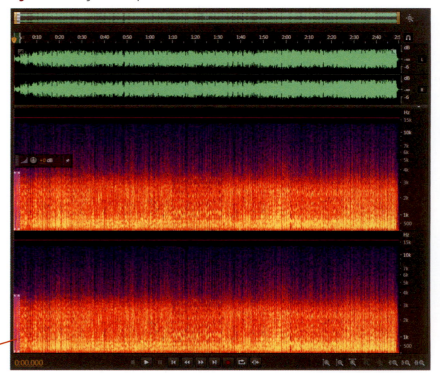 on the
   Tools panel, then select a small portion of the
   area of the spectral frequency display where you
   heard the crackling noise, as shown in Figure 39.

   You are identifying a sample of the noise to create
   a noise print. Compare the colors in the spectral
   display to help you identify your selection. This
   will help you to better remove the crackling noise
   from the larger area in the next step.

   (continued)

Figure 39 *Creating a noise sample*

Selection

Figure © Cengage Learning 2013

Creating a Soundtrack in Adobe Audition CS6

Figure 40 *The Effect-Noise Reduction dialog box*

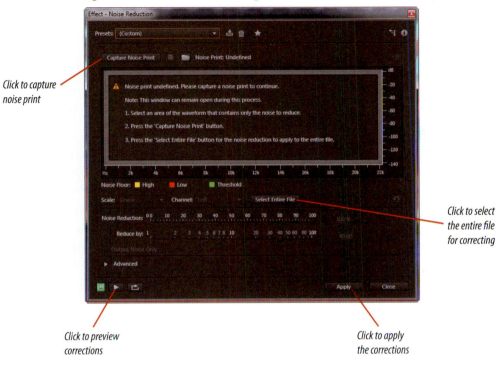

Click to capture noise print

Click to select the entire file for correcting

Click to preview corrections

Click to apply the corrections

7. On the Menu bar, click **Effects**, point to **Noise Reduction / Restoration**, then click **Noise Reduction (process)**.

   The Effect – Noise Reduction dialog box opens, as shown in Figure 40, displaying instructions to capture the noise print.

8. Click the **Capture Noise Print** button.

   This takes a sample of your selection so Audition knows what sound to remove from the file.

9. Click the **Select Entire File** button.

   This selects the entire audio file so that the sample noise print will be applied to the entire file.

10. Click the **Apply button**.

    A progress dialog box is displayed while the crackling noise is being removed.

11. Return the **CTI** to **0:00.000**, then click the **Play button** to hear your results.

    Your results may vary, based on your captured noise print.

12. Click **File** on the Menu bar, click **Save As**, navigate to the drive and folder where you store your Data Files, name the file **PopeyeRestored**, click **Save**, then click **Yes**.

13. Click **File** on the Menu bar, click **Close All**.

You imported an audio file and removed a background artifact noise.

Explore the Audition workspace.

1. Click Start on the Menu bar, point to All Programs, then click Adobe Audition CS6 (Win) or open the Finder from the dock, click Applications from the sidebar, click the Adobe application folder, then double-click Adobe Audition CS6 (Mac).
2. Click Window on the Menu bar, point to Workspace, then click Edit Audio to Video.
3. Continue to click through the various workspaces and notice how the window changes each time.
4. Return the workspace to the Default workspace, then close the Spectral Frequency Display, if necessary.

Work with an audio file.

1. Click the Media Browser panel tab, if it is not already active.
2. On the Media Browser, navigate to the drive and folder where the Chapter 3 Data Files are located.
3. Double-click GrandOldRag.mp3 in the Chapter 3 Data Files Folder.

Switch between the editor views.

1. Click the View Multitrack Editor button.
2. Type **Grand** *your name* in the Session Name text box of the New Multitrack Session dialog box.
3. Click OK to close the New Multitrack Session dialog box.
4. Click the View Waveform Editor button.
5. Click File on the Menu bar, click Close All.

Create a multitrack file.

1. Click File on the Menu bar, point to Import, then click Files.
2. In the Import file dialog box, navigate to the drive and folder where you store your Data Files, open the folder

titled felix, select the contents of the folder, then click Open.
3. In the Files panel, select Felix.mov.
4. In the Files panel, click the New file button, then click New Multitrack Session on the drop-down menu.
5. In the Session Name field, enter **Felix** *your name*, click the Browse button to select the destination folder for your project, then click OK.

Place audio on tracks.

1. Set the workspace to Edit Audio to Video.
2. Click and drag acrobatic.wav from the Files panel to Track 1 on the Editor panel. (*Note:* Click OK to make a copy of the file at the correct sample rate.)
3. Adjust the audio clip as needed so that it starts at 00:00:00.000.
4. Click Video Reference in the Editor panel, then type **Felix**.
5. Rename Track 1 **acrobatic**.
6. Click the Play button on the Editor panel to preview the audio clip with the movie clip, then click the Pause button to stop the preview.
7. Select File on the Menu bar, then click Save to save the Felix *your name* multitrack file.

Adjust the length of an audio clip.

1. In the Editor panel, click Track 2.
2. In the Files panel, select barrel.wav, click the Insert into Multitrack button, then select Felix *your name*. (*Note:* Click OK to make a copy of the file at the correct sample rate.)
3. Adjust the placement of the audio clip so that it begins to play after the acrobatic track ends.

4. Rename the Track 2 layer **barrel**.
5. Hover the mouse pointer over the right edge of the audio clip on the barrel audio track, then drag the clip to the left until the right edge lines up with the end of the video clip on the video track.
6. Adjust the CTI to a location just before the transition between the two clips, click the Play button on the Editor panel to preview the two audio clips, then click the Pause button to stop the preview.

Add Fade In and Fade Out effects.

1. Select the acrobatic clip in the Editor panel, right-click on the Fade Out icon then click Fade Out.
2. Select the barrel clip in the Editor panel, right-click on the Fade In icon then click Fade In.
3. Adjust the placement of the barrel audio clip so that it begins at 2:21.000, as shown in Figure 41.
4. Adjust the CTI to 2:15.00, click the Play button on the Editor panel to preview the two audio clips, then click the Pause button to stop the preview.
5. Adjust the length of the barrel track to match the end of the movie, then add a Fade Out effect to the track.

Apply effects in the multitrack editor.

1. Reset the workspace to Default and make the Effects Rack panel active.
2. Select the acrobatic track.
3. In the Effects Rack panel, click the Track Effects button, select the Preset menu, then click AM Radio.
4. Repeat Step 3 for the barrel track.
5. Click the Play button on the Editor panel to preview the audio clips.

Export an MP3 file.

1. Click File on the Menu bar, point to Export, point to Multitrack Mixdown, then click Entire Session.
2. Navigate to the drive and folder where you store your Data Files, then name the file **Felix-Soundtrack** *your name*.

3. Click the Format arrow, click MP3 Audio (*.mp3), then click OK.
4. Click File on the Menu bar, then click Save All to save all the files that are open on the Files and Editor panels.

5. Click File on the Menu bar, then click Close All to close all the files that are open on the Files and Editor panels.

Figure 41 *Applying Fade Out and Fade In effects*

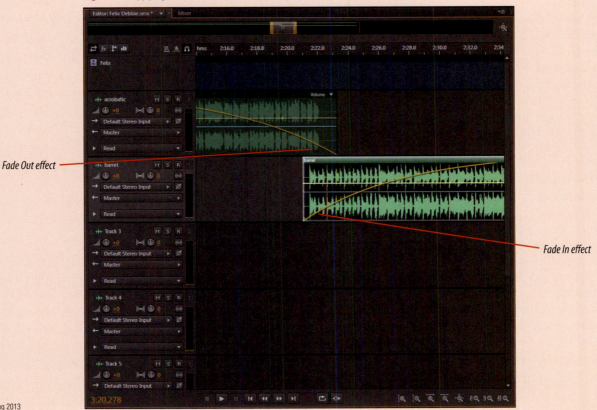

Fade Out effect

Fade In effect

Figure © Cengage Learning 2013

Creating a Soundtrack in Adobe Audition CS6

Work with audio restoration.

1. Click File on the Menu bar, point to Import, then click File.
2. Navigate to the drive and folder where you store your Data Files, click over_there_vbr then click Open.
3. Click the Show Spectral Frequency Display button on the Tools panel, if necessary, to activate the spectral display on the Editor panel.
4. Click the Play button on the Editor panel to hear the audio file, then click the Pause button to stop the preview.
5. Click the Marquee Selection Tool on the Tools panel, then select a small portion of the area of the spectral frequency display where you heard the crackling noise at the very beginning before the music begins.
6. On the Application menu, select Effects, point to Noise Reduction / Restoration, then click Noise Reduction (process).
7. Click the Capture Noise Print button.
8. Click the Select Entire File button.
9. Click the Apply button.
10. Click the Marquee Selection Tool on the Tools panel, then select the purple area at the top of the spectrum, as shown in Figure 42. (Note: The purple runs all the way across and has a narrow black line separating it from the rest of the music.)
11. On the Menu bar, click Effects, point to Noise Reduction / Restoration, then click Noise Reduction (process).
12. Click the Capture Noise Print button.

13. Click the Select Entire File button.
14. Click the Apply button.
15. Click the Play button to hear your results, then click the Pause button to stop the preview.

Figure 42 *Making a selection for a Noise Print*

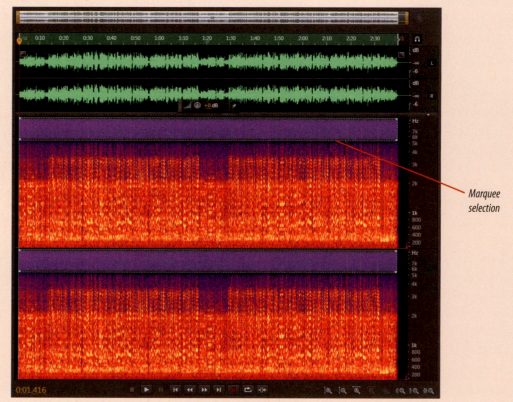

Marquee selection

16. Click File on the Menu bar, click Save As, navigate to the drive and folder where you store your Data Files, name the file **Over-Restored**, click OK then click Yes.
17. Click File on the Menu bar, then click Close All.

Figure © Cengage Learning 2013

You are working on a history project about Martin Luther King, Jr. and plan to incorporate a speech you located online at the John F. Kennedy Presidential Library & Museum. The speech is considered part of the National Archives and therefore part of the public domain, so you do not need to worry about copyright, and you are free to alter the file. Robert Kennedy gave the speech about the assassination of Martin Luther King, Jr. on April 4, 1968 in Indianapolis, Indiana, and you feel the audio needs to be cleaned up before you can use it in your project.

1. Working in the Default workspace, import the file **rfkonmlkdeath45454.mp3** into the Files panel.
2. Double-click **rfkonmlkdeath45454.mp3** on the Files panel to open it on the Editor panel, if necessary.
3. Click the Show Spectral Frequency Display button, if necessary, to turn on the spectral display.
4. Click the Play button to preview the audio clip.
5. Create a Noise Print and apply the Noise/Reduction (process) effect to remove any clicks and static.
6. In the Effect – Noise Reduction dialog box, click the Preview button and adjust the slider during playback to preview your settings. (*Hint:* Click the Power button to hear the audio without the changes.)
7. Click OK when you are satisfied with the results, then compare your Spectral Frequency Display to Figure 43 (your results may vary).
8. Save the file as an MP3 Audio file titled **RFK Speech your name**.

Figure 43 *Completed Project Builder 1*

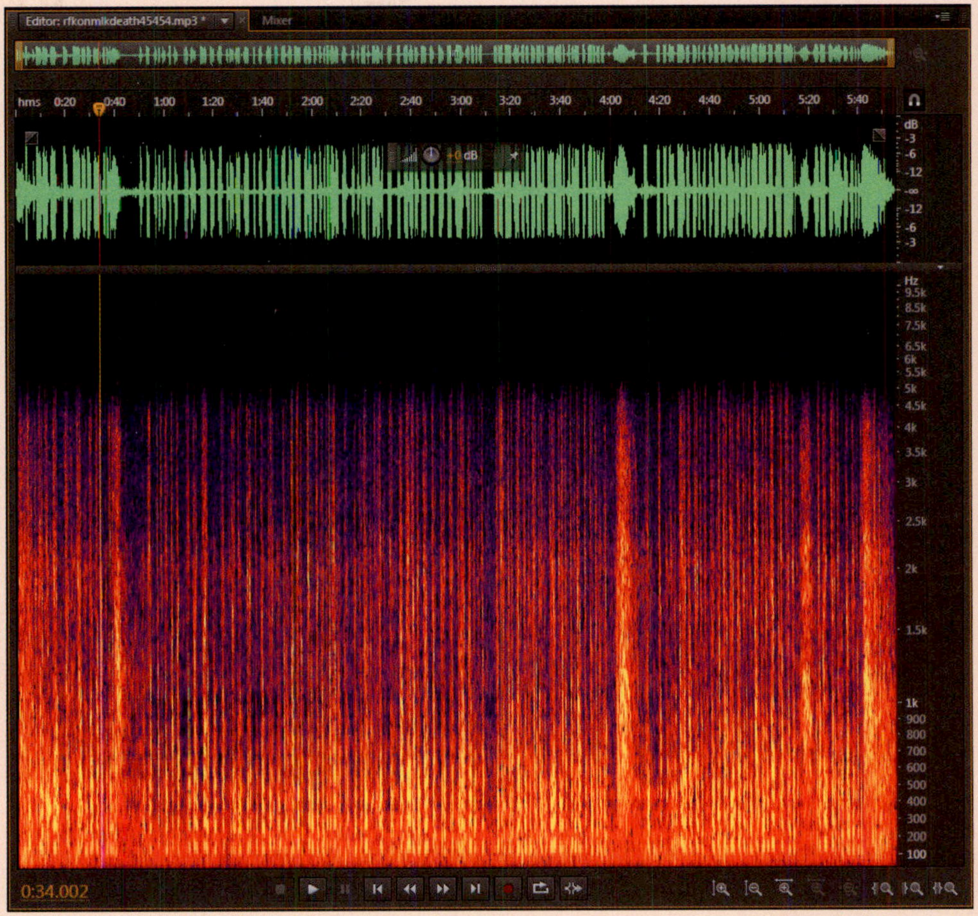

Figure © Cengage Learning 2013

Creating a Soundtrack in Adobe Audition CS6

The elementary school principal in your district loves the video you created for the school's annual awards ceremony in the spring. She has asked you to add some vibrant music to the title sequence to complete the project for her. Explore Public Domain Music (www.pdmusic.org) for music to use in this project.

1. In Audition, open Elementary Title Sequence Final from the drive and folder where your Data Files are stored.

2. Reset the workspace to Edit Audio to Video.

3. Locate music to use in your project.

4. Create a multitrack file and add your video, as shown in Figure 44, and music to tracks.

5. Save the multitrack file as **Elementary Title Sequence Music** *your name*.

6. Edit the score's duration to match the length of the title sequence, then edit the music's effects.

7. Export the multitrack mixdown file as an MP3 file named **Elementary Title Sequence Music** *your name*.

Figure 44 *Beginning of Project Builder 2*

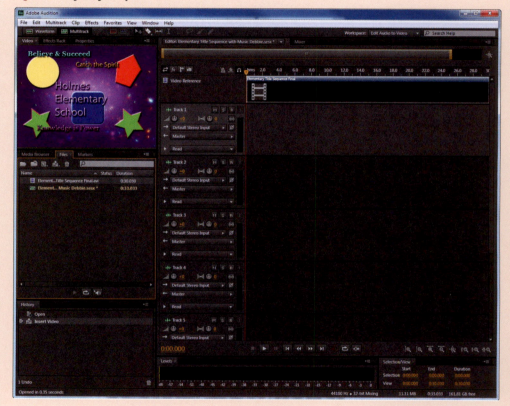

Figure © Cengage Learning 2013

Your Video Production teacher would like you to demonstrate the skills you learned in the Audition chapter. He has asked you to explore the Internet Archive (www.archive.org), as shown in Figure 45, to find public domain resources including a silent film and music. You are to create a musical score with the music you find for the silent film you have chosen.

1. Create a multitrack file and add your video and music to tracks.
2. Save the multitrack file as **Silent Film** *your name*.
3. Preview the film before beginning your project.
4. Organize your audio clips onto separate tracks.
5. Adjust your music so that it overlaps to eliminate any gaps in music.
6. Preview as you work.
7. When you are satisfied with your work, export the multitrack mixdown file as an MP3 audio file named **Silent Film Soundtrack** *your name*.

Figure 45 *Internet Archive Moving Image Archive*

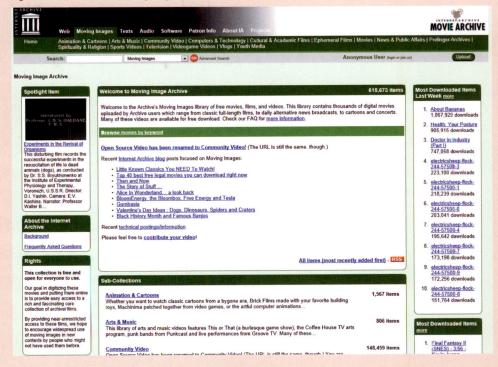

Figure © Cengage Learning 2013

CHAPTER 4

CREATING A DOCUMENTARY
USING PREMIERE PRO & AUDITION CS6

1. Transfer and import video
2. Edit Video
3. Work with Advanced Editing & Video Effects
4. Edit Audio in Audition

CREATING A DOCUMENTARY
USING PREMIERE PRO & AUDITION CS6

In this chapter, you will learn how to edit video in Premiere Pro and integrate your knowledge of Audition to bring life to a video project with audio. You'll practice by working on a film documentary.

The **documentary** is a broad category that describes videos meant to document history.

This may be done through the use of video footage or still images. You will incorporate propaganda footage from World War II, footage filmed using staged reenactments, still photos, archival NASA footage, and audio from primary sources.

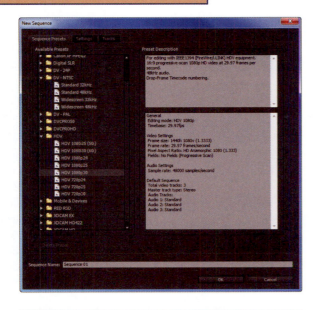

LESSON 1

Transfer and
IMPORT VIDEO

What You'll Do

Figure © Cengage Learning 2013

 In this lesson, you will transfer file-based video and import it into Premiere Pro.

Transferring File-Based Video

To work with video in Premiere Pro, you first need to remove it from your video camera. Bringing footage into a Premiere Pro project may first involve capturing, digitizing, or transferring video files depending on the source of the video. If you are using a camcorder that records on tape, or if you want to get video from a VHS video, then you need to capture and digitize your footage. **Capturing** occurs when you connect a live video camera or an analog tape device, such as a camcorder or VCR that uses videotape, to your computer and you then record the video from the source to a hard disk. The process of converting analog video to digital form is called **digitizing**, and is done so that a computer can process and store it.

Premiere Pro can capture and digitize video if a video capture card is installed in the computer and a device is connected to it. Premiere Pro saves digitized footage to a default location or to a location you designate. For more information about capturing video from an external device, refer to the Adobe Premiere Pro Help.

Importing video is different from capturing video. Digital video cameras that do not use video tape are called **tapeless** or **file-based**. These cameras record video and audio into specific formats with a folder structure specific to the manufacturer such as P2 cards, XDCAM cartridges, SxS cards, RED R3D, or DVDs. Typically, these video cameras record directly to a hard disk, a DVD, or flash memory media as they are recording. Therefore, these files are already digital and no capturing or digitizing is necessary to work with them in Premiere Pro. XDCAM, RED, P2, AVCHD, and HD clips can be mixed and matched on a timeline sequence without rendering.

It is possible to edit the assets on file-based media by attaching the camera to the computer. The computer will then recognize the camera as an external drive, allowing you to work directly with the files. However, it is suggested that a copy of the tapeless media or file-based media folder containing the video and all related files and subfolders be copied to a local hard disk to improve performance. **AVCHD** (advanced video codec high definition) is a format developed by Sony and Panasonic for recording and playback of high definition video and is used in their tapeless video cameras, which record directly to either SD memory cards or hard disk drives. The AVCHD file-based media creates a BDMV folder with subfolders named BACKUP, CLIPINF, PLAYLIST, and STREAM, as shown in Figure 1. XDCAM EX media creates a BPAV folder with subfolders, and a DVD has a VIDEO_TS folder with subfolders, and sometimes an AUDIO_TS subfolder as well.

Importing Video from a File-Based Media Source

Once you have transferred video files from your file-based media you then need to import the files into Premiere Pro to make them available to be used, just as you did with the still images in Chapter 1. Using the Media Browser is the recommended method for importing files that have been transferred from file-based media because of the file structure associated with them.

It is important to keep the file structure of the original file-based media when making your copy.

The Media Browser not only allows you to locate your files more quickly by allowing you to see the structure of your drives and folders, but it filters the folders and files for you by displaying only the video clips, as shown in Figure 2.

Creating a Sequence for AVCHD Video Footage

A sequence may contain different types of assets with different file formats. Premiere Pro performs best if the sequence parameters are set to match the settings for most of the assets that are in the sequence. Therefore, when creating a sequence, use a

Figure 1 *BDMV folder system*

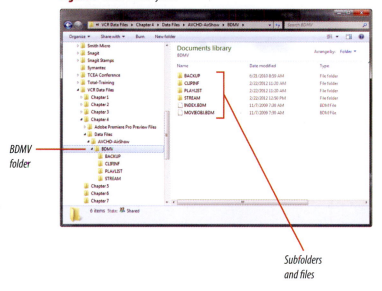

BDMV folder

Subfolders and files

Figure 2 *Viewing file-based media on the Media Browser*

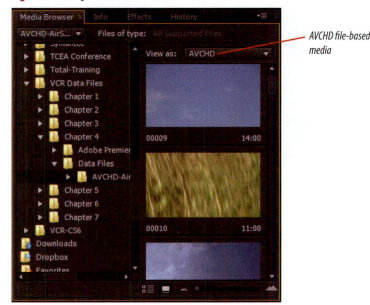

AVCHD file-based media

Figures © Cengage Learning 2013

preset that conforms to the specifications of your original assets to preserve editing quality. The preset you choose sets the frame and pixel aspect ratios for the sequence. For that reason, it is important to choose a preset that most closely matches the parameters of your asset. If necessary, you can customize the preset so that its settings match the asset exactly by clicking the General tab in the New Sequence dialog box. Most settings cannot be modified after the sequence is created so it is extremely important to make sure the settings are accurate.

If you do not know the parameters for the footage you are working with, Premiere Pro has a command called "Get Properties for" that allows you to retrieve that information from either an external clip, as shown in Figure 3, or a clip that is on the Project panel, as shown in Figure 4.

Figure 3 *Viewing the parameters of an external clip*

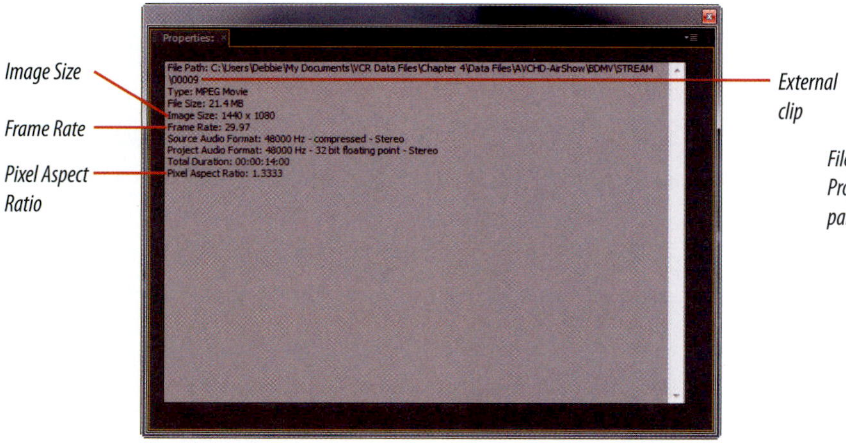

Image Size

Frame Rate

Pixel Aspect Ratio

External clip

Figure 4 *Viewing the parameters for a clip on the Project panel*

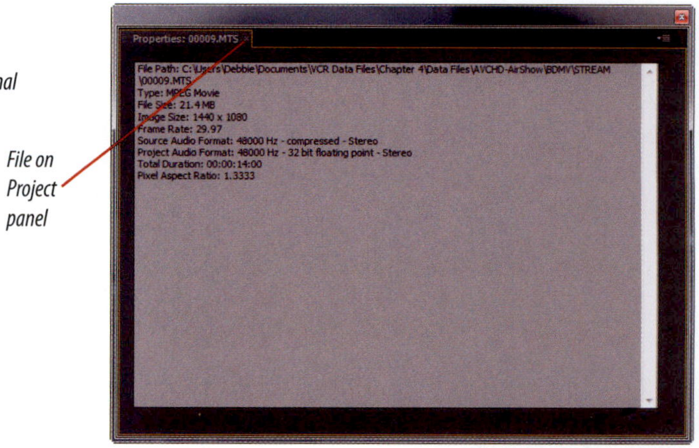

File on Project panel

Figures © Cengage Learning 2013

Creating a Documentary Using Premiere Pro & Audition CS6

The clip in Figure 3 came from an AVCHD file-based media source, which can be identified in the file path name. The parameter settings are Image Size: 1440 x 1080; Frame Rate: 29.97; and Pixel Aspect Ratio: 1.333.

Once you have identified the parameters of the clip, you can open the New Sequence dialog box and begin looking through the presets for a match, as shown in Figure 5. The AVCHD presets do not have any presets that

match the parameters as closely as the HDV presets. However, the HDV 1080p30 preset matches the parameters for the AVCHD file-based media source.

Figure 5 *HDV preset*

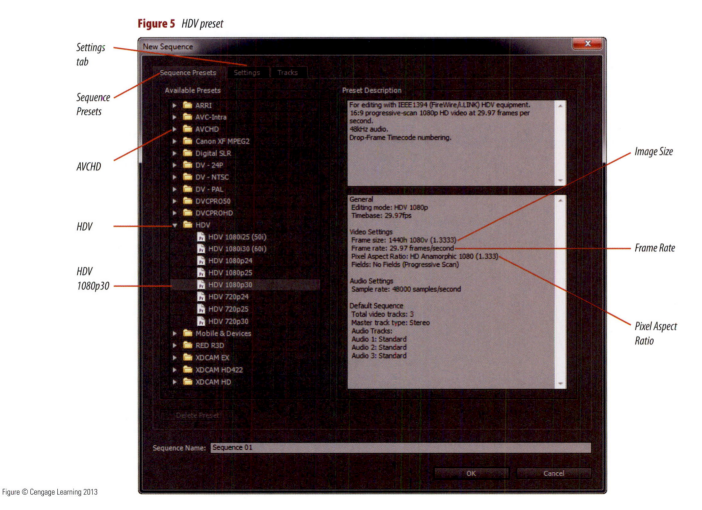

Figure © Cengage Learning 2013

Transfer tapeless video

1. Before starting Premiere Pro, navigate to the location where your Data Files are stored, then locate the Video Clips folder in the Navigation pane, as shown in Figure 6.

   Your Video Clips folder may be in a different location than the one shown in the figure.

2. Open the Video Clips folder, select **AVCHD-AirShow**, click **Organize** on the Toolbar, then click **Copy** (Win) or select the **AVCHD-Airshow** folder, click **Edit** on the Menu bar, then click **Copy** (Mac).

   The AVCHD-AirShow folder and its contents, which were recorded from a hard disk camcorder, are copied.

   (continued)

Figure 6 *Locating the Video Clips folder (Win)*

Windows File Explorer

Toolbar

Organize

Navigation pane

Video Clips folder

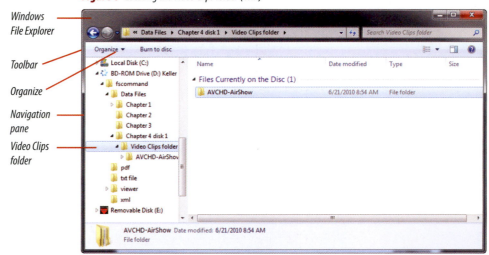

Figure © Cengage Learning 2013

Figure 7 *Copy of AVCHD-AirShow in Chapter 4 Data Files folder (Win)*

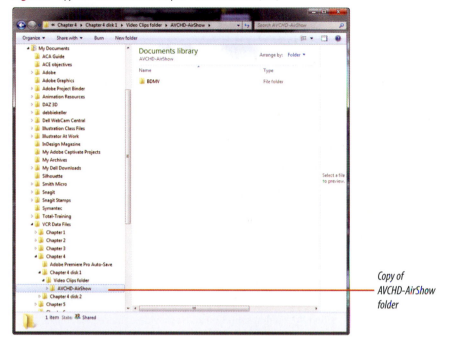

Copy of AVCHD-AirShow folder

3. Select the **Data Files** folder for Chapter 4 using the Navigation pane, click **Organize** on the Toolbar, then click **Paste** (Win) or select the **Data Files** folder for Chapter 4 using the Sidebar, select the **AVCHD-Airshow** folder, click **Edit** on the Menu bar, then click **Paste** (Mac).

This will place a copy of the AVCHD-AirShow folder and its contents to your Chapter 4 Data Files folder, as shown in Figure 7.

You copied AVCHD digital files that were recorded from a hard disk camcorder to your Data Files folder.

24p Workflows in Premiere Pro

Footage that is captured from a video camcorder or by film transfer at approximately 24 non-interlaced (progressive) frames per second (fps) is referred to as **24p footage**. Each frame is built from progressive lines giving it the appearance of a motion-picture film. Premiere Pro has a 24p sequence preset to edit 24p footage; your footage is then captured as usual. To complete the process for playback and keep the motion-picture film effect, Premiere Pro uses a method referred to as a **pulldown scheme** to convert the footage for playback on standard NTSC devices at 29.97 fps.

Two 24p pulldown schemes are available: Interlaced Frame and Repeat Frame. You can select a pulldown scheme when creating a sequence, and you can select or change the scheme in an existing sequence.

Create a sequence for AVCHD video footage

1. Start Premiere Pro, then click **New Project** in the Welcome to Adobe Premiere Pro dialog box.

   The New Project dialog box opens.

2. Click **Browse**, navigate to the drive and folder where your Data Files are stored, then click **OK**.

3. Name the project **Airshow** *your name*, then click **OK**.

   The New Sequence dialog box opens. You will be importing the AVCHD-AirShow video you transferred in the previous exercise.

4. Click the **expander arrow** in front of **HDV**, select **HDV 1080p30**, as shown in Figure 8, then click **OK**.

   The footage was shot in high definition at 29.97 fps and a frame size of 1440 x 1080. Even though the footage is AVCHD, this is the closest available preset.

5. Save your project file and leave it open for the next exercise.

You created a sequence for AVCHD video footage.

Figure 8 *Choosing an HDV preset*

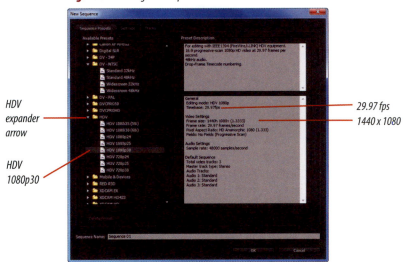

HDV expander arrow

HDV 1080p30

29.97 fps

1440 x 1080

Working with Audio

Premiere Pro has nearly as many options for editing sound as it does for video. You can edit tracks, add effects, and mix together mono, stereo, or 5.1 surround channels. A sequence of clips can contain any combination of mono, stereo, or 5.1 (three front audio channels on the left, center, and right, two rear or surround audio channels on the left and right, and a low-frequency effects audio channel) audio. There are effects in the Effects control panel for each specific channel format.

When editing audio, it sometimes becomes difficult to get the In and Out points in exactly the correct location. Digital audio is not divided into frames like video but into audio samples, which occur far more frequently than frames. The time ruler can be changed from the default Timecode display to Audio Time Units. This time ruler is available in the Source and Program Monitors and the Timeline panel and can be selected from the panel menu.

As you work with different aspects of audio editing in Premiere Pro, a more advanced feature is to map channels of audio tracks using the Source Channel Mappings command before you add a clip to a Timeline sequence. Mapping allows you to decide exactly which channel multichannel tracks go to, giving you better control over stereo or 5.1 surround.

Creating a Documentary Using Premiere Pro & Audition CS6

Figure 9 *Locating the Data Files folder on the Media Browser*

Media
Browser
panel

Chapter 4
folder

Data Files
folder

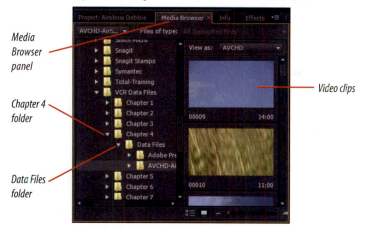

Video clips

Figure 10 *Clip 00029 imported into Project panel*

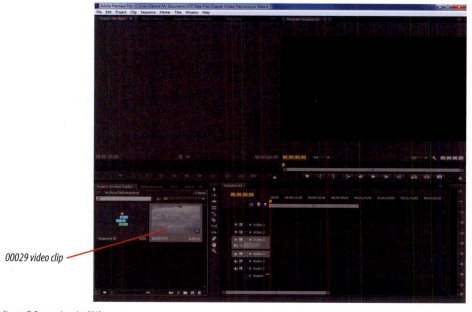

00029 video clip

Import video from a file-based source

1. Open Airshow *your name*, if necessary.

2. On the Media Browser panel, locate your Data Files folder for Chapter 4, then double-click the **AVCHD-AirShow folder**, as shown in Figure 9.

   The View as option on the Media panel automatically changes to AVCHD, filtering the folder and leaving only the video clips on the right side of the panel.

   TIP You may find it easier to work in the Media Browser panel if you change to list view.

3. Double-click **00015**.

   The clip is opened on the Source Monitor for previewing; it is not imported into the Project panel.

4. Click the **Play-Stop Toggle button** ▶ on the Source Monitor to preview the clip.

5. Click the **Source Monitor drop-down menu** then click **Close**.

   The video clip is closed.

6. Select **clip 00029**, click **File** on the Menu bar, then click **Import from Media Browser**.

7. Click the Project panel tab to make the panel active.

   The clip is imported into the Project panel, as shown in Figure 10.

8. Save and close your project file.

You imported video from a file-based source.

Edit
VIDEO

What You'll Do

Figure © Cengage Learning 2013

 In this lesson, you will edit video using the Source Monitor and the Timeline panel.

Trimming Clips on the Source Monitor

As you have already seen, you can preview clips on the Source Monitor. The Source Monitor can also be used for trimming clips. **Trimming** is an editing procedure in which you define In and Out points for a video clip. The In point defines the first frame that is to be included in a sequence and the Out point defines the last frame. Trimming clips is useful when you want to show part of a video clip, not all of it. Trimming a clip does not alter the original clip on the Project panel.

In and Out points are created on the Source Monitor by using the CTI on the time ruler and the Mark In and Mark Out buttons. These buttons are located just below the time ruler on the Source Monitor. There are additional controls to help navigate the In and Out points. The Play In to Out button previews the clip on the Source Monitor from the set In and Out points. You need to click the Button Editor button located on the lower right corner of the Source Monitor to add the Play In to Out button. In addition, there are two buttons to quickly navigate to the In and Out points, Go to In and Go to Out as shown in Figure 11.

Placing Trimmed Clips in a Sequence

Once a clip is trimmed, it can be placed in a sequence on the Timeline. Clips that have been placed in a sequence on the Timeline panel can also be viewed on the Source Monitor. Double-click the clip in the sequence if you would like to view it on the Source Monitor. If the clip has been trimmed, the In and Out points will still be set and can be seen in the Duration display, as shown in Figure 12. The shaded area between the In and Out points on the time ruler on the Source Monitor is called the In/Out Grip and can be dragged to adjust the location of both In and Out points at the same time. Tick marks and numbers are displayed along the time ruler and are based on the timecode display.

The Source menu, on the Source Monitor tab, lists any open clips, and can be accessed by clicking the Source drop-down menu, as shown in Figure 13. Clips opened from a sequence are identified by their sequence name, clip name, and starting time in the sequence. Clips opened from the Project panel are identified by their file name. The Source menu also provides options to clear either the selected clip or all the clips from the Source Monitor.

The Insert and Overwrite buttons are used to place video clips from the Source Monitor into selected tracks at the location of the CTI.

Figure 11 *Source Monitor*

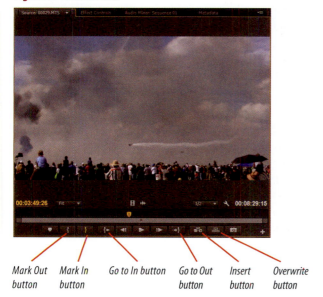

Mark Out button   Mark In button   Go to In button   Go to Out button   Insert button   Overwrite button

Figure 12 *A trimmed clip opened from a sequence*

Clip name

Figure 13 *Source menu*

Source menu

Selected clip

Click arrow to display menu

These buttons are available in the lower portion of the Source Monitor. The Insert button shifts the contents of the selected track to the right, as shown in Figure 14. An edit that involves shifting content to make room for a clip is known as an **insert edit**. The Sync Lock feature retains the relationship between clips in multiple tracks. If you have clips on multiple tracks, and Sync Lock is enabled, the contents of the other tracks also shift to the right by the length of the inserted clip, as shown in Figure 15. As you begin to use advanced editing techniques and make a change to a single clip, Premiere Pro keeps your edits in place by adjusting the other clips

Figure 14 *Insert button with Sync Lock disabled*

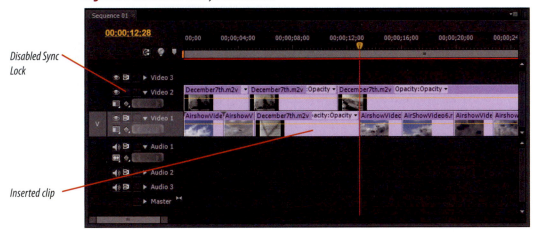

Disabled Sync Lock

Inserted clip

Figure 15 *Insert button with Sync Lock enabled*

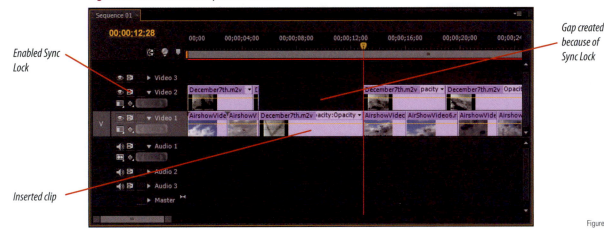

Enabled Sync Lock

Inserted clip

Gap created because of Sync Lock

Figures © Cengage Learning 2013

on the Timeline. Keep in mind that video can have an audio component linked to it.

The Overwrite button places the clip from the Source Monitor over the existing clip, replacing what is already there for the duration of the placed clip, as shown in Figure 16. Sync Lock does not affect the other tracks when using the Overwrite button, as shown in Figure 17. Making an edit using the Overwrite button is referred to as an **overlay edit**.

Figure 16 *Using the Overwrite button with Sync Lock disabled*

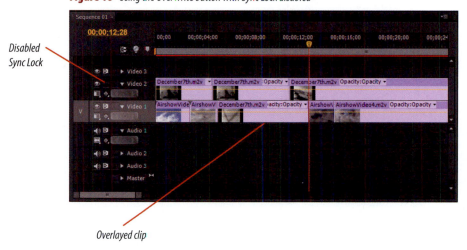

Disabled Sync Lock

Overlayed clip

Figure 17 *Using the Overwrite button with Sync Lock enabled*

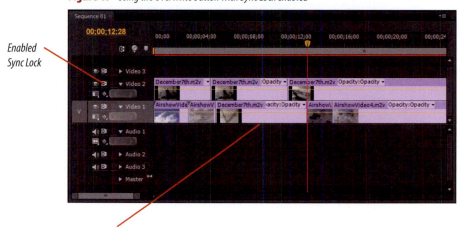

Enabled Sync Lock

Overlayed clip

Trimming on the Timeline Panel

Editing can also be done on the Timeline panel directly on the sequence by using tools from the Tools panel. If you want to trim a video clip's In point or Out point, use the Selection tool. When the cursor is placed over the left edge of a clip, the cursor's appearance changes to the Trim-in icon, as shown in Figure 18, and the Trim-out icon, as shown in Figure 19 is displayed when the cursor is placed on the right edge of a clip. When either icon is displayed, you click and drag to trim the clip. A tool tip displays the number of frames that are being trimmed; this is a negative number when dragging the clip from the right, or a positive number when dragging from the left.

Using the Ripple Edit Tool

The Ripple Edit tool can be used to adjust the cut between two clips; this type of edit is called a **ripple trim**. A ripple trim can move the cut point either backward or forward in time, but only if the clip has frames available. The clip adjacent to the cut line adjusts accordingly, shifting by the amount of the ripple trim either to the left or to the right to compensate.

A ripple trim is performed by positioning the Ripple Edit tool at the cut line in the Timeline panel and dragging either left or right.

Figure 18 *Using the Trim-in icon on the Timeline panel*

Trim-in icon

Tool tip

Figure 19 *Using the Trim-out icon on the Timeline panel*

Trim-out icon

Tool tip

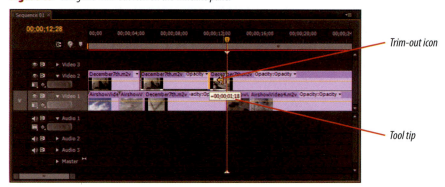

Rearranging Clips on the Timeline Panel

Once you have trimmed your clips you may decide to rearrange their order. In a **rearrange edit**, you click and drag a clip to a new location in the sequence. When you release the clip in place, the existing clips automatically shift to make room for the clip you are placing, as shown in Figure 20. A rearrange edit is performed by pressing and holding [Ctrl][Alt] (Win) or ⌘[option] (Mac) while clicking and dragging the clip, then releasing the mouse button once the clip is in the new location.

Creating Custom Keyboard Shortcuts

Premiere Pro allows you to assign your own custom keyboard shortcut to almost any menu command, button, or tool. This provides you the flexibility to assign shortcuts to commands that currently do not have shortcuts, or to reassign shortcuts to match other software you currently use and are already familiar with.

Premiere Pro does not have keyboard shortcuts like After Effects does to trim clips on a sequence. However, you can create your own keyboard shortcuts in the Keyboard Customization dialog box, which can be found on the Edit menu. You can then quickly create In and Out points at the location of the CTI using your newly created keyboard shortcuts.

Figure 20 *Performing a rearrange edit*

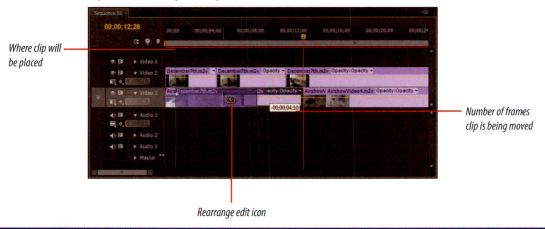

Where clip will be placed

Number of frames clip is being moved

Rearrange edit icon

Slip and Slide Tools

Two more editing tools are the Slip tool and the Slide tool. By dragging a clip's In or Out point with the Slip tool, you can change the clip's starting and ending frames without changing its duration or affecting adjacent clips. In a single action, the **slip edit** moves a clip's In and Out points forward or backward by the same number of frames.

A **slide edit** moves a clip while trimming adjacent clips to compensate for the change. With the Slide tool, as you drag a clip to the left or right, the Out point of the previous clip and the In point of the next clip are trimmed by the number of frames the clip has been moved. The duration of the clip that is being adjusted remains unchanged.

Trim video on the Source Monitor

1. Open Pearl Harbor Reenactment.prproj from your Data Files folder, then rename it **Pearl Harbor Documentary** *your name*.

2. Set the workspace to the **Editing** workspace, if necessary.

   If the Editing workspace is already selected, choose Reset Current Workspace to be sure the workspace is set to the Editing workspace default settings.

3. Double-click **AirshowVideo1.m2v** on the Project panel.

   The video footage opens on the Source Monitor.

4. Click the **Play-Stop Toggle button** ▶ to preview the video clip.

   You want to trim the clip to show the plane when it enters the field of view on the right to when it exits on the left.

5. Click the **Source Monitor panel options button** ☰ and select **Safe Margins** to turn safe margins on if they are not already activated, then repeat if necessary for the Program Monitor.

6. Select the **Button Editor button** ➕, drag the **Play In to Out button** to the bottom row on the button bar, as shown in Figure 21, then click **OK**.

7. Drag the **CTI** on the Source Monitor until the timecode display reads **00;00;02;25**, then click the **Mark In button**.

8. Drag the **CTI** until the timecode display reads **00;00;05;16**, then click the **Mark Out button**, as shown in Figure 22.

(continued)

Figure 21 *Customizing the Source Monitor button bar*

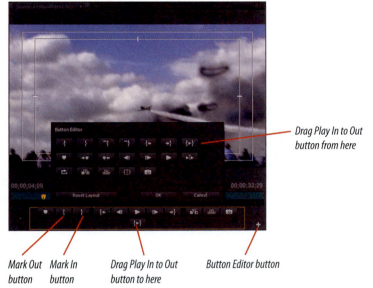

Drag Play In to Out button from here

Mark Out button   Mark In button   Drag Play In to Out button to here   Button Editor button

Figure 22 *Setting an Out point*

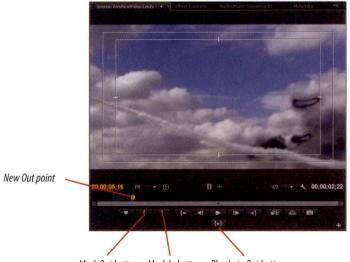

New Out point

Mark Out button   Mark In button   Play In to Out button

Figures © Cengage Learning 2013

Figure 23 *Dragging the In/Out Grip*

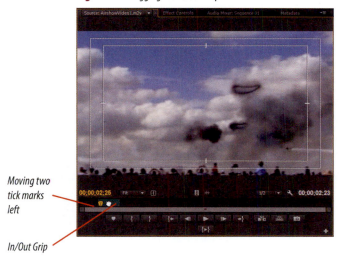

Moving two
tick marks
left

In/Out Grip

Figure 24 *Using the Trim-out icon to adjust the Out point*

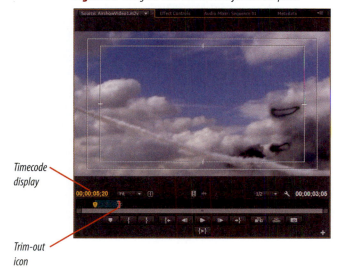

Timecode
display

Trim-out
icon

9. Click the **Play In to Out button** to preview the trimmed clip on the Source Monitor.

   At the beginning of the clip, the plane enters the safe margins. You'll adjust the start time of the clip to display the plane closer to the safe margin, but before the footage becomes shaky.

10. Drag the **In/Out Grip** on the Source Monitor two tick marks to the left to move the In point to the left, as shown in Figure 23.

    The In/Out Grip is the shaded area between the In and Out points you set earlier.

11. Click the **Play In to Out button** to preview the trimmed clip on the Source Monitor and if needed, make any adjustments to the In/Out Grip.

    The Out point moved as a result of dragging the In/Out Grip earlier, so you need to adjust the Out point so that the plane is just leaving the viewing area, but without moving the In point.

12. Hover your mouse over the Out point, then drag the right edge of the clip using the **Trim-out icon** until the timecode display reads approximately **00;00;05;20**, as shown in Figure 24.

13. Click the **Play In to Out button** to preview the trimmed clip on the Source Monitor and if needed, make any adjustments to the Out point.

14. Click the **Insert button** on the Source Monitor to place the trimmed clip in the sequence on the Timeline panel.

    You may want to zoom in on the sequence to get a better look at the clip.

    (continued)

TIP Press [Alt] (Win) or [option] (Mac) and use the scroll wheel on your mouse to zoom in and out on the Timeline panel. You may need to adjust the Zoom bar after adjusting your zoom level. **Note**: Be sure to have the Timeline panel selected first.

15. Press the [**Spacebar**] to preview the clip on the Program Monitor.

16. Save your project file and leave it open for the next exercise.

You created In and Out points on a video clip and then made adjustments to them on the Source Monitor, and finally you placed a trimmed video clip on a sequence.

Edit a clip on the Timeline panel

1. Open Pearl Harbor Documentary *your name*, if necessary.

2. Drag **AirshowVideo2.m2v** to the Video 1 track directly after the AirshowVideo1 video clip on the Timeline panel, as shown in Figure 25.

3. Press the **Down Arrow or Up Arrow key** as necessary to move the CTI to the beginning of the AirshowVideo2 video clip.

4. Press the [**Spacebar**] to preview the video clip on the Program Monitor.

   We will be trimming the clip on the Timeline panel to show the two planes flying in from the right side of the viewing area.

5. Click the **Selection tool** 🔖 on the Tools panel, then place the cursor over the left edge of the AirshowVideo2 video clip.

   (continued)

Figure 25 *Dragging AirshowVideo2.m2v to the Video 1 track*

AirShowVideo2.m2v

AirShowVideo2.m2v

Figure 26 *Trimming a clip from the left on the Timeline panel*

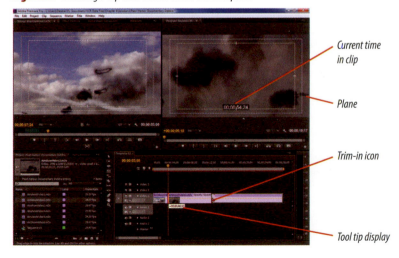

Current time in clip

Plane

Trim-in icon

Tool tip display

Figures © Cengage Learning 2013

Figure 27 *Removing space between video clips*

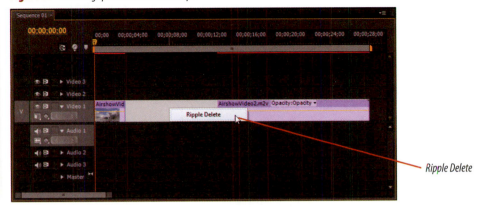

Ripple Delete

Figure 28 *Trimming a clip from the right on the Timeline panel*

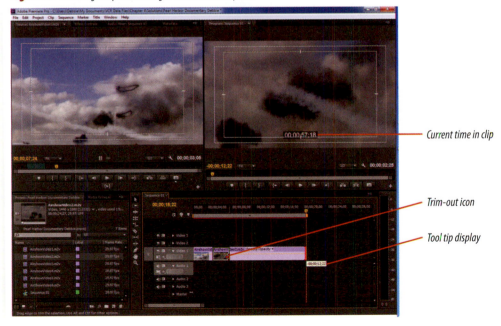

Current time in clip

Trim-out icon

Tool tip display

Figures © Cengage Learning 2013

Lesson 2   Edit Video

6. Once the Trim-in icon appears, drag the left edge to the right until the plane becomes visible in the viewing area, the tool tip display will be approximately **+00;00;09;10,** as shown in Figure 26.

   The Program Monitor previews the video clip as you drag the Trim-in icon to the right.

7. Point the cursor to the blank space between the two video clips on the Video 1 track, right-click, then click **Ripple Delete**, as shown in Figure 27.

   The AirshowVideo2 video clip is shifted to the left, removing the gap.

TIP Pressing the [Delete] key on a gap also performs the Ripple Delete command.

8. Press the [**End**] key (Win) or [**Fn**][**Right Arrow**] keys (Mac) to move the CTI to the end of the AirshowVideo2 video clip.

   You will now trim the clip from the right side.

9. Place the cursor over the right edge of the AirshowVideo2 video clip, then once the Trim-out icon appears, drag the right edge to the left until the second plane leaves the viewing area and the tool tip displays approximately **−00;00;12;22,** as shown in Figure 28.

10. Press [**Spacebar**] to preview the sequence on the Program Monitor.

11. Save your project file and leave it open for the next exercise.

You trimmed a video clip from the left and right on the Timeline panel.

Create keyboard commands to set In and Out points

1. Open Pearl Harbor Documentary *your name*, if necessary.

2. Click **Edit** on the Menu bar, then click **Keyboard Shortcuts** (Win), or click **Premiere Pro** on the menu bar, then click **Keyboard Shortcuts** (Mac).

   The Keyboard Shortcuts dialog box opens, as shown in Figure 29.

3. Scroll down to Trim In Point to Playhead, click **Trim In Point to Playhead**, click the **Edit button** to the right, then press [[] (left bracket), as shown in Figure 30.

   In After Effects, you used the keyboard shortcut [Alt][[] to trim clips. This same shortcut key is not available in Premiere Pro. Instead, you will simply use the left and right brackets without [Alt].

4. Click **Trim Out Point to Playhead**, click **Edit**, press []] then click **OK**.

5. Save your project file and leave it open for the next exercise.

Figure 29 *Keyboard Customization dialog box*

Figure 30 *Creating a keyboard shortcut*

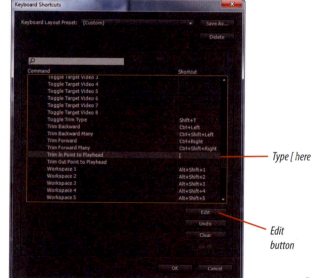

Type [here

Edit button

Figures © Cengage Learning 2013

Figure 31 *Trimming a video clip using a keyboard shortcut*

Plane
leaving
viewing
area

Location
of CTI

Applying the Fast Color Corrector Effect

The Fast Color Corrector effect can be found under the Color Correction bin in the Effects panel and is recommended for making straightforward color corrections that preview quickly in the Program monitor. This effect adjusts a clip's color using hue and saturation controls. In addition, levels controls are available to adjust shadows, midtones, and highlights of an image. A color wheel is used when making adjustments with the hue and balance controls by moving the controls inside the color wheel. The small circle controls the hue balance and the hue angle. It can be adjusted by moving it around the circle and by moving it either away or towards the outer edge of the circle.

Figure © Cengage Learning 2013

Use the CTI to set In and Out points

1. Open Pearl Harbor Documentary *your name*, if necessary.

2. Drag **AirshowVideo3.m2v** after the AirshowVideo2.m2v video clip on the Video 1 track.

3. Preview the AirshowVideo3.m2v video clip, then move the CTI to the beginning of the video clip.

   You need to trim just the right end of the clip.

4. Drag the **CTI** to the location on the Timeline when the plane is just leaving the viewing area on the right, as shown in Figure 31.

5. Press []] on your keypad to set the Out point.

   The right bracket key (]) is the keyboard shortcut you created in the last exercise to set an Out point at the location of the CTI.

6. Press [**Spacebar**] to preview the sequence on the Program Monitor.

7. Save your project file and leave it open for the next exercise.

You trimmed a clip on the Timeline panel at the CTI using a keyboard shortcut.

Trim a video clip with the Ripple Edit tool

1. Open Pearl Harbor Documentary *your name*, if necessary.

2. Drag **AirshowVideo4.m2v** after the AirshowVideo3.m2v video clip on the Video 1 track.

3. Preview the AirshowVideo4.m2v video clip, then drag the **CTI** to the beginning of the video clip.

   This video clip is primarily of the smoke. We want to trim the clip to get footage that has been zoomed in and is not shaky.

4. Click the **Ripple Edit tool** ◄►► on the Tools panel.

   TIP Press [B] on the keyboard to activate the Ripple Edit tool.

5. Place the cursor on the left edge of the **AirshowVideo4.m2v** video clip, then drag the **Ripple Edit icon** to the right until the footage zooms in and becomes less shaky at approximately **+00;00;08;27**, on the tool tip display, as shown in Figure 32.

6. Click the **Selection tool** ► on the Tools panel, place the CTI when you see the footage begin to pan to the left quickly, then press [**]**], to create a Trim out point, as shown in Figure 33.

7. Press [**Spacebar**] to preview the sequence on the Program Monitor.

8. Save your project file and leave it open for the next exercise.

You edited a video clip using the Ripple Edit tool.

Figure 32 *Working with the Ripple Edit tool*

Last frame of outgoing clip

Preview of clip being trimmed

Ripple In icon

Tool tip display

Figure 33 *Creating a Trim Out point*

Trim Out point at CTI

Figures © Cengage Learning 2013

Figure 34 *Setting a Trim Out point*

Timecode display

Trim Out point

Figure 35 *Placing a clip with the Insert button*

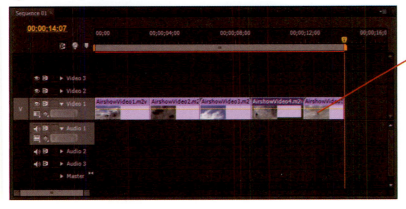

AirshowVideo5.m2v
video clip

Figures © Cengage Learning 2013

Use the Insert button to place a trimmed clip

1. Open Pearl Harbor Documentary *your name*, if necessary.

2. Double-click **AirshowVideo5.m2v** on the Project panel.

3. Click the **Play-Stop Toggle button** ▶ on the Source Monitor to preview the video clip.

   This video clip shows two planes flying in from opposite directions and needs to be trimmed from the right.

4. Move the **CTI** to the point in the clip where the plane on the right leaves the viewing area, as shown in Figure 34, then click the **Mark Out button** { on the Source Monitor.

TIP You can click Step Forward ▶ or Step Back ◀ to adjust the timecode display if you are having trouble getting the image in the frame exactly where you want it.

5. On the Timeline panel, place the CTI at the end of the AirshowVideo4.m2v video clip.

6. Click the **Insert button** 🔳 on the Source Monitor.

   The trimmed AirshowVideo5.m2v video clip is placed at the location of the CTI on the Video 1 track, as shown in Figure 35.

7. Select the sequence, then press [**Spacebar**] to preview the sequence on the Program Monitor.

8. Save your project file and leave it open for the next exercise.

You placed a trimmed clip from the Source Monitor using the Insert button.

Use the Overlay button to place a trimmed clip

1. Open Pearl Harbor Documentary *your name*, if necessary.

2. Open AirshowVideo6.m2v on the Source Monitor and preview the video clip.

   This video clip shows a plane flying in from the left and needs to be trimmed from both sides.

3. Drag the **CTI** until the plane enters the viewing area on the left side, at approximately **00;00;25;07**, then click the **Mark In button**  on the Source Monitor.

4. Drag the **CTI** to just after the plane leaves the viewing area on the right, approximately **00;00;29;00**, then click the **Mark Out button** on the Source Monitor, as shown in Figure 36.

5. On the Timeline panel, place the CTI at the end of the AirshowVideo3.m2v video clip.

6. Click the **Overwrite button** on the Source Monitor to place the video clip on the Timeline panel, as shown in Figure 37.

   This replaces a segment of the AirshowVideo4.m2v video clip with AirshowVideo6.m2v at the location of the CTI, removing a portion of the AirshowVideo4 video clip.

7. Press [**Spacebar**] to preview the sequence on the Program Monitor.

8. Save your project file and leave it open for the next exercise.

You placed a trimmed clip from the Source Monitor using the Overwrite button.

Figure 36 *Setting In and Out points*

In Point

Out Point

Figure 37 *Using the Overwrite button*

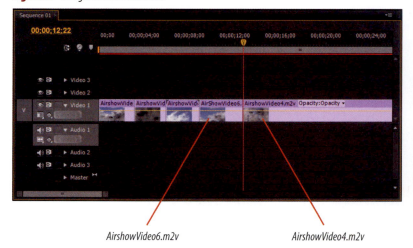

AirshowVideo6.m2v

AirshowVideo4.m2v

Figures © Cengage Learning 2013

Figure 38 *Adjusting the Timeline panel zoom level*

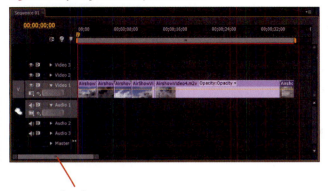

Zoom bar

Figure 39 *Performing a rearrange edit*

Rearrange icon

Figure 40 *New order of video clips*

Figures © Cengage Learning 2013

Perform a rearrange edit

1. Open Pearl Harbor Documentary *your name*, if necessary.

2. Using the Zoom bar, zoom in on the Timeline panel so that you can see all of your video clips at the same time, as shown in Figure 38.

3. Click the **Selection tool** ▶ on the Tools panel, click **AirshowVideo3.m2v**, press and hold [**Ctrl**] [**Alt**] (Win) or ⌘ [**option**] (Mac), drag the video clip in front of **AirshowVideo1.m2v**, then release the mouse button.

   When you press [Ctrl][Alt] (Win) or ⌘ [option] (Mac), the rearrange icon appears, as shown in Figure 39. A tool tip appears when you hover over a video clip, displaying the clip's name, start and end time, and duration.

4. Using the rearrange edit technique, reorder the video clips on the Video 1 track so that they are arranged as follows: AirshowVideo3.m2v, AirshowVideo5.m2v, AirshowVideo1.m2v, AirshowVideo6.m2v, AirshowVideo2.m2v, and AirshowVideo4.m2v, as shown in Figure 40.

5. Press [**Spacebar**] to preview the sequence on the Program Monitor.

6. Save your project file and leave it open for the next exercise.

You rearranged video clips on a sequence using the rearrange edit technique.

LESSON 3

Work with Advanced Editing &
VIDEO EFFECTS

What You'll Do

Figure © Cengage Learning 2013

 In this lesson, you will use advanced editing techniques and apply effects to video clips.

Working with the Razor Tool

If you need to remove a portion of a clip that is not either at the beginning or at the end, you can use the **Razor tool** to split the clip. To do so, you click with the Razor tool pointer. The point that you split the clip is called the **cut point**. A tool tip appears to indicate the In and Out points of the clip and its duration, as shown in Figure 41. Mark as many cut points as needed, then simply select the cut portion that you do not want and press [Delete] on your keyboard. To remove the gap that is left between the remaining clips, use the **Ripple Delete** command; this shifts the clips to the left, removing the empty space. If you have clips on more than one track, the Ripple Delete command is not available unless you disable the Sync Lock and lock the track you are not applying the Ripple Delete command to, as shown in Figure 42.

> **QUICK TIP**
>
> Click the gap and press [Delete] to remove the gap.

Figure 41 *Using the Razor tool*

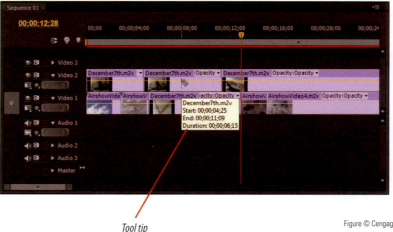

Tool tip

Figure © Cengage Learning 2013

The **Go to Gap** command is a convenient way to jump between gaps and to find gaps that are very short and may be difficult to see. This command can be used on a sequence or on a specific track if multiple tracks are being used.

Rearranging Clips Using the Program Monitor

The Program Monitor can also be used to edit video clips much the same way clips are edited on the Source Monitor. When editing clips on the Program Monitor, the clips being referenced are those already placed on the Timeline panel.

The **Extract button** on the Program Monitor removes a specified area of the sequence marked with In and Out points without leaving a gap in its place. The **Lift button** works in a similar manner to the Extract button, removing a specified area of the sequence; however, the Lift button does leave a gap in its place.

In both cases, the frames that are removed from the sequence are copied to the system clipboard and can then be placed at the location of the CTI with the Paste or Paste Insert command. The **Paste** command behaves like an Overlay edit, and the **Paste Insert** command behaves like an Insert edit.

Nesting a Sequence

Just as you nested compositions in After Effects, you can nest sequences within sequences to create complex groupings. Sequences can be nested inside one another whether or not they share the same presets. However, you cannot nest a sequence inside itself. Nesting sequences can be used as a time-saving technique. You can simply nest a sequence you want to repeat so that you only need to create it once. Nesting sequences can also be used as an organizational tool. If your movie is getting too large, either with many layers or with a long duration, you can break it down into manageable parts with sequences. You can then assemble the final movie in its own sequence.

> **QUICK TIP**
>
> You can use the Sequence from Clip command to have Premiere Pro create a sequence for you based on the clip's properties.

Figure 42 *Using the Ripple Delete command*

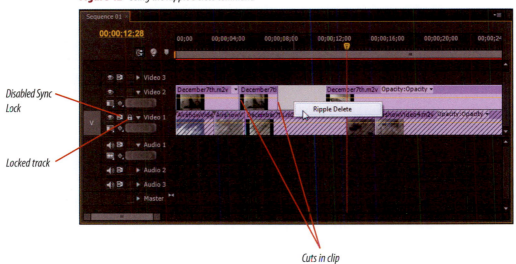

Disabled Sync Lock

Locked track

Cuts in clip

A nested sequence appears as a single linked clip, as shown in Figure 43, and can be treated as such; you can select, trim, move, and apply effects to it. You can also open a nested sequence on the Source Monitor, where you can set In and Out points just as you would with any other clip. If you double-click a nested sequence on the Timeline panel, the source of the sequence opens and becomes the active sequence on the Timeline panel.

QUICK TIP

A nested sequence is displayed in a different color than other clips on a sequence. The color is the same as the Label color in the Project panel.

A nested sequence adds an empty audio track to the Timeline even when your sequence has no audio associated with it. The **Drag Video Only** icon on the Source Monitor allows you to nest the sequence without the empty audio track. Drag Video Only is not a button; it is an icon that provides a place to click when you begin to drag. You click the Drag Video Only icon to initiate the dragging of the clip from the Source Monitor.

Using Keyboard Shortcuts to Preview a Sequence

Most of the playback controls on the Program Monitor have keyboard equivalents. When the Timeline panel is selected, you can use the keyboard shortcuts to preview your sequence on the Program Monitor more efficiently.

You have already used [Spacebar] to toggle between Play and Stop. You can also press [L] to play and [K] to stop. To play a sequence in reverse, press [J]. To increase the speed at which the sequence is playing, press [L] or [J] to play it forward or backward, respectively. If you want to advance or retreat one frame, press and hold [K] and then press either [L] or [J], respectively. In order to play the sequence in slow motion, press and hold the [Shift] key and then press either [L] or [J] to play it forward or backward, respectively.

You can find a list of keyboard shortcuts in the Help file by pressing [F1].

Applying Video Effects

In Chapter 1 you used the standard Motion effects to create panning and zooming effects on still images. Premiere Pro has many additional effects available which include the ability to change the exposure or color of footage, distort images, or remove the background.

Figure 43 *A nested sequence in a sequence*

Reenactment footage

Figure © Cengage Learning 2013

In this chapter, you will modify the color of a video clip to black and white and adjust the lighting effects to make the clip appear darker. The Black & White effect from the Image Control category removes color from a clip and changes it to black and white. There are no controls available for this effect.

Lighting Effects can be found in the Adjust category and can use up to five virtual lights to produce creative effects. Each of these virtual lights can create effects similar to the sun, a light bulb, or a beam of light. The properties that can be manipulated include Lighting Type, Direction, Intensity, Color, Lighting Center, and Lighting Spread. These properties can be manipulated directly on the Program Monitor by clicking the Transform icon on the Effect Controls panel.

You can apply any number of effects to a clip by selecting the effect on the Effects panel and dragging the effect icon to a clip on the Timeline panel. Adjustments are made on the Effect Controls panel, as shown in Figure 44. Not all effects have parameters that can be adjusted.

Working with Transitions

You learned about video transitions in Chapter 1 and you will be using them again as you apply them between cuts in video clips. Transitions are used to piece together two clips that have been cut. Transitions are often used to indicate a change in location, a change

in the rate of the action, or simply the passage of time. Another reason to use transitions is to smooth out minor video or audio errors, which could appear more prominent with just a cut, but which may be less obvious with a well-placed transition such as a dissolve.

There are many transitions to choose from, but most professionals use only simple cuts and crossfades. Using too many transitions can be distracting and can affect the flow of the video. Try to keep transitions as smooth

and as unnoticeable as possible; transitions should not call attention to themselves.

Consider the following when you choose a transition:

- Does the transition fit with the story you are trying to tell?
- Do the clips work well together with the transition?
- Is the transition confusing?
- What do you hope to achieve with the transition?

Figure 44 *Effect Controls panel*

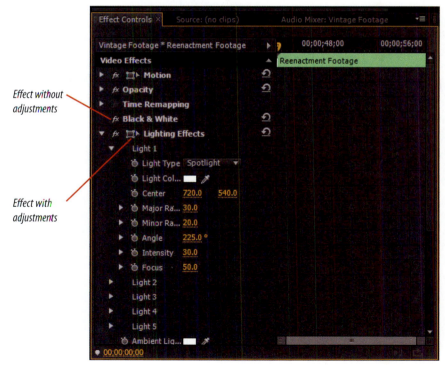

Effect without adjustments

Effect with adjustments

Create a new sequence

1. Open Pearl Harbor Documentary *your name*, and reset the workspace to Editing, if necessary.

2. Click **File** on the Menu bar, click **Import**, navigate to your Data Files folder, select **December7th.m2v**, then click **Open** (Win) or **Import** (Mac).

Leave the clip selected in the Project panel for the next step.

3. Click **File** on the Menu bar, point to **New**, then click **Sequence From Clip**.

A new sequence is created based on the selected clip.

4. Right-click the sequence **December7th.m2v** in the Project panel, click **Rename**, type **Vintage Footage**, then compare your Project panel to Figure 45.

5. Right-click **Sequence 01** on the Project panel, click **Rename**, type **Reenactment Footage**, then compare your screen to Figure 46.

6. Save your project file and leave it open for the next exercise.

You imported a video clip and created a new sequence.

Figure 45 *Project panel with new sequence*

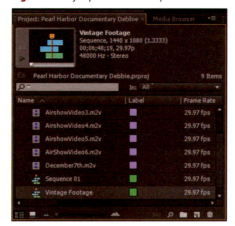

Figure 46 *Project window with the new Vintage Footage sequence*

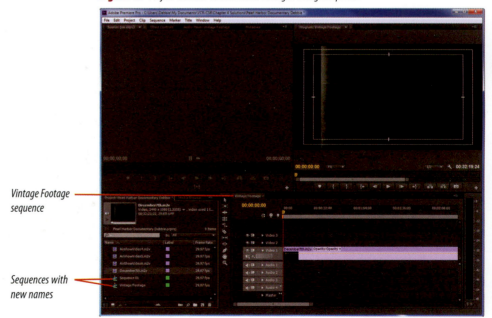

Vintage Footage sequence

Sequences with new names

Figures © Cengage Learning 2013

Figure 47 *Location of first cut line*

Location of CTI

Figure 48 *Making a razor cut*

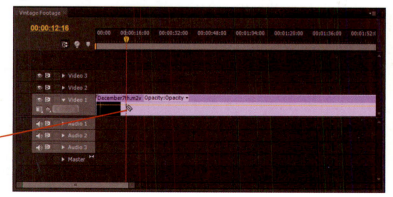

Razor cursor

Use the Razor tool to edit video

1. Open Pearl Harbor Documentary *your name*, if necessary.

2. Click the **Play/Stop Toggle** on the Program monitor to preview the **December7th.m2v** video clip from the Timeline panel.

   You are going to edit this video clip for use with the video of the Pearl Harbor reenactment that you have already edited.

3. Place the **CTI** at the point when you see the plane wreckage after the boat wreckage and the transition ends, approximately **00;00;07;00**, as shown in Figure 47, then click the **Razor tool** on the Tools panel.

4. Place the **cursor** where the CTI overlaps the video clip, as shown in Figure 48, then click.

   The appearance of the cursor changes to that of a razor when over a clip. The clip is cut into two parts. You will continue to move through the video clip making razor cuts.

TIP You can also access the Razor tool by pressing [C].

(continued)

5. Make razor cuts at the following playhead positions: **00;02;06;15**, **00;02;24;15**, **00;04;42;04**, **00;05;51;04**, **00;07;27;20**, **00;09;02;25**, **00;10;19;19**, **00;12;30;18**, **00;16;12;16**, and **00;17;10;29**, then compare your sequence to Figure 49.

You will now remove the clips you do not need.

6. Click the **Selection tool**  on the Tools panel, select the clip with the Start time 00;00;07;00, as shown in Figure 50, then press [**Delete**].

This clip should be the second cut clip in the sequence. Hover the mouse pointer over the clip to see a tool tip displaying the start and end points of the clip. You may need to zoom in on the sequence to see the video clips.

7. Delete the clips with the following start times from the sequence: **00;02;24;15**, **00;05;51;04**, **00;09;02;25**, **00;12;30;18**, and **00;17;10;29**, then compare your Timeline panel to Figure 51.

8. Save your project file and leave it open for the next exercise.

You edited a video with the Razor tool to remove unwanted sections of the footage.

Figure 49 *Sequence with the razor cuts*

Razor cuts

Figure 50 *Selecting a clip to delete*

Start time

Figure 51 *Sequence after video clips deleted*

Gaps from deleted clips

Figures © Cengage Learning 2013

Figure 52 *Using the Go to Gap command*

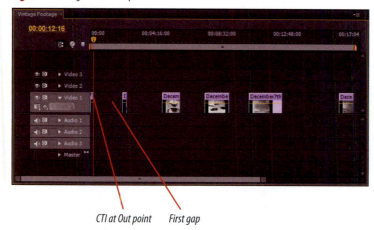

CTI at Out point   First gap

Figure 53 *Using the Ripple Delete command*

Ripple Delete
command

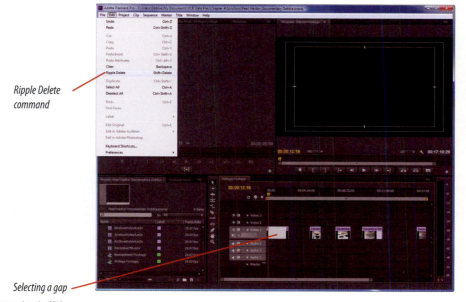

Selecting a gap

Remove gaps between video

1. Open Pearl Harbor Documentary *your name*, if necessary.

   There is a lot of space between the remaining video clips that you now need to remove.

2. Verify that the Vintage Footage sequence is active on the Timeline panel, and that the CTI is at **00;00;00;00**.

3. Click **Sequence** on the Menu bar, point to **Go to Gap**, then click **Next in Sequence**.

   The CTI jumps to the Out point of the first video clip, which marks the beginning of the first gap, as shown in Figure 52.

   Because you have only one track in our sequence, you can choose Next in Sequence. If you were using multiple tracks and needed to distinguish between which tracks you were on, then you would choose Next in Track.

TIP The gaps in this sequence are rather large and easy to see. The Go to Gap command is helpful for finding hard-to-see gaps to verify that there will be no gaps in your final footage.

4. Click the **gap**, click **Edit** on the Menu bar, then click **Ripple Delete**, as shown in Figure 53.

   The gap is removed from the track and the remaining clips shift to the left.

   (continued)

5. Select the remaining gaps on the sequence and then remove them by pressing [**Delete**] so that your Timeline resembles Figure 54.

6. Save your project file and leave it open for the next exercise.

You used the Ripple Delete command to remove gaps left behind from the Razor tool.

Rearrange a clip using the Program Monitor

1. Open Pearl Harbor Documentary *your name*, if necessary.

2. Press [**Spacebar**] to preview the Vintage Footage sequence on the Program Monitor.

   The first cut video clip needs to be moved to the end of the sequence after the attack has taken place.

3. Place the CTI at **00;00;00;00**, then click the **Mark In button** on the Program Monitor.

4. Press [**Down Arrow**], then click the **Mark Out button** on the Program Monitor.

   Notice the color change on the Timeline panel to show the location of the In and Out points that were just set on the Program Monitor, as shown in Figure 55.

5. Click the **Extract button** on the Program Monitor.

   The first cut video clip is removed from the sequence without leaving a gap, as shown in Figure 56.

6. Verify that the Timeline panel is active, press [**End**] to move the CTI to the end of the sequence, click **Edit** on the Menu bar, then click **Paste**.

(continued)

Figure 54 *Sequence with all gaps removed*

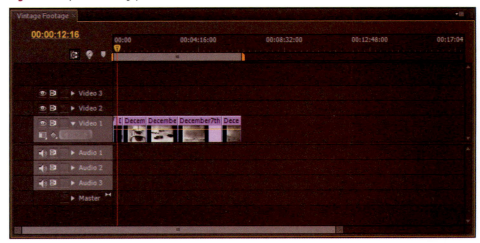

Figure 55 *Specified area of a sequence when setting In and Out points on the Program Monitor*

Specified area of a sequence

Figures © Cengage Learning 2013

Figure 56 *Clip removed with no gap left*

Figure 57 *Searching for a transition*

Cross

Contains field

The extracted clip is placed at the location of the CTI.

TIP You can also use [Ctrl][V] (Win) or ⌘ [V] (Mac) to paste a video clip.

7. Save your project file and leave it open for the next exercise.

You used the Extract button on the Program Monitor and the Paste command to change the location of a video clip in the sequence.

Apply transitions between video clips

1. Open Pearl Harbor Documentary *your name*, if necessary.

   You will add transitions to smooth out the choppiness created by the cut points in the video.

2. Verify that the Vintage Footage sequence is active on the Timeline panel.

3. Change the current workspace to Effects.

4. Drag the **CTI** to **00;00;17;29**.

TIP You can drag the CTI in either the Timeline panel or the Program panel; because both CTIs reference the same information, the CTI in the other panel adjusts automatically to match.

5. Type **Cross** in the Contains field on the Effects panel.

   Entering the keyword *Cross* filters the list to show only transitions that have the word cross in them, as shown in Figure 57. You will be using the Cross Dissolve transition.

6. Click the **Cross Dissolve transition** on the Effects panel, click **Sequence** on the Menu bar, then click **Apply Video Transition**.

   The Cross Dissolve transition is placed at the location of the CTI, as shown in Figure 58.

(continued)

TIP The keyboard shortcut to place the selected transition at the location of the CTI is [Ctrl][D] (Win) or ⌘ [D] (Mac).

7. Place the Cross Dissolve transition at each of the remaining cut points in the sequence: **00;01;26;29**, **00;03;02;04**, **00;05;13;03**, and **00;06;11;16**, as shown in Figure 59.

TIP Another way to place the default transition at the end of each clip is to press [Down Arrow] and then press [Ctrl][D] (Win) or ⌘ [D] (Mac).

8. Place the Dip to Black transition on the last clip in the sequence as an End at Cut transition as shown in Figure 60.

   This will fade the last video clip to black at the end of the sequence.

9. Press [**Spacebar**] to preview the clip on the Program Monitor.

10. Save your project file and leave it open for the next exercise.

You applied a Cross Dissolve transition on the cut lines to remove the choppiness that occurred because of the previous editing.

Nest a sequence

1. Open Pearl Harbor Documentary *your name*, if necessary.

2. Set the current workspace to Editing, then verify that the Vintage Footage sequence is active on the Timeline panel.

3. Right-click the **Reenactment Footage sequence** on the Project panel, then click **Open in Source Monitor**, as shown in Figure 61.

   The sequence opens on the Source Monitor where it can be previewed and edited.

(continued)

Figure 58 *Placing a transition at the CTI*

Cross Dissolve transition

Figure 59 *Cross Dissolve transition between all cut points*

Cross Dissolve transition

Figure 60 *Placing a Dip to Black transition*

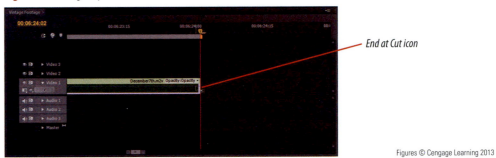

End at Cut icon

Figure 61 *Previewing a sequence on the Source Monitor*

Reenactment
Footage sequence

Vintage
Footage sequence

Figure 62 *Previewing a sequence using keyboard shortcuts*

First frame
of sky

Location of CTI

Figures © Cengage Learning 2013

4. Drag the **CTI** to **00;00;35;00**.

5. Press [**Shift**][**L**] on the keyboard to play the sequence at a slow speed, press [**K**] to stop the sequence from playing, then press [**Shift**] [**J**] to play the sequence in reverse at a slow speed, closely examining just a few seconds of the clip.

   The point where the sailor is looking up at the sky and then planes start to appear in the sky, but are still very faint, would be a good place to insert the reenactment footage.

6. Leave the CTI where you can still see the sailor for the next step.

   You want the CTI to be placed at the exact point where the sailor disappears and the sky appears.

7. Press and hold [**K**], then continue to press [**L**] until you see the first frame of the sky on the Program Monitor, as shown in Figure 62.

8. Click the **Razor tool** on the Tools panel, then click at the location of the CTI to make a cut.

   You are now ready to insert the Reenactment Footage sequence at the location of the cut that you just created.

9. Click the **Insert button** on the Source Monitor to place the Reenactment Footage sequence at the location of the CTI.

   Notice the Reenactment Footage sequence has an empty audio track that was also inserted, as shown in Figure 63.

10. Click **Edit** on the Menu bar, then click **Undo**.

    The sequence is removed from the Timeline panel. You need to place the sequence without the empty audio track.

(continued)

11. Press and hold [**Ctrl**] (Win) or [⌘] (Mac), then click and drag the **Drag Video Only icon** 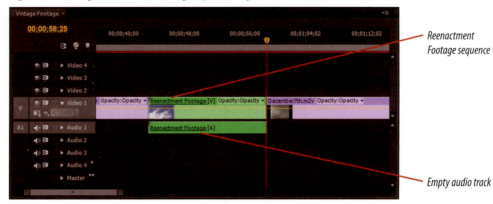 to the location of the CTI to place the Reenactment Footage sequence, as shown in Figure 64.

The sequence is placed without the empty audio track.

12. Press [**Spacebar**] to preview the clip on the Program Monitor.

13. Save your project file and leave it open for the next exercise.

You used keyboard shortcuts to preview a sequence on the Timeline panel and then inserted a sequence using the Drag Video Only icon after creating a razor cut.

Apply a video effect

1. Open Pearl Harbor Documentary *your name*, if necessary.

2. Set the current workspace to Effects, then verify that the Vintage Footage sequence is active on the Timeline panel.

The Reenactment Footage needs to be made black and white.

3. Place the CTI at the beginning of the Reenactment Footage clip on the Timeline panel.

4. If necessary, clear the contents of the Contains field on the Effects panel, click the **expand arrow** in front of Video Effects, then click the **expand arrow** in front of Image Control.

The categories of Video Effects are displayed and the Image Control video effects are also displayed.

(continued)

Figure 63 *Inserting the Reenactment Footage sequence using the Insert button*

Reenactment Footage sequence

Empty audio track

Figure 64 *Dragging video only to sequence with Insert edit command*

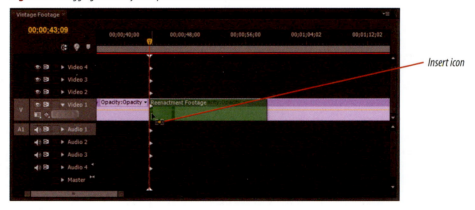

Insert icon

Figures © Cengage Learning 2013

Figure 65 *Applying a Black & White video effect*

Black & White preview

Black & White video effect

Black & White video effect

Drag Black & White effect here

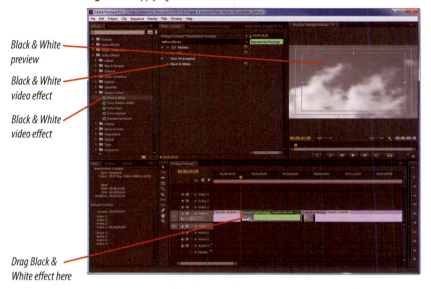

Figure 66 *Applying the Lighting Effects*

Lighting Effects

Light Type drop-down menu

Lighting Effects

Ambience Intensity

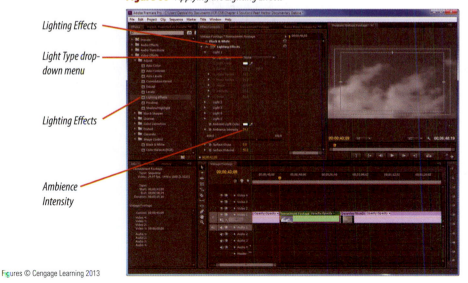

5. Click **Black & White** on the Effects panel, then drag it on top of the Reenactment Footage clip on the Timeline panel.

   As shown in Figure 65, the footage is converted to black and white, which is visible in the preview on the Program Monitor and the Black & White video effect is added to the Effect Controls panel. The effect is a little too bright, so you will make adjustments to it in the next step.

6. On the Effects panel, click the **expand arrow** in front of **Adjust**, then drag **Lighting Effects** on top of the Reenactment Footage clip on the Timeline panel.

   This is the second video effect applied to the Reenactment Footage clip.

7. On the Effect Controls panel, click the **expand arrow** in front of **Lighting Effects**, if necessary, and again in front of **Light 1**, click the **Light Type drop-down menu**, then click **None**.

8. Click the **expand arrow** in front of Ambience Intensity then drag the **slider** to **34.1**, as shown in Figure 66.

   This modifies the appearance of the video footage so that it fits in better with the Vintage Footage sequence with its black-and-white appearance.

9. Press [**Spacebar**] to preview the clip on the Program Monitor.

10. Save your project file and leave it open for the next exercise.

You changed the appearance of a video clip to black and white through the use of video effects.

LESSON 4

Edit Audio
IN AUDITION

What You'll Do

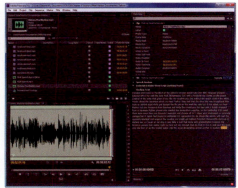

Figure © Cengage Learning 2013

 In this lesson, you will repair an audio file in Audition, then edit the file in Premiere Pro.

Editing an Audio Source File in Audition

If you have either the Master Collection or Production Premium Suite installed—both of which include Audition—you can apply the **Edit in Adobe Audition** command to an audio clip from Premiere Pro, as shown in Figure 67.

The Edit in Audition command can be applied to an audio clip from either the Project panel or the Timeline panel. If you select the clip on the Project panel, the audio is extracted, edits are made on a copy of the audio clip, and the original audio clip is left untouched. If the command is applied to an audio clip on

Figure 67 *Edit in Adobe Audition*

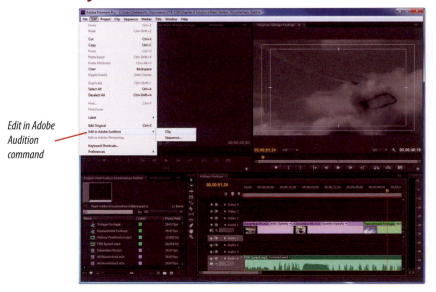

Edit in Adobe
Audition
command

Figure © Cengage Learning 2013

Creating a Documentary Using Premiere Pro & Audition CS6

a sequence, the clip on the Timeline panel is edited in Audition and replaced, leaving the audio clip in the Project panel unchanged. When editing an audio clip in Audition you have two options: clip and sequence. The clip option makes edits to a selected clip from either the Project panel or the Timeline panel. When you save the file in Audition, the clip is automatically updated in Premiere Pro. As long as the file is kept open in Audition, additional edits can be made.

The sequence option allows you to take all clips from a sequence, including any cut lines or just a specified range of time. Premiere Pro and Audition share an XML file with reference information.

Working with Audio Transitions

Transitions are also available for audio in Premiere Pro to add fade-in or fade-out effects. **Crossfades** are audio transitions that fade into or fade out of audio clips. A crossfade is created between two adjoining clips on the same audio track. A fade-in or fade-out effect is created by placing a crossfade transition on either end of a single clip. There are three types of crossfades: Constant Gain, Constant Power, and Exponential Fade, as shown in Figure 68.

The **Constant Gain** crossfade can sound abrupt because it changes the audio at a constant rate in and out as it transitions between clips, as shown in Figure 69. The **Constant Power** crossfade is the default transition. It is analogous to the Dissolve transition between video clips because of the way that it creates a smooth, gradual transition between audio clips. The Constant Power transition works by decreasing the audio for the first clip slowly and then more quickly towards the end of the transition while increasing the audio for the second clip quickly at first and then more slowly toward the end of the transition, as shown in Figure 70. The **Exponential Fade** transition fades out the first clip and fades up the second clip.

Converting Speech to Text

Premiere Pro can convert the spoken word in an audio file into text transcripts. Text transcripts can be used to create closed

Figure 68 *Audio transitions*

Crossfades

Figure 69 *Constant Gain crossfade*

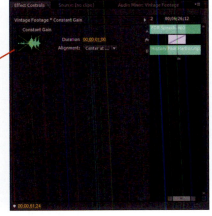

Constant Gain

Figure 70 *Constant Power crossfade*

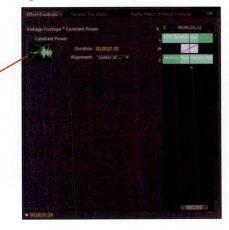

Constant Power

captioning, or as a way to quickly navigate through video or audio clips by searching on the spoken words. In both applications, the Metadata panel is used to initiate the transcription process and to display the transcript when the process is complete. An **XMP metadata file** is generated and shared between all of the Video Suite applications when the transcript is created. **Metadata** includes the text transcript and can also include any additional information, such as the title, author, camera model, and date and time the video or image was taken. Metadata appears on the Metadata panel.

In most cases, not all the transcribed words are accurate, and the accuracy depends on the clearness of the speaker and the quality of the audio. The tools in Audition can be used to clean up the audio before initiating the Convert to Speech option. Generally, the transcription that is generated is useful enough to aid in searching for keywords. However, transcripts can be edited where errors were made in the transcription process if a more accurate transcript is required. If you have a reference script available, you can refer to that file during the transcription process to get a more accurate transcription.

In Premiere Pro, you can convert the spoken word to written text by clicking the Analyze button in the Speech Analysis section of the Metadata panel. The Analyze Content dialog box opens, as shown in Figure 71. There are two quality options in the dialog box; the default is set to High (slower) so the Media Encoder will move at a slower pace as it passes through the audio clip. If you have more than one speaker in the audio clip that you wish to have identified, check the box next to Identify Speakers. Once you click OK, the Media Encoder launches, placing the request in the queue, as shown in Figure 72. When

Figure 71 *Analyze Content dialog box*

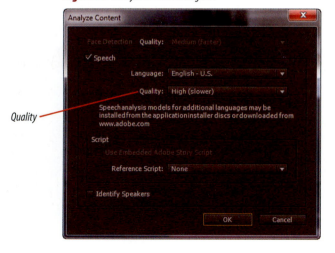

Quality

Figure 72 *Adobe Media Encoder*

Queue

Duration bar

Figures © Cengage Learning 2013

the Media Encoder has finished, you can close the application and return to your project in Premiere Pro. The transcript then appears in the Speech Analysis portion of the Metadata panel, as shown in Figure 73. Having the text available in Premiere Pro allows you to navigate through a clip by selecting keywords or phrases. When a word is highlighted on the Metadata panel, the CTI navigates to that location of the clip. This allows you to quickly jump to a location in a video or audio clip and set In and Out points for the clip, as shown in Figure 74.

If you are going to edit your source file in Audition from Premiere Pro to convert your audio file to a text transcript, you need to export the speech analysis to generate the XMP metadata file, so that when you return to your project the text transcript appears on the Metadata panel in Premiere Pro.

Figure 73 *Metadata panel with transcribed text*

Metadata panel

Transcribed text

Figure 74 *In and Out points and transcribed text*

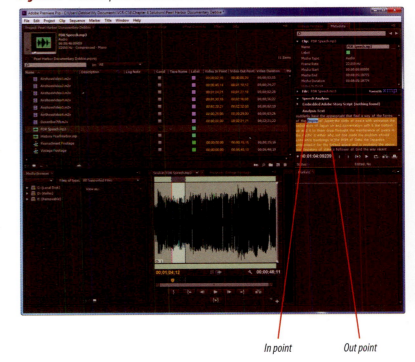

In point

Out point

Figures © Cengage Learning 2013

Import an audio file and preview

1. Open Pearl Harbor Documentary *your name*, if necessary.

2. Set the current workspace to Editing, then verify that the Vintage Footage sequence is active on the Timeline panel.

3. Open the Media Browser, then locate your Data Files folder for Chapter 4.

4. Click **FDR Speech**, press and hold [**Shift**], click **History Pearl Harbor**, as shown in Figure 75 right-click, then click **Import**.

   Both audio files are imported into the Project panel, as shown in Figure 76.

   (continued)

Figure 75 *Locating the Data Files folder for Chapter 4 in the Media Browser*

Media Browser

Data Files folder

Figure 76 *Audio files imported into Project panel*

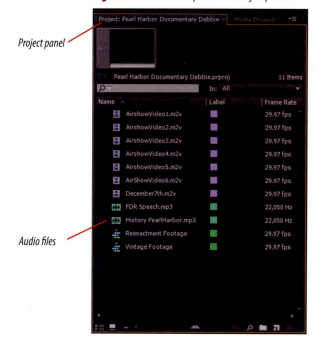

Project panel

Audio files

Figures © Cengage Learning 2013

Creating a Documentary Using Premiere Pro & Audition CS6

Figure 77 *Dragging only the audio to a new audio track*

Drag Audio Only

5. Double-click **FDR Speech** to open it on the Source Monitor, then click the **Play button** ▶ to preview the audio clip.

   You will notice there are some areas of the speech that have scratchy noises that need to be cleaned up in Audition.

6. Click the **Drag Audio Only icon** ⬌ then drag the **FDR Speech** to the **Audio 1** track, as shown in Figure 77.

7. Save your project file and leave it open for the next exercise.

You imported audio files, previewed a file on the Source Monitor, and finally dragged the audio clip to an audio track.

Clean up an audio source file in Audition

1. Open Pearl Harbor Documentary *your name*, if necessary.

2. With the **Selection tool** ▶, click the **FDR Speech audio clip** on the Timeline, point to **Edit** on the Menu bar, click **Edit in Adobe Audition** then click **Edit Clip**.

   Audition opens with the FDR Speech file active on the Editor panel.

(continued)

Working with Sequences in Encore

Adobe Dynamic Link is supported between Premiere Pro and Encore. A Premiere Pro sequence can be sent or imported into Encore for output to DVD, Blu-ray, or SWF. The sequence can then be updated in Premiere Pro and it will be reflected in Encore without rendering. While in Encore, the sequence can be selected for editing by using the Edit Original command.

3. In Audition, choose the Default workspace, then if necessary, click the **Spectral Frequency Display button** ▣ on the Tools panel to show the spectral display on the Editor panel.

Looking at the spectral display, you can quickly determine that there are areas you can remove at the very beginning and at the end of the speech, indicated by black as shown in Figure 78.

4. Click the **Time Selection tool** 工 on the Tools panel, highlight the areas indicated in Figure 78, then press [**Delete**].

The unwanted areas from the audio file are removed; your Editor panel should look similar to Figure 79.

5. Click **File** on the Menu bar, then click **Save**.

The FDR Speech audio clip that you opened from Premiere Pro for editing in Audition is saved.

6. Close Audition, then return to the open project file in Premiere Pro.

7. Keep the file open for the next exercise.

You removed the unwanted areas at the beginning and the end of the FDR Speech in Audition.

Edit an audio clip on the Timeline panel

1. Open Pearl Harbor Documentary *your name*, if necessary.

2. Open the FDR Speech Extracted audio clip, if it is not already open on the Source Monitor.

The edits made in Audition have transferred to the audio file in Premiere Pro.

3. Click the **Play button** ▶ on the Source Monitor to preview the FDR Speech audio file.

(continued)

Figure 78 *Areas to be removed*

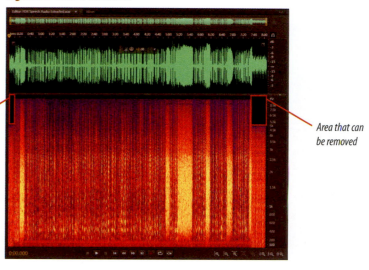

Area that can be removed

Area that can be removed

Figure 79 *Edited source FDR Speech source file*

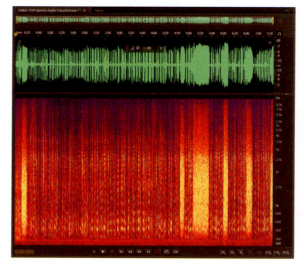

Figures © Cengage Learning 2013

Figure 80 *Viewing the waveform on the audio track*

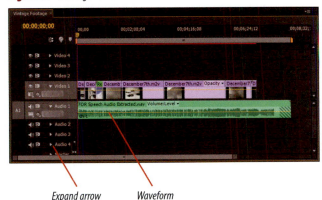

Expand arrow   Waveform

Figure 81 *Deleting applause*

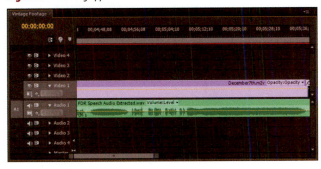

Figure 82 *Shortening the duration of the audio clip*

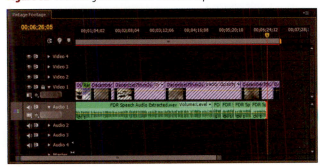

Figures © Cengage Learning 2013

4. Click the **expand arrow** on the Audio 1 track, as shown in Figure 80.

   The waveform is now visible. Notice that the audio clip is much longer than the video. You can correct this by removing some of the applause from the speech. The applause is recognizable in the waveform as large portions of green where the waves are not distinguishable.

5. Click the **Razor tool** on the Tools panel, make cuts before and after the areas of applause, for a total of eight cut lines.

   Be careful not to cut any of the President's speech.

6. Use keyboard shortcut keys to preview the audio clip and make any necessary modifications to the locations of the cuts.

   You will leave the first round of applause when the President is introduced.

7. Lock the Video 1 track, click the **Selection tool** on the Tools panel, right-click between the cut lines, then click **Ripple Delete** to delete the applause using Figure 81 as a guide.

8. Drag the **CTI** to **00;06;23;27**, place the cursor at the right edge of the FDR Speech audio clip, where the President stops speaking, and using the **Trim-out icon**, drag the clip to the CTI, then compare your screen to Figure 82.

   Your time may vary.

9. Save your project file and leave it open for the next exercise.

You edited an audio clip on the Timeline panel using the Razor tool and removed gaps using the Ripple Delete command.

Convert speech to text

1. Open Pearl Harbor Documentary *your name*, if necessary.

2. Change the workspace to Metalogging.

3. Click the **History PearlHarbor audio clip** on the Project panel, as shown in Figure 83, then click the **Analyze button** on the Metadata panel.

   You may need to resize the Metadata panel to see the Analyze button.

4. Without changing the default settings in the Speech Analysis Options dialog box, click **OK**.

   The Adobe Media Encoder opens to perform the transcription, as shown in Figure 84.

5. When the analysis has finished, close the Adobe Media Encoder and return to Premier Pro.

   The text has been added to the Metadata panel in Premiere Pro.

(continued)

Figure 83 *Metadata panel*

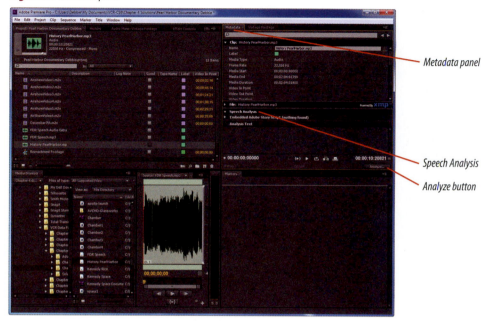

Metadata panel

Speech Analysis

Analyze button

Figure 84 *Analyzing speech dialog box*

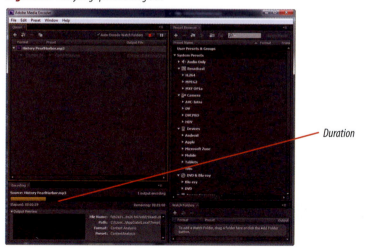

Duration

Figures © Cengage Learning 2013

Figure 85 *Moving the Metadata panel*

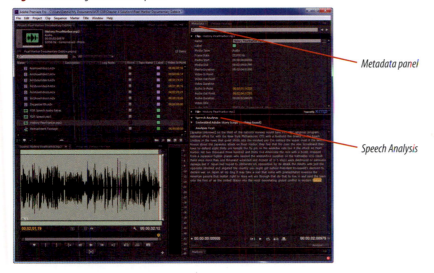

Metadata panel

Speech Analysis

Figure 86 *Highlighting a word in the Speech Analysis to adjust the CTI*

CTI

Highlighted word

Figures © Cengage Learning 2013

6. Expand the Metadata panel so you can see more of the text, as shown in Figure 85.

7. Look through the passage for the part that reads: "through that".

    The transcription has some errors in it. Your transcription may vary. The last statement said by the commentator just after where FDR's speech is played in the clip should be, "the day that will live in infamy became only the first of many as the United States entered the most devastating global conflict in modern history."

8. Click on the "**do**" in the statement.

    The CTI moves to the location of the text you highlight in the Metadata panel, as shown in Figure 86.

9. Click the **Play-Stop Toggle button** ▶ on the Source Monitor to preview the History PearlHarbor audio clip from this point.

    Notice the transcription does not match the spoken word. You will trim the audio clip from this point in the next exercise to use at the end of your video.

10. Save your project file and leave it open for the next exercise.

You converted the speech to text and used the Metadata panel to find text and navigate the CTI to that location.

Edit an audio clip on the Source Monitor

1. Open Pearl Harbor Documentary *your name*, if necessary.

2. Open History PearlHarbor on the Source Monitor.

   You will be editing this audio file on the Source Monitor and then placing it on the Audio 1 track.

3. On the Metadata panel, look through the passage for the part that reads "that do that" and select the word "**do**".

4. On the Metadata panel, click the **Mark In button** .

5. On the Metadata panel, select the last word, **history**.

6. On the Metadata panel, click the **Mark Out button** , then compare your Source Monitor to Figure 87.

7. Set your workspace to Editing.

   The Video 1 track should still be locked.

8. Click in the **header** of the Audio 1 track, if necessary.

   This targets the track by highlighting it and preparing it for the Insert command, as shown in Figure 88.

9. Place the CTI at the end of the audio track.

10. Click the **Insert button** on the Source Monitor.

    The trimmed clip is placed at the location of the CTI on the Timeline panel, as shown in Figure 89.

11. Save your project file and leave it open for the next exercise.

You edited an audio clip on the Source Monitor and then placed it on the audio track.

Figure 87 *Setting In and Out points on the Source Monitor*

In point

Out point

Figure 88 *Targeting the Audio track*

Target track

Figure 89 *Trimmed audio clip inserted from Source Monitor*

Figure 90 *Placing an audio transition*

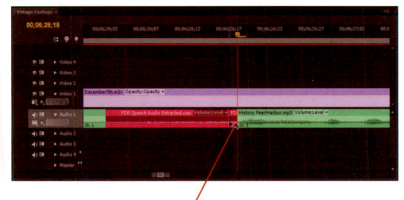

Center at Cut alignment icon

Figure 91 *Preview of sample title on Video 2 track*

Preview of sample title

Apply an audio transition

1. Open Pearl Harbor Documentary *your name*, if necessary.

2. Set the workspace to Effects, click the **Source menu** on the Source Monitor, then click **Close All**.

3. Preview the transition between the last FDR Speech audio clip and the History PearlHarbor audio clip.

   The FDR Speech audio clip needs to fade into the History PearlHarbor audio clip.

4. Click the **expand arrow** in front of **Audio Transitions**, then click the **expand arrow** in front of **Crossfade**.

5. Drag the **Constant Power transition** from the Effects panel and drop it between the last FDR Speech audio clip and the History PearlHarbor audio clip with a Center at Cut alignment, as shown in Figure 90.

   The Constant Power audio transition is analogous to the Dissolve transition used in video.

6. Create a Default Still Title, place it on the Video 2 track to title your documentary, and give yourself credit. One example is provided in Figure 91.

   It is not necessary to provide credits for the clips used in this project; they are all public domain and therefore have no restrictions for their use. The Reenactment footage was filmed by the author and is provided for use as a part of this project.

7. Save and export your movie with the MPEG2 format using the NTSC DV High Quality Preset.

You applied an audio transition between audio clips and exported your final movie with the MPEG2 format.

Transfer tapeless video.

1. Without starting Premiere Pro, navigate to the drive and folder where your Data Files are stored for Chapter 4.
2. Navigate to the Video Clips folder, select AVCHD-Glassworks, click Organize on the Toolbar, then click Copy.
3. Select the Data Files folder for Chapter 4 using the Navigation pane, click Organize on the Toolbar, then click Paste.

Create a sequence for AVCHD video footage.

1. Start Premiere Pro, then click New Project in the Welcome to Adobe Premiere Pro dialog box.
2. Click Browse, then navigate to your Data Files folder.
3. Name the project **Glassworks** *your name*, then click OK.
4. Click the expander arrow in front of HDV, select HDV 1080p30, then click OK.

Import video from a file-based source.

1. Set the workspace to Editing.
2. On the Media Browser panel, locate the Data Files folder for Chapter 4, then double-click the AVCHD- Glassworks folder.
3. Double-click 00003.
4. Click the Source menu on the Source Monitor, then click Close.

5. Select clip 00001, click File on the Menu bar, then click Import from Media Browser.
6. Save and close your project file.

Trim video on the Source Monitor.

1. Open Kennedy SpaceDocumentary.prproj, then rename it **Kennedy Space Documentary** **your name**.
2. Select Workspace on the Menu bar, then choose the Editing workspace.
3. Double-click space1.m2v on the Project panel.
4. Click the Play-Stop Toggle button to preview the video clip.
5. Turn on Safe Margins in both the Source and Program Monitors, if they are not already activated.
6. Drag the CTI until the timecode display reads 00;14;35;05, then click the Mark In button on the Source Monitor.
7. Drag the CTI until the timecode display reads 00;18;48;04, then click the Mark Out button on the Source Monitor.
8. Click the Play In to Out button to preview the trimmed clip on the Source Monitor.
9. Drag the In/Out Grip to the left two tick marks to move the In point to the left.
10. Click the Play In to Out button to preview the trimmed clip on the Source Monitor.
11. Hover your mouse over the Out point, then drag the right edge of the clip with the Trim-out icon until the timecode display reads 00;19;18;02.

12. Click the Play In to Out button to preview the trimmed clip on the Source Monitor.
13. With the CTI at the beginning of the sequence, click the Insert button to place the trimmed clip in the sequence on the Timeline panel.
14. With the Timeline panel selected, press [Spacebar] to preview the clip on the Program Monitor.

Edit a clip on the Timeline panel.

1. Drag space2.m2v to the Video 1 track on the Timeline panel after the existing clip.
2. Press the [Down Arrow] key to move the CTI to the beginning of the space2 video clip.
3. Press [Spacebar] to preview the video clip on the Program Monitor.
4. Click the Selection tool on the Tools panel, then place your cursor over the left edge of the space2 video clip. Once the Trim-in icon appears, drag the left edge to the right until the tool tip displays +00;06;32;02.
5. Point your cursor to the blank space between the two video clips on the Video 1 track, right-click, then click Ripple Delete.
6. Press [Down Arrow] to move the CTI to the end of the space2 video clip.
7. Place your cursor over the right edge of the space2 video clip. Once the Trim-out icon appears, drag the right edge to the left until the tool tip displays -00;00;26;17.
8. Press [Spacebar] to preview the sequence on the Program Monitor.

Create keyboard commands to set In and Out points.

1. Click Edit on the Menu bar, then choose Keyboard Shortcuts. (*Hint*: These keyboard shortcuts have already been created and may already be set on your computer, unless your computer is restored to factory settings.)
2. Click the Keyboard Layout Preset drop-down menu, then click Custom.
3. Scroll down to Trim In Point to Playhead, click Trim In Point to Playhead, click the Edit button, then press [[].
4. Click Trim Out Point to Playhead, press the Edit button, press []], then click OK.

Use the CTI to set In and Out points.

1. Drag space3.m2v after the space2.m2v video clip on the Video 1 track.
2. Preview the space3.m2v video clip and move the CTI to the beginning of the video clip.
3. Move the CTI to 00;08;18;19.
4. Press [[] on your keyboard to create a Trim in point.
5. Move the CTI to 00;08;44;22.
6. Press []] on your keyboard to set a Trim out point.
7. Press [Spacebar] to preview the sequence on the Program Monitor.
8. With the Selection tool, click the gap in front of space3.m2v, then press [Delete].

Trim a video clip with the Ripple Edit tool.

1. Drag space4.m2v after the space3.m2v video clip on the Video 1 track.

2. Preview the space4.m2v video clip, then move the CTI to the beginning of the video clip.
3. Click the Ripple Edit tool on the Tools panel.
4. Place your cursor over the left edge of the space4.m2v video clip, then drag the Ripple Edit icon from the left edge to the right until the tool tip displays +00;04;35;15.
5. Click the Selection tool on the Tools panel, place the CTI at 00;06;45;24, then press []] to create a Trim Out point.
6. Press [Spacebar] to preview the sequence on the Program Monitor.

Use the Insert button to place a trimmed clip.

1. Open space5.m2v on the Source Monitor and preview the video clip.
2. Set the Source Monitor timecode display to read 01;11;00;11, then click the Mark In button on the Source Monitor.
3. Set the Source Monitor timecode display to read 01;11;48;02, then click the Mark Out button on the Source Monitor.
4. On the Timeline panel, place the CTI at the end of the space4.m2v video clip.
5. Click the Insert button on the Source Monitor.
6. Press [Spacebar] to preview the sequence on the Program Monitor.
7. Set the Source Monitor timecode display to read 01;04;14;22, then click the Mark In button on the Source Monitor.
8. Set the Source Monitor timecode display to read 01;04;39;18, then click the Mark Out button on the Source Monitor.

9. On the Timeline panel, place the CTI at the end of the space5.m2v video clip.
10. Click the Insert button on the Source Monitor.

Use the Overlay button to place a trimmed clip.

1. Open space6.m2v on the Source Monitor and preview the video clip.
2. Set the Source Monitor timecode display to read 01;15;33;17, then click the Mark In button on the Source Monitor.
3. Set the Source Monitor timecode display to read 01;19;53;29, then click the Mark Out button.
4. On the Timeline panel, place the CTI at the end of the first space5.m2v video clip.
5. Click the Overwrite button on the Source Monitor to place the video clip on the Timeline panel.

Perform a rearrange edit.

1. Use the Zoom bar to adjust the Timeline panel so that you can see all of your video clips at the same time.
2. Click the Selection tool, click the first space5.m2v, press and hold [Ctrl][Alt] (Win) or ⌘ [option] (Mac), drag the video clip in front of space2.m2v, then release the mouse button.
3. Using the rearrange edit technique, reorder the video clips on the Video 1 track so they are arranged as follows: space1.m2v, space5.m2v, space5.m2v, space2.m2v, space4.m2v, space3.m2v, space6.m2v.
4. Press [Spacebar] to preview the sequence on the Program Monitor.

Create a new sequence.

1. Click File on the Menu bar, click Import, navigate to your Data Files folder for Chapter 4, select apollo launch.m2v, then click Open.
2. On the Project panel, select the apollo launch.m2v video clip, click File on the Menu bar, point to New, then click Sequence.
3. Click the expand arrow in front of DV-NTSC, then click Standard 48kHz.
4. In the Sequence Name box, type **Launch**, then click OK.
5. Right-click Sequence 01 on the Project panel, click Rename, then type **Apollo Flight**.

Use the Razor tool to edit video.

1. Drag the apollo launch.m2v video clip to the Launch sequence on the Timeline panel, then preview the clip on the Program Monitor.
2. Place the CTI at 00;02;07;17 on the Timeline panel, click the Razor tool on the Tools panel, place the cursor over the CTI, then click the video clip.
3. Make razor cuts at the following durations: 00;03;37;14, 00;08;12;02, 00;08;34;22, 00;13;59;29, and 00;16;40;00.
4. Select the clip with the Start time 00;02;07;17, then press the [Delete] key.
5. Delete the clips with the following start times from the sequence: 00;03;37;14, 00;08;34;22, and 00;16;40;00.

Remove gaps between video.

1. Verify that the Launch sequence is active on the Timeline panel, with the CTI at 00;00;00;00.
2. Click Sequence on the Menu bar, point to Go to Gap, then click Next in Sequence.

3. Click the gap, click Edit on the Menu bar, then click Ripple Delete.
4. Select the remaining gaps on the sequence and remove them with the Ripple Delete command.

Rearrange a clip using the Program Monitor.

1. Press [Spacebar] to preview the Launch sequence on the Program Monitor.
2. Place the CTI at 00;00;00;00, click the Mark In button on the Program Monitor, press [Down Arrow], then click the Mark Out button.
3. Press the Extract button on the Program Monitor.
4. Press [End] to move the CTI to the end of the sequence, click Edit on the Menu bar, then click Paste.

Apply transitions between video clips.

1. Change the current workspace to Effects.
2. Move the CTI to the location of the first cut point.
3. Type **Cross** in the Contains field on the Effects panel.
4. Click the Cross Dissolve transition on the Effects panel, click Sequence on the Menu bar, then click Apply Video Transition.
5. Place the Cross Dissolve transition at the remaining cut points in the sequence.
6. Press [Spacebar] to preview the clip on the Program Monitor.

Nest a sequence.

1. Set the current workspace to Editing with the Apollo Flight sequence active on the Timeline panel.
2. Right-click the Launch sequence on the Project panel, then click Open in Source Monitor.

3. Drag the CTI on the Timeline panel to 00;00;00;00.
4. Click the Insert button on the Source Monitor to place the Launch sequence at the location of the CTI.
5. Click Edit on the Menu bar, then click Undo.
6. Press and hold [Ctrl] (Win) or ⌘ (Mac), then click and drag the Drag Video Only icon to place the Launch sequence at the location of the CTI.
7. Press [Spacebar] to preview the clip on the Program Monitor.

Apply a video effect.

1. Set the current workspace to Effects with the Apollo Flight sequence active on the Timeline panel.
2. Place the CTI at the beginning of the Launch clip on the Timeline panel.
3. Clear the contents of the Contains field on the Effects panel, click the expand arrow in front of Video Effects, then click the expand arrow in front of Color Correction.
4. Drag Tint on top of the Launch clip on the Timeline panel.
5. On the Effect Controls panel, adjust the Amount to Tint value to 70.0%.
6. Press [Spacebar] to preview the clip on the Program Monitor.

Import an audio file and preview.

1. Set the current workspace to Editing with the Apollo Flight sequence active on the Timeline panel.
2. On the Media Browser, locate your Data Files folder for Chapter 4.
3. Click Kennedy Space, press and hold [Shift], click Kennedy Rice, right-click, then click Import.

4. Double-click Kennedy Rice to open it on the Source Monitor, then click the Play button to preview the audio clip.
5. Drag the Drag Audio Only icon to the audio track at the beginning of the sequence.

Clean up an audio source file in Audition.

1. Click the Kennedy Rice audio clip on the Timeline panel, click Edit on the Menu bar, point to Edit in Adobe Audition, then click Clip.
2. In Audition, choose the Default workspace, then if necessary, click the Spectral Frequency Display button on the Tools panel to show the spectral display.
3. Use the Marquee Selection tool to take a sample at approximately 10:20.837, where there is a bright vertical line.
4. On the Menu bar, click Effects, point to Noise Reduction/Restoration, then click Noise Reduction (process).
5. Click the Capture Noise Print button.
6. Click the Select Entire File button.
7. Click the Apply button.
8. Click File on the Menu bar, then click Save.
9. Close Audition to return to your open project file in Premiere Pro.

Edit an audio clip on the Timeline panel.

1. Click the Play button on the Source Monitor to preview the Kennedy Rice Audio Extracted file.
2. Click the expand arrow on the Audio track where the Kennedy Rice Audio Extracted file is located.

3. Using the Razor tool make cuts at the following durations: 00;05;26;21, 00;05;37;29, 00;08;40;01, 00;08;48;17, 00;09;14;04, 00;09;21;17, 00;10;57;26, 00;11;03;12, 00;11;44;01, 00;11;48;21, 00;12;01,07, 00;12;09;10, 00;13;07;21, 00;13;12;27, 00;13;21;09, 00;14;21;09, 00;14;27;13, 00;16;03;06, 00;16;12;26, 00;16;52;22, 00;17;00;23, and 00;17;32;21.
4. Lock the Video 1 track and using the Selection tool, right-click between the cut lines, then click Ripple Delete to delete the applause.

Convert speech to text.

1. Change the Premiere Pro workspace to Metalogging.
2. Click the Kennedy Space audio clip on the Project panel.
3. Click the Analyze button on the Metadata panel.
4. Without changing the default settings in the Speech Analysis Options dialog box, click OK. Adobe Media Encoder opens to translate the text.
5. Close the Adobe Media Encoder when the analysis has finished, then return to Premier Pro. The text has been added to the Metadata panel in Premiere Pro.
6. Open the Kennedy Space audio clip on the Source Monitor.
7. Look through the passage for the part that reads: "I believe that this nation"; your analysis may vary.
8. Click the "I" in the statement.

Edit an audio clip on the Source Monitor.

1. Open Kennedy Space on the Source Monitor, reset your workspace to **Editing**.
2. Set the Current-time display on the Source Monitor to 00;03;03;12.
3. Click the Mark In button.
4. Set the Current-time display on the Source Monitor to 00;04;14;11.
5. Click the Mark Out button.
6. Click in the header of the Audio track where the Kennedy Rice audio file is located, and place the CTI at the end of the Kennedy Rice audio clip.
7. Click the Insert button on the Source Monitor.
8. Set the workspace to Effects, then close all open files on the Source Monitor.
9. Preview the transition between the Kennedy Rice audio clip and the Kennedy Space audio clip.

Apply an audio transition.

1. Click the expand arrow in front of Audio Transitions, and again in front of Crossfade.
2. Drag the Constant Power transition and drop it between the last Kennedy Rice audio clip and the Kennedy Space audio clip with a Center at Cut alignment.
3. Create a Default Still Title, place it on the Video 2 track to title your documentary, and give yourself credit. Figure 92 shows one sample.
4. Save and export your movie with the MPEG2 format.

Figure 92 *Completed Skills Review*

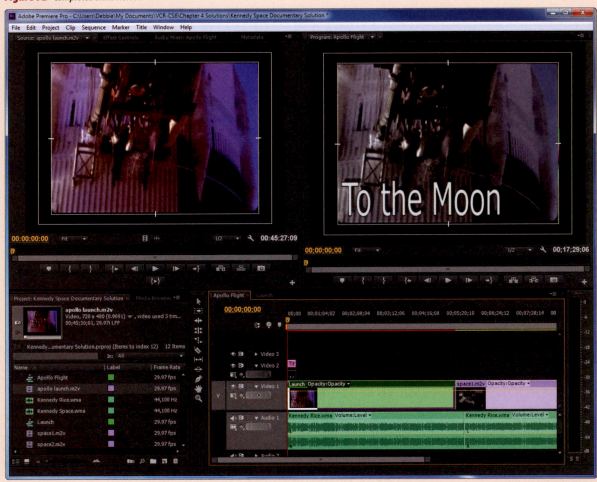

The Chamber of Commerce has announced that they are having their first annual air show to coincide with the 4th of July celebrations to honor America and our military. They have contacted your advertising firm to create a 20-second commercial using some footage they shot at another air show.

The Chamber has provided the beginning Premiere Pro project file, which includes the video clips they would like you to edit into the 20-second spot. They own the footage, so no credits are necessary. They plan to run this ad on television and on the Internet, and therefore need you to supply the final version in F4V and MPEG2 formats.

1. Open Chamber.prproj, then save it as **Chamber Commercial** *your name*.
2. Preview the various video clips on the Source Monitor to decide how you will compose your 20-second spot.
3. Trim the video clips using the techniques you have learned in this chapter.
4. Add a title announcing this as the **First Annual 4th of July Air Show**.
5. Export your movie to the F4V and MPEG2 formats.

Figure 93 *Sample Project Builder 1*

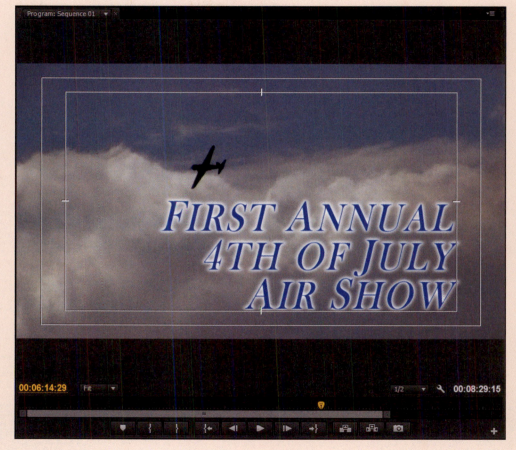

Creating a Documentary Using Premiere Pro & Audition CS6

Your speech teacher is doing a unit on famous speeches and the phrases that have become a part of our everyday lives: Martin Luther King Jr.'s "I have a dream," Douglas MacArthur's "Old soldiers never die," Ronald Reagan's "Tear down this wall," and Lou Gehrig's "Today I consider myself the luckiest man on the face of the earth."

You have decided to use your knowledge of Premiere Pro and your Internet shrewdness to create an audio compilation of 10 of your favorite phrases from famous speeches. You'll use the Metadata panel and the Analyze button to transcribe each speech and share the result with your speech teacher. Figure 94 shows a website that could be used for this project.

1. Research and download 10 famous speeches from the Internet that are in the public domain.
2. Open Premiere Pro and import the files into the Files panel.
3. Preview the audio files, then if any of the files need to be restored, use the Edit in Audition command to make restoration corrections in Audition.
4. Change the workspace to Metalogging. (*Hint*: This makes the Metadata panel easily accessible.)

5. Open the first audio file on the Project panel, then click the Analyze button on the Metadata panel.
6. Repeat this process for the other nine audio clips.
7. Create a new multitrack file, then place the 10 edited clips on the multitrack.

8. Use the information in the transcription to locate a key phrase in each speech, edit the audio clips, and add transitions.
9. Export your Audio file as an MP3 file titled **Great Speech Phrases** *your name*.

Figure 94 *Sample website for Project Builder 2*

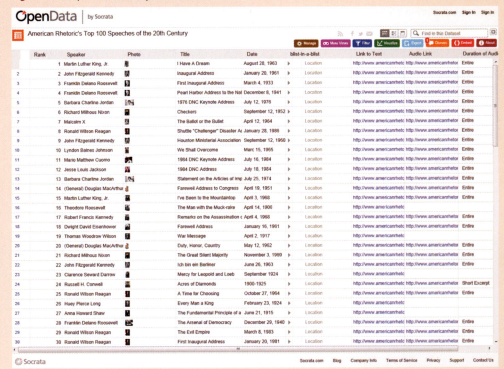

Figure © Cengage Learning 2013

Your history teacher was quite impressed with the video montage you created about the space program. He would like you to use your new audio and video editing skills to create a documentary about the holocaust using information from the United States Holocaust Memorial Museum (http://ushmm.org). There are plenty of materials that can be found by choosing Collections and Archives under the Research link, as shown in Figure 95.

You will need to trim and combine video clips with appropriate transitions and create an audio narration with audio files you are able to find at this website.

In addition, your instructor would like you to do the following:

1. Place an appropriate title at the beginning of the documentary.
2. Provide credits for the sources used in your documentary.
3. Make the documentary at least 20 minutes in length.
4. Place your Production Company Logo (created in Chapter 2) at the end of your documentary.
5. Export to the MPEG2 format with the NTSC DV High Quality Preset.

Figure 95 *Portfolio Project*

"Everyone would believe my pictures": The Legacy of Julien Bryan , Courtesy of the United States Holocaust Memorial Museum Photo Archives.

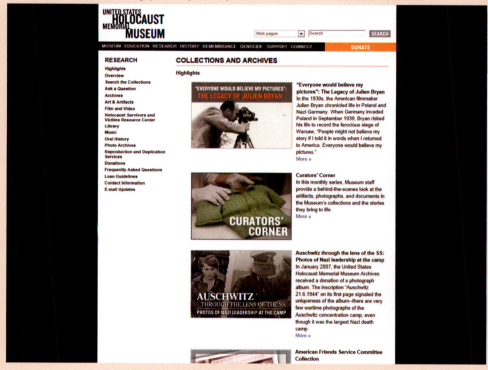

CHAPTER 5

DEVELOPING A PSA AND COMMERCIAL USING PREMIERE PRO & AFTER EFFECTS CS6

1. Edit a public service announcement

2. Edit a commercial for television

3. Edit a commercial developed for the Internet

CHAPTER **5**

DEVELOPING A PSA AND
COMMERCIAL USING PREMIERE PRO & AFTER EFFECTS CS6

In this chapter, you will work with the film concepts of the commercial and the public service announcement (PSA) like those that you see on television or the Internet. You will continue to use the editing techniques you have learned in Premiere Pro and you will learn advanced techniques in After Effects to add special effects to a commercial and a PSA.

A **commercial** is a short film broadcast used as a marketing device to raise awareness of a consumer product, service, or issue. **Public service announcements (PSAs)** are intended to modify public attitudes by raising awareness about specific issues. The most common topics of PSAs are health and safety. A typical PSA is part of a public awareness campaign to inform or educate the public about an issue such as smoking or compulsive gambling.

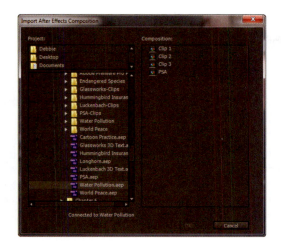

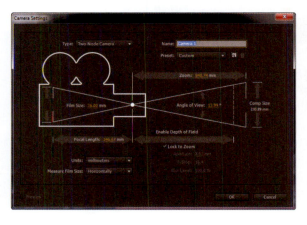

Edit a Public Service
ANNOUNCEMENT

What You'll Do

Figure © Cengage Learning 2013

 In this lesson, you will edit a public service announcement by using advanced techniques in After Effects and creating a voice over in Premiere Pro.

Working with the Cartoon Effect

The Cartoon effect in After Effects creates a stylized effect that resembles vector art by simplifying and smoothing the shading and colors in an image and adding strokes to the edges between features. You may have seen this technique a few years ago in the Charles Schwab television commercials and the full-length movie *A Scanner Darkly*. The result can produce an image that may resemble a sketch or a cartoon, as shown in Figure 1.

The Cartoon effect is in the Stylize category on the Effects & Presets panel. Figure 2 shows the default Cartoon settings applied to video footage. A good rule of thumb when working with the Cartoon effect is to begin with the Fill properties. The Shading Steps and Shading Smoothness properties simplify the shading and coloring in the image, a process known

Figure 1 *Example of Cartoon effect*

Resembles a sketch

Resembles a cartoon

Figure © Cengage Learning 2013

as **posterization**, creating a more cartoon-like effect. The Shading Smoothness property can overrule the Shading Steps settings if the Shading Smoothness value is placed too high, returning the image to a more realistic look. The Detail Radius and Detail Threshold properties work with blurs and soften the image. The Edge properties determine what is considered an edge and how strokes are applied to edges. The Width property is the thickness that is added to an edge, like a thin pencil or a thick marker. Softness is the transition between the edge's stroke and the surrounding colors. Opacity can reduce the appearance of the stroke that is applied to the edge.

Each property has an expand arrow which when clicked reveals a slider, as shown in Figure 3. This may provide greater flexibility when making adjustments on the various properties. It is also a good practice to try different combinations of settings as you work with the effect.

Working with the Levels Effect

After applying the Cartoon effect, it may need a little help to look more cartoon-like. The Cartoon effect relies heavily on color and contrast to detect the edges of the objects or people in the footage. Most footage does not have enough color and contrast for the Cartoon effect to work effectively. The Levels effect, which helps to create contrast, is almost always necessary.

Figure 2 *Cartoon effect with default settings*

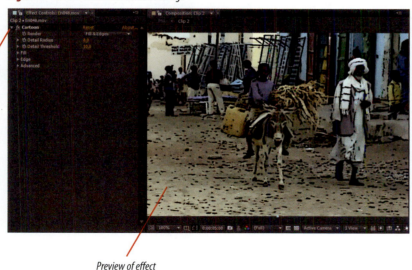

Cartoon effect

Preview of effect

Figure 3 *Revealing the slider*

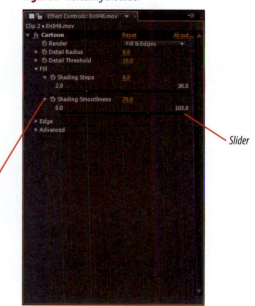

Expand arrow

Slider

The Levels effect, once applied, needs to be moved above the Cartoon effect so that it is applied to the footage first and thus aids the Cartoon effect in picking up contrast.

Apply the Levels effect after you've worked with the Cartoon effect. The Cartoon effect works with the color and contrast of the footage; this will help you make the proper levels adjustments while being able to preview the effect as it is applied with the Cartoon effect.

The Levels effect displays a **histogram**, which is a chart that represents the changes in color from dark to light in the image, as shown in Figure 4. (*Note*: You may need to expand the Effect Controls panel if you are unable to see the entire histogram.) The left side of the histogram shows how much black (or even dark gray) is in the image, and the right side how much white. The triangles at the bottom of the histogram are Input controls that adjust the contrast of the image. The triangle on the left is the Input Black control and on the right is the Input White control. The center triangle is the Gamma control, which adjusts the midtones. Dragging the Gamma control to the left increases the brightness of the image, while dragging it to the right reduces the brightness.

As you work with the histogram controls, you will notice the values displayed for Input Black, Input White, and Gamma adjust as you move the controls. Sliders are also available, as shown in Figure 5, by clicking the expand arrows for these properties.

Figure 4 *Levels effect histogram*

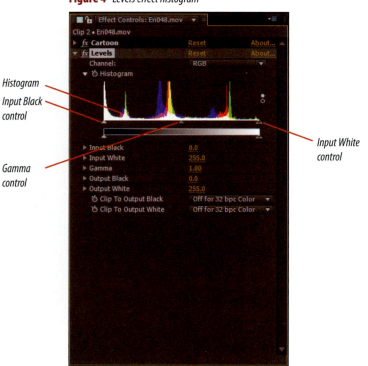

Figure 5 *Levels effect histogram with sliders*

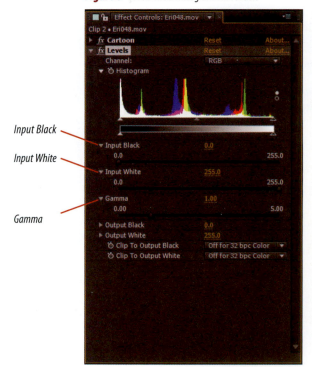

Figures © Cengage Learning 2013

Working with the Hue/Saturation Effect

The Hue/Saturation effect is another color correction effect, which adds to the overall Cartoon effect. This effect is based on the color wheel. Adjusting the color, or hue, is represented by moving along the edge of the color wheel. Adjusting the saturation, or intensity, of the color is represented by moving across the radius of the color wheel. The Master Hue color wheel and Master Saturation setting change the overall hue and saturation of the image, as shown in Figure 6. The value above the color wheel indicates the number of degrees of rotation around the wheel from the original color. A positive value means the wheel was rotated in a clockwise rotation, while a negative value indicates a counterclockwise rotation.

Working with the Channel Mixer Effect

The Channel Mixer effect, in the Color Correction category, is another option that allows more subtle shading for the overall Cartoon effect. Unlike Hue/Saturation, which makes overall changes to the image, the Channel Mixer effect works on specific color channels.

Figure 7 uses a simple red square to show how the Channel Mixer effect works on an image. The true color red is shown in the upper-left square and the Red-Red, Green-Red, and Blue-Red property values are all set to 50 for comparison. When the Red-Red value is reduced to 50, half of the red is removed from the red channel, making the color darker. When green is added to the red in the

Figure 7 *Channel Mixer Red property*

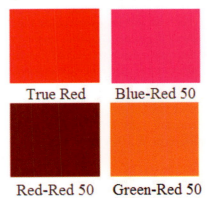

True Red   Blue-Red 50

Red-Red 50   Green-Red 50

Figure 6 *Hue/Saturation effect*

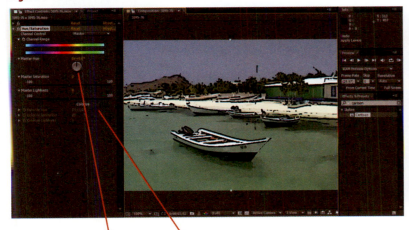

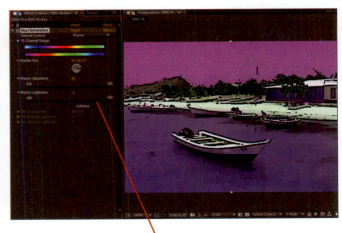

Master Hue color wheel   Default settings

Modified settings

Green-Red channel by changing the value to 50, the red appears orange. Finally, when you change the value to 50 in the Blue-Red channel, the color appears pink.

The color on the left is the input color. The color on the right is the output color, before any effects are applied. As you adjust the color by raising the value (a positive number) you add the input color. If you reduce the value (a negative number) you remove the input color.

Each channel also has a constant value, abbreviated as *Const*. This channel increases the constant color with every other color combination in that color channel. For

example, a Blue-Const setting of 100 saturates the blue channel by adding 100 percent blue.

Figure 8 shows a comparison between two images with the default Channel Mixer settings on the left and with some of the color channels modified on the right. As you can see, a more subtle effect is obtained using the Channel Mixer than when applying the Hue/Saturation effect. In this case, in the red channel, red was added to the green channel and subtracted from the blue channel. In the case of the green channel, green was added to the red channel and removed from the blue channel and in addition, the Green-Const

value was adjusted to a value of 12, adding 12 percent green to all of the green channels. Finally, in the blue channel, blue was added to the green channel.

Importing an After Effects Project to Premiere Pro

Adobe Dynamic Link is a feature available between Premiere Pro, After Effects, and Encore if installed as part of the Creative Suite Production Premium or Master Collection. A change made in an After Effects composition that is dynamically linked in a Premiere Pro project is updated immediately. The same is

Figure 8 *Channel Mixer effect*

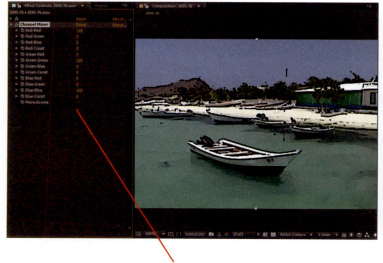

Default settings

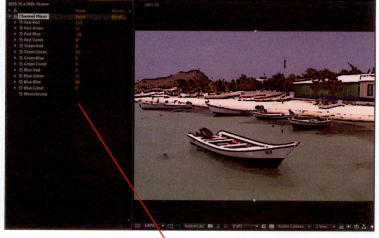

Modified settings

Figure © Cengage Learning 2013

true for a change to a Premiere Pro sequence that is dynamically linked to an After Effects composition. Therefore, it is unnecessary to render or save changes in order for the updates to take place between applications.

Dynamic links are created when a file is imported from one of the programs into another. The file appears with a unique icon and label color, as shown in Figure 9. In this figure, an After Effects file named PSA/PSA was imported into Premiere Pro. The colorful file icon indicates the dynamic link established.

You can link an existing After Effects composition into a Premiere Pro project by clicking Dynamic Link on the File menu, and then clicking the Import After Effects Composition command. If the After Effects project has multiple compositions, you have the option to choose one or more of the compositions, as shown in Figure 10.

To make changes to the linked composition in this example, you would select the composition on the Project panel or Timeline panel and choose the Edit Original command. This launches After Effects with the composition active; you can then switch between the two applications to view changes.

Figure 9 *File with dynamic link*

Dynamic
link icon

Figure 10 *Import After Effects Composition dialog box*

Compositions
available for
import

After Effects
project file

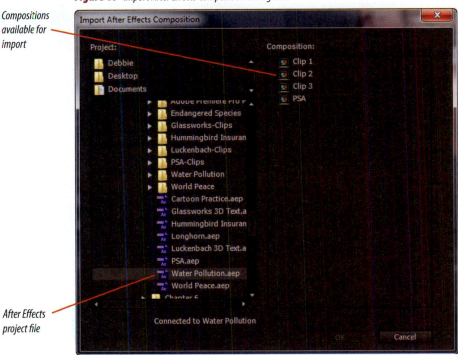

Like any other asset, dynamic links may become unlinked. This happens if a file is moved or renamed. If you need to relink a dynamic link, as shown in Figure 11, right-click the dynamic link and choose Link Media. The Link Media to dialog box opens, as shown in Figure 12, allowing you to locate the missing file.

Dynamically linked files can be manipulated like any other asset. They may be previewed on the Source Monitor, trimmed, and placed on the Timeline panel. As with other assets, the linked files may also be edited on the Timeline panel and may be unlinked from associated audio tracks if needed.

Creating a Voice Over in Premiere Pro

You can record audio directly into Premiere Pro to an audio track in a new sequence or to an audio track in an existing sequence. The recording (WAV file) is saved to your project folder, and an audio clip is added to the sequence in your project and to the Project panel.

Figure 11 *Missing dynamic link*

Missing link

Figure 12 *Link Media to dialog box*

Name of file

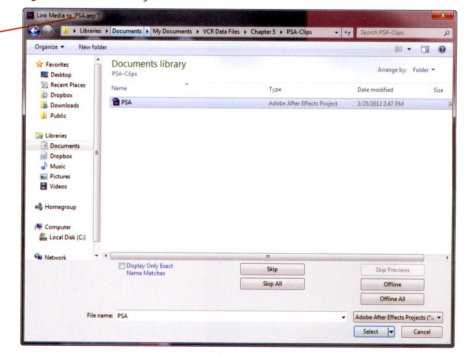

Figures © Cengage Learning 2013

On the Audio Mixer panel you will need to indicate which audio track you want to record to by enabling the track, as shown in Figure 13. The red R icon indicates that the Audio 1 track is enabled for recording. The yellow S icon indicates that the other tracks are muted. It is important to remember to turn down your speakers while you are recording to prevent feedback and echo. While you are recording, you can preview the video on the Program Monitor to assist with timing.

There are two steps in the recording process. You first need to click the Record button, which then begins to blink; then, when you are ready to record, you click the Play-Stop Toggle button to begin recording. To stop the recording process, you click the Play-Stop Toggle button again. The audio clip then appears on the Project panel and at the location of the CTI on the audio track.

Figure 13 *Audio Mixer panel*

Specifying the Default Audio Input Device

A microphone needs to be set as the default audio device in the Audio Hardware section of the Preferences dialog box in Premiere Pro. Premiere Pro uses the ASIO (Audio Stream Input Output) specifications for Windows and Core Audio devices for the Mac OS. Set up your microphone, referring to your operating system's Help for assistance, before starting Premiere Pro, so that Premiere Pro recognizes the settings for your device.

Apply the Cartoon effect

1. Open the PSA.aep file from the drive and folder where you store your Data Files, then save it as **PSA** *your name*.

   Notice there are five compositions already created: Clip 1, Clip 2, Clip 3, Clip 4, and PSA.

   TIP If you see an error that four movie clips are missing, click OK, re-link the missing footage with the movie clips found in the PSA-Clips folder, then follow the instructions in Steps 2 and 3. If you do not receive this error and your movie clips are linked, but you cannot see the preview of a movie clip, right-click on the movie clip in the Project panel and choose Reload Footage, then skip to step 4.

2. Right-click **Ban044.mov** on the Project panel, point to **Replace Footage**, then click **File**.

3. Navigate to the PSA-Clips folder, click **Ban044.mov**, then click **Open**.

   The other three clips should update automatically; if necessary, repeat for the remaining three .mov files.

4. Use the Composition Navigator to select **Clip 1**.

   The Cartoon, Levels, and Hue/Saturation effects have already been applied to this clip as an example for you to preview, as shown in Figure 14.

5. Use the Composition Navigator to select **Clip 2**, then verify that the Effects workspace is in place.

   You will be applying the Cartoon effect to Clip 2.

   You may need to select the Timeline panel and move the CTI to the 00;00;00;00 position to activate the video footage on the Composition panel.

   (continued)

Figure 14 *Example of Cartoon effect applied to Clip 1*

Levels effect

Cartoon effect

Hue/Saturation effect

Clip 1 composition

Figure 15 *Cartoon effect applied to Clip 2*

Cartoon effect

Clip 2 composition

Figures © Cengage Learning 2013

Figure 16 *Shading Steps and Shading Smoothness properties modified in Clip 2*

Shading
Steps

Shading
Smoothness

Figure 17 *Softness, Detail Radius, and Threshold modified in Clip 2*

Detail Radius

Detail
Threshold

Softness

6. Click the **Selection tool** [cursor icon] on the Tools panel, then click the **video footage** on the Composition panel.

7. Click **Effect** on the Menu bar, point to **Stylize**, then click **Cartoon**.

   The Cartoon effect is added to the Effect Controls panel with the default settings, as shown in Figure 15.

8. If necessary, click the **Fill expand arrow**, then click the **Shading Steps** and **Shading Smoothness expand arrows**.

   The sliders become visible for the Shading Steps and Shading Smoothness properties.

9. Adjust the Shading Steps value to **4.5** and the Shading Smoothness value to **60.4**, then compare your screen with Figure 16.

   The Shading Steps property sets the level of posterization in the color fill areas. A higher Shading Smoothness value blends the colors together with more gradual transitions.

10. If necessary, click the **Edge expand arrow**, then change the Softness value to **74.0**.

    The transition between the edge's stroke and surrounding colors is softened.

11. Change the Detail Radius value to **9.0** and the Detail Threshold value to **8.4**, then compare your screen to Figure 17.

    The Detail Radius setting applies a blur to the image and the Detail Threshold setting removes some of the detail.

12. Save your project and leave it open for the next exercise.

You applied the Cartoon effect to Clip 2 in the PSA file and then customized the effect.

Customize the Cartoon effect

1. Open the PSA *your name*.aep file, if necessary.

2. Use the Composition Navigator to select **Clip 3**, then verify that the Effects workspace is in place.

   You may need to select the Timeline panel and move the CTI to 00;00;00;00 to activate the video footage on the Composition panel.

3. Click the **Selection tool** ![selection tool icon] on the Tools panel, then click the **video footage** on the Composition panel.

4. Right-click the **Composition panel**, point to **Effect**, point to **Stylize**, then click **Cartoon**.

   The Cartoon effect is added to the Effect Controls panel with the default settings.

5. If necessary, click the **expand arrow** in front of **Fill**, then click the **Shading Steps** and **Shading Smoothness expand arrows**.

6. Drag the **Shading Steps slider** to the right and to the left to see how it affects the video footage on the Composition panel.

7. Drag the **Shading Smoothness slider** to the right and to the left to see how it affects the video footage.

   You may want to go back and forth between changing the Shading Steps value and the Shading Smoothness value to see how the details can change as a result.

8. Change the Shading Steps value to **4.2**, change the Shading Smoothness value to **80.0**, then compare your screen to Figure 18.

9. If necessary, click the **Edge expand arrow**, then expand the following properties: Softness, Detail Radius, and Detail Threshold.

   (continued)

Figure 18 *Shading Steps and Shading Smoothness values for Clip 3*

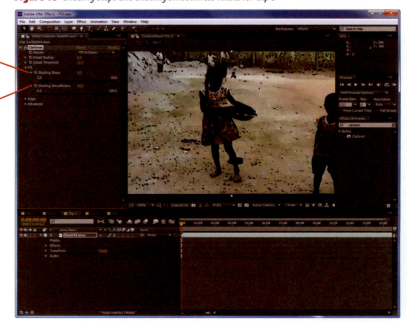

Shading Steps Value 4.2

Shading Smoothness Value 80.0

Figure © Cengage Learning 2013

Figure 19 *Cartoon effect values modified for Clip 3*

Detail Radius value 2.7

Detail Threshold value 16.1

Softness value 57.6

Edge Enhancement value 28.0

Edge Contrast value 0.51

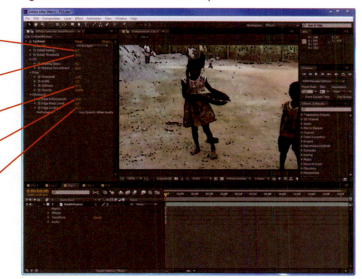

Figure 20 *Searching for the Cartoon effect*

Cartoon in search field

10. Click the **Advanced expand arrow**, then expand the following properties: Edge Enhancement and Edge Contrast.

    The slider becomes visible for each of these properties. You will adjust these values to fine tune the Cartoon effect further.

11. Drag the **sliders** to the left and right for the following parameters: Softness, Detail Radius, Detail Threshold, Edge Enhancement, and Edge Contrast.

    You can switch between properties and change values to see the effect.

12. Change the following properties to the specified values: Softness: **57.6**; Detail Radius: **2.7**; Detail Threshold: **16.1**; Edge Enhancement: **28.0**; and Edge Contrast: **0.51**, then compare your screen to Figure 19.

13. Save your project and leave it open for the next exercise.

You applied the Cartoon effect to Clip 3 in the PSA file, and then customized it.

Search for the Cartoon effect

1. Open the PSA *your name*.aep file, if necessary.

2. Use the Composition Navigator to select **Clip 4**.

    You may need to select the Timeline panel and move the CTI to 00;00;00;00 to activate the video footage on the Composition panel.

3. Click the **Selection tool** on the Tools panel, then click the **video footage** on the Composition panel.

4. Type **cartoon** in the search field on the Effects & Presets panel, as shown in Figure 20.

(continued)

The search feature filters the Effects & Presets panel, showing only the Cartoon effect under the Stylize category.

5. Select the **Cartoon effect** on the Effects & Presets panel, then drag it to the Composition panel, as shown in Figure 21.

   You see an inverted triangle indicating that you are placing the effect on the video footage, and the Cartoon effect appears on the Effect Controls panel.

6. Enter the following values: Shading Steps: **4.0**; Shading Smoothness: **60.0**; Softness: **75.2**; Edge Enhancement: **7.0**; Detail Radius: **5.0**; and Detail Threshold: **12.4**, as shown in Figure 22.

7. Save your project and leave it open for the next exercise.

You searched for the Cartoon effect on the Effects & Presets panel and applied the effect to Clip 4 in the PSA file.

Figure 21 *Applying the Cartoon effect*

Figure 22 *Cartoon effect values modified for Clip 4*

Detail Radius value 5.0

Detail Threshold value 12.4

Shading Steps value 4.0

Shading Smoothness value 60.0

Softness value 75.2

Edge Enhancement value 7.0

Figures © Cengage Learning 2013

Figure 23 *Levels effect applied to Clip 4*

Levels effect

Figure 24 *Moving the Levels effect above the Cartoon effect*

Drop line

Rectangle

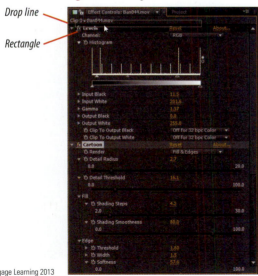

Apply the Levels effect

1. Open the PSA *your name*.aep file, if necessary.

2. Use the Composition Navigator to select **Clip 2**.

3. Click the **Selection tool** on the Tools panel, then click the **video footage** on the Composition panel.

4. Click **Effect** on the Menu bar, point to **Color Correction**, then click **Levels**.

   The Levels effect is used for improving the contrast in an image, which is very important for the Cartoon effect to be effective. The Levels effect is added to the Effect Controls panel, as shown in Figure 23.

5. Drag the **Levels effect** above the Cartoon effect on the Effect Controls panel.

   A white rectangle appears around the effect you are moving and a black drop line shows you where the effect will be placed when you release the mouse button, as shown in Figure 24. The Levels effect is moved above the Cartoon effect so that it is applied to the image before the Cartoon effect and therefore influences the Cartoon effect.

   (continued)

6. On the Effect Controls panel, drag the **Input Black control** to the right, just before the pink line begins, until the Input Black value is **12.0**, as shown in Figure 25.

The Input controls are the triangles directly underneath the histogram: the black on the left, the gray in the middle, and the white on the right.

TIP You may need to resize the Effect Controls panel so that it is wide enough to see the entire width of the histogram display and the Input controls.

7. Drag the **Input White control** to the left of the yellow lines just before the green until the Input White value is **210.0**.

8. Drag the **Input Gray control** to the left to adjust the shadows until the Gamma value is **1.07**, as shown in Figure 26.

9. Save your project and leave it open for the next exercise.

You applied and customized the Levels effect using the Input controls on the histogram for Clip 2 to improve the Cartoon effect.

Customize the Levels effect

1. Open the PSA *your name*.aep file, if necessary.

2. Use the Composition Navigator to select **Clip 3**, then verify that you can see the video footage on the Composition panel.

3. Click the **Selection tool** on the Tools panel, then click the **video footage** on the Composition panel.

4. Right-click the **Composition panel**, click **Effect**, point to **Color Correction**, then click **Levels**.

(continued)

Figure 25 *Adjusting the Input Black control*

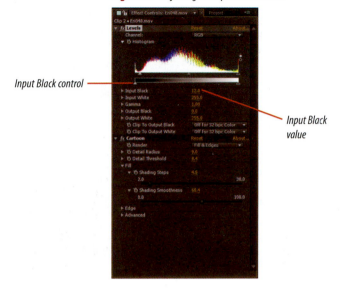

Input Black control

Input Black value

Figure 26 *Customizing the Levels effect on Clip 2*

Input White control
Input Gray control
Input Black control
Input Black value
Input White value
Gamma value

Figures © Cengage Learning 2013

Figure 27 *Customized Levels values for Clip 3*

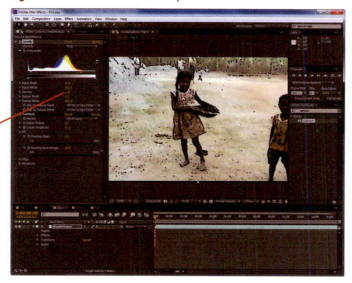

Gamma value
1.37

Figure 28 *Customized Levels values for Clip 4*

Input White
value 217.0

Gamma
value 1.11

5. Drag the **Levels effect** above the Cartoon effect on the Effect Controls panel.

6. Click the **expand arrows** in front of **Input Black**, **Input White**, and **Gamma**.

   The sliders become visible for each of the Input values.

7. Adjust the Input White slider by dragging it to the left and the Input Black slider by dragging it to the right.

   You are trying to improve the contrast in the image.

8. Drag the **Input White slider** to **202.0**, then drag the **Input Black slider** to **10**.

9. Drag the **Gamma slider** to the left and right to adjust the shadows.

10. Drag the **Gamma slider** to **1.37**, then compare your image to Figure 27.

11. Use the Composition Navigator to select **Clip 4**, then verify that you can see the video footage on the Composition panel.

12. Locate and drag the **Levels effect** above the Cartoon effect on the Effect Controls panel.

13. Enter the following values: Input Black: **21.5**; Input White: **217.0**; and Gamma: **1.11**, as shown in Figure 28.

14. Save your project and leave it open for the next exercise.

You applied and customized the Levels effect using the slider controls to adjust the Input Black, Input White, and Gamma levels to Clip 3 and Clip 4 to improve the Cartoon effect.

Apply the Hue/Saturation effect

1. Open the PSA *your name*.aep file, if necessary.

2. Use the Composition Navigator to select **Clip 2**, then verify that you can see the video footage on the Composition panel.

3. Click the **Selection tool** ![selection tool icon] on the Tools panel, then click the **video footage** on the Composition panel.

4. Click **Effect** on the Menu bar, point to **Color Correction**, then click **Hue/Saturation**.

   The Hue/Saturation effect is added to the Effect Controls panel, as shown in Figure 29.

5. On the Effect Controls panel, click the **Master Hue dial**, then drag it counterclockwise until you reach the value **0x -40.0°**, as shown in Figure 30.

TIP Dragging the dial counterclockwise produces a negative number, while dragging clockwise produces a positive number.

(continued)

Figure 29 *Hue/Saturation effect applied to Clip 2*

Hue/Saturation effect

Figure 30 *Adjusting the Master Hue in Clip 2*

Master Hue value

Developing a PSA and Commercial Using Premiere Pro & After Effects CS6

Figure 31 *Adjusting the Master Saturation in Clip 2*

Master Saturation
value

Figure 32 *Customizing the Hue/Saturation effect on Clip 4*

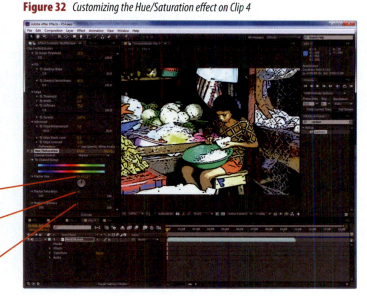

Master Hue value

Master Saturation
value

Master Lightness
value

6. Drag the **Master Saturation slider** until the value is **49**, as shown in Figure 31.

   The footage is brighter.

7. Use the Composition Navigator to select **Clip 4**, then verify that you can see the video footage on the Composition panel.

8. Locate and apply the Hue/Saturation effect.

9. Change the following values: Master Hue: **0x +11.0°**; Master Saturation: **-6**; and Master Lightness: **1**, as shown in Figure 32.

10. Save your project and leave it open for the next exercise.

You applied and customized the Hue/Saturation effect to correct the colors and shadows of the Cartoon effect applied to Clip 2 and Clip 4.

Apply the Channel Mixer effect

1. Open the PSA *your name*.aep file, if necessary.

2. Use the Composition Navigator to select **Clip 3**, then verify that you can see the video footage on the Composition panel.

3. Click the **Selection tool** on the Tools panel, then click the **video footage** on the Composition panel.

4. Right-click the **Composition panel**, click **Effect**, point to **Color Correction**, then click **Channel Mixer**.

(continued)

5. On the Effect Controls panel, change the following values for the Channel Mixer effect, as shown in Figure 33: Red-Green: **20**; Red-Blue: **15**; Green-Red: **10**; Green-Blue: **-15**; Blue-Red: **-10**; and Blue-Green: **10**.

   The Channel Mixer effect is much more subtle than the Hue/Saturation effect, and is able to work on specific channels of color by adding red to the footage and removing some of the blues and greens.

6. Save your project and leave it open for the next exercise.

You applied and customized the Channel Mixer effect to Clip 3.

Import an After Effects composition into Premiere Pro

1. Open the PSA.prproj file, then save it as **PSA** *your name*.

2. Click **File** on the Menu bar, point to **Adobe Dynamic Link**, then click **Import After Effects Composition**.

   The Import After Effects Composition dialog box opens.

3. Locate the PSA *your name* After Effects project file, select the **PSA composition**, as shown in Figure 34, then click **OK**.

   The linked After Effects composition appears on the Project panel.

(continued)

Figure 33 *Customizing the Channel Mixer effect on Clip 3*

Channel Mixer

Figure 34 *Import After Effects Composition dialog box*

Import After Effects Composition dialog box

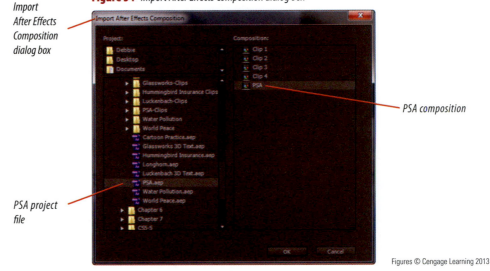

PSA composition

PSA project file

Figures © Cengage Learning 2013

Developing a PSA and Commercial Using Premiere Pro & After Effects CS6

Figure 35 *Previewing the After Effects composition on the Source Monitor*

PSA After Effects composition

Figure 36 *Placing the After Effects composition on the Video 1 track*

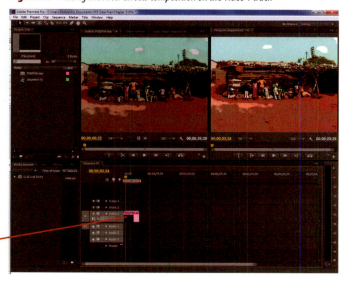

PSA After Effects composition

Figures © Cengage Learning 2013

4. Double-click the **PSA After Effects composition** on the Project panel to preview the composition on the Source Monitor as shown in Figure 35.

5. Click the **Drag Video Only icon** ⊞ on the Source Monitor, place the After Effects composition on the Video 1 track, then in the Clip Mismatch dialog box, click **Change Sequence settings**.

   The After Effects composition is placed on the video track without the audio track, as shown in Figure 36.

6. Click the **Play-Stop Toggle Button** ▶ on the Program Monitor to preview the sequence.

7. Save your project and leave it open for the next exercise.

You imported the After Effects project into Premiere Pro and placed it onto a sequence.

Create a voice over in Premiere Pro

1. Open the PSA *your name*.prproj file, if necessary.

2. Open the PSA Script.txt file.

   You will be reading the text into a microphone to record this into your PSA project. You may want to print the file.

3. Make sure your microphone is plugged into the microphone jack, then verify that your microphone is working.

   Check your computer's documentation if you are not sure how to record with your microphone.

4. Click the **Audio Mixer panel options button** ⊟, then click **Meter Input(s) Only**.

   This activates the sound meter and will allow you to see the input levels of your microphone.

5. On the Audio Mixer panel, under the Audio 1 track, click the **Enable track for recording button** R and the **Solo Track button** S, as shown in Figure 37.

   This enables the Audio 1 track for recording and will place the wav file that is generated automatically at the location of the CTI on that track when you have finished recording.

6. Click the **Record button** ◉ on the Audio Mixer panel.

   The Record button begins to blink.

7. Verify that the CTI is at 00;00;00;00.

   The video will play on the Program Monitor while you are reading the script.

   (continued)

Figure 37 *Audio Mixer panel*

Solo Track button

Enable track for recording button

Play-Stop Toggle button

Record button

Figure © Cengage Learning 2013

Figure 38 *Recording voice over*

Sound Meter

Play-Stop
Toggle button
toggled to Stop

Record button
active

Figure 39 *Audio clips from voice over*

8. Click the **Play-Stop Toggle button** ▶ on the Audio Mixer panel, as shown in Figure 38, then read the PSA script.

   If you make a mistake, you can undo your last action and return to Step 6.

9. Click the **Play-Stop Toggle button** ▶ on the Audio Mixer panel when you have finished recording.

   The audio clip appears on the selected audio track and on the Project panel, as shown in Figure 39. The wav file is also saved to the location of the project file.

10. Preview your project on the Program Monitor.

    If you are not happy with your recording, you can delete the track from the audio track and the Project panel and record it again. Keep in mind that copies of each of your recordings will still be saved in your projects folder.

11. Save your project file, export your final project to the **MPEG2** video format, then exit Premiere Pro.

You created a voice over narration in Premiere Pro to describe your PSA.

Edit a Commercial
FOR TELEVISION

What You'll Do

Figure © Cengage Learning 2013

 In this lesson, you will edit a commercial designed for television with advanced After Effects techniques.

Creating an After Effects Composition in Premiere Pro

There may be times when you are working in Premiere Pro and decide that you would like to add a special effect to a sequence in After Effects. You can create a new After Effects composition in Premiere Pro, and it becomes dynamically linked. Select the clips in the sequence that you want in the composition, choose the Adobe Dynamic Link command,

then select Replace with After Effects Composition. If After Effects is already open, it creates a new composition in the existing project. If After Effects is not open, the Save As dialog box opens, prompting you to name the After Effects project file.

The new After Effects project file with the composition is created based on the sequence settings in Premiere Pro and inherits all of its settings, as shown in Figure 40. The new

Figure 40 *Creating a composition from clips in Premiere Pro*

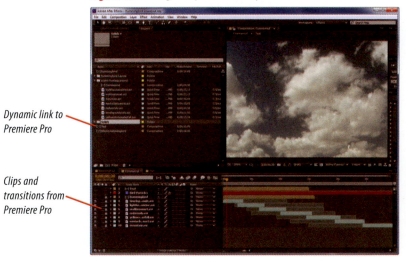

Dynamic link to Premiere Pro

Clips and transitions from Premiere Pro

Figure © Cengage Learning 2013

After Effects project file replaces the clips on the sequence with the dynamic link, as shown in Figure 41. (*Note*: The composition duration is set to 30 seconds by default when you create a dynamically linked After Effects composition.)

Stabilizing Motion with the Warp Stabilizer Effect

The Warp Stabilizer effect was introduced in After Effects CS5.5 to stabilize footage to remove camera shake from a handheld camera during filming.

You can find the Warp Stabilizer effect under the Distort submenu. After Effects automatically analyzes the clip, displaying a message while doing so, as shown in Figure 42. The amount of time the analyzing process takes depends on the amount of footage to be analyzed.

Figure 41 *Composition dynamically linked*

Dynamic link to After Effects

Figure 42 *Applying the Warp Stabilizer effect*

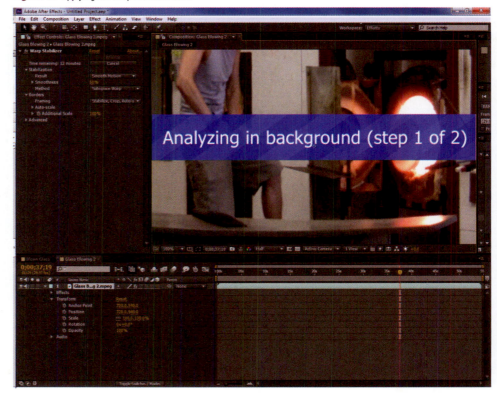

Once After Effects has completed analyzing the footage, a second banner is displayed while stabilization is applied, as shown in Figure 43.

The Warp Stabilizer effect has settings that can be customized, as shown in Figure 44. The following is an overview of some of these settings; refer to After Effects help for more information.

Figure 43 *Stabilizing process*

Figure 44 *Warp Stabilizer effects settings*

Analyze button

Stabilization settings

Borders settings

Advanced settings

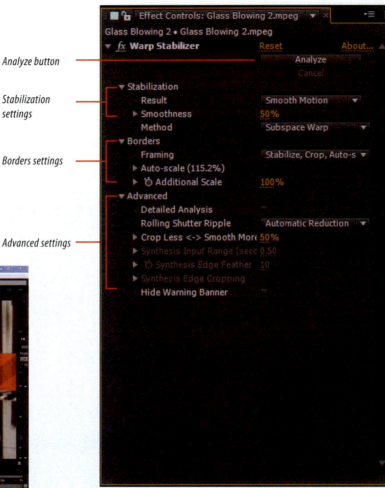

Figures © Cengage Learning 2013

The Analyze button is automatically applied for you when you first apply the effect. If you make any changes to the footage, such as marking In or Out points, the button can be used to reanalyze the footage.

The Stabilization settings allow you to make adjustments to the stabilization process. The Result menu options, Smooth or No Motion, control the final result of the footage. Smooth is the default option and retains the original camera movement while making it appear smoother. The No Motion option tries to remove all camera motion from the footage. When this option is selected, the Crop Less <-> Smooth More function is not available under the Advanced setting.

The Smoothness value determines how much of the camera's original motion is stabilized. This is only available when Smooth Motion is selected. The higher the value, the smoother the result, and the lower the value, the closer the result will be to the original camera motion.

Method determines the complexity of the stabilization analysis. Subspace Warp, the default setting, uses different parts of the frame to stabilize the footage. The most basic method is Position which, just as its name implies, creates tracking data based on position. Position, Scale, and Rotation use data based on position, scale, and rotation. Finally, Perspective uses a method of stabilization that creates corner pins to analyze the footage. If the selected method does not have enough area to track, the previous method is automatically selected for you.

If, after stabilizing your footage, the edges of your footage show artifacts or blank areas, framing can be adjusted. Stabilize, Crop, Auto-scale, the default option, crops the moving edges and scales the image to fill the frame. Stabilize, Synthesize Edges fills any blank space by creating content from information found from frames before and after the blank area, working in much the same manner as Content-Aware in Photoshop.

Creating 3D Text

The Shatter effect is an effect that is applied to give the illusion of exploding images, but it can also be customized to create 3D text. To create 3D text, you need three layers. The first layer is a Text layer, which is referenced by the Shatter effect text. The second layer is a Solid layer and is where you choose the text color. (The text color can always be changed later by selecting the layer and choosing Solid Settings on the Layer menu.) The last layer is a Camera layer, which is used to create a virtual camera to get different views of the Solid layer. Figure 45 shows the Shatter effect applied to the Solid layer.

To customize the Shatter effect and make the text 3D, you need to customize some settings on the Effect Controls panel, as shown in Figure 46. The Rendered View option allows you to preview the final output. Under the Shape property, you can customize the pattern to reference the text on the text layer if you are not using a pattern and want to display text.

A Camera layer allows you to view 3D objects from any angle by moving and rotating a camera around the scene to get different views of a 3D object. The camera preset is the type of camera named according to the focal length of the lens. All cameras are based on the behavior of a 35mm camera with a different lens. The Camera System option allows you to reference a Camera layer rather than working with the camera within the Shatter effect, providing more flexibility.

You must disable the Strength and Gravity values in the Shatter effect if you do not want to see the text explode.

Animating 3D Text with the Orbit Camera Tool

By adjusting the location of the camera, you can cause the 3D text and Light layer

Figure 45 *Applying the Shatter effect*

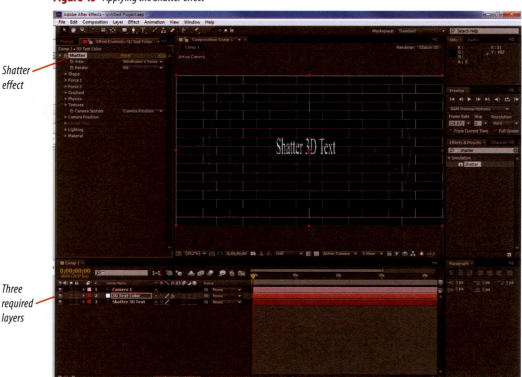

Shatter effect

Three required layers

to follow the camera. You need to use the Orbit Camera tool to adjust the camera; you do not need to be on the Camera layer when making adjustments. The Orbit Camera tool is found below the Unified Camera tool on the Tools panel, or can be retrieved by pressing the letter [c] on the keyboard. Pressing [c] repeatedly cycles through the four camera tools. If you create an initial keyframe on the Position property, then each time you move the CTI and make changes to the position of the camera in the Composition panel, a keyframe is automatically created.

Working with a Light Layer

The Light layer can be used to add lighting effects and cast shadows on the footage. The Light layer needs to be placed above the layer that you want the light to shine on. There are four types of lights to choose from: parallel, spot, point, and ambient. The **parallel** type approximates the light from a source like that of the sun. The **spot** type gives off light that is constrained by a cone, like a flashlight or spotlight. The **point** type is unconstrained, like a bare light bulb.

Figure 46 *Creating 3D text with the Shatter effect*

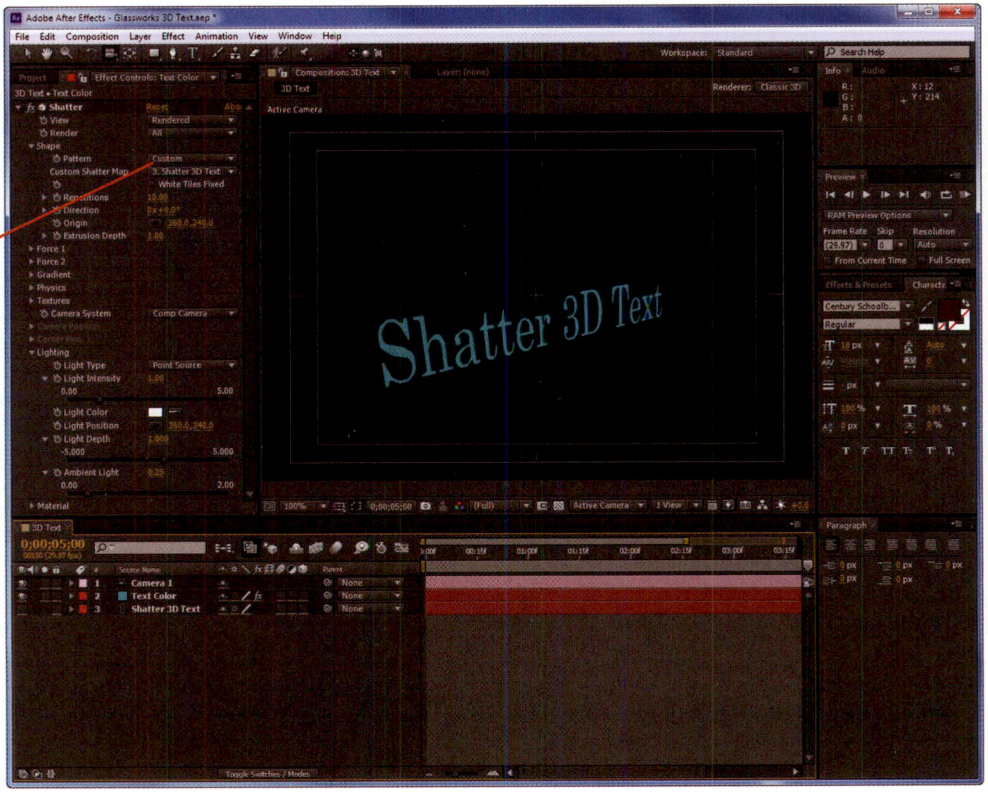

Pattern is set to Custom

Finally, the **ambient** type has no source but simply contributes to the overall brightness and casts no shadows.

The light can be adjusted on the Composition panel, as shown in Figure 47. Three colored arrows at the tip of the cone represent the x, y, and z planes. The light can be adjusted by dragging any of these arrows. The distance of the cone from the text can be modified by selecting the crosshairs. As you move the lighting, the light and shadows move across the text.

Enhancing 3D Text

After creating 3D text using the Shatter effect, you may want to enhance the appearance of your text. Effects can be added to the Solid layer. There are many effects to choose from. Two options are the CC Light Sweep effect and the Color Emboss effect.

The Color Emboss effect works like the Emboss effect without overriding the original colors of the image the effect is being applied

to. The Relief setting controls the maximum width of the highlighted edges, and the Contrast setting determines the sharpness of the image.

The CC Light Sweep effect creates a light reflection along the layer, as shown in Figure 48. By adding a keyframe to the Center control on the Timeline panel, you can adjust the light reflection at various durations and animate the CC Light Sweep effect.

Figure 47 *Working with the light on the Composition panel*

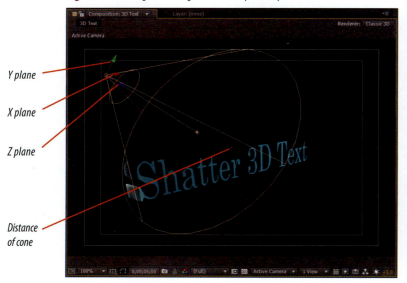

Y plane

X plane

Z plane

Distance of cone

Figure 48 *Applying the CC Light Sweep effect*

Figures © Cengage Learning 2013

Figure 49 *Save As dialog box*

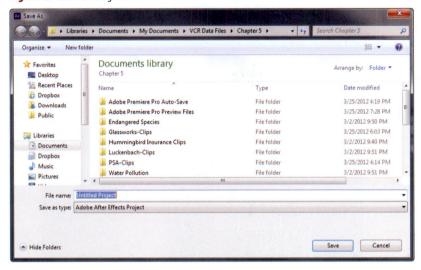

Figure 50 *New composition in After Effects*

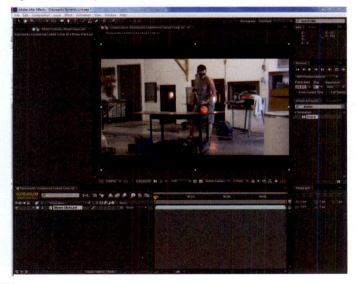

Figures © Cengage Learning 2013

Create an After Effects composition in Premiere Pro

1. Start Premiere Pro, open the Glassworks Commercial.prproj project file, then save it as **Glassworks Commercial *your name***.

2. Preview the video clip on the Program Monitor.

   You will use Adobe Dynamic Link to work with this file between Premiere Pro and After Effects. You will remove the camera shake in the video when the man is molding the glass on the table, then add some 3D animated text. You will first create a new After Effects composition.

3. Click the **Selection tool** on the Tools panel, then select the **Blown Glass clip** on the sequence.

4. Click **File** on the Menu bar, point to **Adobe Dynamic Link,** then click **Replace with After Effects Composition**.

   The Save As dialog box opens, as shown in Figure 49.

5. Name your project **Glassworks Dynamic Link *your name***, then click **Save**.

   TIP Save the file to the same location as your Premiere Pro project file.

   Adobe After Effects launches with the composition created and active, as shown in Figure 50.

6. Click **File** on the Menu bar, point to **Import**, then click **File**.

   The Import File dialog box opens. You will import a Photoshop file to create a frame around the video.

(continued)

7. Locate the Frame.psd file located in the Glassworks-Clips folder, verify the **Import As** drop-down menu is set to **Footage**, then click **Open**.

The Frame.psd dialog box opens.

8. Click **OK** to accept the default settings.

9. Drag **Frame.psd** from the Project panel to the Timeline panel above the Blown Glass.avi layer, then compare your screen to Figure 51.

10. Click the **Premiere Pro icon** on the taskbar (Win) or dock (Mac) to return to Premiere Pro.

The After Effects composition is dynamically linked in the Premiere Pro project, as shown in Figure 52.

11. Save Glassworks Commercial *your name* and then close Premiere Pro.

You should now be in After Effects.

12. Save Glassworks Dynamic Link *your name* and leave it open for the next exercise.

You created a new After Effects composition from Premiere Pro and dynamically linked it to Premiere Pro.

Figure 51 *Setting up the Glassworks dynamic link composition*

Frame.psd layer

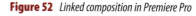

Null Object layer assigned as parent

Figure 52 *Linked composition in Premiere Pro*

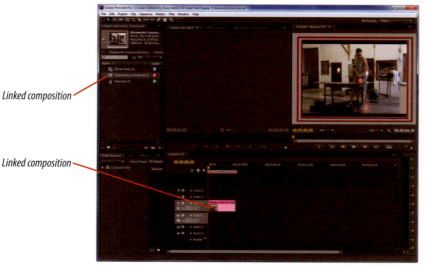

Linked composition

Linked composition

Figure 53 *Starting the Warp Stabilizer effect*

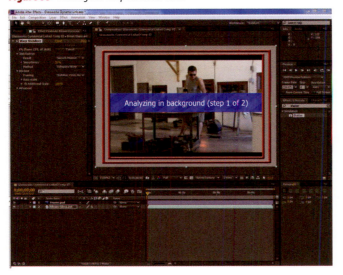

Figure 54 *Stabilizing step in Warp Stabilizer*

Stabilize footage with the Warp Stabilizer effect

1. Start After Effects, then open the Glassworks Dynamic Link *your name*.aep file, if necessary.

2. Click the **Selection tool** ▶ on the Tools panel, then click the **video footage** on the Composition panel.

3. Press [**Spacebar**] to preview your footage.

   The footage is shaky when the glass blower is working with the furnace.

4. Select the **Blown Glass.avi layer**, click **Effect** on the Menu bar, point to **Distort**, then click **Warp Stabilizer**.

   The Warp Stabilizer effect is added to the Effect Controls panel with the default settings, as shown in Figure 53.

5. When the Stabilizing step shown in Figure 54 is complete, preview your footage in the Composition panel.

   The shake has been removed from the footage.

6. Save your project, then close it.

You stabilized shaky footage.

Create 3D text

1. Open the Glassworks 3D Text.aep file, and then save it as **Glassworks 3D Text *your name***.

   The composition and the first Text layer have already been created.

2. Click **Layer** on the Menu bar, point to **New**, then click **Solid**.

   The Solid Settings dialog box opens, as shown in Figure 55.

3. In the Name box, type **Text Color**, click the **color picker**, select a dark red color, then click **OK** twice.

   The Solid layer appears above the Text layer on the Timeline panel.

TIP If you wish to change the color, click Layer on the Menu bar with the Solid layer selected, then click Solid Settings.

4. Type **Shatter** on the Effects & Presets panel search field, drag the **Shatter preset** onto the Text Color layer, then compare your screen to Figure 56.

5. Expand the Shatter effect on the Effect Controls panel if necessary, then click the **View drop-down arrow**, then click **Rendered**.

   This shows a preview of the final effect.

6. Click the **Shape expand arrow**, click the **Pattern list arrow**, then click **Custom**.

   You will now apply the Custom shape to the Text layer that you created earlier.

(continued)

Figure 55 *Solid Settings dialog box*

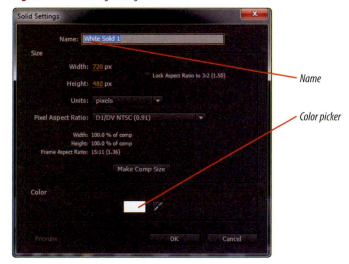

Name

Color picker

Figure 56 *Applying the Shatter effect*

Shatter effect

Render property

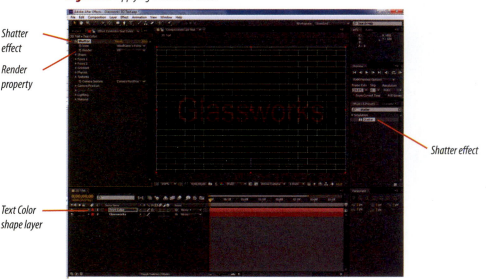

Shatter effect

Text Color shape layer

Figures © Cengage Learning 2013

Figure 57 *Customizing settings for Shatter effect*

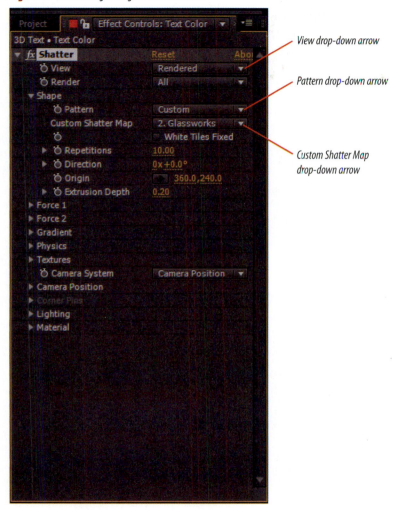

View drop-down arrow

Pattern drop-down arrow

Custom Shatter Map drop-down arrow

7. Click the **Custom Shatter Map drop-down arrow**, then click **2. Glassworks**, as shown in Figure 57.

   The text you created is now referenced to the Shatter effect, so you no longer need to view the Text layer that you created earlier.

8. If necessary, reposition the text to the center of the Compositon panel.

9. On the Timeline panel, to the left of Layer 2, click the **Video Switch button** 👁 on Layer 2.

10. Click the **Play/Pause button** ▶ on the Preview panel to preview the 3D text.

    You are using the Shatter effect to create 3D text. However, you do not want it to shatter, so you will need to make changes to some settings.

11. Click the **expand arrow** in front of **Force 1**, **Force 2**, and **Physics**, change the Strength and Gravity values to **0.00**, then collapse these properties when you have finished.

    Changing these values to 0.00 will remove the Shatter effect for the duration of the video.

12. Click the **Play/Pause button** ▶ on the Preview panel to preview the 3D text.

    You can no longer see the 3D effect. You will add camera and lighting layers in the next step.

13. Save Glassworks 3D Text *your name* and leave it open for the next exercise.

You created 3D text for the Glassworks commercial.

Animate 3D text with a Camera layer

1. Open the Glassworks 3D Text *your name*, if necessary, then verify that the CTI is at **00;00;00;00**.

2. Right-click the **Timeline panel**, click **New**, then click **Camera**.

   The Camera Settings dialog box opens.

3. Click the **Preset list arrow**, click **35mm**, then click **OK**, as shown in Figure 58.

   This preset will behave like a 35mm camera with a standard lens.

4. Select the **Text Color layer** on the Timeline panel, on the Effect Controls panel click the **Camera System drop-down menu**, then click **Comp Camera**.

   This references the Camera layer you created. If you do not reference the Camera layer when you make adjustments to your camera, the text will not move.

5. Click and hold the **Unified Camera tool** on the Tools panel, then click the **Orbit Camera tool**.

6. Click **Glassworks** on the Composition panel, drag to the left and down, then compare your image to Figure 59.

   Your screen may vary.

   (continued)

Figure 58 *Camera Settings dialog box*

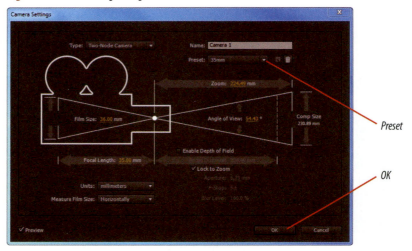

Preset

OK

Figure 59 *Adjusting the camera with the Orbit Camera tool*

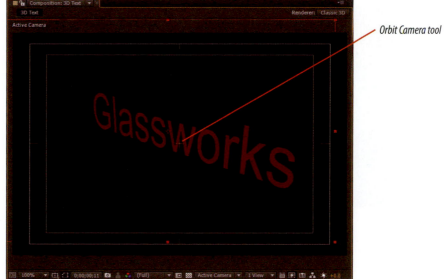

Orbit Camera tool

Figures © Cengage Learning 2013

Developing a PSA and Commercial Using Premiere Pro & After Effects CS6

Figure 60 *Adjusting the light with the Selection tool*

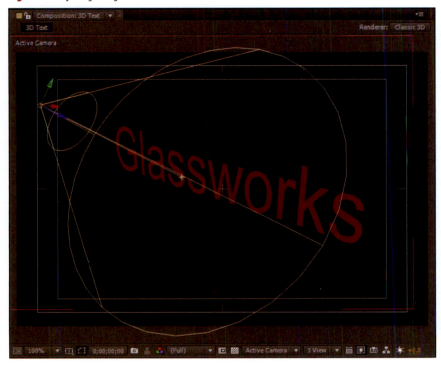

7. Click the **Text Color layer**, then, on the Effect Controls panel, change the Extrusion Depth to **1.00**.

   This increases the thickness of the text.

8. Right-click the **Timeline panel**, point to **New**, then click **Light**.

   The Light Settings dialog box opens.

9. Click **OK** to accept the default settings in the Light Settings dialog box.

   You will move the light on the Composition panel to add a spotlight and brighten the text.

10. Click the **Selection tool** on the Tools panel, move the light to the upper-left area of the Composition panel, then compare your screen to Figure 60.

    Notice as you hover the mouse over the different colored arrows, letters pop up to tell you which plane you will be moving the lighting on, x, y, or z.

11. Click the **Text Color layer** on the Effect Controls panel, click the **Lighting expand arrow**, click the **Light Type list arrow**, then click **First Comp Light**.

    First Comp Light references the Lighting layer you created.

    (continued)

12. Click the **Camera layer**, press the **[P]** key, then click the **Time-Vary stop watch** ⏱.

    This creates a keyframe on the Camera layer for position. Keyframes are automatically created at the location of the CTI when position settings are changed.

13. Click the **Orbit Camera tool** 🔘 on the Tools panel, drag the **CTI** to **0;00;01;00**, then adjust the Glassworks text on the Composition panel so it appears as shown in Figure 61.

    The light will automatically follow the camera, and your text will be animated.

14. Make additional adjustments with the Orbit Camera tool 🔘 at 2 seconds, 3 seconds, 4 seconds, and 5 seconds.

15. Click the **Play/Pause button** ▶ on the Preview panel to preview the 3D text.

16. Save Glassworks 3D Text *your name* and leave it open for the next exercise.

You animated the 3D text by adding a Camera layer and a Light layer for the Glassworks commercial.

Figure 61 *Adjusting the Glassworks text at 1 second*

Figure 62 *Adding the Color Emboss effect*

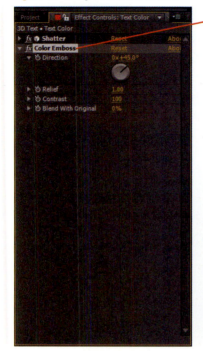

Color Emboss effect

Figure 63 *Adding the CC Light Sweep effect*

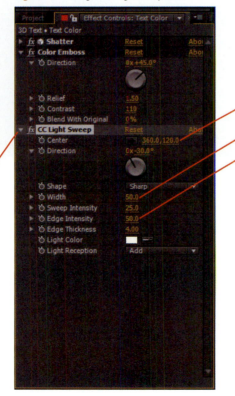

CC Light Sweep

Center value

Width value

Edge Intensity value

Enhance 3D text

1. Open the Glassworks 3D Text *your name* file, if necessary.

2. Select the **Text Color layer**, place the **CTI** at **00;00;00;00**, then collapse the Shatter effect on the Effect Controls panel.

3. Click **Effect** on the Menu bar, point to **Stylize**, then click **Color Emboss**.

   The Color Emboss effect is added to the Effect Controls panel below the Shatter effect, as shown in Figure 62.

4. Change the Relief value to **1.50** and the Contrast value to **110**.

5. Click **Effect** on the Menu bar, point to **Generate**, then click **CC Light Sweep**.

   The CC Light Sweep effect is added to the Effect Controls panel below the Color Emboss effect, as shown in Figure 63.

6. Set the Width value to **25.0** and the Edge Intensity value to **25.0**.

   This softens the effect of the light.

7. Click the **Toggle Animation button** in front of Center to create a keyframe.

(continued)

8. Click the **Effect Control point**, as shown in Figure 64, on the Composition panel to move the location of the light.

9. Make additional adjustments with the Effect Control point at 2 seconds, 3 seconds, 4 seconds, and 5 seconds.

10. Save the Glassworks 3D Text *your name* project, then close After Effects.

You made enhancements to the 3D text for the Glassworks commercial.

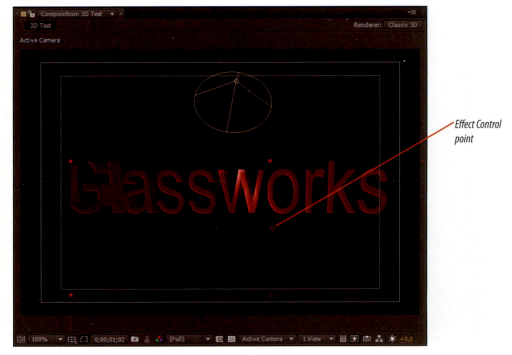

Effect Control point

Figure 65 *Import After Effects Composition dialog box*

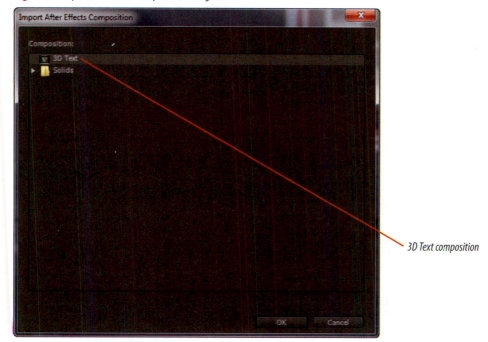

3D Text composition

Import an After Effects composition

1. Start Premiere Pro, then open the Glassworks Commercial *your name* file.

2. Verify that the workspace is set to Editing and that the CTI is at 00;00;00;00.

3. Click **File** on the Menu bar, then click **Import**.

   The Import dialog box opens.

4. Locate the Glassworks 3D Text *your name* file, then click **Open**.

   The Import After Effects Composition dialog box opens.

5. Select the **3D Text composition** as shown in Figure 65, then click **OK**.

   This dynamically links the After Effects composition.

6. Double-click the **3D Text/Glassworks 3D Text** linked composition on the Project panel to open the file on the Source Monitor.

7. Click the **Drag Video only icon** 📧 on the Source Monitor, then drag to the Video 2 layer at the location of the CTI.

   This is the beginning of a television commercial.

8. Preview your project on the Program Monitor.

9. Save your project, export your final project to the MPEG2 video format without audio, then close Premiere Pro.

You imported your 3D Text After Effects file into your Premiere Pro project and exported your project to the MPEG2 video format.

LESSON 3

Edit a Commercial
DEVELOPED FOR THE INTERNET

What You'll Do

Figure © Cengage Learning 2013

 In this lesson, you will edit a commercial that is designed to be published on the Internet. You will also learn animation techniques in After Effects.

Animating with the Puppet Pin Tool

The Puppet tools are used to add natural motion to raster images and vector graphics. This can include still images, shapes, and text characters as well as imported Photoshop and Illustrator files.

The Puppet Pin tool works by deforming parts of an image. A **deform pin** is a type of pin that you can place or move with the Puppet Pin tool. It is best to plan ahead before using the Puppet Pin tool. For example, you may want to remove an image from its background, and if possible, divide different parts of the image onto separate layers, as shown in Figure 66.

When the first deform pin is placed, a mesh is created, which is divided into triangles. Each part of the mesh is linked with pixels in the image, so the image moves with the mesh.

Figure 66 *Using the Puppet Pin tool*

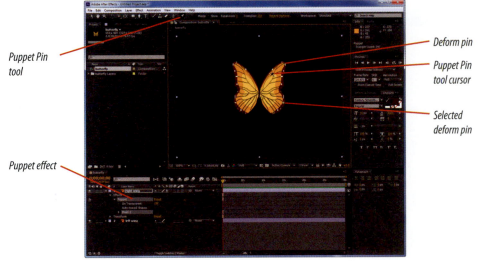

Puppet Pin tool

Puppet effect

Deform pin

Puppet Pin tool cursor

Selected deform pin

Figure © Cengage Learning 2013

The mesh changes shape to conform to the movement of the image based on the location of the deform pin(s).

Similar to using Motion Sketch as you did in a previous chapter, you can sketch the motion path of the deform pins as well. When you have the Puppet Pin tool selected, the Record Options setting becomes available. The Speed setting sets the ratio of the speed to the recorded motion. If the speed is set at 100%, the motion plays back at the speed it was recorded. If the speed is less than 100%, the motion plays back faster. The Smoothing setting removes unnecessary keyframes that are created and makes a smoother motion. When you are ready to record, press and hold [Ctrl] (Win) or [⌘] (Mac) as you click and drag a deform pin. Recording stops when you release the mouse button.

Customizing the Particle Playground Effect

The **Particle Playground effect** is used to animate an object by reproducing it randomly—for instance, creating a flock of birds from the image of a single bird. The Particle Playground effect can be used to duplicate a vector graphic that was animated with the Puppet Pin tool, as shown in Figure 67. The Particle Playground effect

Figure 67 *Particle Playground effect*

Particle Playground effect

generates three kinds of particles: dots, layers, or text characters. There are four particle generators, which are the four properties listed at the top of the Particle Playground effect on the Effect Controls panel: Cannon, Grid, Layer Exploder, and Particle Exploder. By default, Cannon is the only generator active, but you may have all of them active if you choose. However, you can specify only one kind of particle per particle generator. By default, dot particles are created. The movement of the particles is determined by the settings under Gravity, Repel, Wall, and Property Mapper.

The controls you will be using are Cannon, Layer Map, and Gravity. The following Cannon controls create particles in a continuous stream from a single point:

Position: The Position control specifies the x and y coordinates from which particles are created.

Barrel Radius: The Barrel Radius control sets the size of the barrel radius; a negative value creates a circular barrel and a positive value creates a square barrel.

Particles per Second: The Particles per Second control specifies how often particles are created. A value of zero results in no particles being created; a high value increases the density of the particle stream. Keyframes can be set on the Timeline for this control to set the value to zero when you may not want particles created.

Direction: The Direction control sets the angle that the particles are fired from.

Direction Random Spread: The Direction Random Spread control specifies how much a particle direction deviates from the cannon direction.

Velocity: The Velocity control specifies the initial speed at which the particles fire from the cannon, in pixels per second.

Velocity Random Spread: The Velocity Random Spread control specifies the amount of random velocity of particles; a higher value results in more variation in velocity.

By default, the Particle Playground creates dot particles, as shown in Figure 68. The following Layer Map controls replace the dots with a layer of your choosing in the composition:

Use Layer: The Use Layer control specifies the layer on which you want to place the particles.

Time Offset Type: The Time Offset Type control specifies how you want to use the frames of a multiframe layer. For the example of a butterfly flapping its wings, if you were

Figure 68 *Particle Playground effect default dot particles*

to leave the default setting of Relative and the Time Offset at zero, all of the butterflies would be flapping their wings at the same time; they would be synchronized. For simplicity, you'll consider just the random options.

Relative Random: The Relative Random control starts playing the layer from a frame chosen at random. The frame is chosen from within a range between the current time of the effect layer and the Random Time Max you specify.

Absolute Random: The Absolute Random control starts playing the layer from a frame chosen at random. The frame is chosen from a range between zero to the Random Time Max you specify.

Time Offset: The Time Offset control specifies the frame to start playing sequential frames from the layer.

The following Gravity controls accelerate particles in the direction of gravity:

Force: The Force control specifies the force of gravity. A positive value increases the force; a negative value reduces the force.

Direction: The Direction control specifies the angle along which gravity pulls; the default is 180°, simulating the real world.

Here is a summary of the other properties in the Particle Playground effect:

The **Grid generator** works like the Cannon generator, except that it creates particles in a continuous stream from a set of grid intersections.

The **Layer Exploder** and **Particle Exploder** generators create new particles based on a layer. The Particle Exploder then has the ability to explode a particle into more new particles.

The **Repel control** specifies how nearby particles repel or attract each other, simulating adding a positive or negative magnetic charge to each of the particles. The **Wall control** creates an area restricting where the particles can move.

The **Property Mapper** control gives you the ability to control specific properties by using a layer map.

Working with a Pre-Composed Layer

If you want to group some or all of the layers in a composition, you can pre-compose those layers into a new composition. Pre-composing the layers keeps all of the attributes that were applied to the layers and replaces the layers with a new single layer nested composition, as shown in Figure 69.

Figure 69 *Pre-composed layers*

Before

After

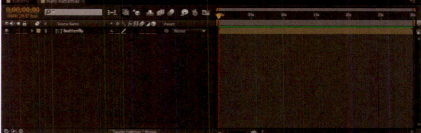

One benefit of creating a pre-composed layer is that you can apply Transform properties, such as Scale, to the pre-composition and all of the layers in the pre-composed layer are affected by the transformation.

Placing Text on a Path

In After Effects, you can place text on a path just as you can in Photoshop and Illustrator. However, in After Effects, you have the ability to animate the text once it is placed on the path. The path is created with the Pen tool. To create text on a path, you must first select the text on the Composition panel before you select the Pen tool. This draws the path as a mask, which makes the stroke transparent when you attach the text to the path. Once you select the Pen tool, the RotoBezier check box needs to be checked. The **RotoBezier** option makes paths easier to draw and makes the curves smoother.

Once you have drawn a path for your text, like the one shown in Figure 70, you expand the Text controls on the Timeline panel. If you successfully drew a mask, the Path Options

control should be an option. Select the Path drop-down menu, choose Mask 1, and your text will align to the path.

Animating Text on a Curved Path

Once you have created text on a path, you may want to animate it. To animate text on a path,

Figure 70 *Placing type on a path*

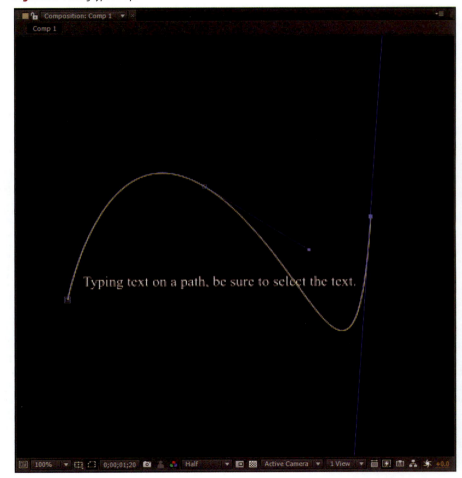

you can adjust the text with the properties found under the Path Options property group on the Timeline panel. The Path Options properties allow you to specify a path and to alter the way individual characters appear on the path. Text can appear perpendicular to the path, aligned left or right, reversed, or with the First or Last Margins adjusted to a specific location, as shown in Figure 71. Keyframes can be created for any of these properties to animate text along a path. For example, select the First Margin control on the Timeline panel, click the Time-Vary stop watch to activate keyframes, then point to the text on the path on the Composition panel, as shown in Figure 72. As you move the CTI and adjust the text on the path, another keyframe is automatically created.

Figure 71 *Path Options controls*

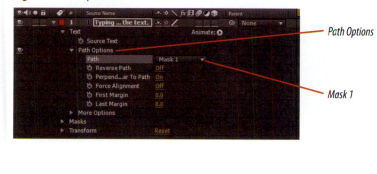

Path Options

Mask 1

Figure 72 *Adjusting text on a path*

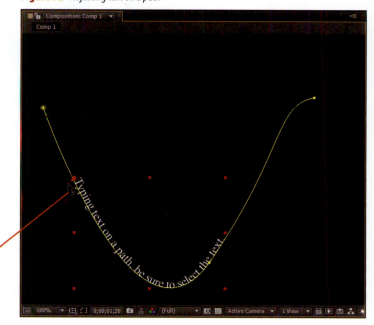

Adjustment cursor

Animate with the Puppet Pin tool

1. Open Hummingbird Insurance.aep from the drive and folder where your Data Files are stored, then save it as **Hummingbird Insurance** *your name*.

   The file has compositions already created and it is dynamically linked to Premiere Pro.

2. Click the **Composition Navigator**, then click **hummingbird**.

3. Click the **hummingbird composition** on the Timeline panel.

   Three layers in this composition make up the hummingbird, the body and the two wings.

4. Select the **Left Wing layer**, click the **Puppet Pin tool** on the Tools panel, point to the **tip of the wing**, then click to place a deform pin, as shown in Figure 73.

5. Click to place two more deform pins on the left wing near the body, one towards the head and the other in the bright green area, as shown in Figure 74.

   These two deform pins will help stabilize the wing when you create the animation to simulate flapping.

   (continued)

Figure 73 *Placing a deform pin*

Deform pin

Figure 74 *Placing deform pins to stabilize*

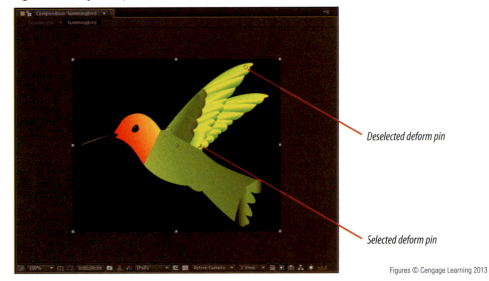

Deselected deform pin

Selected deform pin

Figures © Cengage Learning 2013

Figure 75 *Animating the left wing*

Puppet Sketch tool   Keyframes generated

Figure 76 *Placement of deform pins on the right wing*

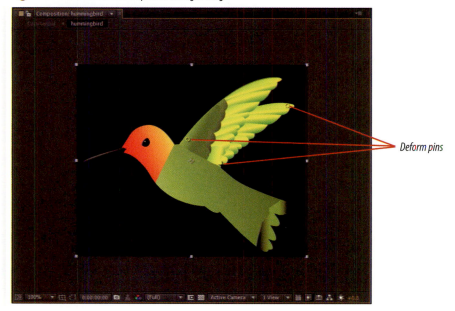

Deform pins

Figures © Cengage Learning 2013

6. Verify that the **CTI** is at **00;00;00;00**, select the deform pin at the tip of the wing, then press and hold [**Ctrl**] (Win) or ⌘ (Mac) while dragging the tip of the wing up and down until the CTI reaches the end of the Timeline.

   Pressing and holding [Ctrl] (Win) or ⌘ (Mac) activates the Puppet Sketch tool, which looks like a stopwatch. Keyframes are automatically recorded as you move the deform pin up and down, as shown in Figure 75.

7. Click the **Play/Pause button** ▶ on the Preview panel to preview the animation.

8. Click the **Video button** 👁 on Left Wing layer to hide the hummingbird's left wing.

   You will be adding deform pins to the Right Wing layer, and hiding the left wing will make it easier to see the right wing.

9. Select the **Right Wing layer**, click the **Puppet Pin tool** 📌 on the Tools panel, if necessary, then place three deform pins at the corners of the wing, as shown in Figure 76.

(continued)

10. Click **Record Options** on the Tools panel.

    The Puppet Record Options dialog box opens, as shown in Figure 77.

11. Change the Speed value to **50%** and the Smoothing value to **20**, then click **OK**.

    If the speed value is set to less than 100%, the motion plays back faster than it was recorded. Setting a higher smoothing value removes keyframes as the motion is created.

12. Click the **deform pin** at the tip of the wing, then press and hold [**Ctrl**] (Win) or ⌘ (Mac) while dragging the tip of the wing up and down until the CTI reaches the end of the Timeline.

13. Click the **Video button** 👁 on Left Wing layer.

14. Click the **Play/Pause button** ▶ on the Preview panel to preview the animation.

15. Save Hummingbird Insurance *your name* and leave it open for the next exercise.

You animated the wings of the hummingbird with the Puppet Pin tool.

Figure 77 *Puppet Record Options dialog box*

Speed value

Smoothing value

Figure 78 *Working with the Particle Playground effect*

Particle Playground

Bird Particles layer

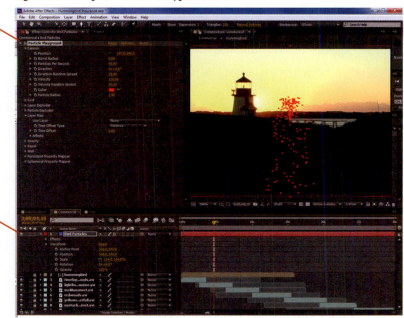

Customize the Particle Playground effect

1. Open the Hummingbird Bird Insurance *your name*.aep project file, if necessary, then select the **Effects workspace**.

2. Click the **Commercial composition** on the Timeline panel, then click the **Play/Pause button** ▶ on the Preview panel to preview the animation.

   A Solid layer has been created with the Particle Playground effect (the random red dots) already applied, as shown in Figure 78.

3. Drag the **CTI** to **0;00;05;00**, then select the **Bird Particles layer**.

   Using the Particle Playground effect, you will duplicate the hummingbird you animated earlier.

4. On the Effect Controls panel, click the **Cannon expand arrow**, then change the following values: Barrel Radius: **25**; Particles Per Second: **3**; Direction: **-90x +0.0°;** Direction Random Spread: **360.00**; Velocity: **200.00**; and Velocity Random Spread: **100.00**.

   These values determine how far apart the birds will fly, how often they will appear, and at what speed and direction.

   (continued)

Figure © Cengage Learning 2013

5. Click the **Gravity expand arrow**, then change the Force value to **7**.

This will slow the speed of the birds.

6. Click the **Layer Map expand arrow**, click the **Use Layer drop-down menu**, then click **2.hummingbird**.

7. Click the **Time Offset Type drop-down menu**, click **Relative Random**, then change the Random Time Max setting to **2.40**.

Your settings should match those shown in Figure 79.

The hummingbird layer is assigned to the Particle Playground effect and the red dots are replaced with hummingbirds. The Relative Random setting brings in the birds at random intervals.

8. Click the **Play/Pause button** ▶ on the Preview panel to preview the animation.

9. Save Hummingbird Insurance *your name* and leave it open for the next exercise.

You customized the Particle Playground effect to display multiple instances of the hummingbird that you animated earlier.

Figure 79 *Particle Playground effect modified settings*

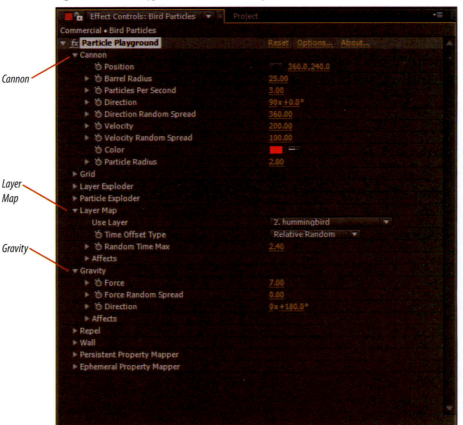

Cannon

Layer Map

Gravity

Figure 80 *Pre-compose dialog box*

New composition name

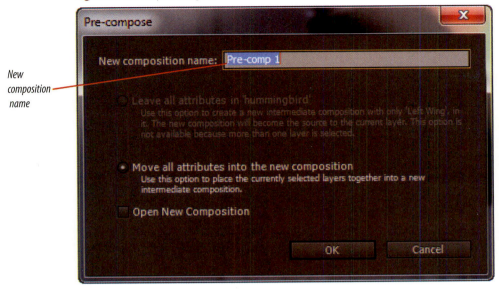

Create a pre-compose layer

1. Open the Hummingbird Bird Insurance *your name*.aep file, if necessary.

2. Select the **hummingbird composition** on the Composition panel, then select the **Left Wing**, **Right Wing**, and **hummingbird layers** on the Timeline panel.

   You will create a pre-compose layer from these three layers.

3. Click **Layer** on the Menu bar, then click **Pre-Compose**.

   The Pre-compose dialog box opens, as shown in Figure 80.

4. In the New composition name text box, type **Whole Hummingbird**, then click **OK**.

   The layers are grouped inside the new composition and are now more manageable. The Whole Hummingbird layer appears on the Timeline.

5. Press [**S**] on the keyboard to reveal the Scale property, then change the value to **50.0%**, as shown in Figure 81.

6. Select the **Commercial composition** on the Composition panel, then click the **Play/Pause button** ▶ on the Preview panel to preview the animation.

   The hummingbirds are now smaller.

7. Save Hummingbird Insurance *your name* and leave it open for the next exercise.

You created a pre-compose layer using the three hummingbird layers, and used it to scale the Particle Playground effect.

Figure 81 *Changing the Scale property*

New composition

Place text on a path

1. Open the Hummingbird Bird Insurance *your name*.aep file, if necessary.

2. Turn on the Title/Action Safe grid.

3. Select the **Text composition** on the Composition panel, click the **Selection tool** 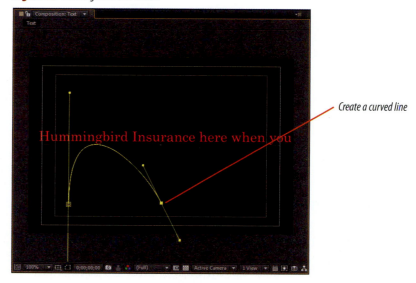 on the Tools panel, then select the text on the Composition panel.

4. Click the **Pen Tool** on the Tools panel, then verify that the RotoBezier check box is unchecked on the Tools panel.

   You are going to draw a curved path to attach the text inside the title safe area.

5. In the lower-left area of the Composition panel, press and hold the mouse button, then move the cursor in an upward direction.

   A vertex, which is represented by a yellow square, appears each time you click the mouse button.

TIP This allows you to create a curved line in the next step similar to that in Figure 82.

6. Using Figure 82 as a guide, click and drag where the second vertex appears in the figure to create the first curve.

7. Using Figure 83 as a guide, continue to draw the curved line until you get to the edge of the viewing area, holding the mouse button for the creation of the second curve.

   Your curved path may vary from the figure.

(continued)

Figure 82 *Drawing with the Pen tool*

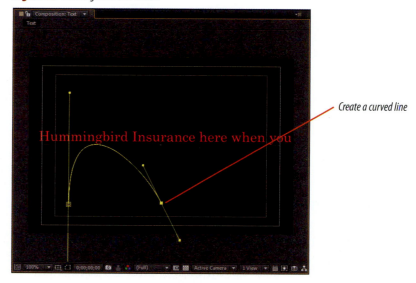

Create a curved line

Figure 83 *Curved line*

Figures © Cengage Learning 2013

Developing a PSA and Commercial Using Premiere Pro & After Effects CS6

Figure 84 *Attaching text to a path*

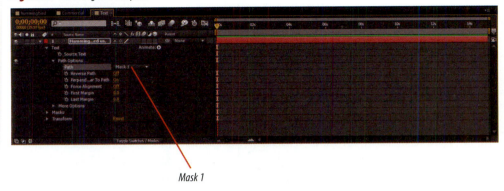

Mask 1

Figure 85 *Text attached to a path*

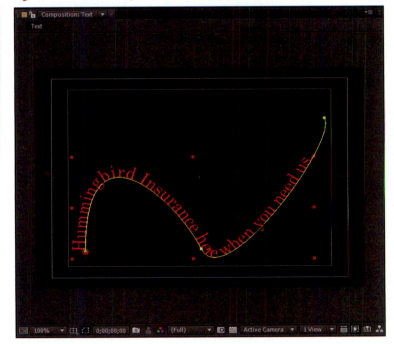

8. On the Timeline panel, expand the Text layer (Hummingbird Insurance here when you need us.), then expand the Text property.

9. Click the **Path Options expand arrow**, click the **Path drop-down menu**, then click **Mask 1**, as shown in Figure 84.

   Your text should now be attached to the curved path, as shown in Figure 85.

10. Save Hummingbird Insurance *your name* and leave it open for the next exercise.

You created a curved path and attached text to the path.

Animate text on a curved path

1. Open the Hummingbird Insurance *your name*.aep file, if necessary.

2. Select the **Text composition**, then expand the Path Options property if necessary.

3. Verify that the CTI is at **00;00;00;00**, then click the **Time-Vary stop watch** in front of First Margin to activate keyframes.

4. Place keyframes at **8 seconds** and **14 seconds** by clicking the **Add or remove keyframe at current time button**.

5. Return to the first keyframe.

6. Click the **Selection tool** on the Tools panel, point to the red rectangle to the left of the letter "H" in "Hummingbird" on the yellow path on the Composition panel, then click and drag the text along the path, as shown in Figure 86.

7. Click the **Go to Next Keyframe button** to jump to the second keyframe, then drag the text along the path as shown in Figure 87.

(continued)

Figure 86 *Adjusting first margin for first keyframe*

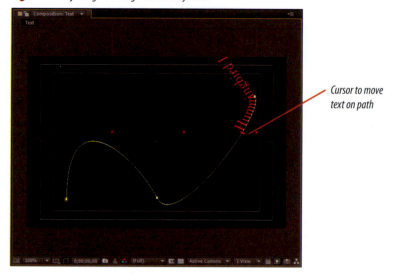

Cursor to move text on path

Figure 87 *Adjusting first margin for second keyframe*

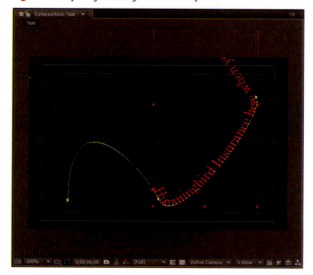

Figures © Cengage Learning 2013

Developing a PSA and Commercial Using Premiere Pro & After Effects CS6

Figure 88 *Adjusting first margin for third keyframe*

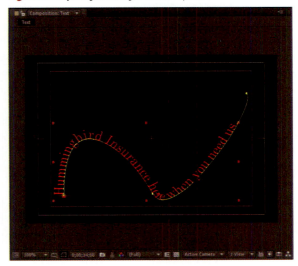

Figure 89 *Text composition added to Commercial composition*

8. Click the **Go to Next Keyframe button** ▶ to jump to the third keyframe, then drag the text along the path as shown in Figure 88.

9. On the Timeline panel, select the **Commercial composition**, then drag the **Text composition** to the top of the stacking order as shown in Figure 89.

10. Click the **Play/Pause button** ▶ on the Preview panel to preview the animation.

11. Click **Composition** on the Menu bar, click **Add to Render Queue**, set the Output Module as an **FLV**, title your file **Hummingbird Insurance Commercial** *your name*, then click the **Render button**.

12. Save your project file and close After Effects.

You added motion to text on a curved path and saved your project as an FLV movie for the Internet.

Figures © Cengage Learning 2013

Apply the Cartoon effect.

1. Start After Effects, open the Water Pollution.aep file, then save it as **Water Pollution** *your name*.
2. Use the Composition Navigator to select Clip 1, then verify that the Effects workspace is in place.
3. Click the Selection tool on the Tools panel, then click the video footage on the Composition panel.
4. Click Effect on the Menu bar, point to Stylize, then click Cartoon.
5. Click the Fill expand arrow, then change the Shading Steps value to 18.0 and the Shading Smoothness value to 65.0.
6. Click the Edge expand arrow, then change the Softness value to 60.0.
7. Change the Detail Radius value to 2.2 and the Detail Threshold value to 50.0.
8. Save your work.

Customize the Cartoon effect.

1. Use the Composition Navigator to select Clip 2, then verify the Effects workspace is in place.
2. Click the Selection tool on the Tools panel, then click the video footage on the Composition panel.
3. Right-click the Composition panel, click Effect, point to Stylize, then click Cartoon.
4. Click the expand arrow in front of Fill, then click the expand arrows in front of Shading Steps and Shading Smoothness.
5. Drag the Shading Steps slider to the right and to the left to see how it affects the video footage on the Composition Panel.

6. Drag the Shading Smoothness slider to the right and to the left to see how it affects the video footage on the Composition Panel.
7. Click the expand arrow in front of the following properties: Edge, then Softness; Detail Radius; Detail Threshold; Advanced, then Edge Enhancement and Edge Contrast.
8. Drag the sliders to the left and right for the following properties: Softness, Detail Radius, Detail Threshold, Edge Enhancement and Edge Contrast.

Search for the Cartoon effect.

1. Use the Composition Navigator to select Clip 3 and verify the Effects workspace is in place.
2. Click the Selection tool on the Tools panel, then click the video footage on the Composition panel.
3. Type **Cartoon** in the search field on the Effects & Presets panel.
4. Select the Cartoon effect on the Effects & Presets panel, then drag it to the Composition panel.
5. Enter the following values: Shading Steps: 4.3; Shading Smoothness: 79.0; Softness: 60.0; Edge Enhancement 1.0; Detail Radius: 6.5; and Detail Threshold: 22.0.

Apply the Levels effect.

1. Use the Composition Navigator to select Clip 1, then verify that you can see the video footage on the Composition panel.
2. Click the Selection tool on the Tools panel, then click the video footage on the Composition panel.

3. Click Effect on the Menu bar, point to Color Correction, then click Levels.
4. Drag the Levels effect above Cartoon on the Effect Controls panel.
5. On the histogram, drag the Input Black control to the right, just before the pink line begins so that your Input Black value is 7.0.
6. Drag the Input White control to the left until the Input White value is 244.0.
7. Drag the Input Gray control to the left to adjust the shadows until the Gamma value is 1.02.

Customize the Levels effect.

1. Use the Composition Navigator to select Clip 2, then verify that you can see the video footage on the Composition panel.
2. Click the Selection tool on the Tools panel, then click the video footage on the Composition panel.
3. Right-click the Composition panel, click Effect, point to Color Correction, then click Levels.
4. Drag the Levels effect above the Cartoon effect on the Effect Controls panel.
5. Click the expand arrows in front of Input Black, Input White, and Gamma.
6. Adjust the Input Black slider by dragging it to the right and the Input White slider by dragging it to the left.
7. Adjust the Gamma slider by dragging it to the left and right to adjust the shadows.
8. Select the Levels effect on the Effects & Presets panel, then drag it to the Composition panel to apply it to the Clip 3 composition.

9. Drag the Levels effect above the Cartoon effect on the Effect Controls panel.

10. Enter the following values: Input Black: **9.0**; Input White: **182.0**; Gamma: **0.79**.

Apply the Hue/Saturation effect.

1. Use the Composition Navigator to select Clip 1, then verify that you can see the video footage on the Composition panel.

2. Click the Selection tool on the Tools panel, then click the video footage on the Composition panel.

3. Click Effect on the Menu bar, point to Color Correction, then click Hue/Saturation.

4. Click the Master Hue dial then drag it clockwise until you reach the value 0x +337.0°.

5. Drag the Master Saturation slider until the value is 42.

6. Save your project and leave it open for the next step.

Apply the Channel Mixer effect.

1. Use the Composition Navigator to select Clip 2, then verify that you can see the video footage on the Composition panel.

2. Click the Selection tool on the Tools panel, then click the video footage on the Composition panel.

3. Right-click the Composition panel, click Effect, point to Color Correction, then click Channel Mixer.

4. Change the following values: Red-Const: -15; Green-Const: -23; Blue-Const: 31.

5. Select the Clip 3 composition, then double-click the Hue/Saturation effect on the Effects & Presets panel to apply the effect.

6. Change the following values: Master Hue: 0x -48.0°; Master Saturation: -21; Master Lightness: -20.

7. Save your project, then close After Effects.

Import an After Effects composition into Premiere Pro.

1. Start Premiere Pro, open the Water Pollution.prproj file, then rename it **Water Pollution** *your name*.

2. Click File on the Menu bar, point to Adobe Dynamic Link, then click Import After Effects Composition.

3. Locate the Water Pollution *your name* After Effects project file, click the PSA composition, then click OK.

4. Double-click the PSA/Water Pollution After Effects composition on the Project panel to preview the composition on the Source Monitor.

5. Click the Drag Video Only icon on the Source Monitor, then place the After Effects composition on the Video 1 track.

6. Click the Play-Stop Toggle button on the Program Monitor to preview the sequence.

Create a voice over in Premiere Pro.

1. Open the Water Pollution Script.txt file.
2. Make sure your microphone is plugged in to the microphone jack input.
3. Click the Audio Mixer panel options button then click Meter Input(s) Only. On the Audio Mixer panel, under the Audio 1 track, click the Enable track for recording button and the Solo Track button.
4. Click the Record button on the Audio Mixer panel.
5. Click the Play-Stop Toggle button on the Audio Mixer panel, then read the Water Pollution script.
6. Click the Play-Stop Toggle button when you have finished recording.
7. Preview your project on the Program Monitor. Figure 90 shows a sample completed project.
8. Export your final project to the MPEG2 video format.

Create a new After Effects composition in Premiere Pro.

1. Open the Luckenbach Commercial.prproj file, then save it as **Luckenbach Commercial** *your name*.
2. Preview the video clip on the Program Monitor.
3. Click the Selection tool, then select the Luckenbach clip in the sequence.
4. Click File on the Menu bar, point to Adobe Dynamic Link, then click Replace with After Effects Composition.

5. Name your project **Luckenbach Dynamic Link** *your name*, then click Save.
6. Click File on the Menu bar, point to Import, then click File.
7. Locate the Frame.psd file located in the Luckenbach-Clips folder, then click Open.

8. Drag Frame.psd from the Project panel to the Timeline panel above the video layer.
9. Click the Premiere Pro icon on the taskbar (Win) or dock (Mac) to return to Premiere Pro, save, then close the file.

Figure 90 *Completed Skills Review, Water Pollution PSA*

Figure © Cengage Learning 2013

Stabilize Footage with the Warp Stabilizer effect.

1. Start After Effects, then open the Luckenbach Dynamic Link *your name*.aep file, if necessary.
2. Click the Selection tool on the Tools panel, then click the video footage on the Composition panel.
3. Press [Spacebar] to preview your footage.
4. Select the Luckenback.avi layer, click Effect on the Menu bar, point to Distort, then click Warp Stabilizer.
5. When the Stabilizing step is complete, preview your footage in the Composition panel.
6. Save your project and close After Effects.

Create 3D text.

1. Open the Luckenbach 3D Text.aep file, then save it as **Luckenbach 3D Text *your name***.
2. Click Layer on the Menu bar, point to New, then click Solid.
3. In the Name text box, type **Text Color**, click the color picker, select a dark green color, then click OK twice.
4. In the Effects & Presets panel search field, type **Shatter**, then drag the Shatter preset onto the Text Color layer.
5. On the Effect Controls panel, click the View drop-down menu, then click Rendered.
6. Click the expand arrow in front of Shape, click the Pattern drop-down menu, then click Custom.
7. Click the Custom Shatter Map drop-down menu, then click 2. Luckenbach.
8. Click the Video Switch button on Layer 2.
9. Click the Play/Pause button on the Preview panel to preview the 3D text.

10. Click the expand arrow in front of Force 1, Force 2, and Physics, then change the Strength and Gravity values to 0.00.
11. Collapse these properties when you have finished.
12. Click the Play/Pause button on the Preview panel to preview the 3D text.

Animate 3D text with a Camera layer.

1. Right-click the Timeline panel, point to New, then click Camera.
2. Click the Preset drop-down menu, click 35mm, then click OK.
3. Select the Text Color layer on the Timeline panel, click the Camera Position drop-down menu, then click Comp Camera.
4. Click the Unified Camera tool on the Tools panel, click Luckenbach on the Composition panel, then drag to the left and down.
5. Select the Text Color layer, then change the Extrusion Depth to 1.20.
6. Right-click the Timeline panel, point to New, then click Light.
7. Click OK to accept the default settings in the Light Settings dialog box.
8. Using the Selection tool, move the light to the upper-left area of the Composition panel.
9. Select the Text Color layer, then, in the Effect Controls panel, click the expand arrow in front of Lighting.
10. Click the Light Type drop-down menu, then click First Comp Light.

11. Select the Camera layer, press [P], then click the Time-Vary stop watch button.
12. Move the CTI to 0;00;01;00, click the Unified Camera tool on the Tools panel, then adjust the Luckenbach text on the Composition panel.
13. Make additional adjustments with the Orbit Camera tool at 2 seconds, 3 seconds, 4 seconds, and 5 seconds.
14. Click the Play/Pause button on the Preview panel to preview the 3D text.

Enhance 3D text.

1. Select the Text Color layer, place the CTI at 00;00;00;00, then collapse the Shatter effect on the Effect Controls panel.
2. Select Effect on the Menu bar, point to Stylize, then click Color Emboss.
3. Change the Relief value to 2.10, then change the Contrast value to 120.
4. Click Effect on the Menu bar, point to Generate, then click CC Light Sweep.
5. Change the Width value to 25.0, the Sweep Intensity to 10.0 and the Edge Intensity value to 25.0.
6. Click the Time-Vary stop watch button in front of Center to create a keyframe, then click the Effect Control point on the Composition panel to move the location of the light.
7. Make additional adjustments with the Effect Control point at 2 seconds, 3 seconds, 4 seconds, and 5 seconds.
8. Save the Luckenbach 3D Text *your name* project and close After Effects.

Import an After Effects composition.

1. If necessary, start Premiere Pro, then open the Premiere Pro project Luckenbach Commercial *your name*.
2. Verify that the workspace is set to Editing and that the CTI is at 00;00;00;00.
3. Click File on the Menu bar, then click Import.
4. Locate the Luckenbach 3D Text *your name* project file, then click Open.
5. Select the 3D Text composition, then click OK.
6. Double-click the 3D Text/Luckenbach 3D Text linked composition on the Project panel to open the file on the Source Monitor.
7. Click the Drag Video only icon, then drag to the Video 2 layer at the location of the CTI, as shown in Figure 91.
8. Preview your project on the Program Monitor.
9. Save your project, export your final project to the MPEG2 video format without audio, then close Premiere Pro.

Animate with the Puppet Pin tool.

1. Open World Peace.aep, then save it as **World Peace** *your name*.
2. Select the Dove composition on the Timeline panel.
3. Select the Left Wing layer, click the Puppet Pin tool on the Tools panel, then click the tip of the wing to place a deform pin.
4. Place two more deform pins on the left wing, one on the left near the head and another at the right near the branch.

5. Click the deform pin at the tip of the tip of the wing, then press and hold [Ctrl] (Win) or ⌘ (Mac) while dragging the tip of the wing up and down until the CTI reaches the end of the Timeline.

6. Select the Right Wing layer, click the Puppet Pin tool, if necessary, then click the tip of the wing to place a deform pin.

Figure 91 *Luckenbach Commercial*

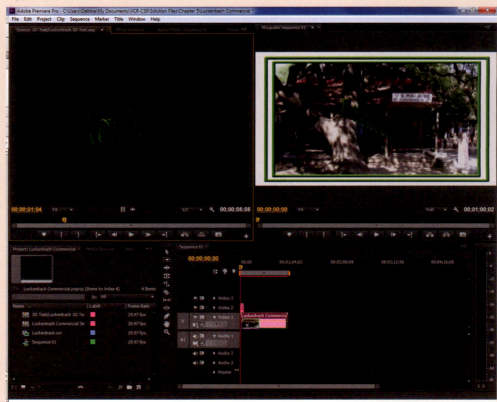

Figure © Cengage Learning 2013

7. Click to place two more deform pins on the right wing, one near the head and another near the base of the wing near the body.

8. Click the Play/Pause button on the Preview panel to preview the animation.

9. Click Record Options on the Tools panel to open the Puppet Record Options dialog box.

10. If necessary, change the Speed value to 50%, change the Smoothing value to 20, then click OK.

11. Click the Selection tool, select the deform pin at the tip of the right wing, then press and hold [Ctrl] (Win) or ⌘ (Mac) while dragging the tip of the wing up and down until the CTI reaches the end of the Timeline.

12. Click the Play/Pause button on the Preview panel to preview the animation.

Customize the Particle Playground effect.

1. Select the Effects workspace.

2. Select the World Peace composition on the Timeline panel, then click the Play/Pause button on the Preview panel to preview the animation.

3. Move the CTI to 0;00;05;00 in the Current time display, then select the Dove Particles layer.

4. On the Effect Controls panel, click the expand arrow in front of Cannon, then change the following values: Barrel Radius: 175; Particles Per Second: 4; Direction: 60x +0.0°; Direction Random Spread: 150.00; Velocity: 300.00; Velocity Random Spread: 250.00.

5. Click the expand arrow in front of Gravity, then change the Force value to 6.

6. Click the expand arrow in front of Layer Map, click the Use Layer drop-down menu, then click 2. Dove.

7. Click the Time Offset Type drop-down menu, click Relative Random, then change the Random Time Max value to 2.40.

8. Click the Play/Pause button on the Preview panel to preview the animation.

Work with a pre-compose layer.

1. Select the Dove composition, select the three layers on the Timeline panel, click Layer on the Menu bar, then click Pre-compose.

2. In the New composition name text box, type **Whole Dove**, then click OK.

3. Press [S] to reveal the Scale property, then change the value to 35.0%.

4. Select the World Peace composition, then click the Play/Pause button on the Preview panel to preview the animation.

Place text on a path.

1. Open the Text composition, then select the text on the Composition panel.

2. Select the Pen tool on the Tools panel, then if necessary, click the RotoBezier check box on the Tools panel.

3. Click in the lower-left area of the Composition panel, move the cursor, click again, move the cursor again and this time hold the mouse button while you click to create a curved line.

4. Continue to draw the curved line until you get to the edge of the viewing area, holding the mouse button for the creation of each vertex.

5. On the Timeline panel, expand the Text layer properties.

6. Click the Path Options expand arrow, click the Path drop-down menu, then click Mask 1.

7. Select the Text composition, then expand the Path Options properties, if necessary.

8. Verify that the CTI is at 00;00;00;00, then click the Time-Vary stop watch button in front of First Margin to activate keyframes.

9. Place keyframes at 15 seconds and 30 seconds by clicking the Add or remove keyframe at current time button.

10. Select the Selection tool and return to the first keyframe, then drag the text along the path until the text is all the way to the right.

11. Click the Go to Next Keyframe button to jump to the second keyframe, then drag the text along the path until it reaches the middle of the path.

12. Click the Go to Next Keyframe button to jump to the third keyframe, then drag the text along the path and return it to where it began.

13. Select the World Peace composition, then drag the Text composition to the top of the stacking order. An example of the composition is shown in Figure 92.

14. Click the Play/Pause button on the Preview panel to preview the animation.

15. Click Composition on the Menu bar, then click Add to Render Queue.

16. Set the Output Module as an FLV and title your file **World Peace Commercial** *your name*, then click the Render button.

17. Save your project file, then close After Effects.

Figure 92 *Completed Skills Review, World Peace Commercial*

Figure © Cengage Learning 2013

Your multimedia instructor would like you to practice your skills with the Cartoon effect on the After Effects project file titled Cartoon Practice. The Cartoon effect has already been applied to the footage with the default settings for you.

1. Start After Effects, open Cartoon Practice.aep, then save it as **Cartoon Practice *your name*.aep**.
2. Set the workspace to Effects.
3. Select the footage on the Composition panel, then make any necessary adjustments to the Cartoon effect on the Effect Controls panel that you feel appropriate.
4. Add the Levels effect to the footage and place it above the Cartoon effect.
5. Make appropriate adjustments to the Levels effect.
6. Add the Hue/Saturation effect to adjust the color.
7. Preview your final composition and save your project. A sample project is shown in Figure 93.
8. Export your project to the FLV file format named **Cartoon Practice *your name***.

Figure 93 *Sample Project Builder 1*

Develop a PSA & Commercial Using Premiere Pro & After Effects CS6

A local steakhouse has contracted you to create a 30-second Internet commercial featuring a sculpture of a longhorn. They would like you to animate the longhorn using the Puppet Pin tool. They would also like you to create some animated 3D text with the name of their restaurant to play above the longhorn for the first 10 seconds of the commercial. For the remaining time, they would simply like the address and the phone number of the restaurant featured. Since this will loop on the Internet, they do not want any sound.

A file has been provided titled Longhorn. aep with the necessary compositions already created for you to work with.

1. Open Longhorn.aep, then save it as **Longhorn your name.aep**.
2. Select the Longhorn composition, then using the Puppet Pin tool, animate the four legs on the Longhorn layer.
3. Select the 3D Text composition, select the Text Color layer, and on the Effect Controls panel, modify the Shatter effect to create 3D text. (*Hint*: The text has already been created for you.)

4. Select the Final composition, then drag the Longhorn and 3D Text compositions into this composition to compile the commercial spot. (*Hint*: The layers with the address and phone number are already created.)

5. Preview your Final composition to be sure you have placed the layers in the correct order. A sample project is shown in Figure 94.
6. Save your project and export as an FLV file named **Longhorn Commercial Spot** *your name*.

Figure 94 *Sample Project Builder 2*

Figure © Cengage Learning 2013

The zoo in your area has contracted you to create a PSA they would like to air on local television and on their Web site to bring public awareness to a campaign about endangered animals. They are providing you with 12 video clips featuring animals they would like included in the commercial. A sample workspace is shown in Figure 95.

Using your skills in Premiere Pro and After Effects, create a 30-second commercial with appropriate text and a voice over from your own research concerning these endangered animals. You will need to export your movie in the MPEG2 and FLV file formats.

Figure 95 *Sample Portfolio Project*

1. Import the video clips into Premiere Pro.
2. Trim clips and combine them on a sequence (needs to be 30 seconds).
3. Use Adobe Dynamic Link to create an After Effects composition from the Premiere Pro sequence.
4. Add special effects of your choosing in After Effects.
5. Add appropriate text either in Premiere Pro or in After Effects.
6. Return to Premiere Pro and add a voice over.
7. Export as an MPEG2 and FLV.

WORKING WITH SPECIAL EFFECTS TO ENHANCE VIRAL VIDEOS - ADOBE PREMIERE PRO & ADOBE AFTER EFFECTS CS6

CHAPTER **6**

1. Adjust speed in Premiere Pro
2. Work with weather effects in After Effects
3. Animate lips on an animal in After Effects

WORKING WITH SPECIAL EFFECTS
TO ENHANCE VIRAL VIDEOS - ADOBE PREMIERE PRO & ADOBE AFTER EFFECTS CS6

A **viral video** is a video that gains popularity on the Internet through the process of sharing via Web sites and email. Viral videos have also become a popular means for marketing, showing off new bands and promoting music, and even as instructional aids in education. Special effects are often used to enhance videos that become viral.

In this chapter, you will work in Premiere Pro and After Effects to add special effects such as adjusting the speed of a clip, adding weather effects footage, and making an animal appear to sing.

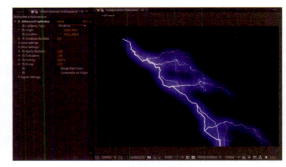

Figures © Cengage Learning 2013

Adjust Speed
IN PREMIERE PRO

What You'll Do

Figure © Cengage Learning 2013

In this lesson, you will use Premiere Pro to adjust the speed of a video clip.

Adjusting Speed in Premiere Pro

Adjusting the speed of a video clip is a popular editing technique. Increasing the speed of a clip is a creative way to indicate the passage of time. Common examples include accelerating the movement of clouds, street traffic, or crowds of people. Decreasing the speed of a clip can enhance emotional and dramatic moments, such as scenes from a wedding or highlights from sporting events.

The playback rate compared to the rate at which a video was recorded is called the **speed**. The speed is identified in percentages. 100% is the recorded playback speed; the speed of a clip can be adjusted to play faster by making the value greater than 100% or slower by making the value less than 100%. Adjusting the speed of a video clip does not adjust the audio and may cause the audio to be out of sync.

Premiere Pro offers three options for adjusting speed: the Time Remapping effect, the Rate Stretch tool, and the Clip Speed/Duration dialog box.

Applying the Time Remapping Effect to a Clip

The Time Remapping effect is used on clips that are on the Timeline panel. This effect can be used to speed up, slow down, play backward, or freeze portions of a video clip. The Time Remapping effect has the flexibility to vary the speed across the duration of an entire clip. You can also ease the speed changes in or out.

When the Time Remapping effect is applied to a clip, the clip's appearance changes. The white speed control track at the top of the clip includes the speed keyframes. It is also where you see left-pointing angle brackets if the clip is set to play in reverse. The rubber band is a line on the Timeline panel that, by default, represents 100% speed. The area above the rubber band represents speeds higher than 100%, and the area below the rubber band represents speeds less than 100%. A speed keyframe is created by pressing [Ctrl] and clicking (Win) or pressing ⌘ and clicking (Mac) at any point on the rubber band. A speed keyframe is identified by a dotted line and a pair of handles in the speed control track, as shown in Figure 1. The rubber band controls the speed of the clip and can be dragged on either side of the keyframe to increase or decrease the speed (the speed on the other side remains the same). Adding keyframes allows the speed to vary, as shown in Figure 2. (*Note*: The duration of the clip automatically adjusts to accommodate the new speed(s). If there is no available space to the right of the clip, and the speed is reduced, thus increasing the length of the clip, then the overall clip duration remains the same and the adjusted clip is trimmed where the next clip begins.)

Playing a Clip Backward then Forward

You can play a clip backward then forward by [Ctrl]-dragging (Win) or ⌘-dragging (Mac) a speed keyframe to the place in the clip where you want the backward motion to end. The Program Monitor displays a split screen; the left frame displays the static frame where the drag was initiated and the right frame previews the reverse playback, as shown in Figure 3. When the mouse button is released to define the segment of backward motion, an additional segment is automatically added to replay the

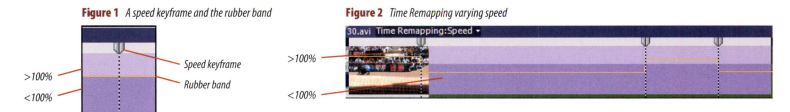

Figure 1 *A speed keyframe and the rubber band*

>100%
<100%

Speed keyframe
Rubber band

Figure 2 *Time Remapping varying speed*

30.avi   Time Remapping:Speed ▾

>100%
<100%

Figure 3 *Playing a clip backward*

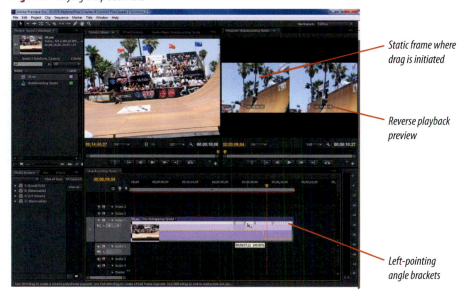

Static frame where drag is initiated

Reverse playback preview

Left-pointing angle brackets

forward motion. Left-pointing angle brackets appear in the speed control track, as shown in Figure 4, to indicate which segment of the clip plays in reverse. You can use the Razor tool or the Trim tool to remove the segment of the clip that replays the forward motion if you want the clip to play only in reverse.

Adding a Speed Transition

After creating a speed change using time remapping, you can create a smoother transition between the different speeds. When you create a speed keyframe, it has two handles joined together on the speed control track. Drag either of these handles left or right to create a transition area, as shown in Figure 5. A blue curve control appears in the middle. Drag either of the handles on the curve control to smooth the transition—the speed change will then ease in and out, creating a smoother transition. The line between two handles is referred to as the **speed ramp**.

Using the Rate Stretch Tool

The Rate Stretch tool is used to change the duration of a clip on the Timeline while simultaneously adjusting the speed to compensate. Using the Rate Stretch tool you can stretch the clip until it fills the gap. Dragging the clip edge to shorten it increases its speed; dragging the clip edge to lengthen it decreases its speed. The clip's In and Out points are not changed, only its speed.

Figure 4 *Left-pointing angle brackets*

Left-pointing
angle brackets

Figure 5 *Adjusting speed transitions*

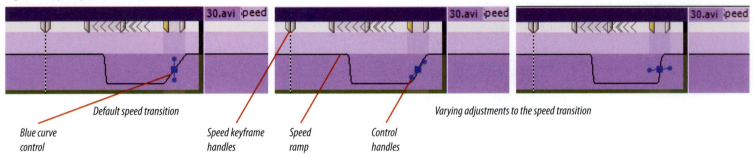

Default speed transition

Varying adjustments to the speed transition

Blue curve
control

Speed keyframe
handles

Speed
ramp

Control
handles

You can view the clip's speed by hovering the mouse pointer over the clip until a tool tip appears, as shown in Figure 6.

Adjusting Speed with the Clip Speed/ Duration Dialog Box

The Clip Speed/Duration dialog box allows you to enter the desired speed or duration of a clip, as shown in Figure 7. By default the speed and duration are linked; therefore, if you increase the speed of a clip, the duration shortens. Click the Link/Unlink icon to change either the speed or duration separately. To play the video backwards, check the Reverse Speed check box. The Maintain Audio Pitch option, when selected, prevents the sound from going up or down in pitch

when the speed is adjusted. The Ripple Edit, Shifting Trailing Clips option, when selected, shifts any existing clips already on the track, moving them either to the left if the speed is increased so the next clip

is not trimmed, or to the right if the speed is decreased so there is no gap remaining. Adjusting the playback rate using the Clip Speed/Duration dialog box applies a constant speed across the entire clip.

Figure 6 *Tool tip showing speed*

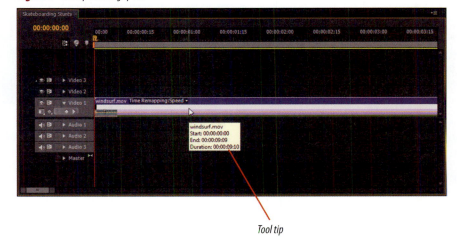

Tool tip

Figure 7 *Clip Speed/Duration dialog box*

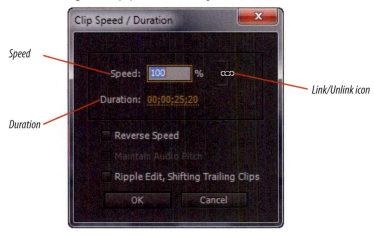

Speed

Duration

Link/Unlink icon

Apply the Time Remapping effect to a clip

1. Open the Speed 1.prproj file from the drive and folder where you store your Data Files, then save it as **Speed 1** *your name*.

   The 42.avi video clip has already been added to the Video 1 track for you.

2. Select the **skateboarding** sequence to activate the Timeline panel, then click the **Play-Stop Toggle button** 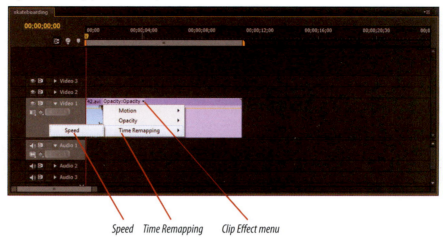 on the Program Monitor to preview the clip.

   You will be adjusting the speed of the clip to highlight the action of the skateboarders.

3. Drag the **CTI** to **00;00;00;00**.

4. On the Timeline panel, click the **Clip Effect menu**, point to **Time Remapping**, then click **Speed**, as shown in Figure 8.

   A yellow horizontal rubber band control appears across the center of the clip, as shown in Figure 9.

TIP Resize the track to get a better view of the rubber band control.

(continued)

Figure 8 *Selecting Speed from the Clip Effect menu*

Speed   Time Remapping   Clip Effect menu

Figure 9 *Rubber band control*

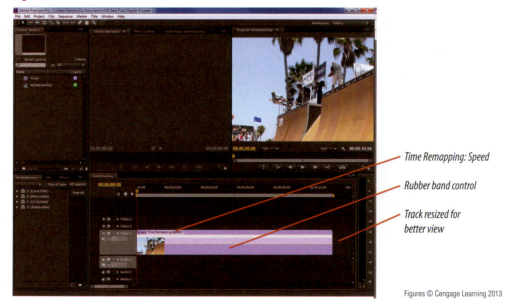

Time Remapping: Speed

Rubber band control

Track resized for better view

Figures © Cengage Learning 2013

Figure 10 *Activating speed keyframes*

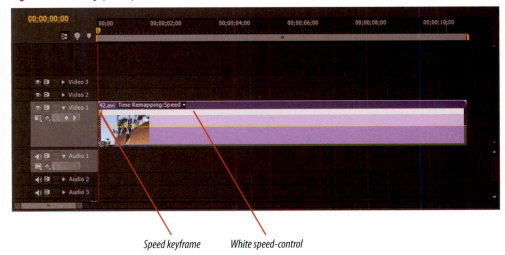

Speed keyframe   White speed-control

Figure 11 *Speed keyframes*

5. [Ctrl]-click (Win) or ⌘-click (Mac) the **rubber band** ☐₊ at the location of the **CTI (00;00;00;00)**.

 Keyframes are activated and a speed keyframe is placed in the white speed control track, as shown in Figure 10.

6. Drag the **CTI** to **00;00;01;15**, then click the **Add-Remove keyframe button** ☐ on the Timeline panel.

 This places a speed keyframe.

7. Add additional speed keyframes at the following times: **00;00;03;08**, **00;00;04;19**, **00;00;07;14**, and **00;00;09;27**, then compare your Timeline to Figure 11.

8. Save your project and leave it open for the next exercise.

You applied the Time Remapping effect to a clip and set speed keyframes on a video clip.

Adjust the speed of a clip

1. Open the Speed 1 *your name*.prproj project file, if necessary.

2. Click the **first rubber band segment** which is between the first and second speed keyframes, then drag in a downward direction until the tool tip reads **25.00%**, as shown in Figure 12.

   The speed of the video clip between the first two speed keyframes is reduced to 25% of the original speed; the overall duration of the clip is extended as a result.

3. Drag the **CTI** to **00;00;00;00**, then click the **Play-Stop Toggle button** ▶ on the Program Monitor to preview the clip.

4. Click the **second rubber band segment**, then drag in an upward direction until the tool tip reads **175.00%**, as shown in Figure 13.

   The speed of the video clip between the second and third speed keyframes is increased to 175% of the original speed; the overall duration of the clip is reduced as a result.

   (continued)

Figure 12 *Decreasing the speed of a clip*

Tool tip – 25.00%

Figure 13 *Increasing the speed of a clip*

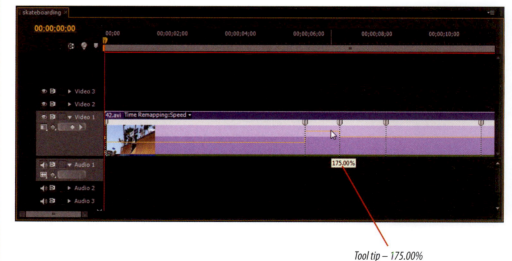

Tool tip – 175.00%

Figures © Cengage Learning 2013

Working with Special Effects to Enhance Viral Videos - Adobe Premiere Pro & Adobe After Effects CS6

Figure 14 *Adjusting the speed of a clip*

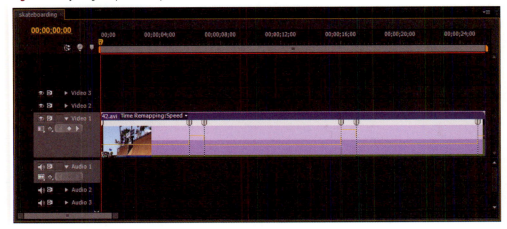

5. Make the following adjustments along the rubber band segments: 3rd segment: **15.00%**, 4th segment: **280.00%**, 5th segment: **30.00%** and 6th segment: **165.00%**, then compare your Timeline panel to Figure 14.

6. Drag the **CTI** to **00;00;00;00**, then click the **Play-Stop Toggle button** ▶ on the Program Monitor to preview the clip.

7. Export your video to the F4V format and name the file **Skateboarding** *your name*.

8. Close the Speed 1 your name.prproj project file.

You adjusted the speed of a video clip by increasing and decreasing the speed in different sections, then exported the file to the F4V format for the Internet.

Play a clip backward then forward

1. Open the Speed 2.prproj file from the drive and folder where you store your Data Files, then save it as **Speed 2 your name**.

   The 30.avi video clip has already been added to the Video 1 track for you.

2. On the Timeline panel, click the **Clip Effect menu**, point to **Time Remapping**, then click **Speed**.

3. Resize the Video 1 track to get a better view of the rubber band control.

4. On the Timeline panel, drag the **CTI** to **00;00;06;27**, then [Ctrl]-click (Win) or ⌘-click (Mac) ⟩₊ the **rubber band** to create a speed keyframe.

5. Drag the **CTI** to **00;00;08;08**, then click the **Add-Remove keyframe button** ◆ on the Timeline panel.

   At the location of this speed keyframe, you will duplicate a portion of the video clip to play it back in reverse.

6. [Ctrl]-click (Win) or ⌘-click (Mac) the **second speed keyframe**, then drag ◀▐▐ to the right until the first portion of the tool tip reads **00;00;09;17**, as shown in Figure 15.

   The Program Monitor shows a split screen. The clip on the right displays the portion of the video clip that is being duplicated. As a result, the location of the speed keyframe has adjusted slightly on the Timeline and is now located at the duration 00;00;08;07. Your time may vary.

   (continued)

Figure 15 *Reversing a portion of a clip*

Tool tip – 00;00;09;17

Figure 16 *Creating a speed transition*

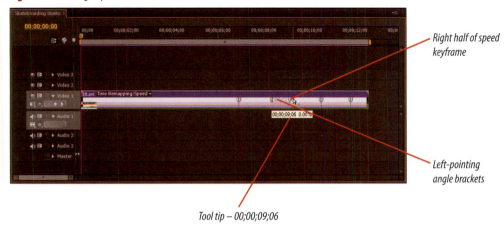

Right half of speed keyframe

Left-pointing angle brackets

Tool tip – 00;00;09;06

Figure 17 *Adjusting the speed transition*

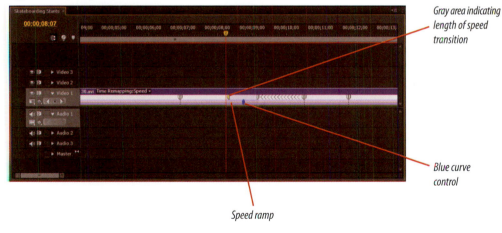

Gray area indicating length of speed transition

Blue curve control

Speed ramp

7. Drag the **CTI** to **00;00;00;00**, then click the **Play-Stop Toggle button** ▶ on the Program Monitor to preview the clip.

8. Save your project and leave it open for the next exercise.

You made a portion of a clip play backwards then forwards.

Add a speed transition

1. Open the Speed 2 *your name*.prproj project file, if necessary.

2. On the Timeline panel, click and drag the **right half of the speed keyframe** that is in front of the left point brackets, until the first portion of the tool tip reads **00;00;09;06**, as shown in Figure 16.

   The distance between the left and right halves of the speed keyframe specifies the duration of the speed transition, and is shown by a gray area.

   A blue curve control appears, which is used to adjust the curvature of the speed ramp, as shown in Figure 17.

3. Drag the **CTI** to **00;00;08;23**, verify that the Timeline panel is active, then press [=] (equal sign) repeatedly to zoom in on the gray area while still seeing both sides of the speed keyframe.

(continued)

4. Click the **right handle of the blue curve control** 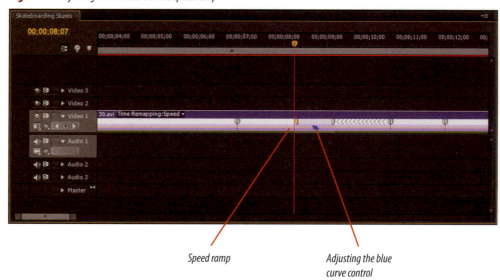, then drag either left or right to adjust the speed ramp, as shown in Figure 18.

   This adjusts the curve of the speed ramp, and the speed change will now ease in and out.

5. With the Timeline panel active, press **[-]** (minus sign) repeatedly to zoom out until you see the entire clip.

   The goal is to see the clip play one time in forward motion and one time in reverse motion.

6. Click the **Razor tool** on the Tools panel, drag the **CTI** to **00;00;10;15** on the Timeline panel, then click at the location of the CTI.

TIP You can also press [C] on the keyboard to activate the Razor tool.

7. On the Timeline panel, drag the **CTI** to **00;00;11;25** then click at the location of the CTI.

   Cut points have been created on either side of the portion of the clip where the clip replays the forward motion.

8. Click the **Selection tool** on the Tools panel, then click the **clip with the cut points** as shown in Figure 19.

9. Click **Edit** on the Menu bar, then click **Ripple Delete**.

   The selected clip is removed without leaving a gap between clips.

10. Drag the **CTI** to **00;00;00;00**, then click the **Play-Stop Toggle button** on the Program Monitor to preview the clip.

(continued)

Figure 18 *Adjusting the curvature of the speed ramp*

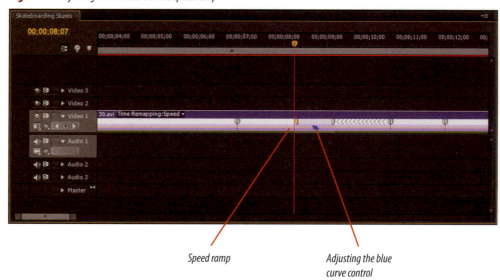

Speed ramp   Adjusting the blue curve control

Figure 19 *Selecting the clip between cut points*

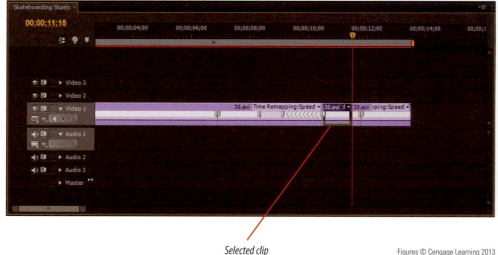

Selected clip

Figure 20 *Using the Rate Stretch tool*

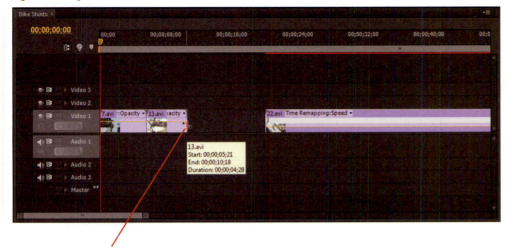

Rate Stretch tool cursor

Figure 21 *Stretching the clip to fill the gap*

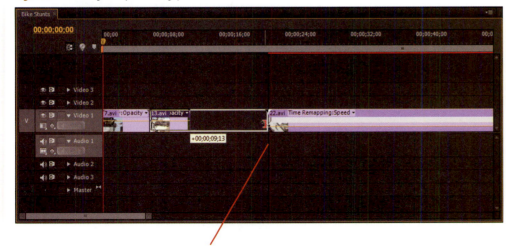

Black line

11. Export your video to the F4V format and name the file **Skateboarding Stunts** *your name*.

12. Close the Speed 2 *your name*.prproj project file.

You adjusted the speed ramp between the clips playing forward and reverse, then you trimmed the clip and exported it for the Internet.

Adjust the speed of a clip with the Rate Stretch tool

1. Open the Speed 3.prproj file from the drive and folder where you store your Data Files, then save it as **Speed 3** *your name*.

   Three video clips have already been added to the Video 1 track for you: 7.avi, 13.avi, and 22.avi. A gap has been left between clips 13.avi and 22.avi, and the 22.avi clip's speed has been adjusted to 12.00%.

2. Click the **Play-Stop Toggle button** ▶ on the Program Monitor to preview the clips.

3. Click the **Rate Stretch tool** on the Tools panel, then point to the right edge of the 13.avi clip on the Timeline.

   The Rate Stretch tool cursor appears, as shown in Figure 20.

TIP You can also press [X] to activate the Rate Stretch tool.

4. Click and drag the **right edge of the 13.avi clip** to the right to fill the gap, then release the mouse button when you see a vertical black line appear, as shown in Figure 21.

(continued)

The vertical black line indicates the length the clip will be when the mouse button is released. The cursor snaps to the left edge of the next clip.

5. Click the **Selection tool** ▶ on the Tools panel.

6. Drag the **CTI** to **00;00;00;00**, then click the **Play-Stop Toggle button** ▶ on the Program Monitor to preview the clip.

   The 13.avi clip speed was adjusted to compensate to fill the gap; the speed was reduced to 34.33%, as shown in Figure 22.

7. Save your project and leave it open for the next exercise.

You adjusted the speed of a clip using the Rate Stretch tool.

Adjust the speed of a clip with the Clip Speed/Duration dialog box

1. Open the Speed 3 *your name*.prproj project file, if necessary.

2. On the Timeline panel, right-click the **7.avi clip**, then click **Speed/Duration**.

   The Clip Speed/Duration dialog box opens as shown in Figure 23.

3. In the Clip Speed/Duration dialog box, change the Speed value to **50%**, click the **Ripple Edit, Shifting Trailing Clips check box**, then click **OK**.

   The speed of the clip is reduced to 50% and the clips on the Video 1 track shift to allow for the necessary adjustment made to the length of the clip. Next you will create a duplicate of the same clip playing in reverse.

   (continued)

Figure 22 *Adjusted speed of clip after using the Rate Stretch tool*

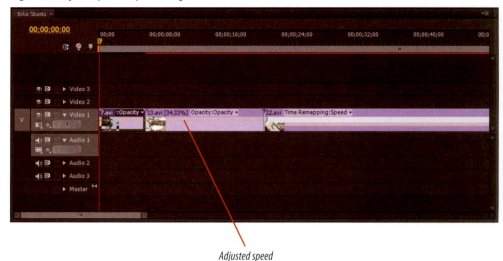

Adjusted speed

Figure 23 *Activating the Clip Speed/Duration dialog box*

Clip Speed/Duration dialog box

Figures © Cengage Learning 2013

Figure 24 *Copying and inserting a clip*

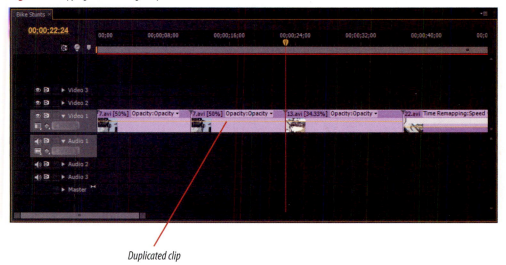

00;00;22;24

Duplicated clip

4. Click the **Selection tool** on the Tools panel, if necessary, then click the **7.avi clip** on the Timeline panel.

5. Click **Edit** on the Menu bar, then click **Copy**.

    A copy of the 7.avi clip is created with the 50% speed duration applied to it.

6. Place the **CTI** at the **cut line** between the 7.avi and 13.avi clips.

7. Click **Edit** on the Menu bar, click **Paste Insert**, then compare your sequence to Figure 24.

    A copy of the 7.avi clip is inserted and the other clips in the sequence are shifted to the right.

8. Right-click the **second instance of the 7.avi clip** on the Timeline panel, then click **Speed/Duration**.

9. In the Clip Speed/Duration dialog box, click the **Reverse Speed check box**, then click **OK**.

    This will cause the clip to playback in reverse.

10. Drag the **CTI** to **00;00;00;00**, then click the **Play-Stop Toggle button** on the Program Monitor to preview the clip.

11. Export your video to the F4V format and name the file **Bike Stunts** *your name*.

12. Close the Speed 3 *your name*.prproj project file.

You adjusted the speed of a clip using the Clip Speed/Duration dialog box. You also copied a clip, inserted it in the sequence, and reversed the playback of a clip. Finally you exported the video for the Internet.

Work with Weather Effects
IN AFTER EFFECTS

What You'll Do

Figure © Cengage Learning 2013

 In this lesson, you will add lightning and rain effects to a video clip.

Working with Weather Effects

Weather effects are another way to establish mood and setting in a video. After Effects includes effects for creating rain, snow, lightning, and fog. In this section, you will explore the CC Rainfall and Advanced Lightning effects. Once you know how to use these effects, you will be able to explore the others on your own.

Applying the Linear Color Key Effect

The **Linear Color Key effect** uses RGB, hue, or chroma information to create a range of transparency across an image based on a specified color. This then allows you to place another image below the layer to replace the color that has been removed, or **keyed**. For example, you could use this effect to remove the clear sky from footage so it could be replaced with footage that better suits a rainy day, such as a gray, cloudy sky.

When applied to a clip, the Linear Color Key effect displays two thumbnail images on the Effect Controls panel, as shown in Figure 25. The thumbnail on the left shows the unaltered image and the one on the right shows a preview of the image with the effect applied. The preview of the image can be one of the following choices from the View menu: Final Output, Source Only, or Matte Only. (*Note*: The View menu is located just below the right thumbnail.) The **Final Output** view displays a preview of the keyed area, the **Source Only** view shows the original footage without the key applied, and the **Matte Only** view shows the alpha channel matte to view holes in the transparency.

The **Key Color** menu has the Key Color swatch and the eyedropper available to select the color that will be keyed. The key color can be selected by clicking a **Key Color swatch**, or by using the **eyedropper** to point to a color in the footage on the Composition panel. The **Matching Tolerance** property determines how closely pixels must match the key color before they become transparent. A value of 100.0% makes the entire image transparent, while a value of 0.0% makes the entire image opaque. The **Matching Softness** property adjusts the softness of the edges between the image and the transparent area. It is suggested that values under 20% usually produce the best results.

To assist in keeping an image opaque, or solid, in the areas where it needs to be, a Photoshop composition can be created and placed below

Figure 25 *The Linear Color Key effect*

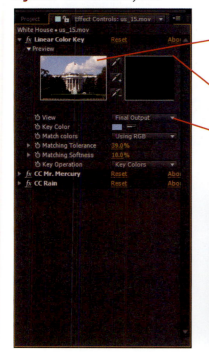

Figures © Cengage Learning 2013

the layer on which the effect is being applied. This method was used in Figure 26 to restore the areas of the footage that were made transparent because the sky and the buildings are so similar in color.

Working with the CC Rainfall Effect

The **CC Rainfall effect** is a self-animating effect that simulates rain. Although the effect is self-animating, keyframes can still be added to customize the effect. The **Amount** property determines the amount of rainfall. A setting of zero stops the rain. The larger the Amount value, the more rainfall. The Speed property

changes the rate at which the rain falls. The angle of the rain can be adjusted with the **Angle** and **Angle Variation** properties. The **Drop Size** property modifies the size of the rain, and the Opacity property blends the rain into footage on which the effect is applied. Finally, the **Source Depth** property gives the illusion that the rain is falling within the footage, not just in front of it.

Using the CC Mr. Mercury Effect

The **CC Mr. Mercury** effect is a particle system that creates ever-changing blobs, which you can make appear like raindrops on a camera lens,

Figure 26 *The Linear Color Key comparison*

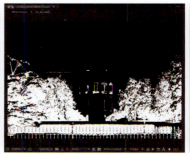

Original Image

Linear Color Key applied

Linear Color Key applied with Photoshop composition

as shown in Figure 27. The properties can be combined to create blobs that behave realistically, splitting up and rejoining, just like real-world liquid particles. The source layer is used as a reflection map for the particles.

The **Radius X** and **Radius Y** properties determine the size of the blob producer based on the X and Y coordinates. The **Velocity** property determines the speed of the blobs at birth. The higher the setting, the faster the blobs move; a setting of zero keeps the blobs stationary.

The **Birth Rate** property determines the number of blobs that are generated at any given point in time. The higher the Birth Rate value, the greater the concentration of blobs.

The **Gravity** property determines how quickly the blobs fall; a negative Gravity value causes them to rise. Setting the Gravity value to zero, along with a zero value for the Velocity property, keeps the blobs from moving.

The **Influence Map** property offers a drop-down menu with options that determine the behavior of the blobs as they appear and disappear. For the effect of water on a lens, the Constant Blobs setting maintains a somewhat constant size from the time they appear to the time they disappear.

The **Blob Birth Size** and **Blob Death Size** properties determine the size of the blobs when they first appear and just before they disappear.

Creating Lightning with the Advanced Lightning Effect

The Advanced Lightning effect, in the Generate category, creates simulations of electrical discharges. The Advanced Lightning effect does not self-animate like the CC Rain and CC Mr. Mercury effects. The **Conductivity State** property changes the path of the lightning and can be used to animate the effect. You must activate keyframes if you want to have some influence over the effect.

The **Lightning Type** property specifies the characteristics of the lightning; the **Direction** and Outer Radius properties change based on this selection.

Figure 27 *An example of the CC Mr. Mercury effect*

Figure © Cengage Learning 2013

The **Origin** property determines the point at which the lightning strike begins.

If the Lightning Type is set to Vertical, the Direction and Outer Radius settings are not available.

The **Outer Radius** property determines the distance the lightning travels from the point of origin. This property is enabled when the Lightning Type property is set to Omni or Anywhere.

The **Direction** property indicates which route the lightning takes. It is available if one of the following Lightning types is selected: Direction, Strike, Breaking, Bouncy, and Two-Way Strike.

The **Alpha Obstacle** property specifies the influence of the alpha channel of the layer the Advanced Lightning effect is being applied to. The **alpha channel** represents the transparent areas on the layer. If the Alpha Obstacle value is greater than zero, the lightning attempts to

wrap itself around the solid areas in the layer by moving through the transparent areas. (*Note*: When setting the value greater than zero, it is not always possible to preview the correct results without selecting Full Resolution in the Preview panel.)

The **Composite on Original** option shows the lightning on the footage as shown in Figure 28. If the Composite on Original check box is not selected only the lightning is visible, as shown in Figure 29.

Figure 28 *Applying the Advanced Lightning effect*

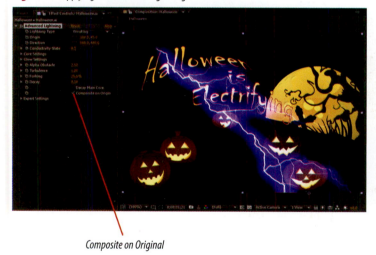

Composite on Original

Figure 29 *Composite on Original option is disabled*

Composite on Original

Figures © Cengage Learning 2013

Apply the CC Rainfall and Linear Color Key effects

1. Open the Weather 1.aep file from the drive and folder where you store your Data Files, then save it as **Weather 1** *your name*.

   The us_5.mov video clip has already been added to the US Capitol composition for you.

2. On the Timeline panel, click the **us_5.mov layer**, click **Effect** on the Menu bar, point to **Simulation**, then click **CC Rainfall**.

   This applies the CC Rainfall effect to the video footage of the Capitol building and activates the Effect Controls panel, as shown in Figure 30.

3. Click the **Play/Pause button** ▶ on the Preview panel to preview the clip.

   Rain has been added to the video footage with the CC Rainfall effect, but the appearance does not change throughout the duration of the footage and the sky is too bright for a rainy day.

4. On the Timeline panel, click the **us_5.mov layer**, click **Effect** on the Menu bar, point to **Keying**, then click **Linear Color Key**.

   You will begin by removing the sky and replacing it with darker clouds.

5. On the Effect Controls panel, click the **Linear Color Key effect** then drag it above the CC Rainfall effect, as shown in Figure 31.

6. On the Effect Controls panel, under the Linear Color Key effect, click the **Match colors drop-down menu**, then click **Using Hue**.

   The transparency will be created based on the hue from the specified color. The Selected View

   (continued)

Figure 30 *Applying the CC Rainfall effect*

CC Rainfall effect

Figure 31 *Applying the Linear Color Key effect*

Linear Color Key effect

Key color swatch

Match colors

Figures © Cengage Learning 2013

Working with Special Effects to Enhance Viral Videos - Adobe Premiere Pro & Adobe After Effects CS6

Figure 32 *Adjusting settings in the Linear Color Key effect*

Key Color swatch

Figure 33 *Placing the US Capitol Mask composition in the active composition*

Project panel

US Capitol Mask
composition

US Capitol Mask
composition

preview becomes dark because the default Key
Color has been applied to the layer and the color
is keyed out.

7. Click the **Key Color swatch**, type **475C82** in the #
   text box in the Key Color dialog box, then click **OK**.

   The Key Color dialog box lets you select a specific
   color to be removed from the footage, in this case
   a light blue, as shown in Figure 32. Holes have
   been created in the Capitol building because
   of the Matching Tolerance level, which allows
   additional pixels that vary from the color selected
   to be removed. The US Capitol composition
   will be used to correct any problems with the
   portions of the building that are transparent;
   therefore, you need only focus on removing the
   sky and the edges of the Capitol building.

8. On the Effect Controls panel, under the Linear
   Color Key effect, verify the Matching Tolerance
   value is **0.0%** and change the Matching Softness
   value to **24.0%**.

   These settings improve the edges around the
   building by making the edges less transparent.

TIP   On the View drop-down menu choose Matte
         Only; this may help you when creating your
         transparency area.

9. Click the **Project panel**, click the **US Capitol
   Mask composition**, then drag it to the US
   Capitol composition on the Timeline, below the
   us_5.mov layer.

   The US Capitol Mask composition should be 2
   in the stacking order, as shown in Figure 33. Notice
   the holes in the building have been corrected.

   (continued)

10. Click the **Project panel**, click the **Storm Clouds.m2v footage**, then drag it to the US Capitol composition on the Timeline, below the US Capitol Mask composition layer.

The Storm Clouds.m2v footage composition should be 3 in the stacking order, as shown in Figure 34.

11. Click the **Play/Pause button**  on the Preview panel to preview the clip.

(*Note*: Color correction techniques learned in an earlier chapter could be applied to the us_5.mov layer to blend the Capitol Building with the storm clouds.)

12. Save your project and leave it open for the next exercise.

You applied the CC Rainfall effect, keyed out the sky, and replaced the sky with storm cloud footage.

Customize the CC Rainfall effect

1. Open the Weather 1 *your name* project file, if necessary, then verify that the Effect Controls panel is visible and that the CTI is at **00;00;00;00**.

2. On the Timeline panel, click the **us_5.mov layer**, click the **Effects expand arrow**, then click the **CC Rainfall expand arrow**.

As adjustments are made on the Effect Controls panel, keyframes will be automatically generated on the Timeline panel, allowing you to see them as they are created.

3. On the Effect Controls panel, in the CC Rainfall effect, click the **Time-Vary stopwatch button** in front of the Drops, Size, and Speed

(continued)

Figure 34 *Placing the Storm Clouds.m2v footage in the active composition*

Storm Clouds.m2v

Storm Clouds.m2v

Figure © Cengage Learning 2013

Working with Special Effects to Enhance Viral Videos - Adobe Premiere Pro & Adobe After Effects CS6

Figure 35 *Changing the CC Rainfall default values*

Drop Size

Speed

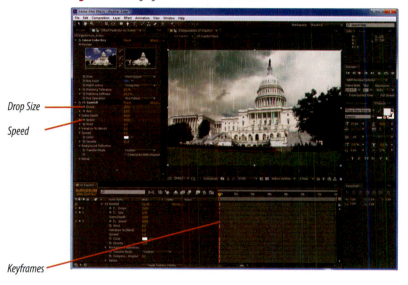

Keyframes

Figure 36 *Reducing the CC Rainfall Amount property to zero*

No rain

Amount
value = 0

properties, then change the values as follows: Drops: **2500**, Size: **5.00**, and Speed: **4000**.

Keyframes for the Drops, Size, and Speed properties are activated and a strong rain begins at the beginning of the video footage, as shown in Figure 35.

4. Drag the **CTI** to **00;00;04;00**, then on the Timeline panel, in the CC Rainfall effect, change Drops to **1500**, Size to **2.00**, and Speed to **1500**.

   You will continue to move through the footage reducing the amount of rain, as the clouds begin to clear.

5. Continue to adjust the CTI, reduce the values at 08 seconds, then reduce the Amount value to zero at 12 seconds.

   By setting the Amount value to zero at the keyframe for 12 seconds, the other values do not need to be updated because the rain has been stopped as shown in Figure 36.

6. On the Timeline and the Effect Controls panels, click the **CC Rainfall collapse arrow** to close the properties.

   It is no longer necessary to have the CC Rain effects expanded in either the Timeline panel or the Effect Controls panel.

7. Click the **Play/Pause button** ▶ on the Preview panel to preview the clip.

8. Save your project and leave it open for the next exercise.

You adjusted the CC Rainfall effect to change the appearance of the rain as the clouds changed.

Apply the CC Mr. Mercury effect

1. Open the Weather 1 *your name* project file, if necessary, then verify that the Effect Controls panel is visible and that the CTI is at **00;00;00;00**.

2. On the Timeline panel, click the **us_5.mov layer**, click **Effect** on the Menu bar, point to **Simulation**, then click **CC Mr. Mercury**.

   The CC Mr. Mercury effect is applied to the layer and the effect appears on the Effect Controls panel. You will need to move this effect above the CC Rainfall effect in order to see the rain that was created earlier.

3. On the Effect Controls panel, click the **CC Mr. Mercury effect**, then drag it above the CC Rainfall effect, as shown in Figure 37.

   This effect gives the impression of drops of water getting on the camera lens during filming.

4. Click the **Play/Pause button** ▶ on the Preview panel to preview the clip.

   Some adjustments need to be made to the effect to minimize the oversized drops or "blob" effect.

5. On the Effect Controls panel, in the CC Mr. Mercury effect, click the **Time-Vary stopwatch button** 🕙 in front of the Birth Rate property to activate keyframes for the Birth Rate property.

   The Birth Rate keyframe is necessary so the effect can be turned off towards the end of the duration of the footage. A keyframe needs to be created only for the Birth Rate property. The property value adjustments will automatically change over time.

   (continued)

Figure 37 *Applying the CC Mr. Mercury effect*

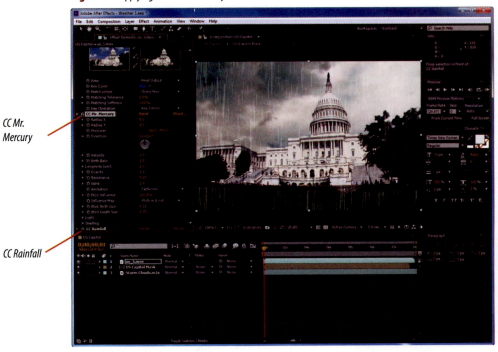

CC Mr. Mercury

CC Rainfall

Figure 38 *Customizing the CC Mr. Mercury effect*

CC Mr.
Mercury

6. On the Effect Controls panel, make the following changes to the property values for the CC Mr. Mercury effect: Radius X: **164.0**, Radius Y: **78.0**, Velocity: **0.0**, Birth Rate: **0.5**, Gravity: **0.0**, Influence Map: **Constant Blobs**, Blob Birth Size: **0.25**, and Blob Death Size: **0.32**, as shown in Figure 38.

These adjustments create drops, keep the drops from moving, slow down the appearance of the drops, and adjust the size of the drops when they are created and when they fade away.

7. Drag the **CTI** to **00;00;12;00**, then on the Effect Controls panel, change the Birth Rate property of the CC Mr. Mercury effect to **0.0**, as shown in Figure 39.

This fades out the appearance of the raindrops.

8. Click the **Play/Pause button** ▶ on the Preview panel to preview the clip.

9. Export your video to the F4V format and name the file **Rain Effects** *your name*.

10. Close the Weather 1 *your name*.aep project file.

You made it appear that there were raindrops on the camera lens during filming, then customized the effect so the rain ended at the end of the clip.

Work with the Advanced Lightning effect on a logo

1. Open the Lightning 1.aep file from the drive and folder where you store your Data Files, then save it as **Lightning 1** *your name*.

The Lightning Logo composition has already been created for you with an Adobe Illustrator document.

(continued)

Figure 39 *Disabling the CC Mr. Mercury effect*

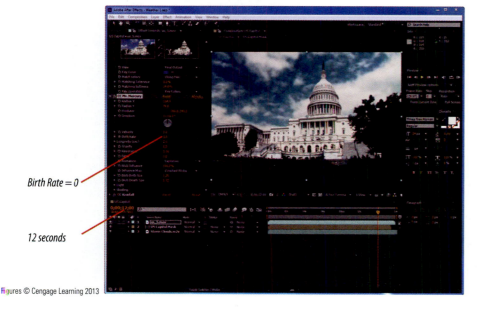

Birth Rate = 0

12 seconds

2. On the Timeline panel, click the **Lightning Logo. ai layer**, click **Effect** on the Menu bar, point to **Generate**, then click **Advanced Lightning**.

The Advanced Lightning effect is applied to the Lightning Logo.ai layer and appears on the Effect Controls panel, as shown in Figure 40.

3. On the Effect Controls panel, click the **Composite on Original check box**.

The lightning is composited with the original layer so the contents of the layer are visible with the lightning. When the layer is not selected, only the lightning is visible.

4. Click the **Play/Pause button** ▶ on the Preview panel to preview the clip.

The Advanced Lightning effect does not self-animate as the CC Rainfall effect did.

5. On the Effect Controls panel, click the **Time-Vary stopwatch button** 🕙 in front of the Conductivity State property.

Keyframes need to be created only for the Conductivity State property to animate the lightning. Keyframes can be activated for other properties if you would like to have additional control over the Advanced Lightning effect.

6. Drag the **CTI** to **00;00;13;00**, then change the Conductivity State value to **3.5** on the Effect Controls panel, as shown in Figure 41.

The Conductivity State setting changes the path of the lightning.

7. On the Effect Controls panel, change the Origin values to **245.0** and **125.0**.

The Origin values specify the x and y coordinates from where the lightning strikes.

(continued)

Figure 40 *Applying the Advanced Lightning effect*

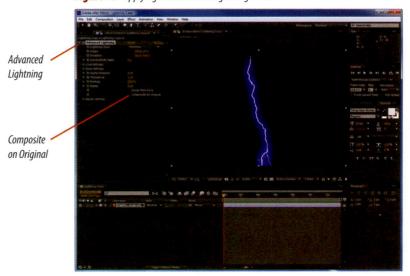

Advanced Lightning

Composite on Original

Figure 41 *Animating the Advanced Lightning effect*

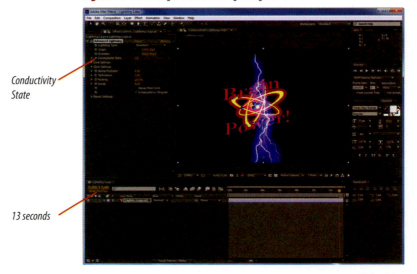

Conductivity State

13 seconds

Figures © Cengage Learning 2013

Figure 42 *Adjusting the Alpha Obstacle property*

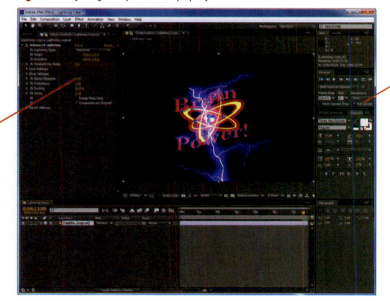

Alpha Obstacle

Full

Figure © Cengage Learning 2013

8. On the Effect Controls panel, change the Direction values to **415.0** and **375.0**.

   The Direction values control specifies the x and y coordinates where the lightning strike ends. The actual end point may vary from the specified x and y based on the lightning type.

9. On the Effect Controls panel, change the Lightning type to **Breaking**.

   With the Breaking type, branches from the lightning are focused towards the Direction point as the distance between the Origin and Direction increases.

10. On the Effect Controls panel, change the Alpha Obstacle property to **4.50**.

    When the Alpha Obstacle value is greater than zero, the lightning attempts to wrap itself around the opaque areas in the layer by moving through the transparent areas.

11. On the Preview panel, change the Resolution to **Full**, as shown in Figure 42.

    If the Alpha Obstacle value is set to a value other than zero, it is important to preview in Full Resolution before exporting your project.

    TIP On the Preview panel, click Full from the Resolution drop-down menu to preview in full resolution.

12. Click the **Play/Pause button** ▶ on the Preview panel to preview the clip.

13. Export your video to the F4V format and name the file **Lightning Logo *your name***.

14. Close the Lightning 1 *your name*.aep project file.

You animated the advanced lightning effect on a logo.

LESSON 3

Animate Lips on an Animal
IN AFTER EFFECTS

What You'll Do

Figure © Cengage Learning 2013

 In this lesson, you will work with a special effect in After Effects that gives the appearance of an animal singing or talking.

Making an Animal Appear to Sing or Talk

A popular effect seen on commercials and the Internet is making babies or animals appear to speak. You have probably seen the E*TRADE baby or the dog in the Bush's Baked Beans commercials. This effect can be accomplished in After Effects. In this lesson, you will make it appear that a dog is singing.

Using the Tracker Panel to Track Motion

Motion tracking is available within After Effects with the Tracker panel. The Tracker panel can be activated by selecting the Motion Tracking workspace, as shown in Figure 43, or by choosing Tracker from the Window menu.

Figure 43 *The Tracker panel*

Tracker panel

Figure © Cengage Learning 2013

Working with Special Effects to Enhance Viral Videos - Adobe Premiere Pro & Adobe After Effects CS6

Motion tracking is used to track the movement of an object identified in footage. Tracking data is generated and then applied to another object in order to follow that same motion. For example, if you would like to add custom signage to a moving vehicle after footage has been shot, you can design your sign in After Effects and then attach the tracking data to the sign so it moves with the vehicle.

The Tracker panel is where you specify settings, control tracking, and apply tracking data. The first decision to be made is whether to choose Track motion or Stabilize motion as the method for tracking the motion of your footage.

Track motion and Stabilize motion are essentially the same processes. The main difference is that the Track motion option allows you to apply the tracking data to another layer, whereas Stabilize motion applies tracking data to the source layer. By default, both processes activate a position, which creates only one track point on the Layer panel, as shown in Figure 44. A **track point** is the area that specifies what is tracked. Selecting either Rotation or Scale activates another track point, which generates tracking data for either the Rotation or Scale property.

A track point contains a feature region, a search region, and an attach point. The **feature region** defines the area in the layer that is tracked. The feature region should be sized to enclose the feature of the tracked region, including as little of the surrounding image as possible. The **search region** is a larger area around the feature region that defines the area where After Effects looks for the feature region. The size and location of

Figure 44 *Moving Track Point 1 over the right eye*

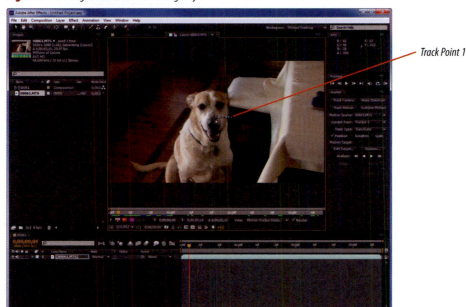

Track Point 1

the search region depends on the movement of the feature being tracked. The larger the search region, the longer the actual process of motion tracking takes. The search region needs to be large enough to accommodate the movement of the tracked feature from frame to frame, not the movement during the duration of the footage. If the movement is gradual, the search region needs to be only slightly larger than the feature region because the track point adjusts to the new location. If the area in the feature region changes position and direction quickly, the search

region needs to be large enough to include the largest position and direction change in any consecutive frames.

The **attach point** is the designated place for the object you plan to attach to the motion. The attach point by default is at the center of the feature region and can be relocated anywhere on the Layer panel before tracking. For example, to animate a thought bubble above a person's head, you would place the attach point above the head and position the feature region on the head. If the attach point

was left in the default position, the thought bubble would be attached to that point and would hide the person's face.

During analysis, the track points may move off of the area you have designated. The analysis can be paused so that adjustments can be made to the track points to improve the tracking data before it is applied. When adjusting the track points, the Selection tool pointer icons change depending on what part of the track point you are moving. Refer to Figure 45 for more details.

Figure 45 *Track Point cursors*

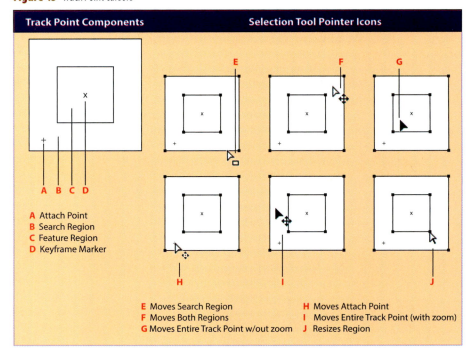

Track Point Components

A Attach Point
B Search Region
C Feature Region
D Keyframe Marker

Selection Tool Pointer Icons

E Moves Search Region
F Moves Both Regions
G Moves Entire Track Point w/out zoom
H Moves Attach Point
I Moves Entire Track Point (with zoom)
J Resizes Region

Working with Reverse Motion Tracking

Reverse motion tracking is a technique used to guarantee that any effects that rely on the motion tracking data stay in place. For example, if a drop shadow were applied to the thought bubble mentioned in the previous example, reverse motion tracking would be necessary to keep the drop shadow effect on the bubble as it moved above the head.

The Stabilize Motion feature generates tracking data for the anchor point, position, and rotation properties, which are part of the Transform group. Oftentimes, after stabilizing, motion-tracking data is applied,

and the tracking data causes the video that was tracked to drift out of the viewing area. This causes footage to be lost and black space to be visible as shown in Figure 46. Reverse motion tracking also is used to correct this problem.

Two compositions are needed to work with reverse motion tracking. The first step is to create a pre-composition based on the layer that the Stabilizing motion-tracking data needs to be applied to. If the video is drifting out of the viewing area, it is necessary to resize the composition to accommodate the movement so that it has room to move

without leaving the viewing area. Next, the workspace needs to be adjusted so that both compositions can be viewed at the same time, as shown in Figure 47; this allows Transform Expressions from the pre-composition to be connected to the main composition. **Expressions** use a scripting language to specify values for a property. A simple expression can be created to connect properties to one another. To add or remove expressions for a property, [Alt]-click (Win) or [option]-click (Mac) the stopwatch button. The Transform Expressions are located under the Transform group on the Timeline panel for each property. The Transform Expressions

Figure 46 *Footage drifting out of viewing area after Stabilize motion applied*

Figure 47 *Viewing two compositions at the same time*

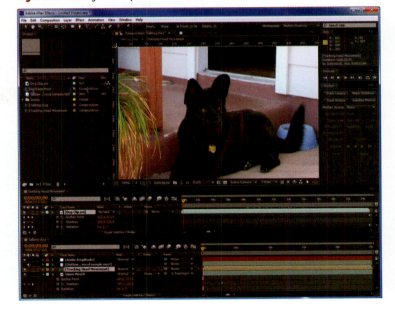

that are connected for reverse motion tracking are Anchor Point, Position, and Rotation. To stabilize motion, it is necessary to connect the properties that are opposites. Anchor Point is the opposite of Position, so those two expressions are connected, Anchor Point to Position and Position to Anchor Point. This reverses the effect of the stabilization on the Anchor Point and Position expressions. Rotation does not have an opposite, so Rotation points to Rotation and a mathematical expression *-1 is added and cancels out any rotation added during the tracking process.

Creating a Garbage Matte

A **garbage matte** is a keying method used to remove portions of an image on a layer; the matte is then animated with the layer. If the image is a still image, the garbage matte can be drawn close to the subject using the Pen tool. When drawing a matte on video, it needs to be drawn loosely to accommodate the motion so the subject does not move outside the matted area.

It is possible to convert a video frame to a still image and create a garbage matte for that individual frame, which then lasts for the duration of the layer. In this case, you can be more exact when drawing your matte because the image will not move. This is done by using the Freeze Frame command. A Hold keyframe is created at the location of the CTI.

Applying the CC Split Effect

The CC Split effect is a distort effect that is often used to make a still image speak. The CC Split effect creates splits or holes in footage. Two crosshairs are provided, as shown in Figure 48, to place the location where the effect

Figure 48 *Adjusting crosshairs for CC Split effect*

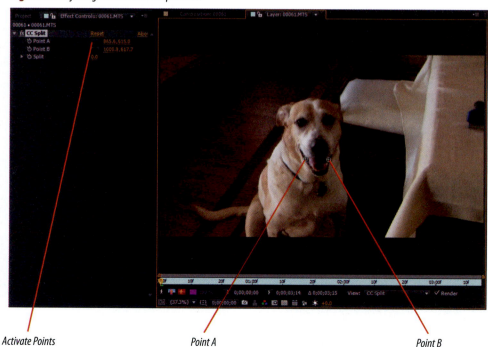

Activate Points   Point A   Point B

Figure © Cengage Learning 2013

Working with Special Effects to Enhance Viral Videos - Adobe Premiere Pro & Adobe After Effects CS6

will create a split or hole in the footage. These crosshairs can be adjusted with keyframes to improve the effect. A garbage matte can be placed below a layer with the CC Split effect to fill the hole and then parented to that layer so the garbage matte follows the hole.

To attach an audio clip, the Split effect needs to be displayed on the Timeline panel and an expression added to the Split property. The next step is to connect the Split effect to one of the sliders on the Audio Amplitude layer. The Pick Whip becomes available when expressions are activated and allows you to create simple expressions easily, by dragging from one parameter to another, as shown in Figure 49. A live link is created from the current parameter with values from the target parameter. For example, dragging the Pick Whip from the Anchor Point property to the Position property creates an expression that copies values from Anchor Point to Position.

(*Note*: If the Pick Whip is not available, [Alt]-click (Win) or [option]-click (Mac) the stopwatch button next to the parameter name in the Timeline.)

Which slider you connect to depends on which audio channel has the audio track. If you have imported a music file, it is probably Both Channels; if you are recording your voice it may be on only one channel. Both channels are produced from audio that is stereo, while one channel is produced if the audio track is mono.

Figure 49 *Attaching the CC Split effect to music*

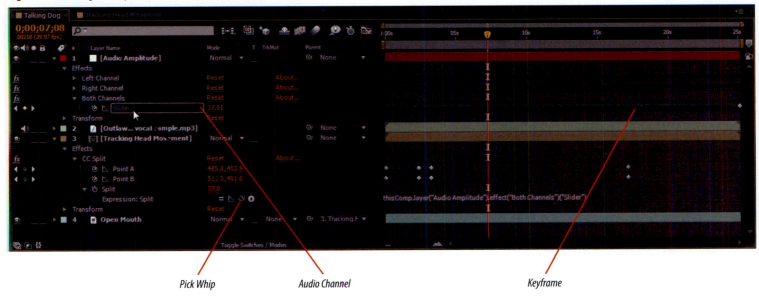

Pick Whip   Audio Channel   Keyframe

Use the Track panel to track motion

1. Open the Talking Dog.aep file from the drive and folder where you store your Data Files, then save it as **Talking Dog** *your name*.

   A project file has already been started for you with two compositions and footage.

2. On the Timeline panel, click the **Tracking Head Movement composition**.

   The Tracking Head Movement composition is a pre-composition that includes the Dog Clip.avi footage. You need to track the movement of the dog's head. (*Note*: If the Tracking Head Movement composition is not on the Timeline panel, double-click it on the Project panel to open it on the Timeline panel.)

3. Click **Window** on the Menu bar, point to **Workspace**, then click **Motion Tracking**.

   The current workspace is reset to Motion Tracking and the Tracker panel becomes available.

4. On the Timeline panel, click the **Dog Clip.avi layer**.

   You will be applying motion tracking to this layer.

5. On the Tracker panel, click the **Stabilize Motion button**.

   A track point appears on the Composition panel; however, you need to track two points and therefore need to activate the Rotation property.

   The first point will track the position and anchor point; the second point will track the rotation.

6. On the Tracker panel, click the **Rotation check box** to activate a second track point, as shown in Figure 50.

   (continued)

Figure 50 *Two track points are created*

Figure 51 *Motion Tracker Options dialog box*

Figure 52 *Moving the Track Point data with zoom feature*

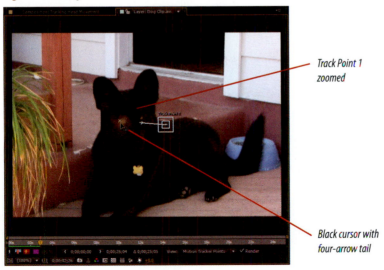

Track Point 1 zoomed

Black cursor with four-arrow tail

7. On the Tracker panel click the **Options button**.

   The Motion Tracker Options dialog box opens, where the tracker can be customized to help improve the tracking analysis as it is being performed.

8. In the Motion Tracker Options dialog box, under Channel, select **Saturation**, on the drop-down menu, select **Stop Tracking**, change the value for If Confidence is Below to **70%**, as shown in Figure 51, then click **OK**.

   The Saturation option is selected because the dog's color does not have much contrast. The Stop Tracking if the Confidence is Below 70% was chosen so that you will be able to adjust the tracking when the analysis stops because the track points will have moved too much from the target.

9. On the Composition panel, click and drag the **Feature Region square** on Track Point 1 over the dog's right eye.

   The cursor's appearance changes to a black cursor with a four-arrow tail, the area within the squares zooms when you click on the inner square's edge, and the entire track point should move together, as shown in Figure 52. (*Note:* If the arrow is white instead of black only the regions will move, but the attach point will not.)

   (continued)

10. Drag **Track Point 2** over the dog's left eye.

You are now ready to track the movement of the dog's head.

11. On the Tracker panel, click the **Analyze forward button** .

This begins the tracking process on the footage. The analysis will stop if the tolerance falls below 70% and the track points will need to be re-adjusted so they are back on the dog's eyes.

TIP Move your cursor between the two boxes to get the four-arrow cursor so you can move both boxes together.

12. When the tracking stops, move the **track points** so they are located on the dog's eyes, as shown in Figure 53, then click the **Analyze forward button**.

TIP Change the magnification of the Composition panel to make the tracking cursors easier to work with.

13. If the track points move too far off of the dog's eyes, stop tracking manually and move the track points back to the dog's eyes.

14. Click the **Analyze forward button** to resume the tracking process and continue to adjust track points if the track points move from the dog's eyes until the CTI reaches the end of the Timeline, then compare your Composition panel tracking data to Figure 54. Your results may vary.

(continued)

Figure 53 *Tracking has stopped*

Track Point 1 needs to be readjusted

Figure 54 *Tracking data on last frame*

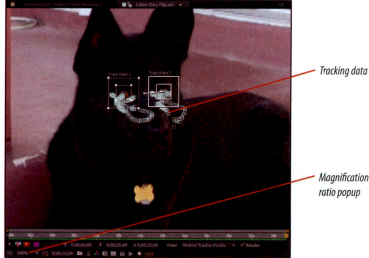

Tracking data

Magnification ratio popup

Figures © Cengage Learning 2013

Working with Special Effects to Enhance Viral Videos - Adobe Premiere Pro & Adobe After Effects CS6

Figure 55 *Tracking data on the Dog Clip.avi*

Tracking data

15. When Motion Tracking has reached the end of the video clip and has stopped, in the Tracker panel, click **Apply**.

    The Motion Tracker Apply Options dialog box opens.

16. Click **OK**.

    The tracking data is placed on the Dog Clip.avi layer, as shown in Figure 55.

17. Save your project and leave it open for the next exercise.

You tracked the movement of the dog's head using the Tracker panel.

Apply reverse motion tracking

1. Open the Talking Dog *your name*.aep project file, with the Tracking Head Movement composition as the active composition, if necessary.

2. Click the **Play/Pause button** 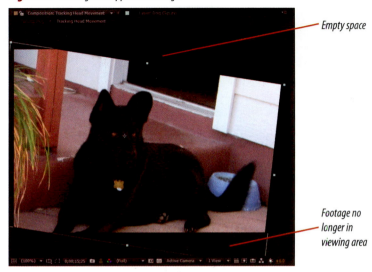 on the Preview panel to preview the footage on the Composition panel.

   Notice the tracking data causes the entire layer to move, and at times causes empty space around the footage or the footage to move out of the viewing area, as shown in Figure 56.

3. Click **Composition** on the Menu bar, then click **Composition Settings**.

   The Composition Settings dialog box opens.

4. Change the Width value to **1000,** verify that the Lock Aspect Ratio check box is checked, then click **OK**.

   This gives the video footage room to move with the tracking data applied to it.

5. On the Timeline panel, click the **Dog Clip.avi layer**, press [A] on your keyboard, press and hold [**Shift**], press [**P**], then press [**R**].

   The Anchor Point, Position, and Rotation properties become visible on the Timeline panel.

6. On the Timeline panel, click the **Tracking Head Movement composition tab**, drag it above the Talking Dog composition until you see the drop zone shown in Figure 57, then release the mouse button. Both compositions should be visible in the Timeline panel.

(continued)

Figure 56 *Tracking data applied to footage*

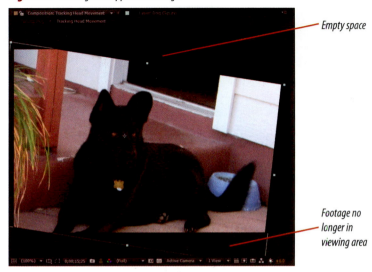

Empty space

Footage no longer in viewing area

Figure 57 *Customizing the workspace*

Drop Zone

Figures © Cengage Learning 2013

Working with Special Effects to Enhance Viral Videos - Adobe Premiere Pro & Adobe After Effects CS6

Figure 58 *Resizing the Timeline panels*

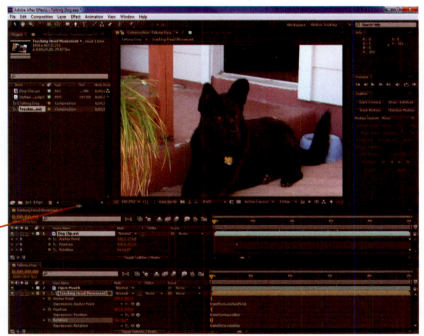

Resize cursor

7. On the Talking Dog Timeline panel, click the **Tracking Head Movement pre-composition**, press [**A**] on your keyboard, press and hold [**Shift**], press [**P**], then press [**R**].

   You will use the Pick Whip to attach these properties from one composition to the other.

8. With the Tracking Head Movement pre-composition still selected, press and hold [**Alt**] (Win) or [**option**] (Mac), then click the **Time-Vary stop watch** 🕐 for the Anchor Point, Position, and Rotation properties.

   This adds an expression for each property.

9. Position your cursor above the Talking Dog Timeline panel tab, when the resize cursor appears, click and drag to resize the panel so you are able to see all of the properties, then do the same for the Tracking Head Movement Timeline, as shown in Figure 58.

TIP   Resize the bottom Timeline panel first; it will size into the panel placed above it.

(continued)

10. On the Talking Dog Timeline panel, click the **Pick Whip** ⊚ for the **Anchor Point property**, then drag to the Position property in the Tracking Head Movement Timeline panel, as shown in Figure 59.

    The Anchor Point property is the opposite of the Position property so you need to connect these two properties to counteract their influence. You need to repeat this process with the Position property.

11. On the Talking Dog Timeline panel, click the **Pick Whip** ⊚ for the **Position property** and drag to the Anchor Point property on the Tracking Head Movement Timeline panel.

12. On the Talking Dog Timeline panel, select the **Pick Whip** ⊚ for the **Rotation property** and drag to the Rotation property on the Tracking Head Movement Timeline panel, then compare your Talking Dog Timeline panel to Figure 60.

    Because there is not an opposite property for rotation, you will enter a mathematical formula multiplying the rotation by -1 to create the opposite.

13. On the Talking Dog Timeline panel, click at the **end of the Rotation expression**, then type ***-1**.

TIP Click anywhere to get out of the Rotation expression or just continue to the next step. Do not press [Enter], which creates another line inside the expression.

14. Click **Window** on the Menu bar, point to **Workspace**, then click **Standard**.

    The workspace is set to Standard and returns the Tracking Head Movement Timeline panel to a stacked tab position.

You used the Pick Whip to attach expressions between two different compositions, and you added a mathematical formula to an expression.

Figure 59 *Using the Pick Whip*

Pick Whip

Figure 60 *Talking Dog properties after using Pick Whip*

Figure 61 *Drawing a garbage matte with the Pen tool*

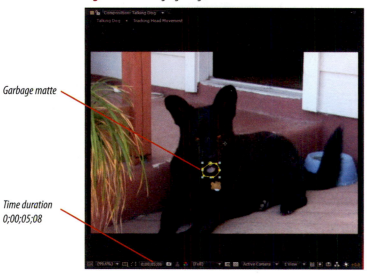

Garbage matte

Time duration
0;00;05;08

Figure 62 *Adjusting the anchor point of the garbage matte*

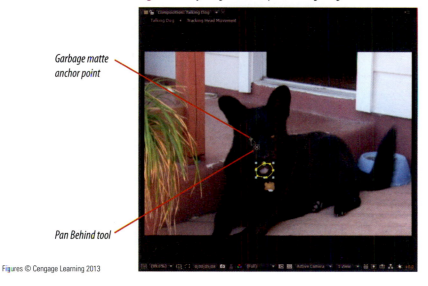

Garbage matte
anchor point

Pan Behind tool

Figures © Cengage Learning 2013

Create a garbage matte

1. Open the Talking Dog *your name*.aep project file, with the Talking Dog composition as the active composition, if necessary.

   The dog's mouth opens just after 5 seconds; you will duplicate this to make your dog talk.

2. On the Timeline panel, click the **Open Mouth layer**, then drag the **CTI** to **0;00;05;08**.

   This is when the dog opens his mouth; you will be drawing a garbage matte around the open mouth.

3. Click the **Pen tool** on the Tools panel, verify that the RotoBezier check box is not checked on the Tools panel, then draw a selection around the open mouth, as shown in Figure 61.

4. On the Timeline panel, right-click the **Open Mouth layer**, point to **Time**, then click **Freeze Frame**.

   A snapshot of the garbage matte you just created is taken.

5. Click the **Pan Behind tool** on the Tools panel, then drag the **garbage matte anchor point** over the right pupil, as shown in Figure 62.

   This attaches the garbage matte anchor point to the Attach point you created during motion tracking over the dog's right eye.

   (continued)

6. On the Timeline panel, on the Open Mouth layer, click the **Parent layer column drop-down menu**, then click **3. Tracking Head Movement**, as shown in Figure 63.

This parents the Tracking Head Movement layer to the Open Mouth layer so that the matte you just created follows the movement of the dog's head. You will make adjustments later to the garbage matte where it moves off track.

7. On the Timeline panel, drag the **CTI** to preview the footage, then drag the **CTI** to **00;00;00;00**.

The open mouth should move with the dog's muzzle.

(continued)

Figure 63 *Setting the Parent layer to the Tracking Head Movement layer*

*Parent Layer
drop-down menu*

Figure 64 *Open Mouth layer moved to bottom of stacking order*

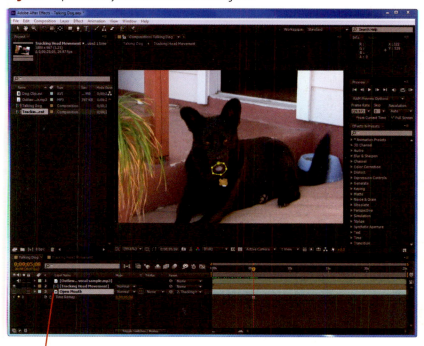

Open Mouth layer

8. On the Timeline panel, drag the **Open Mouth layer** below the Tracking Head Movement layer, then compare your project to Figure 64.

   The Open Mouth layer should now be third in the stacking order.

9. On the Timeline panel, collapse the **Tracking Head Movement layer** and the **Open Mouth layer**.

   The layer properties are no longer in view.

10. Save your project and leave it open for the next exercise.

You drew a garbage matte around the dog's open mouth, created a freeze frame, parented a layer, and reordered the layers.

Apply the CC Split effect

1. Open the Talking Dog *your name*.aep project file, with the Talking Dog composition as the active composition, if necessary.

   You now need to attach coordinates to the dog's mouth to create a hole in the video footage to make it appear he is talking.

2. On the Timeline panel, click the **Tracking Head Movement layer**, click **Effect** on the Menu bar, point to **Distort**, then click **CC Split**.

   The CC Split effect is applied to the Tracking Head Movement layer and appears on the Effect Controls panel.

3. On the Effect Controls panel, click the **CC Split effect**.

   Crosshairs appear on the Composition panel, as shown in Figure 65. These crosshairs adjust the hole that is created in the dog's mouth.

4. Click the **crosshairs** on the left side of the Composition panel, then drag them to the right side of the dog's mouth.

   This is Point A and creates the first reference point to make the mouth open.

   (continued)

Figure 65 *Activating the crosshair points*

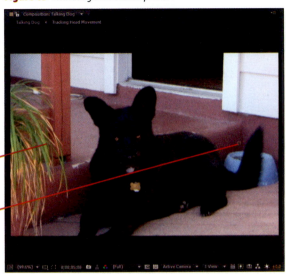

Point A crosshair

Point B crosshair

Working with Special Effects to Enhance Viral Videos - Adobe Premiere Pro & Adobe After Effects CS6

Figure 66 *Placing the Point A and Point B crosshairs*

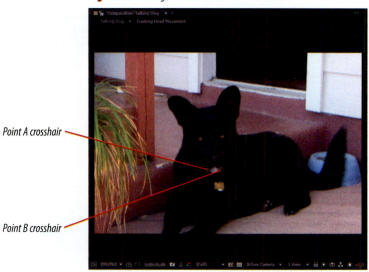

Point A crosshair

Point B crosshair

5. Click the **crosshairs** on the right side of the Composition panel, then drag them to the left side of the dog's mouth, as shown in Figure 66. This is Point B and creates the second reference point to make the mouth open.

6. On the Timeline panel, click and drag the **CTI** to preview the footage, then drag the **CTI** to **00;00;00;00**.

Point A and Point B should move with the dog's muzzle. You will fine tune the movement of the mouth later.

7. Save your project and leave it open for the next exercise.

You applied tracking points to the dog's mouth.

Complete the CC Split effect

1. Open the Talking Dog *your name*.aep project file, with the Talking Dog composition as the active composition, if necessary.

   You now need to make the dog's mouth open in time to the music.

2. On the Timeline panel, click the **first layer** in the stacking order, click **Animation** on the Menu bar, point to **Keyframe Assistant**, then click **Convert Audio to Keyframes**.

   A new layer is created at the top of the stacking order called Audio Amplitude creating keyframes on the audio channels.

3. On the Timeline panel, click the **Tracking Head Movement layer**.

4. Press and hold [**Alt**] (Win) or [**option**] (Mac), then click the **Time-Vary stopwatch button** in front of Split on the Effect Controls panel.

   This activates an expression for the Split property and makes it visible on the Timeline panel, as shown in Figure 67.

   You need to attach this expression to the Audio Amplitude layer to make the mouth open.

   (continued)

Figure 67 *Adding an expression on Split*

Split Time-Vary stopwatch

Split Expression

Working with Special Effects to Enhance Viral Videos - Adobe Premiere Pro & Adobe After Effects CS6

Figure 68 *Expanding the Audio Amplitude layer to expose Slider under Both Channels*

Slider property

5. On the Timeline panel, expand the **Audio Amplitude**, **Effects**, and **Both Channels layers**, as shown in Figure 68.

This exposes the Slider property, which has the keyframes that the CC Split effect needs to reference in order to work. You may need to adjust the size of the panel.

(continued)

Figure © Cengage Learning 2013

6. On the Timeline panel, click the **Pick Whip**  for the **Expression: Split property**, then drag it to the **Slider property**, as shown in Figure 69.

7. On the Preview panel, click the **RAM Preview button** ▶ to preview the mouth opening, then drag the **CTI** to **00;00;00;00**.

   The audio may not play during the first RAM Preview, let it run through and repeat to hear the audio. The mouth needs some adjustments.

8. On the Timeline panel, click **CC Split**, then click the **Time-Vary stopwatch button** ⏱ in front of Point A.

9. On the Timeline panel, click **CC Split**, then click the **Time-Vary stopwatch button** ⏱ in front of Point B.

   Keyframes are now activated for both points. As you move the CTI and make adjustments to the locations of Point A and Point B on the Composition panel, a keyframe will be generated.

   (continued)

Figure 69 *Pointing the Pick Whip for the Expression: Split property to the Slider property*

Slider property   Pick Whip

Figure © Cengage Learning 2013

Figure 70 *Adjusting points on the Timeline*

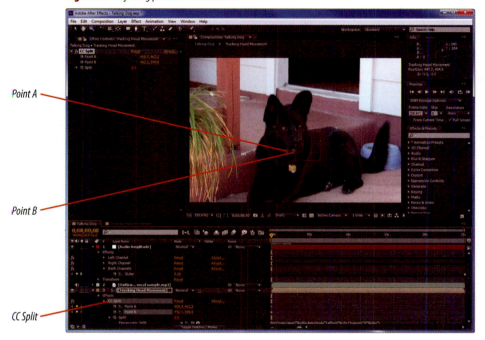

Point A

Point B

CC Split

10. Drag the **CTI** to a location in the footage where the points are not on the mouth.

    The duration in Figure 70 is 0;00;00;00, but yours may vary.

11. On the Composition panel, click **Point A**, then drag to the right corner of the dog's mouth, click **Point B**, then drag to the left corner of the dog's mouth.

    You need to only make adjustments at the times when you see the mouth is opening.

12. On the Timeline panel, drag the **CTI** to locate other areas where Point A and Point B need to be corrected and make corrections as needed.

    The music stops playing at approximately 20 seconds so the mouth should no longer be opening and closing. Therefore you will not need to make adjustments past this point.

13. If necessary, select the **Open Mouth layer** and open the **Position property** (P), activate **keyframes** ◆ , then using the **Selection tool** ▶ adjust the location of the mouth as needed to show when the mouth opens.

14. Export your movie, including the audio, as an F4V resizing it as a Web Video.

You attached the CC Split effect to audio keyframes to make the mouth open and close in time to the music.

Apply the Time Remapping effect to a clip.

1. Open the Speed 4.prproj file from the drive and folder where you store your Data Files, then save it as **Speed 4 *your name***.
2. Select the Bike Tricks sequence to activate the Timeline panel, then click the Play-Stop Toggle button on the Program Monitor to preview the clip.
3. Drag the CTI to 00;00;00;00.
4. On the Timeline panel, click the Clip Effect menu, point to Time Remapping, then click Speed.
5. [Ctrl]-click (Win) or ⌘-click (Mac) the rubber band at the location of the CTI (00;00;00;00).
6. Drag the CTI to 00;00;00;11 and on the Timeline panel, click the Add-Remove keyframe button.
7. Add additional speed keyframes at the following times: 00;00;01;28, 00;00;02;20, and 00;00;04;08.
8. Save your project and it leave open for the next step.

Adjust the speed of a clip.

1. Click the first rubber band segment, then drag in an upward direction until the tool tip reads 315.00%.
2. Drag the CTI to 00;00;00;00, then click the Play-Stop Toggle button on the Program Monitor to preview the clip.
3. Click the second rubber band segment and drag in a downward direction until the tool tip reads 25.00%.
4. Make the following adjustments along the rubber band segments: 3rd - 140.00%, 4th - 35.00%, and 5th - 300.00%.
5. Drag the CTI to 00;00;00;00, then click the Play-Stop Toggle button on the Program Monitor to preview the clip.

6. Export your video to the F4V format and name the file **Bike Tricks *your name***.
7. Close the Speed 4 *your name*.prproj project file.

Play a clip backward then forward.

1. Open the Speed 5.prproj file from the drive and folder where you store your Data Files, then save it as **Speed 5 *your name***.
2. On the Timeline panel, activate Time Remapping on the Clip Effect menu then resize the Video 1 track to get a better view of the rubber band control.
3. On the Timeline panel, drag the CTI to 00;00;02;18 then [Ctrl]-click (Win) or ⌘-click (Mac) the rubber band to create a speed keyframe.
4. Drag the CTI to 00;00;04;03 and on the Timeline panel, click the Add-Remove keyframe button.
5. [Ctrl]-click (Win) or ⌘-click (Mac) the second speed keyframe, then drag to the right until the first portion of the tool tip reads 00;00;05;18.
6. Drag the CTI to 00;00;00;00, then click the Play-Stop Toggle button on the Program Monitor to preview the clip.
7. Save your project and leave it open for the next step.

Add a speed transition.

1. On the Timeline panel, click and drag the right half of the speed keyframe that is in front of the left point brackets, until the first portion of the tool tip reads 00;00;04;20.
2. Drag the CTI to 00;00;04;20, and with the Timeline panel active, press the [=] key three times to zoom in.

3. Click the handle of the blue curve control to adjust the speed ramp.
4. With the Timeline panel active, press the [-] key three times to zoom out.
5. Click the Razor tool on the Tools panel, and on the Timeline panel, drag the CTI to approximately 00;00;07;28 then point and click the location of the CTI to create a cut point.
6. On the Timeline panel, drag the CTI to approximately 00;00;08;20 then point and click the location of the CTI to create another cut point. (*Hint*: You are removing the portion of the clip where there is no action.)
7. Click the Selection tool on the Tools panel, then click the clip with the cut points that were just created.
8. Click Edit on the Menu bar, then click Ripple Delete.
9. Drag the CTI to 00;00;00;00, then click the Play-Stop Toggle button on the Program Monitor to preview the clip.
10. Export your video to the F4V format and name the file **Skateboarding Tricks *your name***.
11. Close the Speed 5 *your name*.prproj project file.

Adjust the speed of a clip with the Rate Stretch tool.

1. Open the Speed 6.prproj file from the drive and folder where you store your Data Files, then save it as **Speed 6 *your name***.
2. Click the Play-Stop Toggle button on the Program Monitor to preview the clip.
3. Click the Rate Stretch tool on the Tools panel, then, on the Timeline panel, point to the right edge of the 18.avi clip.

4. Click and drag the right edge of the 18.avi clip to the right to fill the gap, then release the mouse button when you see the black line.
5. Click the Selection tool on the Tools panel.
6. Drag the CTI to 00;00;00;00, then click the Play-Stop Toggle button on the Program Monitor to preview the clip.
7. Save your project and leave it open for the next step.

Adjust the speed of a clip with the Clip Speed/Duration dialog box.

1. On the Timeline panel, right-click the 1.avi clip, then click Speed/Duration.
2. In the Clip Speed/Duration dialog box change the Speed value to 35%, click the Ripple Edit, Shifting Trailing Clips check box, then click OK.
3. On the Timeline panel, using the Selection tool, click the 1.avi clip.
4. Click Edit on the Menu bar, then click Copy.
5. Place the CTI at the cut line after clip 1.avi.
6. Click Edit on the Menu bar, then click Paste Insert.
7. On the Timeline panel, right-click the second instance of the 1.avi clip, then click Speed/Duration.
8. In the Clip Speed/Duration dialog box, click the Reverse Speed check box, then click OK.
9. Drag the CTI to 00;00;00;00, then click the Play-Stop Toggle button on the Program Monitor to preview the clip.
10. Export your video to the F4V format and name the file **Biking** *your name*.
11. Close the Speed 6 *your name*.prproj project file.

Apply the CC Rainfall and Linear Color Key effects.

1. Open the Weather 2.aep file from the drive and folder where you store your Data Files, then save it as **Weather 2** *your name*.
2. On the Timeline panel, click the us_15.mov layer, click Effect on the Menu bar, point to Simulation, then click CC Rainfall.
3. Click the Play/Pause button on the Preview panel to preview the clip.
4. On the Timeline panel, click the us_15.mov layer, click Effect on the Menu bar, point to Keying, then click Linear Color Key.
5. On the Effect Controls panel, click the Linear Color Key, then drag it above the CC Rainfall effect.
6. On the Effect Controls panel, under the Linear Color Key effect, select the Match colors drop-down menu, then click Using RGB.
7. Click the Key Color swatch, type **8CA5C1** in the # text box in the Key Color dialog box, then click OK.
8. On the Effect Controls panel, under the Linear Color Key effect, change the Matching Tolerance value to 39.0% and the Matching Softness value to 10.0%.
9. Click the Project panel, click the us_15 Mask composition, then drag it to the White House composition on the Timeline below the us_15.mov layer.
10. Click the Project panel, click the StormCloudsGathering2.mpeg footage, then drag it to the White House composition on the Timeline below the us_15 Mask composition layer.

11. Click the Play/Pause button on the Preview panel to preview the clip.
12. Save your project and leave it open for the next step.

Customize the CC Rain effect.

1. Verify that the Effect Controls panel is visible and that the CTI is at 00;00;00;00.
2. On the Timeline panel, click the us_15.mov layer, click the Effects expand arrow, then click the CC Rainfall expand arrow.
3. On the Effect Controls panel, in the CC Rainfall effect, click the Time-Vary stopwatch button in front of the Drops, Size, and Speed properties, then change the Amount value to 0 and the Size to 0.
4. Drag the CTI to 00;00;02;00, and on the Timeline panel, in the CC Rainfall effect, change the Drops to 250 and the Size to 3.5.
5. Move the CTI to 6 seconds then set the following values: Drops: 1000, Size: 5.00, and Speed: 6500.
6. Click the Play/Pause button on the Preview panel to preview the clip.
7. Save your project and leave it open for the next step.

Apply the CC Mr. Mercury effect.

1. Verify that the Effect Controls panel is visible and that the CTI is at 00;00;00;00.
2. On the Timeline panel, click the us_15.mov layer, click Effect on the Menu bar, point to Simulation, then click CC Mr. Mercury.
3. On the Effect Controls panel, click the CC Mr. Mercury effect, then drag it above the CC Rainfall effect.
4. Click the Play/Pause button on the Preview panel to preview the clip.

5. On the Effect Controls panel, in the CC Mr. Mercury effect, click the Time-Vary stopwatch button in front of the Birth Rate property.

6. On the Effect Controls panel, make the following changes to the property values for the CC Mr. Mercury effect: Radius X: 45.0, Radius Y: 395.0, Velocity: 0.0, Birth Rate: 2.0, Gravity: 0.0, Influence Map: Constant Blobs, Blob Birth Size: 0.35, and Blob Death Size: 0.50.

7. Drag the CTI to 00;00;12;00 seconds, then on the Effect Controls panel, change the CC Mr. Mercury effect Birth Rate property value to 3.5.

8. Click the Play/Pause button on the Preview panel to preview the clip.

9. Export your video to the F4V format and name the file **White House Rain** *your name*, which should look like Figure 71.

10. Close the Weather 2 *your name*.aep project file.

Work with the Advanced Lightning effect on a logo.

1. Open the Lightning 2.aep file from the drive and folder where you store your Data Files, then save it as **Lightning 2** *your name*.

2. On the Timeline panel, click the Halloween.ai layer, click Effect on the Menu bar, point to Generate, then click Advanced Lightning.

3. On the Effect Controls panel, click the Composite on Original check box.

4. Click the Play/Pause button on the Preview panel to preview the clip.

5. On the Effect Controls panel, click the Time-Vary stopwatch button in front of the Conductivity State property.

6. Drag the CTI to 00;00;13;00, then on the Effect Controls panel, change the value of the Conductivity State to 2.5.

7. On the Effect Controls panel, change the Origin value to 100.0 and 45.0.

8. On the Effect Controls panel, change the Direction value to 560.0 and 480.0.

9. On the Effect Controls panel, change the Lightning type to Breaking.

10. On the Effect Controls panel, change the Alpha Obstacle value to 2.50.

11. On the Preview panel, change the Resolution to Full.

12. Click the Play/Pause button on the Preview panel to preview the clip.

13. Export your video to the F4V format and name the file **Halloween** *your name*.

14. Close the Lightning 2 *your name*.aep project file.

Use the Tracker panel to track motion.

1. Open the Singing Dog.aep file from the drive and folder where you store your Data Files, then save it as **Singing Dog** *your name*.

2. On the Timeline panel, click the Tracking Head Movement composition.

3. Click Window on the Menu bar, point to Workspace, then click Motion Tracking.

4. On the Timeline panel, click the Singing Dog 2.m2v layer.

5. On the Tracker panel, click the Stabilize Motion button.

6. On the Tracker panel, click the Rotation check box to activate a second tracking point.

7. On the Tracker panel, click the Options button.

8. In the Motion Tracker Options dialog box, under Channel, select Saturation, on the drop-down menu, select Stop Tracking, change the value for If Confidence is Below to 70%, then click OK.

9. On the Composition panel, click and drag the Track Point 1 to an area over the dog's right eye.

10. Drag Track Point 2 over the dog's name tag. (*Note*: Resize the Search Regions to allow for the movement of the dog's head during the video.)

11. On the Tracker panel, click the Analyze forward button.

12. When the tracking stops, adjust the track points as needed.

13. Click the Analyze forward button to resume the tracking process and continue to adjust track points as necessary until the CTI reaches the end of the Timeline.

14. When motion tracking has completed, click Apply.

15. Click OK.

16. Save your project and leave it open for the next step.

Apply reverse motion tracking.

1. Verify that the Tracking Head Movement composition is the active composition.

2. Click the Play/Pause button on the Preview panel to preview the footage on the Composition panel.

3. Click Composition on the Menu bar, then click Composition Settings.

4. Change the Width value to 1500, verify that the Lock Aspect Ratio check box is checked, then click OK.

5. On the Timeline panel, click the Singing Dog 2.m2v layer, press [A] on your keyboard, press and hold [Shift], press [P], then press [R].

6. On the Timeline panel, click the Tracking Head Movement composition tab, then drag it to reposition the Timeline panel so that it is stacked above the Singing Dog composition.

7. On the Singing Dog Timeline panel, select the Tracking Head Movement pre-composition, press [A] on your keyboard, press and hold [Shift], press [P], then press [R].

8. With the Tracking Head Movement pre-composition still selected, while holding the [Alt] (Win) or [option] (Mac) key, click the Time-Vary stopwatch button for the Anchor Point, Position, and Rotation properties.

9. Position your cursor above the Singing Dog Timeline panel tab, then when the resize cursor appears, resize the panel so you are able to see all of the properties, then resize the other Timeline.

10. On the Singing Dog Timeline panel, click the Pick Whip for the Anchor Point property and drag to the Position property on the Tracking Head Movement Timeline panel.

11. On the Singing Dog Timeline panel, click the Pick Whip for the Position property and drag to the Anchor Point property on the Tracking Head Movement Timeline panel.

12. On the Singing Dog Timeline panel, click the Pick Whip for the Rotation property and drag to the Rotation property on the Tracking Head Movement Timeline panel.

13. On the Singing Dog Timeline panel, click at the end of the Rotation expression, then type *-1.

14. Click Window on the Menu bar, point to Workspace, then click Standard.

Create a garbage matte.

1. Verify that the Singing Dog composition is the active composition.

2. On the Timeline panel click the Open Mouth layer, then drag the CTI to 0;00;00;10.

3. Click the Pen tool on the Tools panel, then draw a selection around the open mouth.

4. On the Timeline panel, right-click the Open Mouth layer, point to Time, then click Freeze Frame.

5. On the Timeline panel, click and drag the right edge of the Open Mouth layer to the right until it is the same length as the other layers, if necessary.

6. Select the Pan Behind tool on the Tools panel, then move the garbage matte anchor point over the right pupil.

7. With the Selection tool, adjust the Open Mouth garbage matte to align with the mouth on the Tracking Head Movement pre-composition.

8. On the Timeline panel, on the Open Mouth layer, under the Parent layer column, select 3. Tracking Head Movement from the drop-down menu.

9. On the Timeline panel, drag the CTI to preview the footage, then return the CTI to 00;00;00;00.

10. On the Timeline panel, drag the Open Mouth layer below the Tracking Head Movement layer.

11. On the Timeline panel, click the arrow in front of the label on the Tracking Head Movement layer, then repeat for the Open Mouth layer.

12. Save your project and leave it open for the next step.

Apply the CC Split effect.

1. Verify that the Singing Dog composition is the active composition.

2. On the Timeline panel, click the Tracking Head Movement layer, click Effect on the Menu bar, point to Distort, then click CC Split.

3. On the Effect Controls panel, click the CC Split effect.

4. Click the crosshairs on the left side of the Composition panel, then drag them to the right side of the dog's mouth.

5. Click the crosshairs on the right side of the Composition panel, then drag them to the left side of the dog's mouth.

6. On the Timeline panel, drag the CTI to preview the footage, then return the CTI to 00;00;00;00.

7. Save your project and leave it open for the next step.

Complete the CC Split effect.

1. On the Timeline panel, select the first layer in the stacking order, click Animation on the Menu bar, point to Keyframe Assistant, then click Convert Audio to Keyframes.

2. On the Timeline panel, click the Tracking Head Movement layer.

3. On the Effect Controls panel, while holding the [Alt] (Win) or [option] (Mac), click the Time-Vary stopwatch button in front of Split.

4. On the Timeline panel, click the arrow in front of the Audio Amplitude layer, click the arrow in front of Effects, then click the arrow in front of Both Channels.

5. On the Timeline panel, select the Pick Whip for the Expression: Split property and point it to the Slider property.

6. On the Preview panel, click the RAM Preview button to preview the mouth opening, then return the CTI to 00;00;00;00.

7. On the Timeline panel, click CC Split, then click the Time-Vary stopwatch button in front of Point A.

8. On the Timeline panel, click CC Split, then click the Time-Vary stopwatch button in front of Point B.

9. Drag the CTI to a location in the footage where the points are not on the mouth.

10. On the Composition panel, click Point A, drag to the right corner of the dog's mouth, click Point B, then drag to the left corner of the dog's mouth.

11. On the Timeline panel ruler, drag the CTI to locate other areas where Point A and Point B need to be corrected and make corrections.

12. If necessary, select the Open Mouth layer and open the Position property (P), activate keyframes, then using the Selection tool adjust the location of the mouth as needed to show when the mouth opens.

13. Export your movie as an F4V, resizing it as a Web Video.

Figure 71 *Completed Skills Review, Part 1*

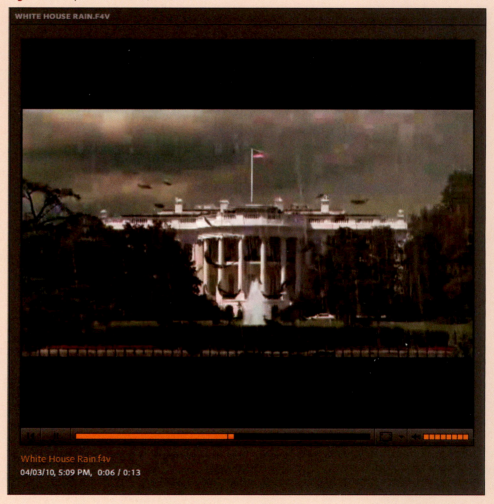

Figure © Cengage Learning 2013

Your multimedia instructor would like to see you try some of the other weather effects that are available in After Effects. Work with the Weather 3.aep file to try your hand at some of the other effects, such as CC Drizzle and CC Snow. (*Note*: The sky in this footage does not need to be removed.)

1. Open the Weather 3.aep project file, then save it as **San Francisco Weather** *your name*.
2. Be creative and apply various weather effects to this video footage.
3. Use keyframes to make adjustments to customize the effects.
4. When you are happy with your work, export your file to the F4V file format. Your completed work may look something like Figure 72.

Figure 72 *Completed Project Builder 1*

Figure © Cengage Learning 2013

PROJECT BUILDER 2

The local zoo would like you to use an antelope video clip to create a Flash video for their Web site of the antelope speaking. They would like you to record your own voice for the clip, inviting people to come to the zoo and see the new antelope exhibit.

1. Open Antelope Talking.aep, then save it as **Antelope Talking** *your name*.
2. Using the Tracker panel, track the movement of the antelope's head on the Antelope Head composition.
3. Apply reverse tracking motion between the Antelope Talking composition and the Antelope Head composition.
4. Apply the CC Clip effect to the Antelope Talking composition.
5. Using Adobe Dynamic Link, create a new Premiere Pro sequence.
6. In Premiere Pro, record a short statement inviting people to the zoo to see the new antelope exhibit.
7. Export the file to the F4V file format with the name **Zoo Promo** *your name*. Your completed work may look something like Figure 73.

Figure 73 *Completed Project Builder 2*

Your multimedia instructor would like you to use the skills you have acquired throughout the course of this book with Premiere Pro, After Effects, and Audition. Using clips available in the Video Clips subfolder titled Sports, shown in Figure 74, create a 90-second highlight video with background music. Use Premiere Pro to edit the footage, After Effects to add special effects, and Audition to create background music.

1. Create a new Premiere Pro project and sequence and save it as **Highlight Video** *your name.*
2. Import the video clips into the Project panel.
3. Using the Source Monitor, preview the various clips and trim and place them on the sequence.
4. Add appropriate video transitions.
5. Use Time Remapping to emphasize various actions in the video footage.
6. Using Adobe Dynamic Link, create an After Effects composition.
7. Using After Effects, add special effects to the video you have edited in Premiere Pro.
8. Export your composition to the MPEG2 format.
9. Using Audition, import the video; then, working with the Edit Score to Video workspace, create a soundtrack for your video.
10. Export your movie and soundtrack as an Audio Mixdown and save it to the MPEG2 file format.

Figure 74 *Portfolio Project*

Figure © Cengage Learning 2013

Working with Special Effects to Enhance Viral Videos - Adobe Premiere Pro & Adobe After Effects CS6

CHAPTER **7**

CREATING AN ELECTRONIC
**PORTFOLIO USING
ADOBE ENCORE CS6**

1. Explore the Encore workspace
2. Create a project
3. Create timelines
4. Build a project

CHAPTER 7

CREATING AN ELECTRONIC PORTFOLIO USING ADOBE ENCORE CS6

Adobe Encore CS6 is a video distribution-authoring tool that allows you to design, author, and build full-featured, menu-driven media projects that are published on a DVD, Blu-ray, or Web DVD. Encore is dynamically linked with Premiere Pro and After Effects, allowing you to work between applications without having to export or render. Alternatively, video and audio files can be used in their existing formats and Encore transcodes them to MPEG-2 video or Dolby Digital audio upon completion of the project.

Encore has a library of resources including menus, buttons, and backgrounds that you can apply to a project. You can also use Photoshop to create and edit customized menus, buttons, and backgrounds. Photoshop supports the specialized naming convention that allows these items to be imported seamlessly.

In this chapter, you will explore the Encore workspace, import assets, and work with the library of available resources to create a custom DVD and a Web DVD.

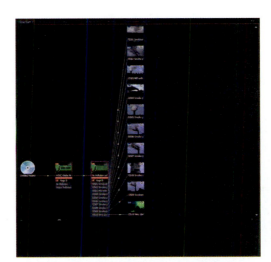

Figures © Cengage Learning 2013

LESSON 1

Explore the ENCORE WORKSPACE

What You'll Do

Figure © Cengage Learning 2013

In this lesson, you will start Encore and explore the workspace.

Exploring the Encore Workspace

Adobe Encore—like Premiere Pro, After Effects, and Audition—includes a number of preformatted and customizable workspaces that optimize the arrangement of panels for particular tasks. Figure 1 shows the default workspace for Encore, which is called Default.

You can change the workspace to another by selecting a preformatted workspace or by rearranging the panels to your individual preferences. Preformatted workspaces are available using the Workspace command on the Window menu or by making a selection from the drop-down menu on the Tools panel.

Panels are moved by clicking and dragging panel tabs. As you drag a panel, the area that you are dragging it to becomes highlighted; this is called the drop zone, and provides a visual reference to where the panel can be placed.

If you wish to save a customized workspace, you may do so by selecting New Workspace from the Workspace menu or from the drop-down menu on the Tools panel.

A basic workflow for creating a project in Encore follows eight steps:

1. Planning the project
2. Importing assets
3. Creating project elements
4. Creating menus
5. Indicating navigation
6. Transcoding audio and video for compatibility
7. Previewing the project
8. Building the project

Understanding Encore Preference Settings

The preference settings in Encore allow you to set a variety of defaults, as shown in Figure 2. The General section of the Preferences dialog box includes the option to set the default television standard to either NTSC or PAL. **NTSC** is the standard used in North America and Japan, and **PAL** is the standard in Europe.

You can change the **Audio/Video Out settings**, allowing projects to be previewed on an external device, if connected using

IEEE 1394 (also known as Firewire). This option, if equipment is available, allows the Menu Viewer to be viewed on the external device to verify the necessary elements remain in the viewing area. The Menu Viewer is a preview panel in Encore that is analogous to the Program Monitor in Premiere Pro.

Figure 1 *Encore Default workspace*

Project panel

Timeline panel tab

Monitor panel

Timeline Viewer

Properties panel

Default workspace

Library panel

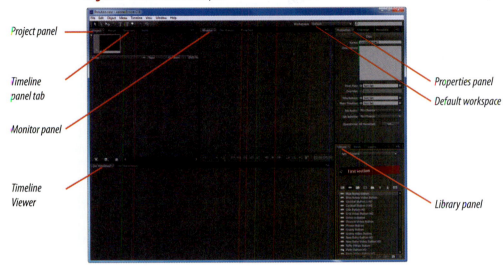

Figure 2 *Preferences dialog box*

Preferences dialog box

Default Television Standard

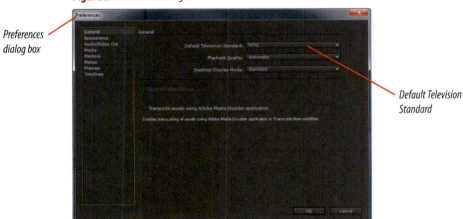

Start Adobe Encore CS6 and explore the workspace

1. Click **Start** 🟢 on the taskbar, point to **All Programs**, then click **Adobe Encore CS6** (Win) or open the **Finder** from the dock, click **Applications** from the sidebar, select the **Adobe applications folder**, then click **Adobe Encore CS6** (Mac).

    You may need to look in a subfolder for Adobe Encore CS6 if you have installed the Video Collection or Master Collection.

    TIP Pressing and holding [Shift][Ctrl] (Win) while starting Encore restores default preference settings. If you are working on a Mac you must instead drag the preferences file to the trash and restart Encore.

2. Click **New Project** in the Adobe Encore CS6 window as shown in Figure 3.

    The New Project dialog box opens.

3. Click the **Browse button**, then navigate to the drive and folder where your Data Files are located.

    The Browse button allows you to choose a destination to save the project to.

    The Browse For Folder dialog box opens, as shown in Figure 4.

    (continued)

Figure 3 *Adobe Encore CS6 window*

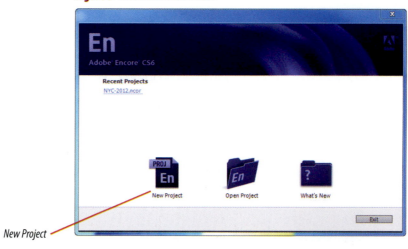

New Project

Figure 4 *Browse For Folder dialog box*

Figures © Cengage Learning 2013

Figure 5 New Project dialog box

Name

Location

Authoring
Mode

Television
Standard

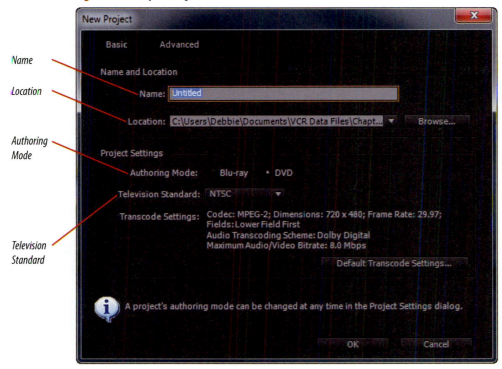

4. Click **OK** to close the Browse For Folder window but keep the New Project dialog box open.

   As shown in Figure 5, the path where the project will be saved is displayed in the Location field.

5. Type **Pollution *your name*** in the Name text box of the New Project dialog box.

6. Click **OK** to accept the default settings.

   The Encore workspace is displayed.

7. Locate the Project panel, the Monitor panel, the Properties panel, and the Library panel.

(continued)

8. Click **Window** on the Menu bar, point to **Workspace**, then click **Menu Design**.

   The Menu Design workspace, shown in Figure 6, is used for designing menus.

9. Click **Window** on the Menu bar, point to **Workspace**, then click **Default**.

   The workspace is reset to the Default workspace.

10. Save your project and leave it open for the next exercise.

You started Adobe Encore CS6, created a new project named Pollution your name, and explored the workspace.

Figure 6 *Encore Menu Design workspace*

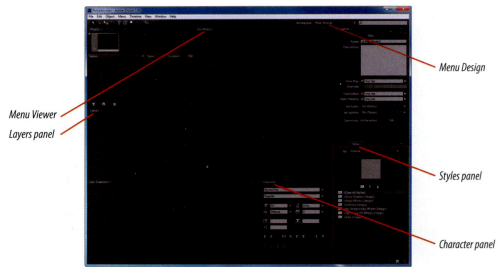

Menu Design

Menu Viewer

Layers panel

Styles panel

Character panel

Figure 7 *Preferences dialog box*

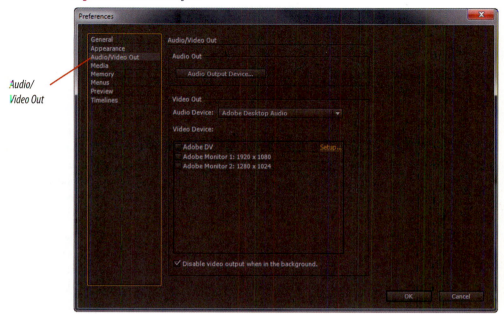

Audio/
Video Out

Figure © Cengage Learning 2013

View the Encore preference settings

1. Open the Pollution *your name*.ncor file, if necessary.

2. Click **Edit** (Win) or **Encore** (Mac) on the Menu bar, point to **Preferences**, then click **General**.

   The Preferences dialog box opens.

3. Verify that Default Television Standard is set to NTSC.

   Encore can be set to preview on an external video source for verifying the appearance of a project.

4. Click **Audio/Video Out** on the left side of the Preferences dialog box, as shown in Figure 7.

   External video and audio devices can be selected in the dialog box if one or more devices are available through an IEEE 1394 connection. The Menu Viewer then previews on the external device.

5. Click **OK** to close the Preferences dialog box.

6. Save your project file, then leave it open for the next lesson.

You explored the Preferences dialog box.

Create A PROJECT

What You'll Do

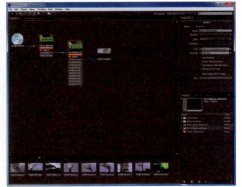

Figure © Cengage Learning 2013

 In this lesson, you will begin an Encore project.

Planning an Encore Project

It is important to plan your project before you begin the authoring process so that you understand what the project will contain and how you will present it. The scope of a project may be as minimal as organizing baby pictures and video, or as complicated as creating an interactive kiosk display. By the end of the planning stage, you should understand the navigation, scheme, playback environment, and type and amount of content for your project.

The **navigation scheme** is the layout of the menus and buttons that provide access to the various sections of the DVD. The navigation scheme should be well organized so that users have obvious and simple access to the content.

The anticipated **playback environment**, or equipment where the final media project will be viewed, is important to know during the planning stage. The playback environment affects what type of content can be included in the project and how it can be accessed. For example, if the project will be accessed only on a computer, you can include content such as data files, which would not be accessible from a television or Blu-ray player. If you are going to export a project to the Flash file format, you can embed Web links.

It is essential to know the type and amount of content that will be included in your project so you know what type of media is needed: a single-layer DVD, a dual-layer (dual-sided) DVD, or a Blu-ray disc. Small projects with mostly audio content generally fit on a single-layer DVD. A project with a feature-length movie and supplemental materials could require a dual-layer DVD or a Blu-ray disc.

It is a good idea to create a storyboard or flowchart on paper first before beginning your project. A **storyboard** is a visual representation that displays the structure of the project from start to end. It should start with the main menu with buttons to access the content. The content can be organized into chapters, like those that are often seen on movie DVDs, requiring additional menus.

For example, Figure 8 shows a storyboard for a DVD to chronicle a couple's new baby. In this example, there is a main menu with three buttons: Photos, Video, and Documents. Under each button, the storyboard shows what the couple plans to put on the next menu. A storyboard can show as much detail as you want to provide. Depending on the project, a storyboard can be simple or quite complex—incorporating, for example, nested submenus. As you become more proficient at designing storyboards and Encore projects, you can add additional details, such as video transitions between menus, slideshows, motion menus, and audio information.

Working with Projects

Encore files are called projects. Projects store links to their content, menus, and timelines, and must conform to either the NTSC (National Television Standards Committee) or the PAL (Phase Alternating Line) television standard. These standards are specifications that any video must conform to in order to be viewed in a particular country or region. These requirements consist of specific frame rates and frame size conditions. The NTSC standard covers the regions of North America and Japan. The PAL standard covers Europe. The final output must conform to one of these standards.

When a project is created, Encore creates a project folder in the same directory where the project file is saved. As assets are imported, menus are created, and files are transcoded, Encore builds additional folders to hold the data. The folders are created in a hierarchy, as shown in Figure 9, and updated as changes are made to them. The Preferences file keeps track of any changes to the Encore interface. The Cache folder contains image files that are used for thumbnails. The Sources folder organizes the data into categories such as video and audio assets, menus, and transcoded files.

Figure 8 *Sample Storyboard*

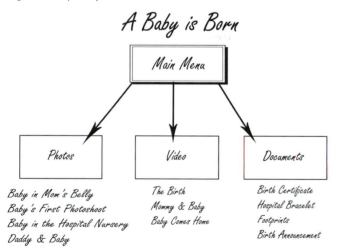

Figure 9 *Sample folder structure*

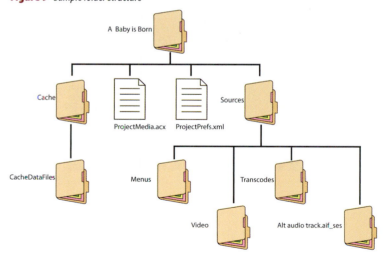

Figures © Cengage Learning 2013

Organizing and Adding Assets

Assets include any type of multimedia, such as video clips, audio clips, and still images, used in an Encore project. Assets are organized in the Project panel, as shown in Figure 10.

Assets that are specific to Encore only include menus, timelines, slideshows, playlists, and chapter playlists. Assets can be used multiple times. They can also be replaced, renamed, and updated.

A **menu** provides viewers with access to the content in a project, as shown in Figure 11. Menus can be created and customized from the templates that are included with

Figure 10 *The Project panel*

Preview

Video clip

Menu

Timeline

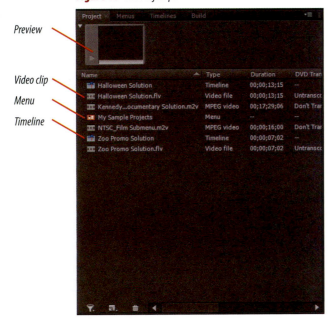

Figure 11 *Preview a menu in the Menu Viewer*

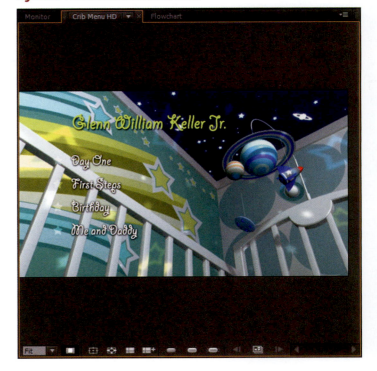

Figures © Cengage Learning 2013

Creating an Electronic Portfolio Using Adobe Encore CS6

ENCORE CS6 SUPPORTED FILE FORMATS

Video

- AVI (Windows)
- DV-AVI (Mac OS)
- H.264
- MPEG-2 (including MPG, MPV, and M2V)
- Apple QuickTime® (MOV; including Reference Movies)—requires QuickTime installed on Windows systems
- WMV (Windows Media File)

Still Images

- Adobe Photoshop (PSD), RGB color space
- Bitmap (BMP)
- GIF
- JPEG
- PICT
- Portable Network Graphics (PNG)
- Targa (TGA)
- TIFF

Note: *PSD files must be 8-bit when imported as image assets; when imported as menus they can be 8-bit or 16-bit. TIFF files cannot be imported as menus.*

Audio

- AC3 (Dolby® Digital)
- Audio Interchange File Format (AIF, AIFF; not AIFF-C)
- Digital Theater Sound (DTS)
- mp3
- MPG or M2P (including MPEG-1, MPA, Layer II)
- QuickTime (MOV)
- WAV (32-bit floating-point files are transcoded; 96-kHz 16/24-bit files are not transcoded)
- WMA

Note: *DTS audio files do not play during Preview in Encore, even though they play from a burned disc.*

Encore. They can also be downloaded from Resource Central, built from assets imported into the project, or designed in Photoshop and imported into Encore.

The Timeline Viewer, or **timeline**, is used to organize the assets that each button or menu item links to. These may include video clips, still images, and audio, as shown in Figure 12.

The Timeline allows you to mark specific points in the project to create chapters or position subtitles.

A slideshow is a sequence of still images enhanced with special effects, such as pans and zooms, transitions and narrations, or music. Slideshows can be organized in the Slideshow viewer, as shown in Figure 13.

A **playlist** is a collection of timelines, slideshows, or chapter playlists set to play sequentially.

A **chapter playlist** is similar to a playlist, but it provides a way to play a single timeline's chapters in non-sequential order.

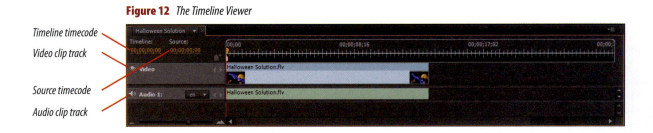

Figure 12 *The Timeline Viewer*

Timeline timecode

Video clip track

Source timecode

Audio clip track

Figure 13 *The Slideshow Viewer*

Slide Number

Preview

Slide Duration

Transition

Creating an Electronic Portfolio Using Adobe Encore CS6

Adding and Customizing Menus

The Library panel includes a variety of categories for organizing the different assets available. These categories, or sets, include all of the items from the same theme and themes have the same design elements—for example "Electric". Menus are one of the many sets available, as shown in Figure 14. The Toggle display buttons filter the various categories for simplified viewing. Menus can be created from either menus or backgrounds. Menus are created by choosing a menu or background in the Library panel and then clicking the New Menu button. After choosing a menu, you can customize it by using the Place button to add buttons, or by using the Text tool to highlight any of the text and then edit it, as shown in Figure 15.

Working with Backgrounds

A background can be added to a project as a menu by clicking the New Menu button on the Library panel. The background is then added to the Menu Viewer as a menu item. Using a background for a menu provides greater flexibility and allows you to customize the layout of the menu. You can choose text items and buttons that complement the

Figure 14 *The Library panel*

Library panel

Toggle displays

Place button

New Menu button

Toggle displays:
a. Menus
b. Buttons
c. Images
d. Backgrounds
e. Layer Sets
f. Text Items
g. Shapes
h. Replacement Layers

Figure 15 *Highlighted text in a menu for editing*

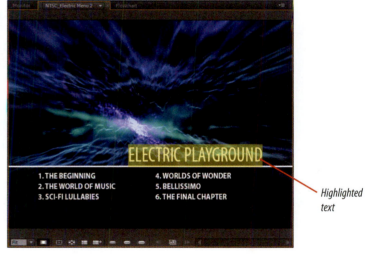

Highlighted text

background, giving it a consistent look, as shown in Figure 16.

(*Note*: The Show Safe margins are available on the Menu Viewer to aid in placement of assets and other visual elements.)

Working with the Flowchart Panel

The Flowchart panel assists with planning a project by showing the menu items and timelines graphically, in a tree structure. As you work with your project, the flowchart continually updates to show the navigation

Figure © Cengage Learning 2013

Figure 16 *Customizing a background with text and button items*

Button item

Text item

Background item

Safe Margins

Show Safe Area

Motion Menus

A Motion menu can also be created. This type of menu includes moving footage or audio. Video can be added to play in the background or in the thumbnail images of buttons. Music or a narration can also be added to play while the menu is displayed.

File Size and Quality

The available space on the destination disc (DVD or Blu-ray) limits the file size of the final project and as a result can influence the quality of the video. The video portion of the content occupies the most disc space. Depending on the data rate, 1 minute of standard-definition video for a DVD project can fill up to 73.5 MB at a rate of 9.8 megabits per second (Mbps). The same length of high-definition video for a Blu-ray can occupy 270 MB, using a data rate of 36 Mbps.

layout of the project. The Flowchart panel can also be used to set project navigation.

The Flowchart panel is divided into two areas: the upper pane and the lower pane. The upper pane displays the elements that are being used in the project and the lower pane displays the elements that are in the Project panel but are not being utilized. The arrows between the elements show how the buttons are connected to the timelines. A white line with an arrow indicates a normal link and a red line with an arrow indicates a broken link, as shown in Figure 17. Broken links occur when an item is removed from a project after a link has already been set. Figure 18 shows a broken link in the Menu Viewer panel and the Properties panel.

Figure 17 *Working with the Flowchart panel*

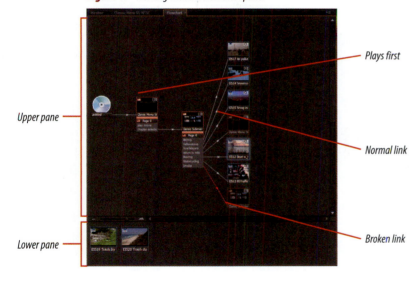

Upper pane

Lower pane

Plays first

Normal link

Broken link

Figure 18 *Missing link in Menu Viewer panel*

Missing Link in properties panel

Missing Link in Menu Viewer panel

Figures © Cengage Learning 2013

Organize and add assets

1. Open the Pollution *your name*.ncor file, if necessary.

2. Click **File** on the Menu bar, point to **New**, then click **Folder**.

   The New Folder Name dialog box opens, as shown in Figure 19.

3. Type **Air Pollution**, then click **OK**.

   A folder named Air Pollution is created on the Project panel.

4. On the Project panel, click the **Create a new item button**  then click **Folder**, as shown in Figure 20.

5. Type **Water Pollution** in the New Folder Name dialog box, then click **OK**.

   The Water Pollution folder is added to the Project panel.

6. Select the Air Pollution folder on the Project panel.

7. Click **File** on the Menu bar, point to **Import As**, then click **Timeline**.

   The Import as Timeline dialog box opens.

(continued)

Figure 19 *New Folder Name dialog box*

Enter name of folder here

Figure 20 *Creating a new folder*

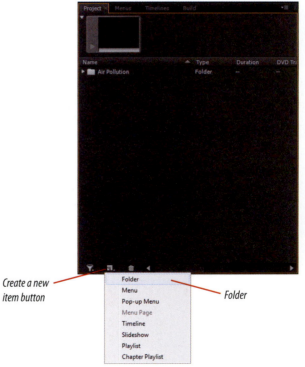

Create a new item button

Folder

Figures © Cengage Learning 2013

Creating an Electronic Portfolio Using Adobe Encore CS6

Figure 21 *Importing assets*

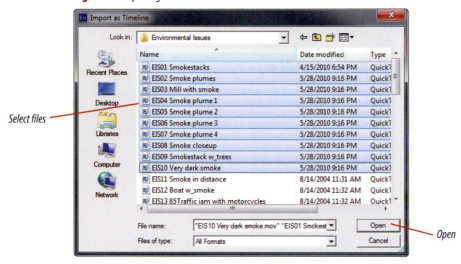

Select files →

← Open

Figure 22 *Air Pollution Timeline assets*

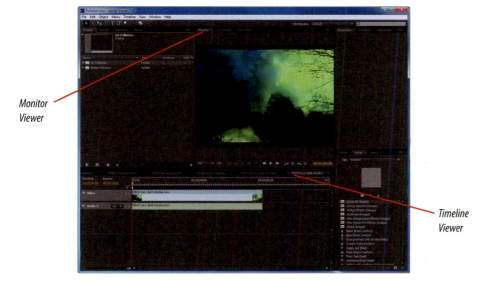

Monitor Viewer →

← Timeline Viewer

Figures © Cengage Learning 2013

8. Navigate to the drive and folder where your Data Files are stored, locate and open the **Environmental Issues folder**, click **EIS01**, press and hold [**Shift**], click **EIS10**, as shown in Figure 21, then click **Open**.

   The video footage is imported into the Project panel and placed inside the Air Pollution folder as a timeline and as individual clips. The Monitor Viewer and Timeline Viewer become active as shown in Figure 22.

9. On the Project panel, right-click the **Water Pollution folder,** point to **Import As**, then click **Asset**.

10. Select the files from EIS18 to EIS24, then click **Open**.

    The video footage is imported into the Water Pollution folder.

11. Save your project file and leave it open for the next step.

You created folders in the Project panel and imported video footage as individual timelines and associated assets into those folders.

Add and customize a menu

1. Open the Pollution *your name*.ncor file, if necessary.

2. Click **Window** on the Menu bar, then click **Library**.

   The Library panel appears in the lower-right side of the Encore workspace.

   TIP The Library panel may already be open.

3. On the Library panel, click the **Set drop-down menu**, then click **Corporate**, if necessary, as shown in Figure 23.

   The Library sets in the Corporate category are made available.

4. On the Library panel, click the **Toggle display of menus button** .

   This filters the Library panel to display only menu templates for the Corporate category.

5. Select **Globe Menu**, then click the **New Menu button** on the Library panel.

   The Globe Menu is added to the Project panel and appears in the Menu Viewer, as shown in Figure 24.

   (continued)

Figure 23 *The Library panel*

Library panel

Set drop-down menu

Figure 24 *Adding a menu template to a project*

Globe Menu

Menu Viewer

Globe Menu

Figures © Cengage Learning 2013

Creating an Electronic Portfolio Using Adobe Encore CS6

Figure 25 *Customizing the Menu Template*

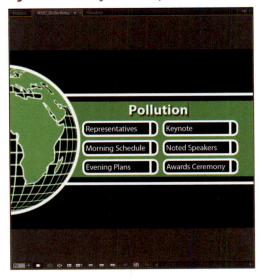

Figure 26 *Modifying the submenu buttons*

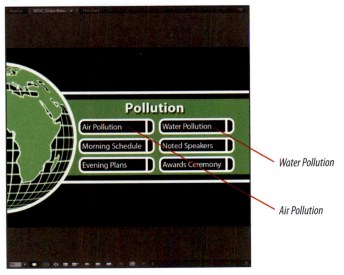

Water Pollution

Air Pollution

Lesson 2   Create a Project

6. Click the **Text tool** T on the Tools panel, then click **to the left of the letter G** in "Global" on the Menu Viewer.

   The text cursor is placed in front of the word Global so that the text can be edited.

7. Highlight the text **Global Sales Meeting**, then type **Pollution**, as shown in Figure 25.

   The title on the main menu is changed to Pollution.

8. Using the same method, change **Representatives** to **Air Pollution** and **Keynote** to **Water Pollution**, as shown in Figure 26.

9. Click the **Selection tool** on the Tools panel, then click **Morning Schedule** in the Menu Viewer.

10. Click **Edit** on the Menu bar, then click **Cut**.

    The Morning Schedule submenu button is removed from the main menu.

    (continued)

11. Using the same method, remove **Noted Speakers**, **Evening Plans**, and **Awards Ceremony**.

    The main menu now has two submenu buttons, Air Pollution and Water Pollution, as shown in Figure 27.

12. Click and drag the **Air Pollution button** down towards the center of the green area to center the button vertically.

13. Click and drag the **Water Pollution button** down towards the center of the green area to center the button vertically.

    The submenu buttons are centered, as shown in Figure 28.

14. Save your project file and leave it open for the next step.

You added and customized a menu template.

Work with backgrounds

1. Open the Pollution *your name*.ncor file, if necessary.

    You will create a custom submenu from a background image.

2. On the Library panel, click the **Toggle display of backgrounds button** .

    The items in the Library panel are filtered to display just backgrounds; these backgrounds are complimentary to the menu templates viewed previously.

3. Click **Globe BG**, then click the **New Menu button** on the Library panel.

    The Globe BG image is added to the Project panel as a blank menu and opens in the Menu Viewer, as shown in Figure 29.

    (continued)

Figure 27 *Modified Main Menu*

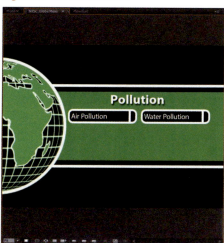

Figure 28 *Adjusting the submenu buttons*

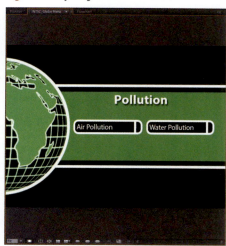

Figure 29 *Adding a background as a menu item*

Globe BG
Globe BG

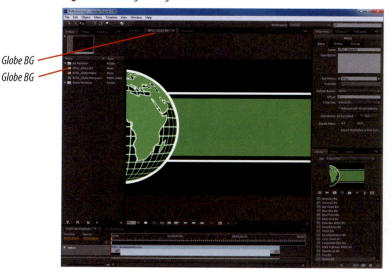

Figures © Cengage Learning 2013

Creating an Electronic Portfolio Using Adobe Encore CS6

Figure 30 *Adding a button to the submenu*

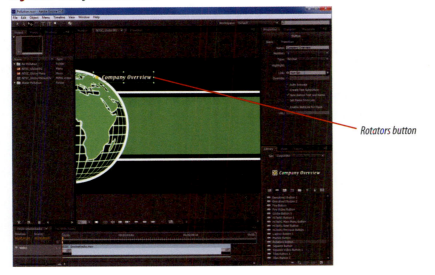

Rotators button

Figure 31 *Moving a button*

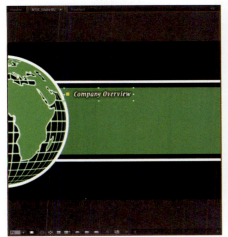

Figure 32 *Globe BG submenu with buttons*

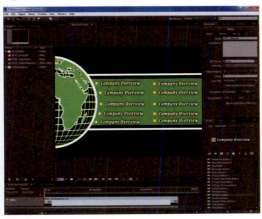

Figures © Cengage Learning 2013

4. On the Library panel, click the **Toggle display of buttons button** .

   The items in the Library panel are filtered to display only buttons.

5. Click **Rotators Button**, then click the **Place button** on the Library panel.

   The Rotators Button is added to the Menu Viewer, as shown in Figure 30.

6. Click the **Move tool** on the Tools panel, then click and drag the **Company Overview** to the green rectangle, as shown in Figure 31.

7. Repeat this process to add 9 more Rotators Button buttons for a total of 10, and arrange the buttons as shown in Figure 32.

   TIP Use the Selection tool and the Align command on the Object menu to help align the buttons.

8. Save your project file and leave it open for the next step.

You added buttons to the Globe BG submenu.

Work with the Flowchart panel

1. Open the Pollution *your name*.ncor file, if necessary.

2. Click the **Workspace drop-down menu**, then click **Navigation Design**.

   This resets the workspace, making the Flowchart panel prominent, as shown in Figure 33.

3. On the Project panel, right-click **NTSC_Globe Menu**, then click **Set as First Play**.

   This sets NTSC_Globe Menu as the item that will play first and replaces EIS01 Smokest in the Flowchart panel, as shown in Figure 34.

4. On the Project panel, right-click **NTSC_Globe BG**, then click **Rename**.

   The Rename Menu dialog box opens.

(continued)

Figure 33 *The Navigation Design workspace*

Flowchart panel

Navigation Design

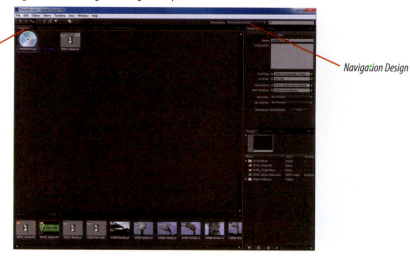

Figure 34 *Setting NTSC_ Globe Menu to play first*

NTSC_Globe Menu

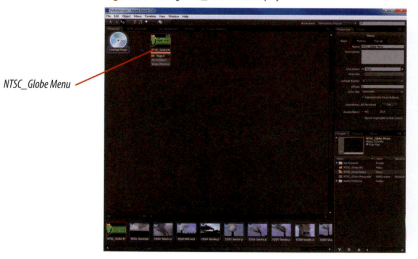

Creating an Electronic Portfolio Using Adobe Encore CS6

Figure 35 *Rename Menu dialog box*

Enter a new Menu name text box

Figure 36 *Linking a button*

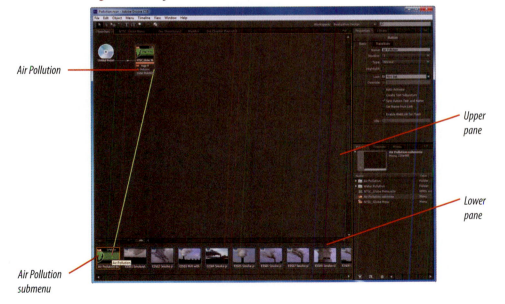

Air Pollution

Upper pane

Lower pane

Air Pollution submenu

Lesson 2   Create a Project

5. Type **Air Pollution submenu** in the Enter a new Menu name text box, as shown in Figure 35, then click **OK**.

   This renames the title of the submenu making it easier to locate.

6. Click the **Selection tool** ▶ on the Tools panel, then click and drag **Air Pollution** from the NTSC_Globe Menu icon on the Flowchart panel to the **Air Pollution submenu** in the lower pane, as shown in Figure 36.

   The cursor changes to the Pick Whip, and the Air Pollution submenu is added to the upper pane with a link connecting the two items.

7. Using the same method, select the **first Company Over** from the Air Pollution submenu and point to **EIS01** in the lower pane.

   The EIS01 timeline is added to the upper pane and the first button on the Air Pollution submenu is linked to the timeline.

   (continued)

8. On the Properties panel, click the **Set Name from Link check box,** as shown in Figure 37.

   This changes the name of the button to EIS01 Smokestacks.

9. Repeat this process for each of the buttons from the Air Pollution submenu in the upper pane, pointing to the timelines in the lower pane in order from the left, then clicking the **Set Name from Link check box** for each button.

10. Compare your Footage panel to Figure 38.

    The timelines are removed from the lower pane once they are selected and moved to the upper pane.

11. Save your project file and leave it open for the next step.

You renamed the buttons and linked them to the appropriate timelines.

Figure 37 *Renaming a button based on Timeline name*

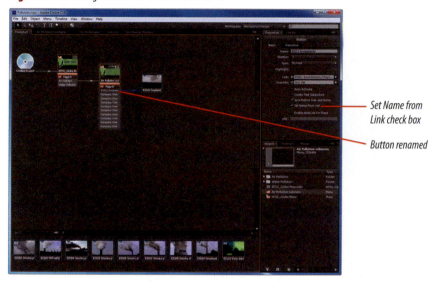

Set Name from Link check box

Button renamed

Figure 38 *All buttons on Air Pollution submenu linked*

Figures © Cengage Learning 2013

Figure 39 *Adding placeholder text to the submenu*

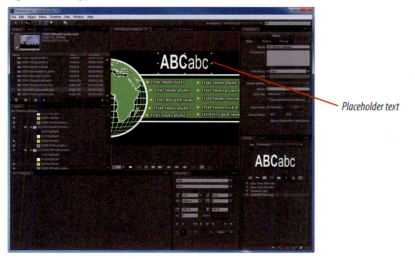

Placeholder text

Figure 40 *Using the Character panel*

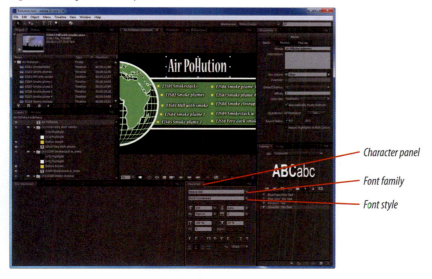

Character panel

Font family

Font style

Figures © Cengage Learning 2013

Edit a menu

1. Open the Pollution *your name*.ncor file, if necessary.

2. Reset the workspace to Menu Design.

   A title and a button to return to the main menu are needed on the Air Pollution submenu.

3. On the Library panel, click the **Toggle display of text items button** ⬛T.

   This filters the items in the Library panel to display only text items.

4. Click **Scientific Title Text**, then click the **Place button** ➡.

   Placeholder text is placed on the Monitor Preview.

5. Click the **Move tool** ⬛ on the Tools panel, then click and drag the **placeholder text** above the button list, as shown in Figure 39.

6. Click the **Text tool** ⬛T on the Tools panel, then change the placeholder text to **Air Pollution**.

7. Click the **Direct Select tool** ⬛ on the Tools panel, click **Air Pollution**, then on the Character panel change the font family to **Nueva Std**, and the font style to **Bold Condensed**, as shown in Figure 40.

(continued)

8. Click the **Direct Select tool** on the Tools panel, then drag the **Air Pollution title** so it is centered over the button titles, as shown in Figure 41.

9. Click **Scientific Title Text**, click the **Place button** , then move the placeholder text to the bottom right of the Menu Viewer.

   You will rename this text placeholder and use it for a button that returns the viewer to the main menu.

10. Click the **Text tool** on the Tools panel, change the placeholder text to **Return to Main Menu**, then change the font family to **Nueva Std**, and the font size to **36**.

11. On the Library panel, click the **Toggle display of buttons button** .

12. Click **HiTech1 Previous Button**, click the **Place button** , then move the button to the left of the Return to Main Menu text, as shown in Figure 42.

(continued)

Figure 41 *Moving the Air Pollution title*

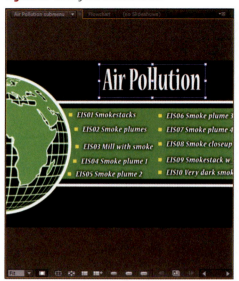

Figure 42 *Creating a Return button with text*

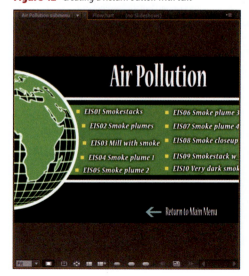

Figures © Cengage Learning 2013

Creating an Electronic Portfolio Using Adobe Encore CS6

Figure 43 *Setting the Return button's action*

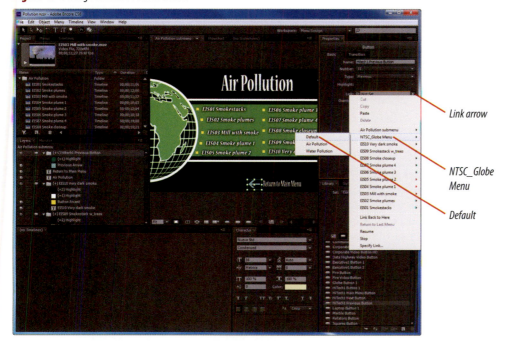

Link arrow

NTSC_Globe
Menu

Default

13. Click the **Selection tool** , click **HiTech1 Previous Button**, then on the Properties panel, click the **Link arrow**, point to **NTSC_Globe Menu**, and choose **Default** as shown in Figure 43.

This sets the button action to return to the main menu. Your figure may vary.

14. Save your project file and it leave open for the next step.

You edited the submenu to include a title and a button to return to the main menu.

Figure © Cengage Learning 2013

LESSON 3

Create
TIMELINES

What You'll Do

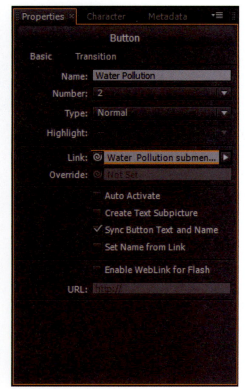

Figure © Cengage Learning 2013

  In this lesson, you will create timelines in Encore.

Previewing a Project

During the process of creating a project and setting links, it is a good idea to preview the project before you build your disc or Flash file. When you preview a project, you will see how it will appear at final output and be able to test the links in the Project Preview window with navigation controls such as Play, Pause, and Skip Forward, as shown in Figure 44.

Working with Timelines

As in Premiere Pro, you can use a timeline in Encore to arrange various assets or to hold a single asset. Every linked asset needs to be placed on a timeline. The Timelines panel shows all the timelines in the current project. When a specific timeline is selected on the Timelines panel, its properties become active on the Properties panel, as shown in Figure 45.

Figure 44 *Project Preview window*

Highlighted button

Navigation controls

Figure © Cengage Learning 2013

Timelines can be created at the same time assets are imported by selecting the Import As Timeline option from the File menu. The asset is imported in its original format and a timeline is created at the same time. Timelines may also be created after assets are imported by using the Create a new item button on the Project panel and then dragging the assets from the Project panel to the timeline.

A timeline needs an action set to control what happens when the clip ends. If an action is not set when the project is built, the video clip remains on a black screen when the clip is finished playing. This action is set in the Properties panel and is called an **end action**.

The end action is set either by using the Pick Whip or by using the End Action drop-down menu to select what the project should play when the video clip ends, as shown in Figure 46.

Figure 45 *Working with Timelines*

Timelines panel

Properties panel

End Action

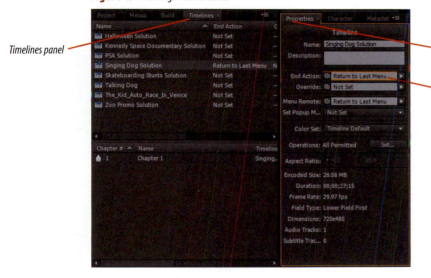

Figure 46 *End Action drop-down menu*

End Action drop-down menu

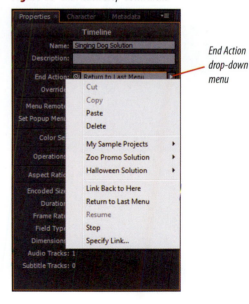

Figures © Cengage Learning 2013

Creating Buttons with Timelines

A button can be created by dragging a timeline from the Project panel to the Menu Viewer. The button that is selected as the default in the set is created automatically when the Timeline is dropped on the Menu Viewer, as shown in Figure 47. The default button can be set by right-clicking the button on the Library panel and then choosing Set as Default Button.

Creating a Playlist

A **playlist** is a group of timelines that are set to play sequentially. A playlist plays back all the elements that have been added to the playlist without stopping. A playlist is created by selecting the timelines on the Project panel while holding [Ctrl] (Win) or ⌘ (Mac). The playlist, when selected, can then be viewed on the Properties panel, as shown in Figure 48. A playlist is an excellent way to give end users the opportunity to view multiple timelines at once.

Figure 47 *Creating a button from a timeline*

Default button

Figure 48 *Creating a playlist*

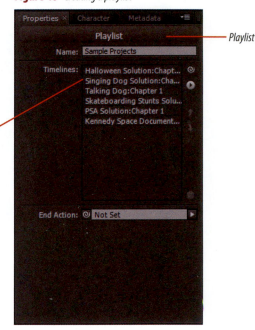

Playlist

Timelines in playlist

Figures © Cengage Learning 2013

Creating an Electronic Portfolio Using Adobe Encore CS6

Figure 49 *Project Preview window*

Figure 50 *Air Pollution submenu displayed in the Project Preview window*

Lesson 3   Create Timelines

Preview a project

1. Open the Pollution *your name*.ncor file, if necessary.
2. Reset the workspace to **Default**.

    The name of each button has been changed to reflect the name of the timeline to which it is linked.

3. Click **File** on the Menu bar, then click **Preview**.

    The Project Preview window opens, as shown in Figure 49.

4. In the Project Preview window, click the **Air Pollution button**.

    The Air Pollution submenu is displayed, as shown in Figure 50.

5. Click the **EIS01 Smokestacks button**, then watch the video clip in its entirety.

    Notice the Project Preview goes to black when the video clip ends. The end action needs to be set so when the clip finishes, the Air Pollution submenu is again displayed.

6. Click the **Exit and return button** to return to the Encore workspace.

7. Save your project file and leave it open for the next exercise.

You previewed your project.

Set an end action for the timeline

1. Open the Pollution *your name*.ncor file, if necessary.
2. Click **Window** on the Menu bar, then click **Timelines**.

    The Timelines panel appears in the upper-left section of the Encore workspace.

(continued)

3. On the Timelines panel, click **EIS01 Smokestacks**, then on the Properties panel, click the **End Action arrow,** point to **Air Pollution submenu**, then click **Default**, as shown in Figure 51.

   The video clip will now return to the Air Pollution submenu when it finishes playing, instead of staying on a black screen.

4. Repeat this process with the remaining timelines on the Timelines panel.

5. Save your project file and leave it open for the next exercise.

You set the end action for each of the timelines in the Timeline panel to return to the Air Pollution submenu.

Create buttons for a submenu with timelines

1. Open the Pollution *your name*.ncor file, if necessary.

2. Reset the Default workspace.

3. Click **File** on the Menu bar, point to **Import As**, then click **Menu**.

   The Import as Menu dialog box opens.

4. Select the **Water Pollution submenu file** from your Data Files folder, then click **Open**.

5. On the Project panel, double-click **Water Pollution submenu** to open it in the Menu Viewer preview panel.

   The Water Pollution submenu has already been created for you; you need to set some links to add functionality.

6. Click the **Selection tool** ![selection tool icon], click the **light blue arrow** in the Menu Viewer, then on the Properties panel, click the **Link drop-down menu**, point to **NTSC_Globe Menu**, then click **Default**, as shown in Figure 52.
   (continued)

Figure 51 *Setting the end action for a timeline*

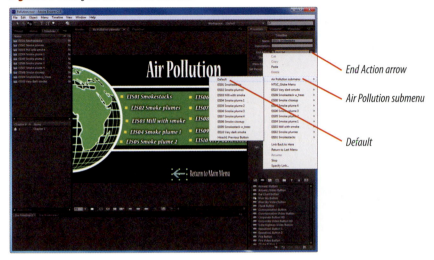

End Action arrow

Air Pollution submenu

Default

Figure 52 *Setting the Link action for the light blue arrow*

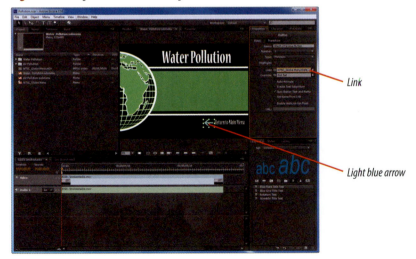

Link

Light blue arrow

Creating an Electronic Portfolio Using Adobe Encore CS6

Figure 53 *Creating a button by dragging an asset from the Project panel*

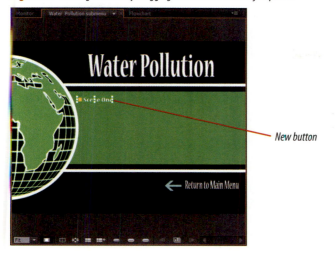

New button

Figure 54 *Button placement on the Water Pollution submenu*

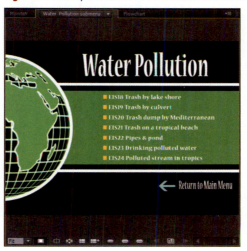

7. On the Library panel, click the **Toggle display of buttons button,** right-click **Fire Button**, then click **Set as Default Button**.

8. On the Project panel, expand the contents of the **Water Pollution folder** to display the video footage assets.

9. Click and drag the **EIS18 Trash by lake shore.mov** video clip to the Water Pollution submenu in the Menu Viewer, as shown in Figure 53.

   A button is created in the Menu Viewer and a timeline is created on the Project panel.

10. Select the button, then on the Properties panel, click the **Set Name from Link check box** to reset the name of the button.

11. Click the **Move tool** on the Tools panel, then move the **EIS18 Trash by lake shore button** to the upper middle area of the green rectangle.

12. Repeat this process with the remaining video clips in the Water Pollution folder so that the buttons look like those shown in Figure 54.

TIP A red rectangle will alert you if you are overlapping buttons. To ensure buttons work correctly they cannot overlap.

(continued)

13. Click the **Menu Viewer drop-down menu**, then click **NTSC_Globe menu**.

    The NTSC_Globe menu is displayed in the Menu Viewer.

14. Click the **Water Pollution menu**, then on the Properties panel, set the Link to **Water Pollution submenu: Default**, as shown in Figure 55.

    This creates the link for the Water Pollution button to go to the Water Pollution submenu.

15. Preview the project to verify all of the buttons are working properly.

    All buttons should go to the appropriate places and all video clips should return to the appropriate submenus.

16. Make corrections if necessary.

17. Save your project file and leave it open for the next step.

You placed video assets on the Water Pollution submenu to create buttons, then you verified that all of the buttons and timelines in the project were working properly.

Create a playlist

1. Open the Pollution *your name*.ncor file, if necessary, then reset the Default workspace if necessary.

2. On the Project panel, expand the **Air Pollution folder**.

3. Select the **EIS01 Smokestacks timeline**, press and hold [**Ctrl**] (Win) or [⌘] (Mac), then select the remaining timelines in order.

4. Click the **Create a New Item button** , then click **Playlist**.

    The New Playlist Name dialog box opens, as shown in Figure 56.

    (continued)

Figure 55 *Setting the Water Pollution link on the main menu to go to the Water Pollution submenu*

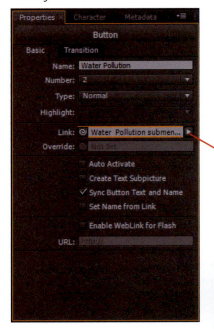

Link

Figure 56 *New Playlist Name dialog box*

New Playlist Name

Figures © Cengage Learning 2013

Creating an Electronic Portfolio Using Adobe Encore CS6

Figure 57 *Setting the end action for a Playlist*

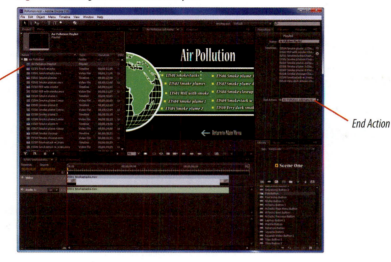

Air Pollution Playlist

End Action

Figure 58 *Moving the Air Pollution Playlist button*

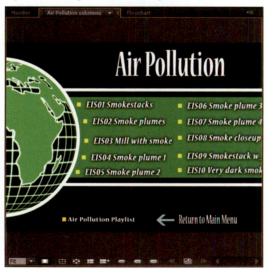

5. Type **Air Pollution Playlist** in the Enter a name for the new playlist text box, then click **OK**.

   The playlist is added to the Air Pollution folder on the Project panel.

6. Select **Air Pollution Playlist**, then on the Properties panel, set the end action to **Air Pollution submenu: Default**, as shown in Figure 57.

7. On the Menu Viewer tab, select the **Air Pollution submenu** from the drop-down menu, if necessary.

   The Air Pollution submenu needs to be active in the Menu Viewer panel.

8. Drag the **Air Pollution Playlist** from the Project panel to the Air Pollution submenu in the Menu Viewer, then click the **Set Name from Link check box**.

9. Click the **Move tool** , then move the **Air Pollution Playlist button** to the location shown in Figure 58.

   All of the Air Pollution video clips will play without stopping.

10. Save your project file and leave it open for the next lesson.

You created a playlist to play all of the Air Pollution video clips in order then return to the Air Pollution submenu.

LESSON 4

Build
A PROJECT

What You'll Do

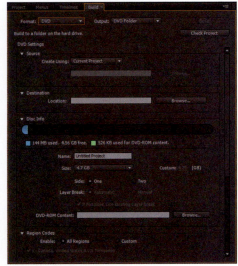

Figure © Cengage Learning 2013

 In this lesson, you will build your final project to the Flash format for the Internet and burn it to a DVD.

Checking the Project

Encore includes a feature called Check Project, which is an important feature to use before actually building a project to its final output. The Check Project feature identifies problems with a project such as missing links or end actions not being set. This feature can be activated from the Build Project panel or from the File menu. You can choose which issues you want to check for by adding and removing check marks in the Check Project panel, as shown in Figure 59. Leaving all of the options

Figure 59 *The Check Project panel*

Figure © Cengage Learning 2013

checked ensures that any possible problems are not missed. Figure 60 shows some problems after running the Check Project feature. Selecting the name of a problem in the Check Project panel allows you to fix that problem on the Properties panel, as shown in Figure 61. Not all problems can be repaired on the Properties panel, though; for instance, an orphaned item like the Orphan Playlist problem shown in Figure 62 would need to be repaired on the Flowchart panel by moving it from the lower pane to the upper pane.

Figure 60 *Check Project results*

Identified problems

Figure 61 *Fixing a problem on the Properties panel*

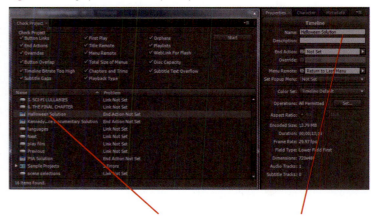

Selected problem

Problem on Properties panel

Figure 62 *Fixing a problem on the Flowchart panel*

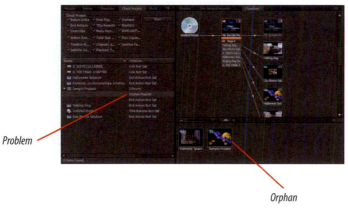

Problem

Orphan

Building a Project to the Flash Format

The Build panel offers the option to export an Encore project to a Flash format for interactive viewing on the Internet, as shown in Figure 63. The F4V and FLV formats are available, along with several presets to set the size and quality of the video. The F4V format is compatible with Flash Player 9 and higher, and is the new standard for published Flash files. The FLV standard is compatible with Flash Player 7 and higher.

In the Build panel, the name of the project is found in the Disc Info section of the panel. A project is named Untitled Project by default; it is not automatically given the same name as your Encore Project file. Templates are available to provide a background for the Flash project, as shown in Figure 64. If a template is not specified the default black background is used.

When a Flash project is built, Encore creates files and a folder within a separate folder named using the project name in the Build panel. These files contain the necessary information for the project to play properly. Every Flash project produces the AuthorContent.xml, flshdvd.swf, and index.html files. In addition, a Sources folder is created, which contains the Flash videos, menu images, and icons needed for the project. (*Note*: The title of the Web page defaults to the name of the template, which can only be changed by editing the HTML code; it cannot be done in Encore.)

Figure 63 *Build panel*

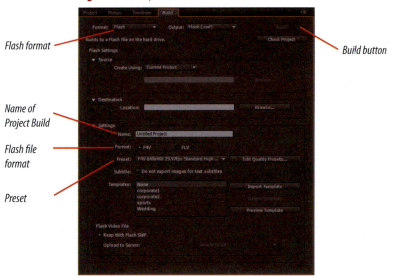

Flash format

Build button

Name of Project Build

Flash file format

Preset

Figure 64 *Published Flash project*

Flash project

Background template

Figures © Cengage Learning 2013

Building a DVD

The Build panel also offers the option to build a project to a DVD, as shown in Figure 65. You can burn the project directly to blank media that is in the appropriate drive. When DVD player software is installed, the resulting DVD plays automatically when inserted into a DVD drive, as shown in Figure 66. You can also burn a DVD project to a folder that can be viewed on a computer with a DVD player.

The Disc Info area of the Build panel indicates if there is enough room on the selected media that has been designated for the project. As with the Flash build, you need to specify the name of the project. You can also copy-protect the disc so that it cannot be copied illegally.

Figure 65 *Build Project for a DVD*

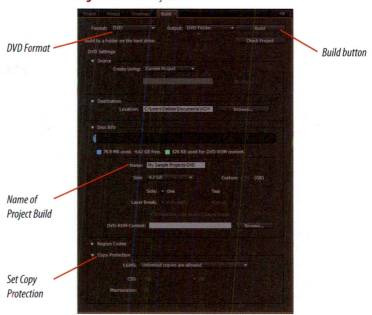

DVD Format

Build button

Name of Project Build

Set Copy Protection

Figure 66 *Published DVD project*

Build a project to the Flash format

1. Open the Pollution *your name*.ncor file, if necessary, then reset the Default workspace if necessary.

2. Click **Window** on the Menu bar, then click **Build**.

   The Build panel becomes active in the upper-left area of the Encore workspace.

3. On the Build panel, click the **Format drop-down arrow**, then click **Flash**.

   The Output drop-down menu automatically updates to Flash (.swf), and the Settings options update to Flash options, as shown in Figure 67.

4. On the Build panel, click the **Browse button**, navigate to the drive and folder where you save your work, then click **OK**.

   (continued)

Figure 67 *The Build panel for Flash*

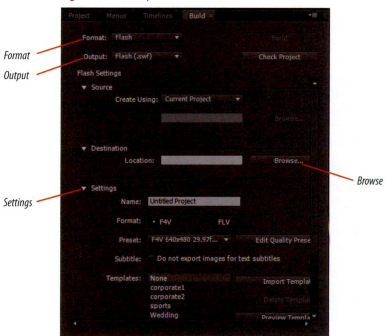

Working with Sequences in Encore

Adobe Dynamic Link is supported between Premiere Pro and Encore. A Premiere Pro sequence can be sent or imported into Encore, for output to DVD, Blue-ray, or SWF. If the sequence is then updated in Premiere Pro, the update is reflected in Encore without rendering. In Encore, the sequence can be selected for editing by using the Edit Original command.

Creating an Electronic Portfolio Using Adobe Encore CS6

Figure 68 *Changing the Settings in the Build panel*

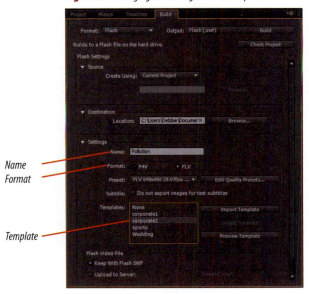

Name
Format

Template

Figure 69 *Checking the project for problems*

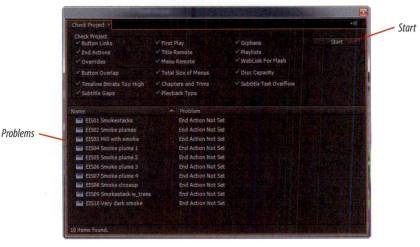

Problems

Start

5. In the Settings section complete the following: Name text box: **Pollution** *your name*, Format: **FLV**, and Templates: **corporate2**, then compare your screen to Figure 68.

6. Click the **Check Project button**.

   The Check Project dialog box opens.

7. Click **Start**.

   Problems are identified, as shown in Figure 69, and need to be repaired before building the project.

   TIP   If there are no errors, skip Steps 8 and 9.

8. In the Problems list select **EIS02**, then on the Properties panel, click the **End Action drop-down menu**, then click **Air Pollution submenu: Default**.

   The Timeline properties become active on the Properties panel when the problem is selected in the Check Project dialog box.

9. Repeat this process for each of the timelines in the Check Project dialog box.

(continued)

Figures © Cengage Learning 2013

10. Click **Start**, then compare your results to Figure 70.

All the problems should be repaired. If you still have to make corrections, click Start again.

11. Close the Check Project dialog box.

12. On the Build panel, click the **Build button**, then click **OK** when the process is complete.

The Save Project dialog box is visible for a short time, then the Build Progress dialog box is displayed to show the progress of the build, as shown in Figure 71.

If you receive an error when attempting to build your project that a folder with that specific name is already taken, modify the name of your project in the Build panel.

(continued)

Figure 70 *Problems have been corrected*

Figure 71 *Build Progress dialog box*

Status of build

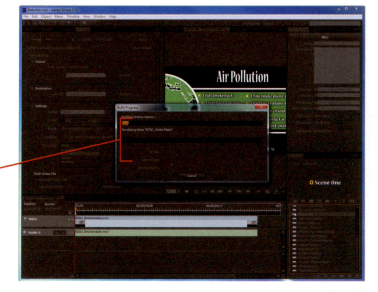

Creating an Electronic Portfolio Using Adobe Encore CS6

Figure 72 *Locating the Pollution your name folder*

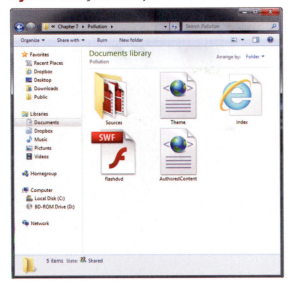

Figure 73 *Final project published for the Internet*

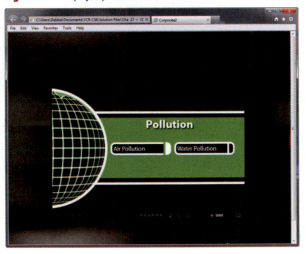

13. Minimize Encore, then navigate to and open the folder where you save your work.

    A folder has been created with the files necessary for the Flash Web page to function properly, as shown in Figure 72.

14. Open the Pollution *your name* folder, then double-click **index.html** to preview your project, as shown in Figure 73.

15. Save your project file and leave it open for the next exercise.

You built a project for the Flash format after verifying and correcting any problems.

Build a DVD

1. Open the Pollution *your name*.ncor file, if necessary.

2. On the Build panel, change the format to **DVD**.

   All the settings change accordingly to support the DVD output, as shown in Figure 74. (*Note*: You will need a blank DVD inserted in your DVD drive.)

   (continued)

Figure 74 *Build panel settings for a DVD build*

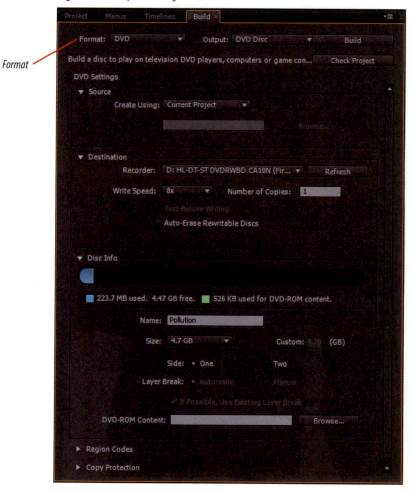

Format

Figure © Cengage Learning 2013

Creating an Electronic Portfolio Using Adobe Encore CS6

Figure 75 *Progress of build to a DVD*

Status of build

Figure 76 *Final project published to a DVD*

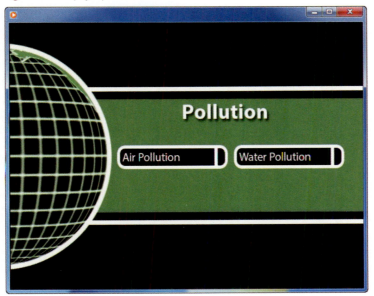

3. Click the **Build button**, then click **OK** when the process is complete.

   The Save Project dialog box is visible for a short time, then the Build Progress dialog box is displayed to show the progress of the build, as shown in Figure 75.

   (*Note*: The project has already been checked for errors before we built to the Flash format. If this was the only build, Check Project should have been completed prior to starting the build process.)

4. Minimize Encore and open the DVD, as shown in Figure 76.

   This disc is ejected upon completion. When you put it back into the drive, the DVD should launch automatically.

5. Save and close your project file.

You published your project to a DVD.

Start Adobe Encore CS6 and explore the workspace.

1. Click Start on the Menu bar, point to All Programs, then click Adobe Encore CS6 (Win) or open the Finder from the dock, click Applications from the sidebar, select the Adobe applications folder, then click Adobe Encore CS6 (Mac).
2. Click New Project in the Adobe Encore CS6 window.
3. Click the Browse button, then navigate to the drive and folder where your Chapter 7 Data Files are located.
4. Click OK to close the Browse for Folder window but keep the New Project dialog box open.
5. Type **Erosion Final** *your name* in the Name text box of the New Project dialog box.
6. Click OK to accept the default settings.
7. Locate the Project panel, the Monitor panel, the Properties panel, and the Library panel.
8. Click Window on the Menu bar, point to Workspace, then click Menu Design.
9. Click Window on the Menu bar, point to Workspace, then click Default.

Organize and add assets.

1. Click File on the Menu bar, point to New, then click Folder.
2. Type **Deforestation**, then click OK.
3. On the Project panel, click the Create a new item button, then click Folder.
4. Type **Desertification** in the New Folder Name dialog box, then click OK.
5. Select the Deforestation folder on the Project panel.
6. Click File on the Menu bar, point to Import As, then click Timeline.

7. Locate the Environmental Issues folder where your Data Files are stored, click EIS28, press and hold [Shift], select EIS37, then click Open.
8. On the Project panel, right-click the Desertification folder, point to Import As, then click Asset.
9. Select the files from EIS51 to EIS56, then click Open.

Add and customize a menu template.

1. Click Window on the Menu bar, then click Library, if necessary, to select it.
2. On the Library panel, click the Set drop-down menu, then click General, if necessary.
3. On the Library panel, click the Toggle display of menus button.
4. Click Sunset Menu, then click the New Menu button on the Library panel.
5. Click the Text tool on the Tools panel, then click to the left of the letter I in "Inspiration" on the Menu Viewer.
6. Highlight Inspirational Thoughts, then type **Erosion**.
7. Using the same method, change the text "play movie" to **Deforestation** and the text "scene selections" to **Desertification**.
8. Click the Selection tool, then click special features in the Menu Viewer.
9. Click Edit on the Menu bar, then click Cut.
10. Using the same method, remove languages.

Work with backgrounds.

1. On the Library panel, click the Toggle display of backgrounds button.
2. Locate and select Sunset BG, then click the New Menu button on the Library panel.

3. On the Library panel, click the Toggle display of buttons button.
4. Locate and select the Sunset Button, then click the Place button on the Library panel.
5. Repeat this process to add 9 more buttons for a total of 10, then arrange the buttons as you like.

Work with the Flowchart panel.

1. On the Project panel, right-click NTSC_Sunset Menu, then click Set as First Play.
2. On the Project panel, right-click NTSC_Sunset BG, then click Rename.
3. Type **Deforestation submenu** in the Enter a New Menu name text box, then click OK.
4. Click the Workspace drop-down menu, then click Navigation Design.
5. Click the Selection tool, select Deforestation from the NTSC_Sunset Menu icon on the Flowchart panel, then drag to the Deforestation submenu in the lower pane.
6. Select the first introductions from the Deforestation submenu on the Flowchart panel, then point to EIS28 in the lower pane.
7. On the Properties panel, check the Set Name from Link check box.
8. Repeat this process for each of the buttons from the Deforestation submenu in the upper pane, pointing to the timelines in the lower pane in order from the left and clicking the Set Name from Link check box for each button.

Edit a menu.

1. Reset the workspace to Menu Design.
2. On the Library panel, click the Toggle display of text items button.
3. Select 36 pt Gold Trajan Pro, then click the Place button.
4. Click the Move tool on the Tools panel, then click and drag the placeholder text above the button list.
5. Click the Text tool on the Tools panel, then change the placeholder text to **Deforestation**.
6. Click the Move tool, then move the Deforestation title so it is centered over the button titles.
7. Select 36 pt Gold Trajan Pro, click the Place button, then move the placeholder text to the bottom right of the Menu Viewer.
8. Click the Text tool on the Tools panel, then change the placeholder text to **Return to Main Menu**, and the font size to 10. (*Note*: Type Return to Main Menu on two lines, pressing [Enter] (Win) or [return] (Mac) after *to*.)
9. Right-click the Return to Main Menu text, then click Convert to Button.
10. Click the Selection tool, click the Return to Main Menu button, then on the Properties panel, click the Link arrow, point to NTSC_Sunset Menu, then click Default.

Preview a project.

1. Reset the workspace to Default.
2. Click File on the Menu bar, then click Preview.
3. In the Project Preview window, click the Deforestation button.

4. Click the EIS28 Slash & burn plot Thailand button, then watch the video clip in its entirety.
5. Click the Exit and return button to return to the Encore workspace.

Set an end action for the timeline.

1. Click Window on the Menu bar, then click Timelines.
2. On the Timelines panel, select the EIS37 Clear-cut hillside WA, then on the Properties panel, click the End Action drop-down menu, point to the Deforestation submenu, then click default.
3. Repeat this process with the remaining timelines on the Timelines panel.

Create buttons for a submenu with assets.

1. Reset the Default workspace.
2. Click File on the Menu bar, point to Import As, then click Menu.
3. Locate the Desertification submenu file from your Data Files folder, then click Open.
4. Click the Direct Select tool, select Return to Main Menu in the Menu Viewer, then on the Properties panel, click the Link drop-down menu, then click NTSC_Sunset Menu: Default.
5. On the Library panel, click the Toggle display of buttons button, right-click Sunset Button, then click Set as Default Button.
6. On the Project panel, expand the contents of the Desertification folder to display the video footage assets.

7. Click and drag the EIS51 Desertification Mai W Africa. mov video clip to the Desertification submenu in the Menu Viewer.
8. Click the Selection tool, select the button, then on the Properties panel, click the Set Name from Link check box to reset the name of the button.
9. Repeat this process with the remaining video clips in the Desertification folder.
10. Click the Menu Viewer drop-down menu, then click NTSC_Sunset menu.
11. Click the Desertification button, then on the Properties panel, click the Link drop-down menu, point to Desertification submenu, then click Default.
12. Preview the project to verify all of the buttons are working properly.
13. Make corrections if necessary.

Create a playlist.

1. Reset the Default workspace if necessary.
2. On the Project panel, expand the Desertification folder.
3. Select the EIS51 Desertification Mai W Africa timeline, press and hold [Ctrl] (Win) or ⌘ (Mac), then select the remaining timelines in order.
4. Click the New Item button, then click Playlist.
5. Type **Desertification Playlist** in the Enter a name for the new playlist text box, then click OK.
6. Select Desertification Playlist, then on the Properties panel, click the End Action drop-down menu, point to Desertification submenu, then click Default.

7. Drag Desertification Playlist from the Project panel to the Desertification submenu in the Menu Viewer, then click the Set Name from Link check box.

8. Click the Move tool, then move the Desertification Playlist button to the bottom of the list of buttons, as shown in Figure 77.

Build a project to the Flash format.

1. Reset the Default workspace if necessary.

2. Click Window on the Menu bar, then click Build.

3. On the Build panel, click the Format drop-down menu, then click Flash.

4. On the Build panel, click the Browse button, navigate to the folder where you save your work, then click OK.

5. In the Settings section, complete the following: Name box: **Erosion** *your name*, Format: **FLV**, and Templates: **corporate2**.

6. Click the Check Project button.

7. Click Start. (*Hint*: If there are no errors, continue to Step 11.)

8. If necessary, in the Problems list, select EIS51 Desertification Mai W Africa, then on the Properties panel, click the End Action drop-down menu, point to Deforestation submenu, then click Default.

9. Repeat this process for each of the timelines in the Check Project dialog box.

10. Click Start.

11. Close the Check Project dialog box.

12. On the Build panel, click the Build button, then click OK when the process is complete.

13. Minimize Encore, then navigate to and open the folder where you save your work.

14. Open the Erosion *your name* folder, then double-click index.html to preview your project.

Build a DVD.

1. On the Project panel, change the format to DVD.

2. Click the Build button, then click OK when the process is complete.

3. Minimize Encore, then open the DVD.

4. Save and close your project file.

Figure 77 *Sample Skills Review*

Figure © Cengage Learning 2013

A colleague has been working on a Flash presentation that will be published for the Internet. Unfortunately, there has been a family emergency and he is not able to finish the project. You have been asked to complete the project so that the deadline is met for the client.

A playlist still needs to be created to play all the video clips sequentially without stopping. The playlist should be linked to the Play Movie button on the Classic Menu SD main menu. The project then needs to be checked for problems and finally built to the Flash format.

1. Open the PB1.ncor project from the drive and folder where you save your Data Files.
2. Create a Playlist named **Issues** that uses all of the clips in sequential order.
3. Create a link on the Play Movie button to the playlist.
4. In the Build panel, name the project **Environmental Issues**.
5. Check the project for problems and correct any problems that you need to. An example is shown in Figure 78.
6. Build the project to the Flash FLV file format.

Figure 78 *Example of the PB1 workspace*

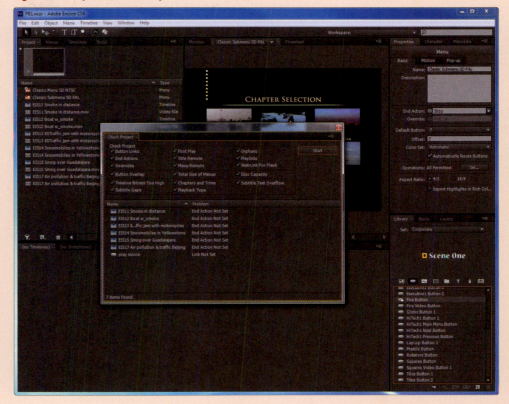

Figure © Cengage Learning 2013

Creating an Electronic Portfolio Using Adobe Encore CS6

You recently went on a trip to San Antonio, Texas and decided to create a slideshow of your pictures from the trip using your skills in Encore.

Using the images found in the Riverwalk folder where your Data Files are located, create a slideshow.

1. Create a new Encore project named *Your Name* **PB2** using the default settings, then set the Workspace to Slideshow Design.

2. Import the images from the Riverwalk folder located in the Chapter 7 data files folder as a slideshow.

3. In the Slideshow Options panel, customize the settings for the slideshow to your liking.

4. Make additional changes in the Properties panel for each slide if you would like. Figure 79 shows an example.

5. Build the project to the Flash FLV file format.

Figure 79 *Example of the PB2 Workspace*

Figure © Cengage Learning 2013

Creating an Electronic Portfolio Using Adobe Encore CS6

Design an electronic portfolio using the portfolio projects you have created through the course of this book. As you create the DVD, use your production logo to start the DVD and then go to the main menu. Include a playlist that plays all of your portfolio projects in order.

1. Create a new Encore project and name it **Your Name Portfolio**, using the default settings.
2. Import one final copy of each portfolio project you have created in either the MPEG-2 or FLV file format as a timeline.
3. Choose a template you would like to use for your project from the Library panel.
4. Modify the menu and submenus as you like. An example is shown in Figure 80.
5. Set the production logo to play first, then go to the main menu.
6. Create a playlist of your portfolio projects.
7. Link the buttons appropriately.
8. Check your project for problems, then fix the problems if there are any.
9. Build your project to the Flash format.
10. Preview your Flash project, then build your project to a DVD.

Figure 80 *Example Submenu for Portfolio Project*

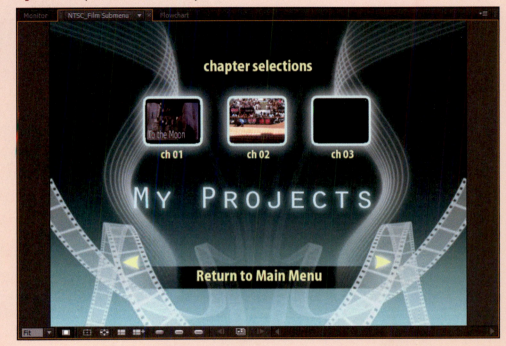

Figure © Cengage Learning 2013

Creating an Electronic Portfolio Using Adobe Encore CS6

VIDEO COLLECTION DATA FILES					
Chapter	Data File Supplied	Support Files	Linked Files	Student Creates File	Used In
Chapter 1	None	None		Earth Day your name.prproj	Lesson 1
	Earth Day your name.prproj*	70s Soft Rock – 60.mp3 Scenic1.jpg Scenic2.jpg Scenic3.jpg Scenic4.jpg Scenic5.jpg Scenic6.jpg Scenic7.jpg Scenic8.jpg Scenic9.jpg Scenic10.jpg Scenic11.jpg Scenic12.jpg Scenic13.jpg Scenic14.jpg Scenic15.jpg Scenic16.jpg Scenic17.jpg Scenic18.jpg Scenic19.jpg Scenic20.jpg Scenic21.jpg Scenic22.jpg Scenic23.jpg Scenic24.jpg Scenic25.jpg Scenic26.jpg Scenic27.jpg Scenic28.jpg Scenic29.jpg	None		Lesson 2 Lesson 3 Lesson 4 Lesson 5

*Created in previous Lesson or Skills Review in current chapter

DATA FILES LIST

(CONTINUED)

Chapter	Data File Supplied	Support Files	Linked Files	Student Creates File	Used In
		VIDEO COLLECTION DATA FILES			
Chapter 1, continued		Scenic30.jpg Scenic31.jpg Scenic32.jpg			
	Earth Day your name.prproj*	Earth Day Text.txt	None	Earth Day your name.mpeg Earth Day your name.flv	Lesson 6
	None	Subtle Storm - 60.mp3 Scenic16.jpg Scenic17.jpg Scenic18.jpg Scenic19.jpg Scenic20.jpg Scenic21.jpg Scenic22.jpg Scenic23.jpg Scenic24.jpg Scenic25.jpg Scenic26.jpg Scenic27.jpg Scenic28.jpg Scenic29.jpg Scenic30.jpg Scenic31.jpg Scenic32.jpg America Text.txt	None	America the Beautiful your name.proproj America the Beautiful your name.mpeg America the Beautiful your name.flv	Skills Review
	Italy.prproj	None	Subtle Storm.mp3 Italy1.jpg Italy2.jpg Italy3.jpg Italy4.jpg Italy5.jpg Italy6.jpg	Italy your name.prproj Italy your name.mpeg Italy your name.flv	Project Builder 1

*Created in previous Lesson or Skills Review in current chapter

VIDEO COLLECTION DATA FILES					
Chapter	**Data File Supplied**	**Support Files**	**Linked Files**	**Student Creates File**	**Used In**
Chapter 1, continued			Italy7.jpg Italy8.jpg Italy9.jpg Italy10.jpg Italy11.jpg Italy12.jpg Italy13.jpg Italy14.jpg Italy15.jpg		
	SA Missions.prproj	None	Flat Calm.mp3 SA_Mission1.jpg SA_Mission2.jpg SA_Mission3.jpg SA_Mission4.jpg SA_Mission5.jpg SA_Mission6.jpg SA_Mission7.jpg SA_Mission8.jpg SA_Mission9.jpg SA_Mission10.jpg SA_Mission11.jpg SA_Mission12.jpg SA_Mission13.jpg SA_Mission14.jpg SA_Mission15.jpg SA_Mission16.jpg SA_Mission17.jpg SA_Mission18.jpg SA_Mission19.jpg SA_Mission20.jpg	SA Missions your name.prproj SA Missions your name.flv	Project Builder 2
	None	None	None	Space Program your name.prproj Space Program your name.mpeg	Portfolio Project

VIDEO COLLECTION DATA FILES					
Chapter	**Data File Supplied**	**Support Files**	**Linked Files**	**Student Creates File**	**Used In**
Chapter 2	GridsPractice.aep	None	None	None	Lesson 1
	None	us_11.jpg		BUG your name.aep BUG Final your name.mpeg	Lesson 2
	Production Logo.aep	Channel 6 Logo.psd	EarthSpin_720x480.mpeg	Logo your name.aep Logo Final your name.flv	Lesson 3
	Title Sequence.aep	None	Nightscape.mp3 us_10.mov Title Sequence Text.psd	Title Sequence your name.aep Title Sequence Final your name.mpeg	Lesson 4
	Nighttime.aep	us_10.jpg Nighttime Logo.psd	Nightscape.mp3 Skyline.jpg	Digital Graphic your name.aep Digital Graphic Final your name.mpeg Nighttime your name.aep Nighttime Final your name.flv	Skills Review
	Demo.aep	None	None	Animation Preset Demo your name.aep Animation Preset Demo Final your name.mpeg	Project Builder 1
	None	None	None	Elementary Title Sequence.aep Elementary Title Sequence Final your name.mpeg	Project Builder 2
	None	None	None	Title of your choice.aep Title of your choice.mpeg Title of your choice.flv	Portfolio Project

Chapter	Data File Supplied	Support Files	Linked Files	Student Creates File	Used In
VIDEO COLLECTION DATA FILES					
Chapter 3	None	PopeyetheSailorMan.mp3	None	Popeye your name.sesx	Lesson 1
	None	pastime_rag.wav dixie_dimples.wav chaplin.mp4	None	Chaplin your name.sesx Chaplin-Soundtrack your name.mp3	Lesson 2
	None	PopeyetheSailorMan.mp3	None	PopeyeRestored.sesx	Lesson 3
	None	GrandOldRag.mp3 over_there_vbr Felix.mov barrel.wav acrobatic.wav		grand your name.sesx Felix your name.sesx Felix-Soundtrack your name.mp3 Over-Restored.sesx	Skills Review
	None	rfkonmlkdeath45454.mp3	None	RFK Speech your name.mp3	Project Builder 1
	Elementary Title Sequence Final your name.mpeg**	None	None	Elementary Title Sequence with Music your name.asnd Elementary Title Sequence with Music your name.mpeg	Project Builder 2
	None	None	None	Silent Film your name.asnd Silent Film Soundtrack Final your name.mpeg	Portfolio Project

**Created in a previous chapter

DATA FILES LIST
(CONTINUED)

VIDEO COLLECTION DATA FILES					
Chapter	**Data File Supplied**	**Support Files**	**Linked Files**	**Student Creates File**	**Used In**
Chapter 4	None	AVCHD-Airshow Folder		Airshow your name.prproj	Lesson 1
	Pearl Harbor Reenactment. prproj		AirshowVideo1.m2v AirshowVideo2.m2v AirshowVideo3.m2v AirshowVideo4.m2v AirshowVideo5.m2v AirshowVideo6.m2v	Pearl Harbor Documentary your name.prproj	Lesson 2
	Pearl Harbor Documentary your name.prproj*	December7th.m2v	None		Lesson 3
	Pearl Harbor Documentary your name.prproj*	History PearlHarbor.mp3 FDR Speech.mp3	None	Pearl Harbor Documentary your name.MPEG	Lesson 4
	None Kennedy Space Documentary. prproj	AVCHD-Glassworks Folder apollo launch.m2v Kennedy Space.mp3 Kennedy Rice.mp3	space1.m2v space2.m2v space3.m2v space4.m2v space5.m2v space6.m2v	Glassworks your name.prproj Kennedy Space Documentary your name.prproj Kennedy Space Documentary your name.mpeg	Skills Review
	Chamber.prproj	None	Chamber1.m2v Chamber2.m2v Chamber3.m2v Chamber4.m2v	Chamber Commercial your name.prproj Chamber Commercial your name.mpeg Chamber Commercial your name.flv	Project Builder 1
	None	None	None	Great Speech Phrases your name.mp3	Project Builder 2
	None	Production Company Logo**	None	Documentary.prproj Documentary.mpeg	Portfolio Project

*Created in previous Lesson or Skills Review in current chapter
**Created in a previous chapter

VIDEO COLLECTION DATA FILES					
Chapter	**Data File Supplied**	**Support Files**	**Linked Files**	**Student Creates File**	**Used In**
Chapter 5	PSA.aep PSA.prproj	PSA Script.txt	Ban044.mov Eri048.mov Eri50.mov Nic038.mov	PSA your name.aep PSA your name.prproj PSA your name.mpeg	Lesson 1
	Glassworks Commercial.prproj Glassworks 3D Text.aep	Blown Glass.avi	Frame.psd	Glassworks Commercial your name.prproj Glassworks Dynamic Link your name.aep Blown Glass.mocha Glassworks 3D Text your name.aep Glassworks Commercial your name.mpeg	Lesson 2
	Hummingbird Insurance.aep	None	scenic footage.prproj commercial.avi hummingbird.ai lighthousesunrise.avi malibusunset.avi mountain.avi nantucketsunset.avi redwoods.avi timelapseclouds.avi yellowstonewaterfall.avi	Hummingbird Insurance your name.aep Hummingbird Insurance your name.flv	Lesson 3
	Water Pollution.aep Water Pollution.prproj LuckenbachCommercial.prproj Luckenbach 3D Text.ae World Peace.ae	Water Pollution Script.txt	EIS19 Trash by culvert.mov EIS21 Trash on a tropical beach.mov EIS25 Brown water from mine.mov frame.psd Luckenbach.avi Dove.avi londonbigben.avi sydneyaustralia.avi us_5.mov	Water Pollution your name.aep Water Pollution your name.prproj Water Pollution your name.mpeg Luckenbach Commercial your name.prproj Luckenbach Dynamic Link your name.ae Luckenback.mocha Luckenbach 3D Text your name.ae World Peace your name.ae World Peace Commercial your name.flv	Skills Review

VIDEO COLLECTION DATA FILES					
Chapter	Data File Supplied	Support Files	Linked Files	Student Creates File	Used In
Chapter 5, continued	Cartoon Practice	None	ELS041.mov	Cartoon Practice your name.aep Cartoon Practice your name.flv	Project Builder 1
	Longhorn.ae	None	Longhorn.psd	Longhorn your name.ae Longhorn Commercial Spot your name.flv	Project Builder 2
	None	EIS62 Endangered Asian rhino.mov EIS63 Endangered African rhino.mov EIS64 Cheetah in grass.mov EIS65 Endangered antelope.mov EIS66 Male gorilla.mov EIS67 Young gorilla.mov EIS68 Mother Orang at Borneo refuge.mov EIS69 Orang with infant.mov EIS70 Panda in Beijing zoo.mov EIS71 Tiger SE Asia.mov EIS72 Manatee FL.mov EIS73 Andean condor.mov		Endangered species commercial.prproj Endangered species.mpeg Endangered species.flv	Portfolio Project

VIDEO COLLECTION DATA FILES					
Chapter	**Data File Supplied**	**Support Files**	**Linked Files**	**Student Creates File**	**Used In**
Chapter 6	Speed 1.prproj Speed 2.prproj Speed 3.prproj	None	42.avi 30.avi 7.avi 13.avi 22.avi	Speed 1 your name.prproj Skateboarding your name.flv Speed 2 your name.prproj Skateboarding Stunts your name.flv Speed 3 your name.prproj Bike Stunts your name.flv	Lesson 1
	Weather 1.aep Lightning 1.aep	None	Storm Clouds.m2v us_5.mov us_5 mask.psd Lightning Logo.ai	Weather 1 your name.aep Rain Effects your name.flv Lightning 1 your name.aep Lightning Logo your name.FLV	Lesson 2
	Talking Dog.aep	None	Dog Clip.avi Outlaw in Black Boots vocal sample.mp3	Talking Dog your name.aep Talking Dog your name.flv	Lesson 3
	Speed 4.prproj Speed 5.prproj Speed 6.prproj Weather 2.aep Lightning 2.aep Singing Dog.aep	None	42.avi 43.avi 1.avi 10.avi 18.avi Halloween.ai StormCloudsGathering2.mpg us_15.mov us_15 mask.psd Boy Band vocals.mp3 Singing Dog 2.m2v Open Mouth 2.avi	Speed 4 your name.prproj Bike Tricks your name.flv Speed 5 your name.prproj Skateboarding Tricks your name.flv Speed 6 your name.prproj Biking your name.flv Weather 2 your name.aep White House Rain your name.flv Lightning 2 your name.aep Halloween your name.flv Singing Dog your name.aep Singing Dog your name.flv	Skills Review
	Weather 3.aep	None	us_7.mov	San Francisco Weather your name.flv	Project Builder 1
	Antelope Talking.ae	None	antelope.mov	Zoo Promo your name.flv	Project Builder 2
	None	None	Sports Folder	Highlight Video your name.prproj Highlight Video your name.mpeg	Portfolio Project

DATA FILES LIST

(CONTINUED)

VIDEO COLLECTION DATA FILES					
Chapter	**Data File Supplied**	**Support Files**	**Linked Files**	**Student Creates File**	**Used In**
Chapter 7	None	EIS01 Smokestacks.mov EIS03 Mill with smoke.mov EIS04 Smoke plume 1.mov EIS05 Smoke plume 2.mov EIS06 Smoke plume 3.mov EIS07 Smoke plume 4.mov EIS08 Smoke closeup.mov EIS09 Smokestack w_trees.mov EIS10 Very dark smoke.mov EIS18 Trash by lake shore.mov EIS19 Trash by culvert.mov EIS20 Trash dump by Mediterranean.mov EIS21 Trash on a tropical beach.mov EIS22 Pipes & pond.mov EIS23 Drinking polluted water.mov EIS24 Polluted stream in tropics.mov Water Pollution submenu.psd	None	Pollution your name.ncor Pollution your name.flv	Lesson 1 Lesson 2 Lesson 3 Lesson 4
	None	EIS28 Slash & burn plot Thailand.mov EIS29 Burning cutover land Tropics.mov EIS30 Detail burning tree Tropics.mov EIS31 Smoke Amazon forest.mov EIS32 Deforested Amazon Brazil.mov EIS33 Slash & burn plot Venezuela.mov EIS34 Cutover hillside Guatemala.mov EIS35 Clear-cut operation OR.mov EIS36 Clear-cut hillside OR.mov EIS37 Clear-cut hillside WA.mov EIS51 Desertification Mali W Africa.mov EIS52 Overgrazed land Sahel Mali.mov EIS53 Desertification the Sahel Mali.mov	None	Erosion your name.ncor Erosion your name.flv	Skills Review

VIDEO COLLECTION DATA FILES					
Chapter	**Data File Supplied**	**Support Files**	**Linked Files**	**Student Creates File**	**Used In**
Chapter 7, continued		EIS54 Disturbed desert floor CA.mov EIS55 Abandoned city Central Asia.mov EIS56 Hot rising sun.mov Desertification submenu.psd			
	PB1	None	EIS11 Smoke in distance.mov EIS12 Boat w_smoke.mov EIS13 85 Traffic jam with motocycles.mov EIS14 Snowmobiles in Yellowstone.mov EIS15 Smog over Guadalajara.mov EIS17 Air pollution & traffic Beijing.mov	Environmental Issues.ncor Environmental Issues.flv	Project Builder 1
	None	Riverwalk_01.jpg Riverwalk_02.jpg Riverwalk_03.jpg Riverwalk_04.jpg Riverwalk_05.jpg Riverwalk_06.jpg Riverwalk_07.jpg Riverwalk_08.jpg Riverwalk_09.jpg Riverwalk_10.jpg Riverwalk_11.jpg Riverwalk_12.jpg Riverwalk_13.jpg Riverwalk_14.jpg Riverwalk_15.jpg	None	Your Name PB2.ncor Your Name PB2.flv	Project Builder 2

DATA FILES LIST

(CONTINUED)

Chapter	Data File Supplied	Support Files	Linked Files	Student Creates File	Used In
Chapter 7, continued	None	Space Program your name.mpeg** (Chapter 1) Title of your choice.mpeg** (Chapter 2) Chaplin Soundtrack Final your name.mpeg** (Chapter 3) Documentary.mpeg** (Chapter 4) Endangered species.mpeg** (Chapter 5) Highlight Video your name.mpeg** (Chapter 6)	None	Your Name Portfolio Project.ncor Your Name Portfolio Project.flv	Portfolio Project

**Created in a previous chapter

A

24-p footage
Footage that is captured from a video camcorder or by film transfer at approximately 24 non-interlaced (progressive) frames per second (fps).

Action safe zone
The outer margin of the safe zone where content is guaranteed to be visible on all television displays.

Adjustment layer
A layer in After Effects that affects all layers that fall below it in the stacking order.

Alpha channel
Represents the transparent areas on the layer.

Alpha Obstacle
A property available with the Advanced Lightning effect in After Effects that specifies the influence of the alpha channel of the layer the Advanced Lightning effect is being applied to.

Ambient (light)
In After Effects, a lighting effect that has no source but simply contributes to the overall brightness without casting shadows.

Amount
A property available with the CC Rainfall effect in After Effects that determines the amount of rainfall.

Angle
A property available with the CC Rainfall effect in After Effects that can be used to set the angle of the rain.

Angle Variation
A property available with the CC Rainfall effect in After Effects that can be used to adjust the angle of the rain.

Animation preset
A collection of animation settings in After Effects that include keyframes and effects that can be applied to a layer.

Anti-aliasing quality
A setting in the Premiere Pro Effect Controls panel that adjusts the smoothness of a transition's edges.

Application window
The main window of an application, comprising the various panels.

Attach point
The designated place for the object you plan to attach to a motion in After Effects.

Audio/Video Out setting
A setting available in the Encore preferences which allows a project to be previewed on an external device that is connected by an IEEE 1394 cable.

AVCHD
Advanced Video Codec High Definition. A format developed by Sony and Panasonic for recording and playback of high definition video, and used in their tapeless video cameras.

B

Bins
Used to organize assets in the Project panel; work much the same way as folders in Windows Explorer or the Mac OS Finder.

Birth Rate
A property available with the CC Mr. Mercury effect in After Effects that determines the number of blobs that are generated at any given point in time.

Blob Birth Size
A property available with the CC Mr. Mercury effect in After Effects that determines the size of blobs as they first appear.

Blob Death Size
A property available with the CC Mr. Mercury effect in After Effects that determines the size of blobs as they disappear.

Border color
A setting in the Effect Controls panel that allows the color of the transition border to be set.

Border width
A setting in the Effect Controls panel that allows for the adjustment of the optional border on a transition.

Buffering
The delay before a video begins to play on the Internet.

Bug
A term used in the United States and Canada for a digital on-screen graphic.

C

Capturing
In Premiere Pro, the process of connecting a live video camera or an analog tape device, such as a camcorder or VCR that uses videotape, and then recording the video from the source to a hard disk.

CC Mr. Mercury effect
An effect available in After Effects that creates ever-changing blobs, which you can make appear like rain drops on a camera lens.

CC Rainfall effect
A self-animating effect available in After Effects that simulates rain.

Clips
See digital assets.

Codecs
Encoders/decoders or compressors/decompressors. Processes used to convert video to a variety of file formats.

Commercial
A short film broadcast used as a marketing device to raise awareness of a consumer product, service, or issue.

Composite on Original
An option available with the Advanced Lightning effect in After Effects that shows the lightning on the footage in the Composition panel.

Composition panel
A panel in After Effects that represents layers spatially, and where compositions are displayed at the location of the CTI on the Timeline panel.

Composition (Comp)
In After Effects, the container that holds all the references for a movie; can be dynamically linked to Premiere Pro or to Encore.

Comp
See Composition.

Conductivity State
The property in the Advanced Lightning effect in After Effects that changes the path of lightning and can be used to animate the effect.

Constant Gain
A type of Crossfade in Premiere Pro; can sound abrupt because it changes the audio at a constant rate in and out as it transitions between clips.

Constant Power
A type of Crossfade in Premiere Pro that serves as the default transition; creates a smooth, gradual transition between audio clips.

Crawl
A title in which text moves horizontally over the footage.

Crossfade
An audio transition used to fade in or fade out an audio clip.

Current-time display
The area on the Timeline panel in Premiere Pro that shows the timecode for the current frame.

Current-time Indicator (CTI)
See play head.

Custom (transition settings)
A setting in the Premiere Pro Effect Controls panel that makes changes specific to a transition.

Custom workspace
A workspace that has been created by a user and saved with a unique name.

Cut
See cut line.

Cut line
In Premiere Pro, the point where a clip has been split. It is marked by a vertical line between two clips and is also referred to as a cut.

Cut point
The point where you split a clip.

———————— **D** ————————

Default crawl
See Crawl.

Default roll
See Roll (title).

Default still
See Still (title).

Deform pin
A type of pin that you can place or move with the Puppet Pin tool.

Digital assets
Video, audio, still images, and Photoshop and/or Illustrator files.

Digital on-screen graphic
A logo overlaid on a portion of the television viewing area to identify the channel, much like a watermark.

Digitizing
The process of converting analog video to digital form so a computer can process and store it.

Direction
A property available with the Advanced Lightning effect in After Effects that sets which route the lightning takes.

Documentary
A video meant to document history.

DOG
See digital on-screen graphic.

Downstream composition
A composition that contains a nested composition.

Drag Video Only
An icon located on the Source Monitor in Premiere Pro that allows you to place a video clip without its audio track.

Drop zone
The area that becomes highlighted as you drag a panel; provides a visual reference to where the panel can be placed.

Duration
The span between the In point and the Out point of a video clip.

Dynamic Link
A command that allows you to share files between applications so that when a file is updated in one program, it is automatically updated in the other.

———————— **E** ————————

Edge selectors
Arrows found on some transitions that change the orientation or direction of the transition.

Edit in Adobe Audition
A command in Premiere Pro used to edit an audio clip in Audition.

Editing (workspace)
The default workspace in Premiere Pro.

Encode
See Encoding.

Encoding
A procedure done during the export process so that other people will be able to view a movie.

End action
An action set in Encore to control what happens when a video clip ends.

End slider
The ending edge of a transition; may be adjusted.

Exponential Fade
A transition that fades out the first clip and fades up the second clip.

Expressions
Values of a property specified using a scripting language.

Extract button
Located on the Program Monitor in Premiere Pro; removes a specified area of the sequence marked with In and Out points without leaving a gap in its place.

Eyedropper
A tool used to select a color from an image or video clip.

—————————— F ——————————

Fading
A basic effect used on images to fade in or out by applying the Opacity effect.

Feature region
Defines the area in a layer in which motion is tracked in After Effects.

File-based
See tapeless.

File-based media
The media to which a tapeless video camera records, such as a hard disk, a DVD, or flash memory.

Final Output (Linear Color Key Effect)
A view that displays a preview of the keyed area.

Footage
The term used for assets in After Effects.

—————————— G ——————————

Garbage matte
A keying method used in After Effects to remove portions of an image or layer; the matte can be animated with the layer.

Go to Gap
A command in Premiere Pro used to jump between gaps and to find gaps that are very short and may be difficult to see.

Gravity
A property available with the CC Mr. Mercury effect in After Effects that determines how quickly the blobs fall; a negative Gravity value causes them to rise.

Grid generator (Particle Playground effect)
Creates particles in a continuous stream from a set of grid intersections.

Guide layer
In After Effects, a layer that provides a visual reference in the Composition panel and that can be used to help position and edit elements; by default, this layer does not become part of the final output.

—————————— H ——————————

Histogram
A chart that represents the changes of color in an image.

Horizontal Zoom bar
The area that corresponds with the visible portion of the Timeline panel and that allows you to quickly move to different parts of a sequence.

—————————— I ——————————

Icon view
In the Premiere Pro Project panel, the view that shows thumbnails or smaller versions of the digital assets that have been imported.

Influence
A setting that regulates the speed of change as motion advances toward and retreats from a keyframe.

Influence Map
A property available with the CC Mr. Mercury effect in After Effects that offers a drop-down menu with options that determine the behavior of the blobs as they appear and disappear.

In point
The marker that indicates the beginning of a layer in After Effects; in Premiere Pro, it defines the first frame that is to be included in a sequence.

Insert edit
In Premiere Pro, a type of edit that shifts the contents of the selected track to the right when an asset is placed on the track.

—————————— K ——————————

Key Color (Linear Color Key effect)
A menu that has the Key Color swatch and the eyedropper available to select a color to be keyed.

Key Color Swatch (Linear Color Key effect)
A palette of colors used to select a color to be keyed.

Keyed
Describes a color that has been removed from an image or video.

Keyframe
A frame with settings that provide a snapshot of how you want a clip to look at a specified time.

L

Layer duration bar
The bar that extends between the In point and the Out point on the Timeline panel.

Layer Exploder (Particle Playground effect)
A generator that creates new particles based on a layer.

Layers
In After Effects, the parts of a composition where footage is added; represented as a bar graph.

Lift button
A button located on the Program Monitor in Premiere Pro that removes the area of a sequence marked with In and Out points, leaving a gap in its place.

Lightning Type
A property available in After Effects that specifies the characteristics of lightning.

Linear Color Key effect
An effect available in After Effects that uses RGB, hue, or Chroma information to create a range of transparency across an image based on a specified color.

Live streaming video
See Streaming video.

M

Master composition
In After Effects, the term used for a composition in which a nested or pre-composition is placed.

Matching Softness (Linear Color Key effect)
A property that adjusts the softness of the edges between an image and a transparent area.

Matching Tolerance (Linear Color Key effect)
A property that determines how closely pixels must match the key color before they become transparent.

Matte Only (Linear Color Key effect)
A view that shows the alpha channel matte to view holes in the transparency.

Menu
A feature of an Encore project that provides viewers with access to the content of the project.

Metadata
Information about an asset that's displayed in the Metadata panel in Audition; may include the text transcript, the title, author, camera model, and day and time the video or image was taken.

Motion path
The visual representation created when animating properties change over space as well as time.

Movie
A term used in After Effects to describe a file that is created by rendering a composition.

N

Navigation scheme
The layout of the menus and buttons that provide access to the various sections of a DVD.

Nesting
Placing one composition inside another.

Non-linear editing
The ability to access any frame in a video in order to make changes to it.

NTSC
National Television Standards Committee. The television standard used in North America and Japan.

Null object
In After Effects, an invisible layer that can have all the properties of a visible layer and can then be applied to other layers.

O

Opacity
The level of transparency on a scale from 0% to 100%; if set to 0%, the clip is completely transparent; at 100%, the clip has no transparency.

Origin
A property available with the Advanced Lightning effect in After Effects that determines the point at which the lightning strike begins.

Out point
Marks the end of a layer in After Effects; in Premiere Pro it defines the last frame that is to be included in a sequence.

Outer Radius
A property available with the Advanced Lightning effect in After Effects that determines the distance the lightning travels from the point of origin.

Overlay edit
In Premiere Pro, a type of edit in which you place a clip over an existing clip already on a track for the duration of the placed clip.

P

PAL
Phase Alternating Line. The television standard used in Europe.

Panel tabs
The tabs found at the tops of panels. You can move panels by dragging panel tabs.

Parallel (light)
In After Effects, a lighting effect that approximates the light from a source like the sun.

Particle Exploder (Particle Playground effect)
A generator that creates new particles based on a layer and then has the ability to explode a particle into more new particles.

Particle Playground effect
An effect in After Effects that is used to animate an object by reproducing it randomly.

Paste
In Premiere Pro, a command that adds frames from the system clipboard by performing an Overlay edit.

Paste Insert
In Premiere Pro, a command that adds frames from the system clipboard by performing an Insert edit.

Pixel
The unit of measurement typically used when designing for video output or the Web; equal to 1/72 of an inch.

Play head
A light blue triangle in the ruler with a vertical red line extending through the video and audio tracks; also known as the Current-time Indicator (CTI).

Playback environment
The equipment on which a final Encore media project will be viewed.

Playlist
In Encore, a collection of timelines and/or slideshows set to play sequentially; may also include chapter playlists.

Point (light)
In After Effects, a lighting effect that has no constraints, like the light from a bare light bulb.

Posterization
A process used to create a cartoon-like effect on a digital image or video.

Pre-composition
A nested composition used to group layers within a composition.

Production logo
An opening or closing logo used by movie and television production companies at the beginning of a theatrical movie or at the end of a television program or movie to brand what they have produced.

Program monitor
In Premiere Pro, the panel that displays the contents of the timeline, i.e., your project in progress.

Progressive downloadable video
A technology used to make video viewable on the Web in which movie player software determines how long it will take to download an entire movie for viewing and begins playing the movie when enough of the movie has been downloaded so it will play back uninterrupted.

Project
A single file in After Effects that stores compositions and references to footage used.

Project file
A Premiere Pro, After Effects, or Encore document.

Project panel
The panel that organizes all the assets for a project in Premiere Pro, After Effects, or Encore.

Property Mapper (Particle Playground effect)
A control that gives you the ability to control specific properties by using a layer map.

Public Service Announcement (PSA)
A type of commercial intended to modify public attitudes by raising awareness about specific issues.

Pulldown scheme
A method used by Premiere Pro to convert footage for playback on standard NTSC devices at 29.97 fps.

——————— **R** ———————

Radius X
A property available with the CC Mr. Mercury effect in After Effects that determines the size of the blob producer based on the X coordinate.

Radius Y
A property available with the CC Mr. Mercury effect in After Effects that determines the size of the blob producer based on the Y coordinate.

Razor tool
In Premiere Pro, a tool used to split a clip at any point and create a cut line.

Rearrange edit
In Premiere Pro, an editing technique that allows you to click a clip and drag it to a new location in a sequence. The existing clips in the sequence automatically shift to make room for the clip that is being placed.

Reference file
A file created to track assets that are referenced in the Premiere Pro Project panel.

Render item
In After Effects, an item that has been added to the Render Queue panel.

Rendering
The process of compiling a composition into its final output from all of its layers and settings; a rendered project plays more smoothly and much closer to real time.

Repel control (Particle Playground effect)
A property that specifies how nearby particles repel or attract each other, simulating a positive or negative magnetic charge on each of the particles.

Reverse
A setting in the Effect Controls panel that allows you to play a transition backward.

Ripple delete
A command that removes a clip from a sequence without leaving any gaps if the clip being removed is located between two other clips.

Ripple trim
In Premiere Pro, a video editing technique that allows you to move the cut point either backward or forward in time (if the clip has frames available). The clip adjacent to the cut line adjusts accordingly, either shifting to the left or to the right by the amount of the ripple edit to compensate.

Roll (title)
A title in which text moves vertically over the footage.

Root composition
The most downstream composition in a nested composition.

RotoBezier
An option used with the Pen tool in After Effects that makes paths easier to draw and makes curves smoother.

Round-trip editing
The process of sharing project files between applications without having to import and export files.

──────── **S** ────────

Safe zone
The viewing area designed to ensure that certain content is not missed when being played on television screens; broken down into two areas: title safe zone and action safe zone.

Scrubbing
Clicking and dragging the CTI to preview a sequence.

Search region
A larger area around the feature region that defines the area in which After Effects looks for the feature region.

Segment
The line or curve that connects two vertices.

Sequence
In Premiere Pro, the section of the Timeline panel where most editing takes place.

Session
An Audition document or project file.

Show actual sources
An option in the Effect Controls panel that displays the starting and ending frames of clips to which a transition has been applied.

Slide edit
A style of edit that moves a clip while trimming adjacent clips to compensate for the change; applied using the Slide tool in Premiere Pro.

Slip edit
A style of edit that moves a clip's In and Out points forward and backward by the same number of frames; applied using the Slip tool in Premiere Pro.

Source monitor
The panel used to preview assets from the project panel or the media browser before being placed in a sequence.

Source Only (Linear Color Key effect)
A view that shows the original footage without the key applied.

Spatial
A type of layer property in After Effects that has the ability to move or add motion across composition space.

Speed
The playback rate compared to the rate at which a video was recorded.

Speed (property)
A property available with the CC Rainfall effect in After Effects that changes the rate at which the rain falls.

Speed ramp
The line between the Speed keyframe's two handles.

Spot (light)
In After Effects, a lighting effect that gives off light that is constrained by a cone, like a flashlight or spotlight.

Standard (workspace)
The default workspace in After Effects.

Start slider
The beginning edge of a transition; may be adjusted.

Still (title)
A title that has fixed text.

Storyboard
A visual representation that displays the structure of a project from start to end; used in the planning stage.

Storyboarding
A way to plan a video by placing clips or digital assets in the order you plan to have them play.

Streaming video
Video played much like a traditional live broadcast and affected by the bandwidth available.

Synthetic layer
In After Effects, a layer that is created without using source footage.

──────── **T** ────────

Tapeless
A type of digital video camera that does not use video tape.

Temporal
A type of After Effects layer property that changes a layer over time.

Thumbnail
A reduced size picture of a digital asset.

Time ruler
A feature of the Premiere Pro Timeline panel that measures the time in a sequence horizontally and displays icons for markers and In and Out points.

Timecode
A feature of the Premiere Pro Timeline panel that marks a specific frame with a unique address and is recorded onto videotape during the recording process.

Timeline panel
The panel where you place various assets and edit them.

Timeline Viewer
The term used for the timeline or Timeline panel in Encore.

Title Actions panel
A part of the Titler in Premiere Pro where you align, center, or distribute objects and text vertically and horizontally.

Title panel
A part of the Titler in Premiere Pro where you design and preview text and graphics; the central panel in the Titler window.

Title properties panel
A part of the Titler in Premiere Pro where you choose a font and change the font size, kerning, leading, or font characteristics such as bold or italics.

Title safe zone
The inner margin of the safe zone that ensures text will be visible on all television displays.

Title sequence
Motion graphics shown at the beginning of a movie or television program to provide the title and credit the actors.

Title Styles panel
A part of the Titler in Premiere Pro where you can apply preset styles to titles and create and save your own titles.

Title tools panel
A part of the Titler in Premiere Pro where the tools are located to draw basic shapes, create text paths, and create vertical or horizontal text.

Titler
In Premiere Pro, a mini-application in a free-floating window used to create titles.

Tools panel
A panel that provides various tools including the Selection tool and the Zoom tool; can be found in every application.

Track point
The area that specifies what is tracked in After Effects.

Tracks
In Audition, the parts of a session where video and audio clips are assembled, edited, and enhanced with effects and transitions.

Transition
The movement from one clip to the next in a sequence; can add additional interest to video and can be as simple as phasing out one image and phasing in another.

Trimming
In After Effects, changing the In and Out points on the Layer panel or the Timeline panel; in Premiere Pro, defining In and Out points for a video clip in the Source Monitor.

U

Upstream composition
A composition nested within another composition.

V

Velocity
A property available with the CC Mr. Mercury effect in After Effects that determines the speed of the blobs at birth.

Vertex
A point at which the direction of a path changes.

Video montage
A video that combines digital images, words, transitions, and music.

Viral video
A video that gains popularity on the Internet through the process of sharing via Web sites and e-mail.

W

Wall Control (Particle Playground effect)
A property of the Particle Playground effect that creates an area restricting where particles can move.

Work area bar
A visual representation of the area of a sequence that you want to preview or export; the selected portion is indicated by brackets just below the Time ruler.

Workspace
The arrangement of the panels in an application window.

Workspace Switcher
The workspace drop-down menu that is used to selected preformatted workspaces.

X

XMP metadata file
The file generated and shared between all video suite applications when a transcript is created.

INDEX